Foundations of Corporate Empire

Is history repeating itself?

By Karl Moore and David Lewis

FINANCIAL TIMES

Prentice Hall

an imprint of Pearson Education

London • New York • San Francisco • Toronto • Sydney • Tokyo • Singapore • Hong Kong
Cape Town • Madrid • Paris • Milan • Munich • Amsterdam

PEARSON EDUCATION LIMITED

Head Office:
Edinburgh Gate
Harlow CM20 2JE
Tel: +44 (0)1279 623623
Fax: +44 (0)1279 431059

London Office:
128 Long Acre
London WC2E 9AN
Tel: +44 (0)20 7447 2000
Fax: +44 (0)20 7240 5771
Website: www.business-minds.com

First published in Great Britain in 2000

© Pearson Education Limited 2000

The right of Karl Moore and David Lewis to be identified as authors
of this work has been asserted by them in accordance
with the Copyright, Designs and Patents Act 1988.

ISBN 0 273 63964 1

British Library Cataloguing in Publication Data
A CIP catalogue record for this book can be obtained from the British Library

10 9 8 7 6 5 4 3 2 1

Designed by George Hammond Design.
Typeset by Northern Phototypesetting Co Ltd, Bolton
Printed and bound in Great Britain by Bell & Bain Ltd, Glasgow

The Publishers' policy is to use paper manufactured from sustainable forests.

Praise for Foundations of Corporate Empire

"This fascinating book should serve as a timely reminder to those who seem to think that tomorrow can be managed with scarcely a backwards glance to yesterday. Compulsive reading for businessmen and politicians."

Sir David Rowland,
President, Templeton College, Oxford University

"*Foundations of Corporate Empire* adds a much needed extension-three thousand years— to business history, enhancing our understanding of modern business."

Professor George Yip
Beckwith Professor of Management Studies, Cambridge University.

"In this well-researched and highly readable book, Moore and Lewis persuasively argue that many of today's global economic institutions and structures are not as new as often proclaimed but the product of a long evolutionary process. Their conclusion that a historical perspective provides important clues about the future of globalization is thought-provoking and worthy of broad debate."

Dean Cornelis A. de Kluyver
Dean, Peter. F. Drucker Graduate School of Management,
Claremont Graduate University

"A fascinating and important work, which deserves to be widely read."

Alister McGrath
Professor of Historical Theology, and Principal,
Wycliffe Hall, Oxford University

"Multinationals and managers are at the heart of globalisation. Moore and Lewis demonstrate that globalisation has been around for ages. In 2000 BC the city-states of Phoenicia developed the first multinational trading organisations. Entrepreneurs flourished in Athenian Greece, as did family-based capitalism in the Roman Empire. The European seafaring nations developed trading companies such as the East India Company as the backbone of their world empires. Finally American multinationals developed as complex multidivisional organisations in the 20th century. Global capitalisation has the ancient roots. Today's business executives can build upon four thousand years of globalisation."

Dr. Alan M. Rugman,
Thames Water Fellow of Strategic Management, Templeton College,
University of Oxford

FINANCIAL TIMES
Prentice Hall

In an increasingly competitive world, it is quality
of thinking that gives an edge – an idea that opens new
doors, a technique that solves a problem, or an insight
that simply helps make sense of it all.

We work with leading authors in the fields of
management and finance to bring cutting-edge thinking
and best learning practice to a global market.

Under a range of leading imprints, including
Financial Times Prentice Hall, we create world-class
print publications and electronic products giving
readers knowledge and understanding which can then
be applied, whether studying or at work.

To find out more about our business and professional
products, you can visit us at www.business-minds.com

For other Pearson Education publications, visit
www.pearsoned-ema.com

Pearson
Education

To Brigitte, Erik and Marie-Ève with love

Contents

Foreword

by Richard Pascale

Organizational performance and corporate culture can not be replicated through an optimal combination of compensation schemes, hiring profiles and spans of control. They are rooted in society and history and these factors are largely ignored or underestimated by academics and managers.

Karl Moore and David Lewis, the former a student of management, the latter of world history, have traced the evolution of commercial activity and organizational forms over the past 5000 years. The long historical perspective reveals that mankind has long wrestled with the issues of initiative and control that preoccupy us today and that solutions are very much subject to fashion. Particular types of enterprises and motivational strategies come and go; an organizational form gains ascendancy, then wanes as it encounters changing societal and historical circumstances for which it is ill-suited.

Foundations of Corporate Empire puts all this under a microscope. The Sumerians invented temple capitalism; the Assyrians made it multinational; the Phoenicians evolved controls; the Greeks leapfrogged with an entrepreneurial model that replace it; the Romans perfected a robust blend of autonomy and regimentation that flourished for four hundred years.

Asia fostered parallel developments and sophisticated organizational forms: India spawned a system that combined central authority and local entrepreneurship; China combined family capitalism and Confucian socialism. By the Middle Ages, both Europe and Asia had perfected flourishing faith-based partnerships and alliances and these gave rise to the first truly corporate forms of organization. By the sixteenth century, this was augmented with joint-stock ownership. The stage was set for the free- standing firm, prototypes of the modern American, European and Japanese multinationals.

The Information Age is changing this context yet again. It ushers forth new models built on electronic networks. this opens a whole new realm of possibility for blending autonomy and control as it allows us to orchestrate virtual armies of independent agents on a global scale.

The policies of nationals and enterprises are shaped by what they *are* as much as by what they do. They adopt new models and modify them to reflect their cultural idiosyncrasies. As winning arrangements succeed, they attract imitators. Imitation spawns over-application – which is inevitably exposed by the superior features of newer models. When organizations fail, we tend to blame them for not working hard enough. The reality is that the rules of the game change and organizations fail to remain in a fluid relationship with the social and historical context. When adaptability succumbs to orthodoxy, decay is not far behind. In a turbulent age, variation is the key to organizational vitality.

Richard Pascale is a writer, a consultant, and an associate fellow of Templeton College, Oxford University, England, where he teaches strategy and organization. He is author of Managing on the Edge *(Simon & Schuster, 1990).*

Acknowledgements

....

A book such as this draws strength from a large number of scholars. We would like to give special thanks to Professors Alan Rugman, John Dunning, Peter Buckley, John Cantwell and Geoffrey Jones from the international business research community. From the field of history we offer thanks to the numerous Oxford history dons who kindly commented on our various drafts. On the management side we would like to extend our appreciation to Richard Pascale, who kindly agreed to write this book's foreword, Keith Grint, Leslie Willcocks and Janine Nahapiet of Oxford University, and Julian Birkinshaw of LBS. The ideas of Henry Mintzberg and Jay Conger, colleagues of Karl's from McGill University, and Gareth Morgan of Toronto's York University have also been very helpful.

Karl's secretary, Carole Priestley, was a stalwart on numerous occasions. We very much appreciate our editor, Jacqueline Cassidy of Financial Times Prentice Hall, and her wisdom along the way. Neil Earle was a pleasure to work with and contributed much invaluable editng skill. The maps are courtesy of Angus Colquhoun and Professor Hawari Mahmoud of the British School of Archaeology in Jerusalem. We would like to thank former Dean Rory Knight and current Dean Marshall Young for their support and the financial help of the Templeton College research fund. David wishes to thank Steve Martens and Hector Roybal for their useful insights into entrepreneurship.

Karl would like to thank his wife, Brigitte, and his children, Erik and Marie-Ève, for their patience, endurance and support.

K.J.M., Oxford, UK
D.C.L., Los Angeles, California

Timeline

	EUROPE	NEAR EAST	INDIAN OCEAN	FAR EAST
3500–300 BCE		Beginnings of Sumerian civilization and commerce		
3000–2500		Urban Revolution in Mesopotamia and Pyramid Age in Egypt. Temple capitalism in Sumer	Indus Valley Harappan Culture	
2500–2000		Early Dynastic states in Sumer, Early Bronze trade between Near East and Harappan India. Beginnings of private merchants in Sumer; Egyptian Middle Kingdom		
200–1500	Akkadian Empire unifies Mesopotamian market, flourishing trade in luxuries with Indus Valley. Old Assyrian merchant colonies in Anatolia pioneer multinational enterprise. Pusu-ken			Formation of Shang culture in China with collectivised agriculture and state bronze industry
1500–1000	Ugaritic trade with Egypt and Aegean; Sinaranu; socialist Minoan and Mycenaean economies	Babylonian commerce in Amarna Age; merchant princes handle diplomacy; Job of Hauran;	Collapse of Indus valley culture and Aryan invasion	

Iron Age Revolution
begins in Cyprus, spreads to Greece and Levant; Rig Veda and ironworking in India

	EUROPE	NEAR EAST	INDIAN OCEAN	FAR EAST
1000–900	Recovery from Greek Dark Age	Rise of Tyrian merchants and alliance with Solomon	Late Vedic period of Brahmanas; Aryan settlers spread eastward along Ganges; painted grey ware found in Indian sites	Zhou Dynasty; casting of iron and rise of early Chinese entrepreneurs

	EUROPE	NEAR EAST	INDIAN OCEAN	FAR EAST
900–800	Euboean trade with Syria	Itobaal; Tyrian investment in Near East		
800–700	Tyrians colonise Carthage, Malta, Sardinia, Sicily and Spain; foundation of Pithekoussai by Euboeans and Tyrians; Greek colonise Italy			
700–600	Homer highlights Helleni c Market Revolution in *Odyssey*; Greeks colonise Black Sea; coined money spreads from Lydia to Aegean	Tyrian collaboration with Neo-Assyrian Empire		
650–500	Age of tyrants and early democratic reforms in some Greek *poleis*			Laozi outlines first natural-law philosophy
500–400	Athenian Empire dominates Aegean; Carthage dominates western Mediterranean	Athenians rout Tyrian seapower	Early urbanization in Gangetic cities; Siddhartha Gautama teaches Buddhist principles	Iron introduced in China
400–300	Private banking in Greece Pasion; Roman conquest of Italy and militarization of Roman enterprise	Graeco-Macedonian conquest of Near East	Maurya Dynasty established by Chandragupta	Confucius articulates ethic of bureaucratic gentleman; copper coins in use

	EUROPE	NEAR EAST	INDIAN OCEAN	FAR EAST
300–200	First and Second Punic Wars; Roman publican firms grow rich on military contracts; Barcids in Spain	Hellenistic monarchies practise state capitalism in Egypt and mixed enterprise in Seleucid realm	Mauryan Empire in India; under Asoka state and private enterprise mixed; spreads Buddhism and commerce; Buddhist traders reach South-East Asia; Qin Dynasty unifies China for first time; construction of Great Wall and repression of Confucians; Kautilya formulates *Artashastra*	
200–100	Third Punic War; Rome eradicates Carthage, absorbs Greek world in Aegean	Parthians conquer much of Iran and Iraq, emerge as middleman in Asian economy	Indo-Greek and Saka rule in north-west India; Hellenistic traders from Egypt sail to south India; Menader (Milinda) in Buddhist literature	Early Han Dynasty; Emperor Wudi expands Chinese power deep into Central Asia; Confucianism becomes orthodoxy; silk trade with India and West; monopolies on salt and iron
1001–1	Roman expansion across Western Europe and Near East; heyday of publican firms; Cicero; Sestii		Extensive Indian trade links with Rome; earliest date for Laws of Manu which define role of castes in commerce	Debate on salt and iron
1–100 CE	Roman World economy in full bloom: Italy at hub of European trade; direct Roman commerce with India, trade with Han China through Parthian middlemen; Later Han Dynasty			
100–200	Climax of Pax Romana; wealth and business activity shifting from Italy to the provinces; Roman Indian Ocean trade bypasses Parthians; production of paper in China			

	EUROPE	NEAR EAST	INDIAN OCEAN	FAR EAST
200–300	Growing insability of Roman Empire following Persian revolt; decline of investment climate		Roman trade fades from India; probable date of published *Arthashastra*	Decline of Han Empire
300–400	Temporary stability of Roman Empire but with regimented economy	Indian Ocean economy dominated by Gupta Empire, Persians, Ethiopians southern Arabs; Faxian visits India from China; Kalidasa; Arab traders in Mecca manage caravan trade between Mediterranean and Indian Ocean		Political fragmentation in China; power in hands of generals and warring kingdoms
400–500	Collapse of Roman Empire in West			
500–600	Byzantium inherits remnants of East roman trade			
600–700	Islamic expansion isolates Europe from Near Eastern commerce; Frisians trade in North Sea	Prophet Muhammad mobilises Arabia; successors conquer Near East and North Africa	End of northern hedgemony in India	Grand Canal built under Sui; beginnings of Tang Dynasty, military expansion; Muslim traders settle in Canton
700–800	Abbasid Caliphate expands trade with Indian Ocean; Tang Empire in China; massive southward migration of population; temporary Dark Age revival under charlemagne; stirrup introduced into Europe; unrest affects Muslim trade with China; great interstate conflicts in India; Arab mathmaticians formulate algebra			
800–900	Apex and decline of Muslim world economy linking Iraq with Egypt and China; Viking traders expand throughout much of Europe; Otthere Jewish Radhanite traders form networks stetching from Spain to China; collapse of Tang; Hindu monarchy in Sumatra			

	EUROPE	NEAR EAST	INDIAN OCEAN	FAR EAST
900–1000	Amalfi, Genoa, Venice revive European trade; rise of commercial entrepreneurs and towns in England, northern Europe	Wealth and power in Islamic world shift to Fatimid Caliphate	Chola Dynasty in India	Period of disunity in China; printed books
1000–1100	Waterpower transforming northern Europe; Cistercians form multinational enterprise and help diffuse technology; faith-based partnership alliancesin Italian, Islamic trade; Europe rejoining world trade		Chloa Empire rules not only in India but also in Sumatra and Malaya	Song Empire; flourishing Chinese entrepreneurs in south China Confucianism accepts commerce; silk and porcelain exports to West
1000–1200	Crusader capitalism; cathedral building	Seljuk Turks emerge as force in Near East	Muslim armies invade north and east Inda	
1200–1300	The medieval world economy: Venice and Genoa leading European revival; Mongols create empire stretching from China to Near East; Marco Polo seeks trade opportunities in China; Italian supercompanies, Bardi, Peruzzi, Acciaiuoli, operate as multinationals; Yuan China continues trade in porcelain and silk with India and Europe			
1300–1400	World Depression ends medieval economic expansion: in wake of Black Death; Muslim sultanates in Delhi and elsewhere rule large parts of India; Mongols devastate Iraq and precipitate economic decline in Near East; Ottoman Turks conquer Anatolia and invade Europe; Italian firms such as Datini adapt to Depression with alliance model; Hanseatic trading colonies across Northern Europe; Hildebrand of Veckingchusen; clocks introduce time management into European business			

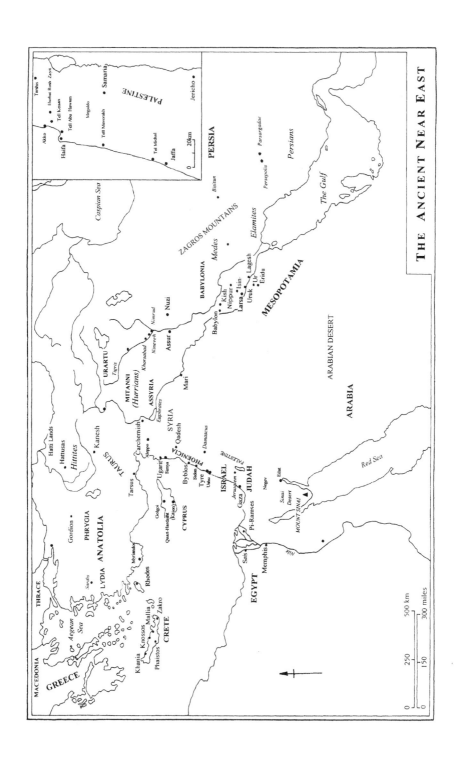

THE ANCIENT NEAR EAST

PALESTINE

Tarbès
Horbat Rosh Zayit
Tell Keisan
Samaria
Akko
Tell Abu Hawam
Megiddo
Haifa
Tell Mevorakh
Jericho
Tel Michal
Jaffa

20km
0

PERSIA

Caspian Sea

Bisitun
Parsargadae
Persepolis
Persians

The Gulf

ZAGROS MOUNTAINS

Elamites

Medes

BABYLONIA
Kish
Nippur
Isin
Larsa
Uruk
Lagesh
Ur
Eridu

Babylon

URARTU

Tigris
Khorsabad
Nimrud
Nuzi
Nineveh
Assur

MITANNI
(Hurrians)

MESOPOTAMIA

ASSYRIA
Euphrates
Mari

SYRIA
Qadesh
Damascus

ARABIAN DESERT

Hatti Lands
Hattusas
Hittites
Kanesh

TAURUS

Carchemish
Aleppo
Sumra

ARABIA

PHOENICIA
Ugarit
Byblos
Sidon
Tyre
Ubu

PALESTINE

Tarsus

Red Sea

ISRAEL
Jerusalem
JUDAH
Gaza

Golgoi
Quri-Hardadat (Katon)
CYPRUS

Eilat

Negev

GREECE

THRACE
MACEDONIA

Gordion
PHRYGIA
ANATOLIA

Sardis
LYDIA
Meriandos
Rhodes

Sinai Desert
MOUNT SINAI

Pi-Ramses

Aegean Sea

Khania
Knossos
Mallia
Zakro
CRETE
Phaistos

Sais
Memphis

Nile

EGYPT

500 km
250
0

300 miles
150
0

[xviii]

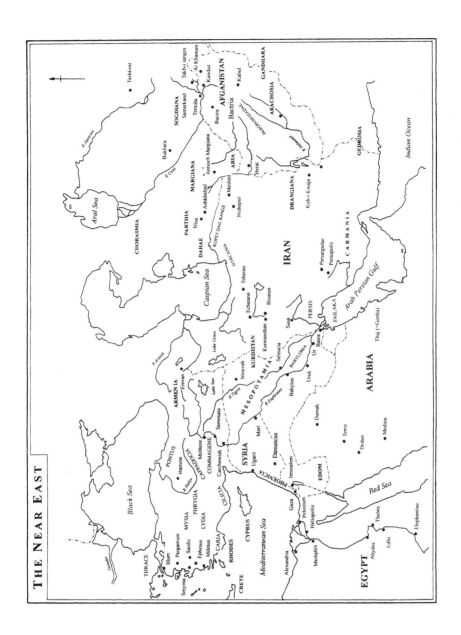

THE NEAR EAST

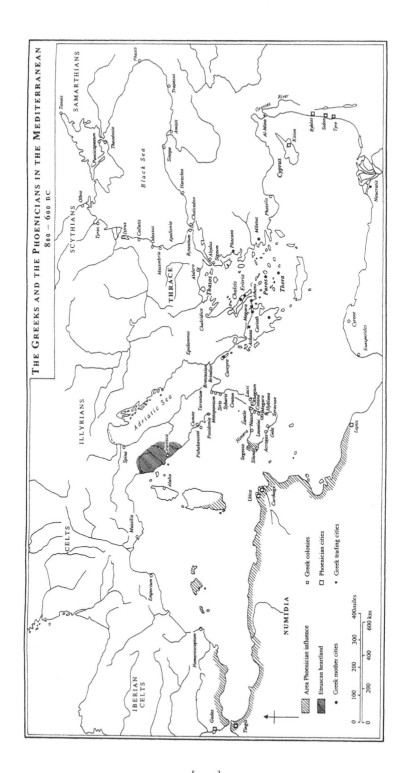

THE GREEKS AND THE PHOENICIANS IN THE MEDITERRANEAN
800 – 600 BC

SAMARTHIANS

Phasis

Tanais

Panticapaeum

Theodosia

Trapezus

Amisis

Black Sea

Sinope

SCYTHIANS

Olbia

Heraclea

River

Orontes

Al-Mina

Byblos

Sidon

Tyre

Kition

Tyras

Istrus

Callatis

Odessus

Apollonia

Chalcedon

Byzantium

Cyprus

THRACE

Mesembria

Sigeum

Abydus

Phocaea

Miletus

Phaselis

Abdera

Thasos

Chalcis

Eretria

Athens

Paros

Thera

Cyrene

Euesperides

Naucratis

ILLYRIANS

Chalcidice

Epidamnus

Megara

Corinth

Adriatic Sea

Brundisium

Brentesion

Corcyra

Tarentum

Locri

Rhegium

Siris

Metapontum

Sybaris

Croton

Zancle

Himera

Naxos

Catane

Segesta

Selinus

Leontini

Megara

Acragas

Hyblaea

Gela

Syracuse

Cumae

Posidonia

Pithekoussai

Spina

Corsica

Aleria

Leptis

CELTS

Massilia

IBERIAN
CELTS

Emporion

Hemeroscopium

Gades

Tingis

NUMIDIA

Utica

Carthage

Area Phoenician influence

Etruscan heartland

• Greek mother cities

o Greek colonies

□ Phoenician cities

• Greek trading cities

| 0 | 100 | 200 | 300 | 400 miles |

| 0 | 200 | 400 | 600 km |

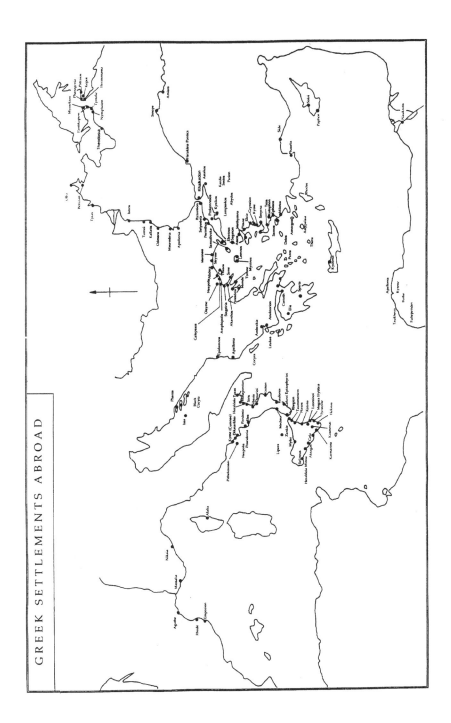

GREEK SETTLEMENTS ABROAD

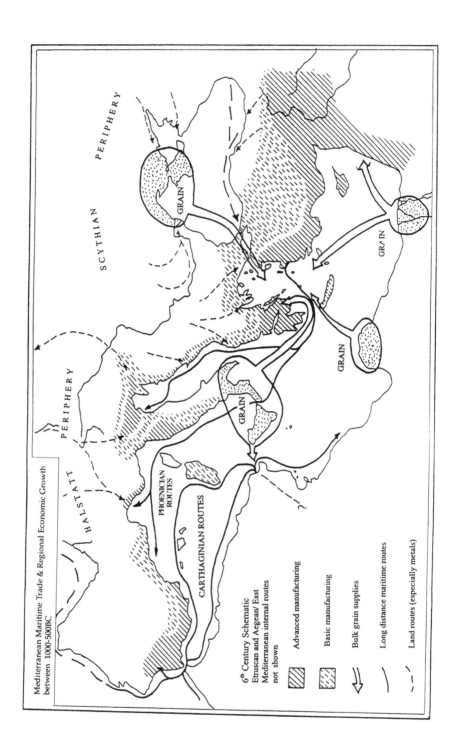

Mediterranean Maritime Trade & Regional Economic Growth between 1000-500BC

6th Century Schematic
Etruscan and Aegean/East
Mediterranean internal routes
not shown

Advanced manufacturing

Basic manufacturing

Bulk grain supplies

Long distance maritime routes

Land routes (especially metals)

PERIPHERY

SCYTHIAN

PERIPHERY

HALSTATT

PHOENICIAN ROUTES

CARTHAGINIAN ROUTES

GRAIN

GRAIN

GRAIN

GRAIN

GRAIN

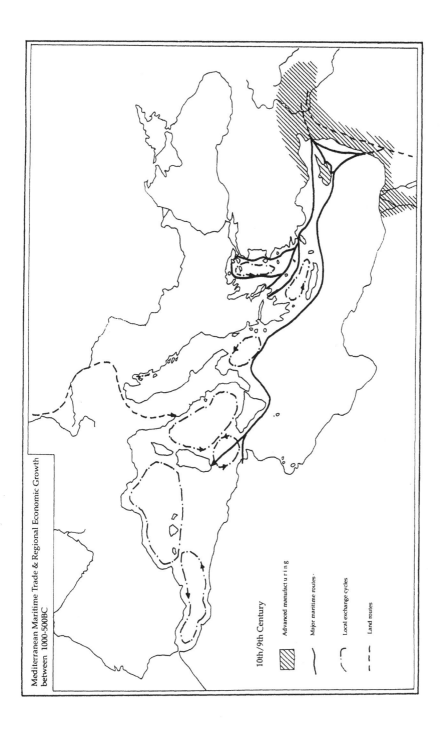

Mediterranean Maritime Trade & Regional Economic Growth between 1000-500BC

10th/9th Century

▨ Advanced manufacturing

⌐ Major maritime routes

⌐ Local exchange cycles

-- Land routes

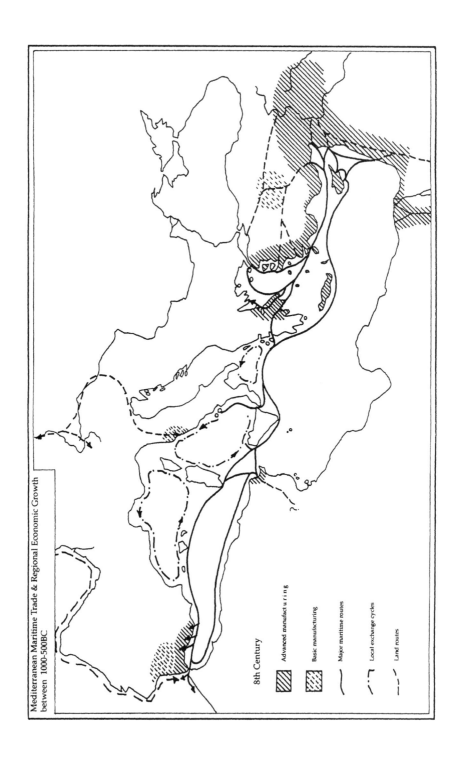

Mediterranean Maritime Trade & Regional Economic Growth
between 1000-500BC

8th Century

Advanced manufacturing

Basic manufacturing

Major maritime routes

Local exchange cycles

Land routes

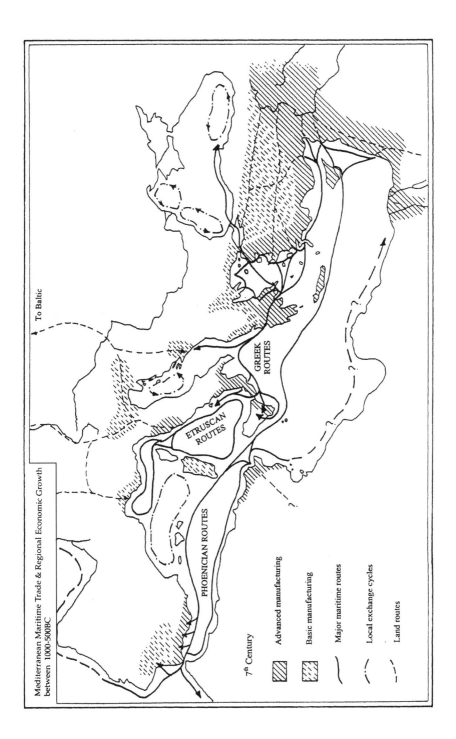

Mediterranean Maritime Trade & Regional Economic Growth between 1000-500BC

To Baltic

GREEK ROUTES

ETRUSCAN ROUTES

PHOENICIAN ROUTES

7th Century

Advanced manufacturing

Basic manufacturing

Major maritime routes

Local exchange cycles

Land routes

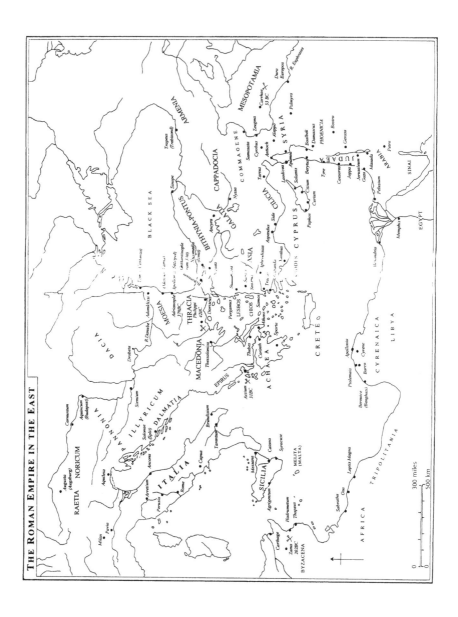

THE ROMAN EMPIRE IN THE EAST

THE ROMAN EMPIRE IN THE WEST

ANTONINE WALL

HADRIANS WALL

Carlisle

Eburacum (York)

Deva (Chester)

Lindum (Lincoln)

BRITANNIA

GERMANIA

Verulamium (St Albans)

Camuiodumum (Colchester)

Aquae Sulis (Bath)

Londinium

BELGICA

Vetera (Xanten)

R. Rhenus (Rhine)

Augusta (Trier)

LUGDUNENSIS

Lutetia (Paris)

GALLIA

R. Liger (Loire)

AQUITANIA

Augustadunum

Augusta (August)

Lugdunum (Lyon)

R. Rhodanus (Rhone)

Vienna (Vienne)

Pavia

R. Garumna (Garonne)

Arausio

NARBONENSIS

TARRACONENSIS

R. Ebro

Nemausus (Nimes)

Numantia

Narbo

Massilia (Marseilles)

Caesaraugusta

LUSITANIA

Emporiae (Ampurias)

R. Tagus

CORSICA

Aleria

Olisipo

Tarraco

HISPANIA

Saguntum

Olbia

Augusta Emerita

Corduba

B A E T I C A

Ebusus

SARDINIA

Ilipa 206BC

Hispal

BALEARES

Caralis

Gades (Cadiz)

Carthago Nova (Cartagena)

Nora

Tingis (Tangier)

Caesarea (Cherchel)

Hippo Regius

Cirta

NUMIDIA

M·AURETANIA

Timgad

Madaurus

0   100   200 miles

0   100   200   300 km

N

1

Introduction:
la Longue Durée

FOR more than two decades we have heard of it. A diverse cross-section of academics, management gurus and business executives have proclaimed its coming – the dawning of a new economic age, a global knowledge economy ushered in on the wings of technology.

The future belongs, say these seers, to an economy dominated by a mix of transnational giants and fleet-of-foot small and medium-sized business operations adept at networking their way to the top of the heap. The prophets of this emerging new economy present their vision as an entirely new and modern phenomenon. But is this true?

In this book we argue that many of today's economic structures existed in prototype form several thousand years ago. To make our point, we sketch the history of international business from the emergence of ancient Assyria around 2000 BCE through the Phoenician, Carthaginian and Grecian periods up to the time of the Roman Imperium under Augustus, and then on to the medieval and modern eras ending with today's post-modern time. We survey the first 'multinationals', run by the Assyrians. We focus on the Phoenician penchant for transnational enterprise, a business dynamic dependent upon a shrewd maximization of multiple sources of innovation. Then we analyse the Western world's first entrepreneurial culture, that of ancient Greece. We move on with a study of the vitality of family capitalism in ancient Rome. After the fall of Rome the state enterprises of China overshadowed the multinational. The multinational would return in a more advanced form, aided by discoveries of new markets and technologies in the late Middle Ages and early modern times. By 1550 one could speak of a world economy dominated by Europe encompassing the entire globe. With the Industrial Revolution and Electric/ Petroleum Revolutions of the 19th and 20th centuries the modern multi-national, especially in its American form, came into its own.

Our view of globalization differs from that of Thomas Friedman in his best-selling book *The Lexus and the Olive Tree*. He argues that there have been only two ages of globalization: the current one that started after 1945, and the age from the mid-1880s, when Britain was the super-power of the world, to the 1920s when the Depression and protectionism brought it to an abrupt end. We agree that those are two important ages of globalization and that today's current version, especially since the fall of communism, is qualitatively different. However, we believe that globalization, or at least known-world globalization, existed long before the 20th century. We believe that our readers will be surprised by the extent of international business activity in the near and ancient past.

> Many of today's economic structures existed in prototype form several thousand years ago

Our quest to study the past was spurred by a statement of Professor John Dunning, perhaps the leading international business academic. In a recent work on multinational enterprises (MNEs) Dunning stated that 'earlier examples of embryonic MNEs can, most surely, be found in the colonizing activities of the Phoenicians and the Romans, and before that, in the more ancient civilizations'. This sort of history, added Dunning, 'remains to be written''. This book represents a tentative historical probe in that direction. There is, of course, a considerable literature on the evolution of MNEs in early medieval Europe. Orlin, Larsen and Aubet have written very competent economic histories of the ancient world. Yet, as Dunning remarked, little has been written about the earliest recorded MNEs and their wide-ranging, multifaceted activities.

This book attempts to fill that gap. One of us is a contributor to inter-national business theory with a strong background in the practical, high-pressure field of IBM mainframe computer sales. The other is a historian with a speciality in European studies. This blending of our research fields and interests offers, we feel, an unusual perspective through which to explore the economic life of the ancient and modern worlds. The lens with which we will view international business history is the *Eclectic Paradigm* – a leading framework used by international business scholars.

This we see as a key model for exploring the roots and rise of ancient multinationals.

In the closing chapter we suggest parallels between ancient and modern economies. We ask the question: has the Anglo-American model 'won' the battle for economic leadership, as Alan Greenspan has recently suggested? Our conclusion is that, in the light of world history, Greenspan's suggestion might appear rather naïve. We have added managerial lessons as short insets, on topics such as knowledge management, virtual corporations and leadership; we are sure that most readers will be struck by the way that many of the issues we wrestle with today have parallels in history.

> There is nothing to be lost and everything to be gained from setting the history of business in as wide a frame as possible, from a concentration upon what French writers once called *la Longue Durée* – the Long View

Before outlining our evidence, however, we must turn to an important topic. Therefore first will be an introduction to the leading framework of analysis of the multinational enterprise, the Eclectic Paradigm. For international business scholars, our next chapter will be a review. We believe that there is nothing to be lost and everything to be gained from setting the history of business in as wide a frame as possible, from a concentration upon what French writers once called *la Longue Durée* – the Long View.

In the fast-moving business environment of the 21st century there will be less time to ponder the lessons of the past. We offer them here as both handy synthesis and pivotal scene setting.

FOOTNOTES TO CHAPTER 1

1. Dunning, J. (1993) *Multinational Enterprise and the Global Economy.* Wokingham: Addison-Wesley, 96.

Foundations of Corporate Empire is supported by an extended online version with additional information and footnotes. The address is **www.businessminds/foundations**

2

International business and the Eclectic Paradigm

T HE world of international business is nothing if not dynamic. From trade to countertrade and from factoring to forfeiting, the lexicon of global commerce is often bewildering and baffling to an outsider. It comes as no surprise, then, to learn that competing theories exist about why and how the world's multinationals operate and how they set up their international activities.[1]

John Dunning's Eclectic Paradigm is a most useful model for helping us to understand the economic life of the ancient world. Dunning is considered by many to be the unofficial dean of international business studies. His Eclectic Paradigm is the result of over 40 years of research into the kaleidoscopic world of international business and is considered among the leading frameworks in the field.

The Eclectic Paradigm can be summarized by the acronym OLI – *ownership, location* and *internalization* advantages. For Dunning, the existence and arrangement of these core advantages will encourage or discourage a firm to undertake foreign activities and thus evolve (or not evolve!) into a true multinational. To get a better handle on this concept it is good to begin at the beginning. We need to define terms. What precisely is meant by the term 'multinational enterprise'? Fortunately, there is a widely accepted definition of MNE used by two leading centres of research on the global economy. These are the Organization for Economic Co-operation and Development (OECD) and the United Nations Centre for Transnational Corporations (UNCTC). According to these sources, an MNE is 'an enterprise that engages in foreign direct investment (FDI) and owns or controls value-adding activities in more than one country'.[2]

Next we need to pinpoint more clearly the two factors in this definition, especially since this will have direct application to the arguments given below. Simply put, 'foreign direct investment' refers to the more or less straightforward investment of resources of money, people or time, in other countries. 'Value-adding activities' refers to any and all activities that increase the value of an item. This definition can encompass a lot – from the refining of raw ore into a finished or semi-finished metal to dyeing a piece of cloth with Phoenician purple dye. It can also refer to distribution functions of the kind provided by

> From trade to countertrade and from factoring to forfeiting, the lexicon of global commerce is often bewildering and baffling to an outsider

Walmart and Tesco. 'Value-adding activities' as an umbrella term also includes service activities, ancient and modern. It encompasses the work of a Xerox service rep fixing a copier in Helsinki or the painstaking dedication of a Greek in the time of Plato creating a copy of a piece of Corinthian pottery. It also includes knowledge based activities, a control plank of the new economy and also, as we shall show, of the ancient economy. Many countries today, EU countries in particular, impose value-added taxes (VAT) reflecting governmental attempts to generate revenues from these productive, profitability-oriented procedures.

So much for the basics. The next order of business is to clarify those three types of advantage central to the Eclectic Paradigm. First, *ownership advantages*. This term refers to those firm-specific advantages (FSAs) that comprise the strategic competencies of a business organization.[3] Put more simply, FSAs are the capabilities and assets that provide competitive advantage to a company and that allow it to succeed in the marketplace. Some examples are the economies of scale and scope of Daimler Benz; Intel's proprietary knowledge of semiconductor manufacture; Benetton's subcontracting relationships combined with powerful brand-name recognition; Nokia's ability to combine technologies; and 3M's innovative capabilities. Researchers set forth striking potential advantages held by companies richly blessed with strategic competency. These include advantages associated with the size of firm (e.g. economies of scale, product diversification); management of organizational expertise; carefully guarded brand names; the ability to acquire and upgrade resources; labour-intensive or mature small-scale intensive technologies; product differentiation; marketing economies; and, finally, access to domestic markets. Other analysts would add the ability to anticipate and thus maximise global production and marketing opportunities; capital availability and financial expertise; access to natural resources; and the ability to adjust to structural changes.[4]

For most multinationals it works like this: as a firm expands it seeks out new opportunities to earn additional profits ('rents' is the technical term) from its FSAs. In most cases a company attempts to expand first inside its home country. Over time however, the easier opportunities in the home country are exhausted. Firms then typically turn to foreign markets to keep growth rates healthy and avoid stagnation.[5] In today's globally linked economy the process of foreign expansion is accelerated by a dynamic new factor: the threat of foreign competition in the firm's home market. This spurs the expansion of activities outside the home country where competition is often not as intense. Plus, overseas development often has a beneficial side effect: it often positions a company to learn more about foreign competitors and thus prepares the firm to compete more effectively in the crucial home market.

> Overseas development often has a beneficial side effect: it often positions a company to learn more about foreign competitors and thus prepares the firm to compete more effectively in the crucial home market

The plot soon thickens. By entering a new international market, a foreign company suffers at first from disadvantages in comparison to its local competitors. Domestic competitors, after all, at first enjoy considerable natural advantages. They are much more familiar with the local culture, industrial structure, governmental requirements and other aspects of doing business in a country. Existing relationships with customers, suppliers, regulators and other key players are advantages that foreign firms must either match or overcome in order to be successful. Thus, a firm must have strong FSAs to be successful in entering a foreign market. This is one reason why the Eclectic Paradigm places so much weight on FSAs in a company's decision to 'go international' and evolve into a true multinational enterprise.

Internalization advantages are those advantages a firm gains when it seeks to maximise its own inherent ownership-specific advantages. Rather than sell goods outright or allow other companies that right the organization 'internalises' its operations. To internalise is to bring diverse operations within the hierarchy of the firm rather than exploit them through arm's-length relationships in the market, licensing agreements, strategic alliances or any of the relationships shown in Figure 2.1.

HIERARCHY

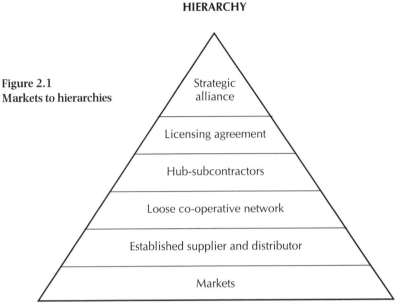

Figure 2.1
Markets to hierarchies

Source: David Faulkner, Oxford University

Theorists of internalization operate on the premise that firms grow by replacing imperfect (or non-existent) external markets by internal ones.[6] The implications here are many.

First is the argument that internalized firms can be their own most efficient means of production when imperfect market conditions exist. The most important imperfect market condition affecting individual firms is when the company generates proprietary information (most often through the organization's research and development department or R&D). That information then takes on many of the attributes of a public good. Proprietary information includes, most vitally, specialized knowledge developed by the technical and marketing branches of R&D, managerial experience, new production techniques, production differentiation and market awareness.

A firm must have strong FSAs to be successful in entering a foreign market

Whether one studies the closed-door methods that produced Stealth Bomber technology or the right mixture of tempered steel necessary to produce the Roman double-edged sword, the principles apply. A public good is defined as a good for which consumption by one party does not reduce the consumption of others. Knowledge is considered a public good because it can be applied by any person or organization to a specific problem without

[7]

destroying the ability of others to do the same. But here's the rub: the price of a public good is zero. The market cannot price a public good; hence an imperfect market condition exists, as in the hypothetical case of ABC Electronics spending many millions of pounds to develop a new way of making computer chips. If ABC's process becomes common knowledge and is adopted by its competitors, the firm's potential to maximise its profits is greatly reduced. They may barely recover the costs of R&D.

Here is where internalization comes into play. In order to profit from investment in knowledge development, ABC Electronics 'internalises'; i.e. it uses its internal market to monitor and control the deployment of the new process across the firm's internal market organization. New processes and strategies are most often internalized to allow the firm to maximise the control exerted over its employees, to monitor the process and to control its introduction to the marketplace. In the language of tennis: advantage – ? The firm. Of course, ABC Electronics has the option of selling its new process to its competitors in the open market. The difficulty here is obvious: it is loss of control over what the competitor does with the new procedure and loss of control over resale at a lower price. The new low price would benefit the competition but undercut ABC's full profitability potential.

The above is a not uncommon scenario of imperfect market conditions at work. Other market imperfections include government regulations, national and local taxes, controls, tariffs, non-existent futures markets, and an inequality between buyers' and sellers' knowledge of the value and quality of the product. In the last 25 years, through eight rounds of General Agreement on Tariffs and Trade (GATT), and at the regional level through the EU and NAFTA, the world has enjoyed a general reduction of certain types of government-erected barriers. However, many tariff barriers still exist. These still significantly distort market prices and act as additional incentives to internalization. So far we have been addressing market imperfections at the nation-state level, discrepancies that affect foreign firms coming into a country much more than already-ensconced national firms. The larger truth is that internalization advantages are relevant for any firm and help to explain why we more often see hierarchies at work in the world of business rather than pure markets. Yet the internalization advantages for MNEs are obvious, and these advantages encourage firms to expand into foreign markets not through foreign agents, joint ventures and other non-hierarchical forms, but through their own internal organization in the form of foreign subsidiaries.[7]

Finally, we turn to *location advantages* or, as they are also known, country-specific factors. These have been popularized by Harvard's Michael Porter with his important work on the 'national competitiveness diamond'.[8] Simply put, this factor relates to the advantages a firm gains from operating in a particular country. In the last two decades global-oriented firms in many industries have moved considerable parts of their activities overseas in order to take advantage of location factors. Prominent examples include seeking out lower workers' wage rates in South-East Asia and Mexico, and trying to gain competitive advantage in newly emerging markets such as China. Head offices have moved from Sweden and France to the UK in order to avoid higher tax rates in their home countries. Some companies have located for the purpose of increasing organizational learning by starting up R&D labs in Silicon Valley, or in partnership with universities such as Oxford and Cambridge. Here the focus is on what economists call the national factor endowments of a nation.

In a more formal sense, potential advantages might include: lower input costs (such as low labour wages and inexpensive national resources); increased labour productivity; the size and character of markets; reduced transport costs; and the physical distance from key markets and the home country of the MNE. Other factors affecting location advantages are: tariff barriers; the taxation structure; risk factors; attitudes toward FDI; and the structure of national competition within an industry. A lot of this can be summed up under the rubric of market-seeking and resource-seeking activities. These have been the twin engines driving MNEs both ancient and modern. A recent example of market-seeking behaviour was the renaissance of an 1890s dream, 'the China market'. Many firms set up ventures in China in the early 1990s in order to be in a position to secure a market of more than one billion potential consumers. Resource-seeking behaviour of recent note surely includes major oil companies setting up subsidiaries far from their home base to secure petroleum supplies for their downstream retail marketing activities – that is, the local petrol or gas station.

But was the emphasis on resource-seeking and market-seeking behaviour as important in ancient times as it is today in the age of turbo-charged capitalism? Is there evidence for the bold claim that such modern-sounding concepts as foreign direct investment and OLI were extant, at least in principle, in the world of Ashur and Augustus? Read on. The answers will surprise you.

NOTES TO CHAPTER 2

1. Two other important theories that seek to explain foreign activities of firms are the internationalization theory of the MNE (see Buckley, P. and Casson, M. (1976) *The Future of the Multinational Enterprise*. London: Macmillan; Hennart, J. F. (1982) *A Theory of Multinational enterprise*, Ann Arbor, MI: University of Michigan Press) and the macro-economics theory of foreign direct investment (consult Kojima, K. 'Reorganization of North-south Trade: Japan's Foreign Economics Policy for the 1970s' in (1973) *Hitosubasi Journal of Economics*, 23: 630–40; and his 'Japanese Direct Investment Abroad' in (1990) *Social Science Research Institute Monograph* Series 1. Tokyo: International Christian University).

2. Dunning, J. (1993) *Multinational Enterprises and the Global Economy*. Workingham, UK: Addison-Wesley, 3.

3. The term *strategic competencies* comes from Barlett, C. and Ghoshal, S. *Managing across Borders: The Transnational Solution*, Harvard Business School Press, Boston, 1989. Kay, J. (1995) in his *Foundations of Corporate Success* (Oxford University Press) uses the term *distinctive capabilities*.

4. Dunning, J. (1993) *Multinational enterprises and the Global Economy*. Workingham, UK: Addison-Wesley; Buckley, P. and Casson, M. (1976) *The Future of the Multinational Enterprise*, New York: Holmes and Meier.

5. They also, or alternatively, turn to using their FSAs in allied markets: what might be called horizontal extension. An example is Virgin's expanding in its home market of the UK by buying a rail line; in this case there has been the question of the extendability of the competencies of their ventures into running a rail line.

6. Buckley, P. (1993) 'The Role of Management in Internalization Theory' in *Management International Review*, 33, 3, 197–207.

7. We use the term *foreign subsidiaries* here broadly to include forms short of subsidiaries such as a sales office.

8. see Porter, M. (1990) *The Competitive Advantage of Nations*. Boston: The Free Press.

3

Cradles of civilisation ... and capitalism

The international economy of the Copper and Bronze Age: 3500–1600 BCE

C APITALISTS – in the Bronze Age? Entrepreneurs in ancient Mesopotamia? Aren't we exaggerating a little here? For today's sophisticated venture capitalist, whose fortunes change hands at the flick of a cursor, it must certainly seem like it.

But truth is often stranger than fiction. Almost as far back in time as we want to go, the business of the world – with apologies to Calvin Coolidge – was business. Human civilizations, including commerce, arose in the valleys of the Nile, Indus, Yellow, Tigris and Euphrates rivers during what is known as the Copper Age, around 3500 BCE. The Sumerian culture of Mesopotamia would become the most dynamic of these civilizations, for it and its daughter civilizations of Babylon and Assyria would lay the foundations of both Western civilization and Western capitalism for 3000 years – half of recorded human history. So why did Mesopotamian Iraq, the Land of the Two Rivers, come to excel in world politics and trade while more fertile and protected regions such as Egypt, India and China remained peripheral?

Much of the answer lies in its geographical position: it occupied a favourable strategic position in terms of potential trade routes. The towns of Egypt were flanked on the east and west by the foreboding African desert, a savage terrain relieved only by the narrow and fertile Nile valley; by gaining control of the northern and southern exits of the Nile, a single ruler could control the approaches to Africa. This is precisely what happened. A line of strong Pharaohs, beginning with Menes, seized total control in Egypt, suppressed local initiative and autonomy in the Delta and beyond, and erected a permanent centralized bureaucracy that

The resource-based view of the firm, or history matters

Core competencies, core capabilities and administrative heritage are among the hottest terms in strategic management. Organizations from large multinationals to government agencies work hard to figure out the areas where they compete with the best, on a world-class level. After sorting out what their core capabilities are, many organizations then move to outsource the majority of the other activities that fall outside those capabilities. The theory is that an organization will contribute more if it focuses on where it brings the greatest value, the result being profits for a firm and stakeholder support for a non-profit or government agency.

Popularized by LBS's Gary Hamel and Michigan's C.K. Prahalad in the early 1990s in their book *Competing For the Future* (Boston: Harvard Business School Press, 1994) and in a series of *Harvard Business Review* articles, the concept of core competencies is a well marketed packaging of what is called the resource-based view of the firm. This academic theory is, arguably, the most widely studied by strategic-management scholars today.

Over the past 20 years two major schools of analysis have been very important for corporate strategic thinking. The first was a result of the hugely influential (1980) *Competitive Strategy* by Harvard's Michael Porter (New York: The Free Press). In it Porter turned industrial economics on its head; traditionally this branch of economics was concerned with the problems created by monopolies, typically the view of government. Porter took the tools of industrial economics and used them to help a firm understand the dynamics of an industry so that it could improve its profits – an altogether different concern from that of the government! This led to a focus on the industry and an understanding that Porter called the *five forces* that dominate a given industry, namely: *Barriers to Entry*, that is how hard it is for a new competitor to enter an industry; *The Threat of Substitutes*, how easy it is for customers to turn to other products if the price becomes too high; *The Power of Suppliers & The Power of Customers*, which refers to the relative power of suppliers and customers and their ability to upset the power-structure of the industry as it is today; and finally, *The Degree of Rivalry Between Competitors*, that is the intensity of competition in an industry.

What would often happen is that senior executives in a firm would use high-flying management consultants like McKinsey or Bain to undertake a rigorous industry analysis as a central input to the development of the firm's strategy. What came to the fore towards the end of the 1980s was that what a firm should do, what strategy it should adopt, depended on who it was. An IBM and a Dell both compete in the PC market, and could well receive the same report from a management consultancy about the dynamics of the PC industry, but should adopt very different approaches because they have different strengths and weaknesses or, as academics put it, a different set of resource stocks with which they compete in the marketplace, hence the resource-based view of the firm. In retrospect this seems like common sense, but like many things, it didn't appear quite as obvious in the cut and thrust of the time.

This focus on the resources of the firm has been called a number of things: one, from Sumantra Ghoshal and Chris Bartlett, being the administrative heritage of the firm. We think that their term captures a key idea: that for an organization properly to develop a strategy that is the way forward it must keep firmly in mind its past, because it is in the past that the resource base was built and it is this from which it will launch its future successes. To develop an effective strategy for a particular organization, strategists would do well to study the history of the firm and how it ended up where it is today.

monopolized commerce and turned the state's best minds to the service of the imperial cult. Egypt's leaden authoritarianism became the forerunner of the centrally directed and semi-communistic empires of more modern times: the Sassanid Mongol, Ottoman, Manchu, Moghul, Aztec and Inca despotisms, and perhaps contributed to the cultural style of both Czarist and Soviet Russia.[1]

As for China, it was hardly a promising candidate for either techno-logical or commercial pre-eminence. For 2000 years, throughout the Bronze Age and much of the Iron Age, its economy developed in a self-contained world. While the Egyptians, Sumerians and Indus Valley civilizations were building pyramids and ziggurats and trading with each other, the Longshan (Lung Shan) people (late 3rd and early 2nd millennia BCE) were forming walled settlements along the Yellow River, raising cattle and sheep and learning the art of working in bronze.[2] Ancient China left us only a few business records written on shell and bone; it entered the age of cities and commerce almost two millennia after the Sumerians.

The first historic Chinese dynasty, the Shang, ruled all of northern China from the city of Anyang after 1766 BCE.[3] Even in these early times, Chinese economics had a tradition of regimented state enterprise, and emphasis was on the family and a kinship unit known as the *zu* (*tsu*). All *zu* were subject to the king in Anyang. This kinship structure, in which the king was patriarch of all, controlled economic as well as political life. Land was owned not by private farmers but by the king himself, who spoke of 'my lands' or 'our lands'. New land was cleared and sown on his orders by farmers bound to 'agricultural collectives, controlled by the rulers. Their lives and posses-sions were controlled by the king and the nobles, being in essence their tools and possessions.'[4] Chinese industry was also centralized in two major workshops situated at Anyang. The Shang approach to bronzeworking was radically different from that of the Sumerians. Instead of forging tools, vessels and implements piece by piece, the royal smiths poured molten copper and tin into elaborate moulds that created *cast* bronze products of much greater beauty and quality than those to the west. There was, at this point, no significant trade with the west, and royal control of the Yellow River valley allowed Anyang to monopolise what trade did occur with other Far Eastern kingdoms.[5]

But in Sumer, Babylon and Assyria, and possibly India, history took a different turn. These areas were destined to become the true cradles of private economic initiative. The oldest written documents of civilization itself (dating from 3200 BCE if not earlier) show early business transactions arising north of the swampy coastline of the Persian Gulf. The slow-moving waters of the Euphrates were easy to channel for irrigation water, allowing the first Sumerian villages to arise.[6] Both the Tigris and Euphrates and their adjoining canals formed webs of land- and water-routes that would 'tend to strengthen local or regional units and impede the trend towards [Sumerian political] unification'. Thus Mesopotamian geography and agriculture allowed the rise of *multiple* power centres along the Fertile Crescent, something unknown or temporary in China, Egypt, and perhaps, the Indus valley.[7]

It is simplistic, however, to assume that geography alone led to the rise of capitalism in Mesopotamia. It did not. What it did do was make political consolidation more difficult. No single municipality or settlement or bureaucratic entity could easily monopolise access to the outside world, a fact that allowed an environment of competition to develop between the various Sumerian towns. This was a decisive factor in generating the technological revolution that, after 3100 BCE, would help usher in the Bronze Age. Before this, Sumerians and others in ancient Mesopotamia lived in an almost completely rural subsistence economy in towns along or near the river valleys, or wherever sufficient rainfall and moisture permitted them to settle. Only one or two towns such as Eridu and Uruk merited the status of a city.[8]

As the Bronze Age urban revolution gained momentum (between 3100 and 2900 BCE), however, the Sumerian landscape began to change dramatically. The Tigris–Euphrates valley and the western edge of modern-day Iran steadily acquired dense clusters of farms and towns. At least a dozen thriving cities sprang up whose names are known to history, such as Kish, Ur, Lagash, Umma, Awan, Hamazi and Shuruppak. This take-off was also to take place nearby, in northern Mesopotamia, Syria, Anatolia, the Indus valley and even Egypt; but the Sumerians, now crowded into their burgeoning cities in search of both new economic opportunities and military security, led the world in the arts of capital formation, technological innovation and urban development.[9]

Tall oaks from little acorns grow! The early chapters of Genesis echo events in Sumerian times, as noted by Yale historians William J. Hallo and William Kelly Simpson, among others. The Genesis writers' accounts of Cain's 'building a city' and, six generations later, of Tubal Cain's making 'all kinds of tools out of bronze and iron' are seen by Hallo and Simpson as a reference to the beginnings in Sumer of urbanization and the invention of bronze.[10] Foundries with fires heated to 590 °C and 790 °C made metallurgy possible; Sumerian smiths, accustomed to forging copper tools, began to discover that soft red-brown copper ore forged with tin would produce an even harder metal alloy.[11] The more tin that was added, the yellower and harder the new metal became. Now they could make sturdy ploughs, sickles, donkey-carts, tools and cookware that vastly increased human productivity. The very map of Sumer itself was redrawn by the new bronze tools. Farmers could grow enough wheat and barley to feed the new sculptors, artisans, carpenters, leather-workers, bricklayers, scribes and others, who were now able to earn a living in places such as Uruk.[12]

We know a lot about the dawn of civilization and business in the Near East from thousands of clay tablets found in places like Ur, Shuruppak, Girsu near Lagash, and the site of Ebla in Syria. Most documents date from 2500–2300 BCE, and are written in the wedge-shaped characters of cuneiform, which evolved from pictograms.[13] The focus of individual tablets is often narrow, but taken in their totality, they are legible and detailed enough to provide an eye-witness commentary on history's first urban society, its evolving economy, and even its domestic and international political order.[14] Sumer's politics, diplomacy, war and business, although different from our own, are still recognisable. Commonplace household items, too, such as vases decorated with images of ears of corn and stalks of wheat, speak volumes about the economic life of the time.[15]

At the centre of the communities were the temples of the gods and the palaces of their *lugals* – 'big men', or kings. The temple clergy dispensed relief to the poor, while considering all their subjects merely servants created for the pleasure of the air-god Enlil, Enki and other powerful deities.[16] Political power rested in the hands of tribal chiefs who built temples and public works to enhance their personal prestige and upstage their rivals. However, although historians used to think that these city-states were 'socialist' theocracies, in which temples had all the power and owned all the land, by the 1960s archaeologists realized that individual and family property and commercial markets were part of the Mesopotamian economy from the beginning. Early capitalist networks worked alongside and in perfect harmony with the public enterprises of palace and temple. The average Sumerian peasant was more than capable of supporting himself and his family from his poultry and the wheat and vegetables grown on his small irrigated plot, which he would have owned: real estate was a thriving business as far back as Early Dynastic times.[17] Sumerians were neither communists nor *laissez-faire* capitalists. The ancient tablets show us a mixed economy where entrepreneurs had certain freedoms within a framework of strongly regulated commerce, much of it state-run:

'All sectors of production, from agriculture to industry, stand subject to an iron-handed administration which ... not only controls and registers every phase of the work, but also plans and promotes it.'[18]

The building programmes of the chiefs stimulated both commerce and the growth of towns. By 2500 BCE the vast majority of Mesopotamians lived in cities. Shuruppak, home of the legendary Ut-Napishtim, the Babylonian Noah, grew in area from 40 hectares in 3000 BCE to between 70 and 100 hectares by 2300 BCE. Some Sumerian cities quite possibly contained within their mud-brick walls some 15–30 000 people.[19]

As the city-states perfected the arts of weapon-making and political organization, they soon equipped humankind's first armies. Armies enforced the ambition of the rulers and deterred the ambition of their neighbours. Tribal democracies became monarchies as the 'big men' claimed hereditary and even semi-divine powers. No longer just servants of the gods, the kings of Sumer became first supermen and then semi-divine 'sons of God'.[20]

As early as 2500 BCE, the city-states began to evolve into nation-states, controlling large tracts beyond their urban cores. Smaller states became vassals of more powerful domains. Ebla became a huge commercial empire that exercized control over much of Syria, northern Mesopotamia and even part of Anatolia, rich in wheat, barley, cattle, silver, gold and textiles.

The fierce power struggles endured in Sumer accelerated the development of her international business and long-distance trade. Warring 'men of renown' such as Gilgamesh and Eannatum needed endless supplies of copper and bronze for their chariots, battle-axes, swords, spears, daggers, shields and arrows. The cities of Sumer had plenty of food but were far from deposits of precious stones, copper and tin; so Kish, Ur, Uruk and their neighbours set up trading networks with distant places and bartered their surplus food and textiles for the resources they needed. Thus began what we today call resource-seeking behaviour and the quest for competitive advantage.[21]

> 'At least as important as these local resources was the lack of other
> important raw materials, which all had to be imported. South
> Mesopotamia has no source of metals, no trees that produced
> suitable timber for larger constructions and only insignificant
> amounts of stone. The focus of much documented commercial and
> imperial activity was the acquisition of these items.'[22]

The first international economy was in place shortly after 3000 BCE. Goods floated up and down the Tigris and Euphrates in reed boats, travelled overland by donkey, and headed off to destinations as far west as the Aegean and as far east as India and Afghanistan. The existence of this network of commerce is confirmed not only by the artefacts of Sumer and Ebla but by Sumerian and Babylonian literature. The Sumerian poem *Enmerkar and the Land of Aratta* spoke of a long-distance venture in which King Enmerkar of Uruk bartered his city's abundant grain for the minerals of the distant land of Aratta to the east (modern-day Afghanistan). Huge deposits of copper, tin and precious stones such as lapis lazuli, together with evidence of mining, have been found in Iran, Uzbekistan and Afghanistan.[23] Because Indus-valley smiths were smelting bronze at the same time as their counterparts in Sumer (3100 BCE), it seems that both Sumerians and Indians exported tin from Aratta: if the evidence in *Enmerkar* is correct, Sumerian merchants were involved in a true export–import trade in the fourth millennium BCE. It is not difficult to conjure up impressions of aggressive Mesopotamian traders packing foodstuffs and cloth wares in leather bags on the sides and backs of their donkeys to head out across the Iranian plateau, to secure supplies of tin and precious stones from Afghanistan and India some 3000 years before the Christian era.

Similar long-distance trade routes developed between Mesopotamia, Syria and other kingdoms to the west. Precious metals existed in Anatolia (now Turkey). Early Bronze Age Anatolia was as much a battleground for competing trade-hungry dynasties as Sumerian Iraq. Their situation was simply the reverse: lacking food and textiles, but having abundant reserves of silver and tin, Anatolian princes welcomed a chance to trade the latter for the former.[24]

Ebla and northern Mesopotamia were Anatolia's best customers. From 2600 to 2300 BCE the Eblaites ruled some seventeen kingdoms that included all of Syria, large portions of Palestine, northern Mesopotamia, and a section of Anatolia itself. Archaeology shows the scale of this early trade network: weapons in northern Mesopotamia and Syria were identical to Sumerian types; lapis lazuli from the east was unearthed at Mari; stone sculptures in northern Iraq were identical to those further south.[25]

The region of Syria around Ebla produced enough wheat, barley, wine and olives to feed millions. Ebla abounded in livestock, the royal herds alone boasting 80 000 cattle and 80 000 sheep. It was no less successful in industry, its textile mills being equal, if not superior, to those of Sumer. It also possessed enormous reserves of silver and gold – the preferred medium of exchange, even at this time. Through bilateral trade agreements with its neighbours, Ebla provided the world's first documented legal framework for international commerce. Trading as far south as Sinai, as far west as Cyprus and as far north as Kanesh, the Eblaite dynasty linked these regions with the new cities of Mari and Ashur. So, a fixed system of prices based on silver and gold, and an elaborate treaty system, created an early form of Common Market *and* a sophisticated body of international law by which trade routes were safeguarded and the flow of merchants and goods guaranteed.[26]

Despite its vast domain, Ebla's empire lasted no more than seven decades. Rich and liberal by ancient standards, she was dethroned by her more warlike rivals. In her place arose an empire led by the Mesopotamian usurper calling himself *Sharrukenu*, or Sargon. Conquering a domain that stretched from the Mediterranean to the Persian Gulf from his new royal city of Akkad, Sargon provided a model for supranational empires to come. He introduced permanent military garrisons, strategically placed forts, a centralized form of government and a personal claim to renown and world rule that outraged the priests of Nippur.[27]

The kings of Akkad were as noteworthy for their expansion of trade as they had been for their conquests. Akkad became the hub of a flow of goods, money, knowledge and resources that moved in all directions. Mesopotamian commerce was now carried on by sea as well as on land. State-subsidized vessels from Lagash, Larsa, Umma and Ur carried Sumerian wheat and textiles to points along the Gulf as far as the Indian Ocean. These venturous exporters brought back copper, tin and precious stones in quantities far greater than donkeys could ever dream of carrying. Temple records tell the story: the god Enki in the mythical tale of *Enki and Ninhursag* confers a blessing on the land of Dilmun (modern Bahrain), the trading destination for the wares of eight different countries, including Magan (Oman), Meluhha (India), Elam and, of course, Sumer.[28] *Enki and the World Order* again alludes to seaborne trade, conducted by Dilmun-boats, Magan-boats and *magilum*-boats sailing back and forth between India, the Horn of Arabia and the river-ports of Sumer. In a revealing passage, the god Enki includes the Gulf trade as part of the global order over which he presides:

> *The l[ands] of Magan and Dilmun*
> *Looked up at me, En[ki],*
> *Moored (?) the Dilmun-boat to the ground (?),*
> *Loaded the Magan-boat sky high;*
> *The* magilum-*boat of Meluhha*
> *Transports gold and silver,*
> *Brings them to Nippur for Enlil, the [king] of all the lands.*[29]

India entered the world of international commerce as Meluhha, which supplied the merchants of Sumer with wood, copper, gold, silver, carnelian and cotton. Its cities, its ceramic and copper industries, and its trade evolved in tandem with those of Sumer. Excavations of the great Indus-valley cities of Harappa and Mohenjo-Daro in the 1920s revealed a genuine urban society and a capitalist culture that were tightly organized and well-managed from the outset. Indus-valley cities were laid out in neat rectangular streets and had the best sewage system in the ancient world. Uniform weights and measures were based on both binary and decimal systems.[30]

Further excavations have shown that the Indus culture extended into Afghanistan and even Central Asia. After 3000 BCE, the Indus cities were engaging in a form of 'semi-industrial mass production' of ceramics. Towns and cities, whose homes were made with adobe bricks and standardized courtyards, doubled in size, and trade with Sumer intensified. Towards the end of the 3rd millennium BCE the port of Lothal on the Indus served as 'an emporium of trade between the Indus civilization and Mesopotamia'.[31] Lothal seems to have supplied the Indus cities with cotton from Gujarat and copper from Rajasthan at a time when raw materials were very much in demand. Up to about 2500 BCE, the cities of Mohenjo-Daro, Harappa and Kalibangan served as capitals of their regions in the way that Uruk, Kish and other cities did in Sumer. From

2500 BCE on, the uniformity of pottery and other artefacts suggests that Mohenjo-Daro had unified the Indian civilization of its time in the manner that the Mauryans and Guptas would do in later centuries.[32]

Sargon's traders journeyed west as well as east, absorbing the region of Ebla into the world of Sumer. The Enki myths show both the importation of copper, exotic goods and gold from the east and the developing trade between Sumer, Ebla and cities on the Mediterranean. Enriched by a growing import–export business, the cities of Mesopotamia were connected by an extensive river-borne commerce, as revealed in the tale that follows the route of the god Enki as his boat journeyed along the Tigris and Euphrates, from Ur in the south to Ashur in the north.[33] Evidence exists of trading posts in northern Iraq, in Syria, on the Upper Euphrates and in Turkey, in which Akkadians founded settlements among the resident population.

Tablets dating from Sargon's time say little about Anatolia, just enough to hint that he got his silver and tin from a place called Purushkanda. A monument shows Akkadian soldiers leading captives whose hair, daggers and drinking vessels are Anatolian, but Sargon was unlikely to have occupied the region, preferring instead to control the strategic Taurus mountain passes.[34] Asia Minor was now an integral part of a web of commerce stretching from the Hellespont to the Hindu Kush. Mesopotamia became the breadbasket and workshop of the world, trading finished goods for raw materials. The international money economy pioneered in Ebla was continued in Akkad. All goods, loans and commodities were priced and quoted in terms of silver. Silver was eagerly exchanged in the form of ingots or as rings worn by parties to various transactions. Where silver was not available, grain, cattle and the perennial pigs or donkeys substituted as the universal currency.[35]

Age of the merchant-princes

Just who were the dynamic traders in this extensive and evolving Bronze Age trade? Was there a state enterprise left in the hands of the temples and royal palaces, or did it eventually become the work of self-supporting private individuals seeking profit on their own initiative? Was the eager Bronze Age Sumerian *dam-gàr* (merchant-prince – Akkadian a public employee or was he free to trade on his own behalf as an entrepreneur?

Giving a precise definition to the role and dimensions of merchants in Bronze Age society is a bit of a divining act for those of us accustomed to debating the merits of individualism versus collectivism and state control versus privatization. We have to be careful not to look at the bottom of the well of history and see our own image as freebooting capitalists looking back. Yet the evidence is fascinating. The Mesopotamian trader was neither a paid civil servant nor a totally independent entrepreneur in the sense that we understand these terms today. When he first emerged on the Mesopotamian social scene in about 3000 BCE, the larger *dam-gàr* generally operated in the employ of his city's temple or palace. Temples, we should not forget, were repositories of wealth given as offerings and for safe keeping. They functioned as banks do today. The tablets of Akkad show the rise to prominence of a new class of *tamkāru* able to profit from both state contracts and private commercial arrangements.

> We have to be careful not to look at the bottom of the well of history and see our own image as freebooting capitalists looking back

The export trade still rested in the hands of crown functionaries and temple officials. Public institutions, funded by state taxes and temple tithes, provided both the capital and the organizational skill for long, perilous journeys by boat or donkey-caravan to Anatolia, Meluhha or Aratta.

> Temples, we should not forget, were repositories of wealth given as offerings and for safe keeping. They functioned as banks do today

As economic links expanded and developed, however, the *tamkārum* was in a position to accumulate more and more of his own capital and gradually to assume the role of creditor, moneylender and independent agent. From the Akkadian period on, the records suggest the emergence of an independent trading class throughout Mesopotamia. While many merchants continued to take advantage of state- and temple-sponsored transactions, a growing number began to act on their own initiative. Many merchants became independently wealthy through buying, selling and speculating, while still tied to transactions involving throne and temple. We read of Ur-Sara of Umma, for example, raising livestock for state consumption. Ginunu, his contemporary, traded in grain and silver, while Sunitum dealt in barley and other foodstuffs. Women with names such as Ana-é dealt in real estate, metals and grain. Yet the burgeoning *tamkāru* class does not appear in the list of state households in Akkadian times. They were regarded as government customers and agents, not public employees.[36]

The Akkadian Empire collapsed after 2200 BCE. The Gulf trade continued under a succession of Middle Bronze Age states led by Ur, Isin, Larsa and, eventually, Babylon, under the reign of Hammurabi. Hammurabi! Even today, who has not heard of Hammurabi's Law Code making adroit and skilful use of warfare and diplomacy, this celebrated ruler left the most complete records yet of the trading life of early antiquity.

The picture emerging from these records is astonishing. Textiles and food from Mesopotamia still flowed east and the copper, tin and luxuries of India, Afghanistan and the Gulf still flowed west – with a difference! Much of the produce shipped eastward – fish, textiles, barley and wheat – became classified as exchangeable goods. The palace stewards of Ur-Nammu, Shulgi and their heirs reigning as the Third Dynasty of Ur (UR III) assigned to them a fixed value by weight of silver. In contrast, however, many other items such as copper, tin, lumber, spices, wines and cattle fluctuated greatly according to their markets.

The merchants involved in this lucrative export–import trade, however, grew more specialized and independent. This was a key Bronze Age development. International trade began to pass from priests and palace functionaries to self-employed merchant-princes. Privatization would accelerate in the Old Babylonian period, as this city on the Euphrates became dominant between 1800 and 1600 BCE.

It is noteworthy that, whereas the rulers of pre-Sargonic Lagash and of Akkad talk of direct trade with Meluhha, Magan and Dilmun, in Ur III times the Mesopotamian ships reach only to Magan, and in Old Babylonian times no further than Dilmun. This may reflect conditions in the Gulf, but it may also have to do with a shift within Mesopotamia from publicly supported ventures to private enterprise, which would probably imply less capital investment.

Then, as now, politics began to affect trade. At mighty Ur, for example, a burgeoning bureaucracy helped stifle the life of the city. The once-great Ur-Nammu dynasty gave way to the less powerful kingdoms of Isin and Larsa around 2000 BCE. These new kings possessed neither the capital nor the trained personnel to renew state-sponsored international commerce on a large scale. Yet Sumer and its heir, Babylon, always had to trade or die.

Mesopotamia, the 'land between the rivers', was susceptible to crop failure, drought, infestation and freebooting raiders. It is not surprising, then, that something akin to the 1990s trend towards privatization in the Western economy took place. The merchant community itself stepped forward to fill the vacuum left by the public sector.[37] The leadership in international trade devolved upon a newly emergent commercial institution known as the *kāru*. The *kāru* is a term best translated as 'harbour'. The *kāru* originated from communities of traders living alongside the docks of large Sumerian port cities such as Ur, Umma and Lagash. In the face of political instability and economic necessity, these informal associations of *tamkāru* were granted semi-official status by the local kings. The *kāru* were headed by a chief commercial magnate, the *orwakil tamkāru*, who was granted adminis-trative authority from the crown to conduct and regulate commerce. *Kāru* in various cities were empowered to exercise the commercial, legal and administrative duties the public sector could no longer afford to sustain. It was equivalent to the British Crown's giving wide legal and administrative powers to the factors and entrepreneurs of the Hudson's Bay Company in 18th-century British North America. Meanwhile, all across Mesopotamia, donkey-caravans and Dilmun-boats continued to carry the copper, tin, wheat and textiles that had sustained the region for generations.[38]

The rise of a capitalist economy, international trade and the devolution of state power and enterprise to the realm of the private *kāru* in Babylonia was paralleled in the north and west, in regions once dominated by Ebla. In past centuries, the neo-Sumerian realm of Ur had controlled the city of Ashur. Ur's successor states of Isin and Larsa were too weak to do so. Around 2000 BCE, the ruler Puzur-Ashur fortified the wall of Ashur (modern-day Qal'at Sharqat) and thus Assyria made its not-so-modest bow into history. It soon became a commercial power in its own right as heir to the northern economic sphere, which included Anatolia, Mari and Ebla. This area would become a famous cockpit of history in the ancient Near East and the cradle of the first multinational enterprises.

NOTES TO CHAPTER 3

1. Larsen, M.T. 'The Tradition of Empire in Mesopotamia; in *idem*, ed (1979) *Power and Propaganda: a Symposium on Ancient Empires*. Copenhagen: Akademisk Forlag, 47–7.

2. Chinese names are transliterated by either traditional spellings or the new *pinyin*, which is now adpted in China itself. Under *pinyin*, which is generally used (except for authors cited or note references) in this book, Fukien, for example is rendered as Fujian, Sung as Song, Ch'in as Quin, Cheng Ho as Zheng He, Yangtze as Yangzi, Kwangtung as Guangdong, Chou as Zhou, etc. The *Pinyin* spelling will be presented first followed by the tradktional spelling, if it is different.

3. Hucker, C.O. (1997) *China's Imperial Past*. Stanford, CA: Stanford University Press, 21–30; Kwang-chich (1980) *Shang Civilizaton*. New Haven, CT: Yale University Press, 69–73.

4. Chang Cheng-lang 'P'u-tz'u p'ou t'ien chi ch'i hsiang-kuan chu wen-ti in (1973) *K'ao ku Hsüeh-pao* (1): 93–118, in Chang, Kwang-chih, 226–7.

5. Chang, Kwang-chih (1980) *Shang Civilization*. New Haven, CT: Yale University Press. 233–40.

6. Kuhrt. A. (1994) *The Ancient Near East, c. 3000–330 BC*. London: Routledge, Volume I, 19–21.

7. *Ibid.*, 21; Larsen, M.T. 'The Tradition of Empire in Mesopotamia' in *idem*, ed. (1979) *Power and Propaganda: a Symposium on Ancient Empires*. Copenhagen: Akademisk Forlag, 47, 77.

8. Halo, W.W. and Simpson, W.K. (1971) *The Ancient Near East: a History*. New York: Hartcourt, Brace and Jovanich, 12–13; Mallowan, M.E.L. (1971) *Early Mesopotamia and Iran*. New York: McGraw-Hill, 25°8; Nissen, H.J. (1983) *The Early History of the Ancient Near East: 900–2000 BC*. Chicago: University of Chicago Press, 39–64.

9. Hallo, W.W. and Simpson, W.K. (1971) *The Ancient Near East: a History*. New York: Harcourt, Brace and Jovanich, 31–4.

10. Gen. 4:17–23. Biblical references are from the *New International Version* here and throughout.

11. Hallo, W.W. and Simpson, W.K. (1971) *The Ancient Near East: a History*. New York: Harcourt, Brace and Jovanich, 20–33.

12. *Ibid.*, 27–33; Nissen, H.J. (1983) *The Early History of the Ancient Near East: 900–2000 BC*. Chicago: University of Chicago Press, 39–64; Pettinato, G. (1981) *The Archives of Ebla: an Empire Inscribed in Clay*, with an afterword by Dahood, M. Garden City, NY: Doubleday and Co., 174; Childe, V.G. (1953) *New Light on the Most Ancient East*. New York: Frederick A. Praeger, 129.

13. Kuhrt, A. (1994) *The Ancient Near East, c. 3000–330 BC*. London: Routledge, Volume I, 28.

14. *Ibid.*, 43.

15. *Ibid.*, 23–5.

16. Orlin, L.L. (1970) *Assyrian Colonies in Cappadoci*a. The Hague, 46–7.

17. Kramer, S.N. (1963) *The Sumerians, their History, Culture and Character*. Chicago:

University of Chicago Press, 75; Limet, H. 'Les schemas du commerce neo-sumerien', *Iraq*, 39, part 1 (1977), 51–3.

18. Pettinato, G. (1981) *The Archives of Ebla: an Empire Inscribed in Clay*, with an afterword by Dahood, M. Garden City, NY: Doubleday and Co., 179–80.

19. Kuhrt, A. (1994) *The Ancient Near East, c. 3000–330 BC*. London: Routledge, Volume I, 25, 31–2.

20. Hallo, W.W. and Simpson, W.K. (1971) *The Ancient Near East: a History*. New York: Harcourt, Brace and Jovanich, 33–49; Kramer, S.N. (1963) the *Sumerians, their History, Culture and Character*. Chicago: University of Chicago Press, 73–4.

21. Larsen, M.T. 'The Tradtion of Empire in Mesopotamia' in *idem*, ed. Propaganda: *a Symposium on Ancient Empires*. Copenhagen: Akademisk Forlag, 76.

22. Kuhrt, A. (1994) *The Ancient Near East, c. 3000–330 BC*. London: Routldge, Volume I, 21.

23. Stech, T. and Piggott, V.C. 'The Metals Trade in Southwest Asia in the Third Millennium BC', *Iraq*, (1986), 40–5; Kramer, S.N. 'Commerce and Trade: Gleanings from Sumerian Literature', *Iraq*, 39, part 1 (1977), 61.

24. Özgüç, T. 'Early Anatolian Archaeology in the Light of Recent Research', *Anotlia*, VII, (1963) 10–11.

25. Kuhrt, A. (1994) *the Ancient Near East, c. 3000–330BC*. London: Routledge, Volume I, 40–1.

26. Pettinato, G. (1981) *The Archives of Ebla: an Empire Inscribed in Clay*, with an afterword by Dahood, M. Garden City, NY: Doubleday and Co., 184, 226–6.

27. An acient city of Mesopotamia, now in south-eastern Iraq. it was never a political capital, but it played a dominant role in the religious life of Mesopotamia, as the seat of the workshop of Enlil.

28. Kramer, S.N. (1963) *The Sumerians, their History, Culture and Character*. Chicago: University of Chicago Press, 276–84; Forster, B.R. 'Comercial Actvities in Sargonic Mesopotamia' *Iraq*, 39, Part 1 (1977), 38–9.

29. 'Enki and the World Order' in Kramer, S.N. (1963) *The Sumerians, their History, Culture and Character*. Chicago: University of Chicago Press, 176.

30. Kulke, H. and Rothermund, D. (1993) *History of India*. London: Routledge, 24.

31. *Ibid.*

32. *Ibid.*, 24–6.

33. Larsen, M.T. 'The Tradition of Empire in Mesopotamia' in *idem*, ed. (1979) *Power and Propaganda: a Symposium on Ancient Empires*. Copenhagen: Akademisk Forlag, 77–9.

34. Mellnik, M. 'An Akkadian Illustration of a Capaign in Cilicia?', Anatolia, VII (1963), 101–2, 110–1.

35. Forster, B.R. 'Commercial Activities in Sargonic Mesopotamia, *Iraq*, 39, *Part 1* (1977), 35–6.

36. *Ibid.*, 32–3, 36–7.

37. Postgate, G.N. (1992) *Early Mesopotaia: Society and Economy at the Dawn of History*. London: Routledge, 220–1.

38. Garelli, P. (1963) *Les Assyriens en Cappadoce*. Paris: Librarie Adrien Maissoneuve, 171–2; Postgate, G.N. (1992) *Early Mesopotamia: Society and Economy at the Dawn of History*. London: Routledge, 220–1.

4

Cradle of multinational enterprise

Assyria and Babylonia: 2000–1000 BCE

T HE Assyrians! The ancient world rang with the terror of their name. The Hebrew prophets knew them well and sketched their ravaging ways in vivid and unforgettable language. Listen to Isaiah:

'Here they come, swiftly and speedily! Not one of them grows tired or stumbles, no one slumbers or sleeps ... Their arrows are sharp, all their bows are strung; their horses' hoofs seem like flint, their chariots' wheels like whirlwind. Their roar is like that of the lion, they roar like young lions; they growl as they seize their prey and carry it off with no one to rescue (Isaiah 5:26–29).

Isaiah's Assyria (Ashur) – the terror of the ancient Near East – is well known to history. But Ashur the resource-seeking, market-driven international trader is not well known at all. It's time we met him. As they formed their numerous commercial colonies in foreign lands, these deft merchant traders of the second millennium BCE perfected a thousand-year-old system of private enterprise inherited from Sumer and Babylon. The commercial structures they created may rightly be described as the first genuine multinational enterprises in recorded history.

With few natural resources, no outlet to the sea, a lack of defensible borders and a series of powerful, hostile neighbours, Assyria lived in constant danger of impoverishment, an impoverishment that required trade to remedy it. Little was known of Old Assyrian life until the 1920s, when the Czech Bedrich Hrozny uncovered a huge find of some 10 000 clay tablets on the site of the Anatolian city of Kanesh, right in the heart of Turkey. The Kanesh tablets, written in the Assyrian language, spoke of contracts, partnerships, profits, orders and other transactions of the business district of a prosperous trading city. University of Ankara excavations continued throughout the 1950s and 1960s and beyond, unveiling a large colony of resident Assyrian merchants who were some of the foremost businessmen of the ancient world.[1]

Ilushuma, Erishum and other Old Assyrian kings adopted both the northern half of Sargon's trading network and the Sumerian–Babylonian *kāru* system. Large-scale and international trade was in the hands of a private sector making up 'the first experiment of free enterprise on a large scale'.[2] The lion's share of ventures was borne by private merchant associations more than willing to accept the risks and profits of long-distance commerce far beyond Assyria's borders.

> The lion's share of ventures was borne by private merchant associations more than willing to accept the risks and profits of long-distance commerce far beyond Assyria's borders

Bronze Age Assyria lacked the means to wage a Sargonid war of conquest to obtain markets and resources, seeking salvation instead in the flourishing model of the 'factor' method embodied in the *kāru*. Assyrian merchants cultivated the favour of a foreign prince, obtaining legal rights to settle as permanent residents in an organized body where they were ideally placed to supervise economic activity directly. In this entrepreneurship with a vengeance, everybody profited: the host-country, Assyria and the merchants themselves. A *kāru* at Nuzi gave Assyrian merchants access to tin mines; a second *kāru* in the Akkadian city of Sippar cemented its trade in clothing and foodstuffs in Assyrian hands.[3]

Most Assyrian *kāru* lay far to the north-west of Ashur and Nineveh, targeting the forests and mines of Syria and Anatolia. Rather than importing the precious copper and tin needed for a Bronze Age economy across Iran or via a Sumerian-dominated Gulf, hundreds of Assyrian merchants invested closer to home. In the decades following 1950 BCE (traditional dating) hundreds of Assyrian merchants flung out a score of commercial *kāru* and factoring sites along the rich caravan routes of the day. Trails wound across Syria, Cilicia and Anatolia, over a thousand kilometres from Ashur itself.[4]

Kārum Kanesh

Archaeology shows that both the Old Assyrian state and the Assyrian presence in Kanesh began within a few decades of the collapse of the neo-Sumerian kingdom of Ur. Digging at Kanesh, the Turkish archaeological teams uncovered four layers of occupation, which can be seen in Table 4.1.

Table 4.1 The Assyrian merchant colonies at Kanesh[5]

Kanesh Level I:	Middle Bronze: destruction, Assyrian occupation, followed by more destruction (1800–1600 BCE) coinciding with Babylonian defeat of Assyria.
Kanesh Level II:	Middle Bronze: thriving Assyrian business district, 2000–1800 BCE, contemporary with Old Assyrian kingdom.
Kanesh Level III:	Early Bronze: economic upsurge to 2000 BCE; Akkadian and Ur periods; commercial links with Syria, Ashur.
Kanesh Level IV:	Early Bronze: early occupation, coinciding with Sumerian Early Dynastic.

Level II contained the most important discoveries for business historians: a well-planned city with a thriving business district. Kanesh was neatly separated into various quarters, divided by streets wide enough for carts. The city centre contained large workshops, foundries and restaurants. Sunlight and fresh air entered scores of windowless brick dwellings, which served as the Assyrian business district. Within their closely bunched six- to eight-room homes the traders stored enormous numbers of business tablets, filed in vases in special rooms. Assyrian living spaces were clearly divided – the family went about its activities in one part of their home and trading offices were maintained in another.

By the time of the Assyrian ruler Erishum (around 1960 BCE, traditional dating) an extensive network of Assyrian *kāru* and lesser trading posts formed a trail of settlement stretching from northern Iraq to the southern shore of the Black Sea.[6] A series of *kāru* in the former territory of Ebla followed the Euphrates upstream to where it met the upper reaches of the Halys. Hattusas lay near the future capital of the Hittite Empire. The largest and most important Assyrian outpost was Kārum Kanesh, situated on the Halys athwart the river and land routes of Asia Minor.[7]

Ashur's colonies were not the result of military conquest, but of trading settlement planted among self-governing Anatolian princes. Bilateral trading and international marketing arrangements were the hallmark of the Assyrian connection. The market-seeking traders opening up the rich treasure-bearing regions of Anatolia did what no other power had done before, systematically knitting together a vast trading 'empire' in a foreign area without recourse to war.[8]

> The market-seeking traders opening up the rich treasure-bearing regions of Anatolia did what no other power had done before, systematically knitting together a vast trading 'empire' in a foreign area without recourse to war

Assyrian resident aliens in Kanesh took on many native ways, even though they were still governed by Assyrian law, and tended to keep to themselves. Their clannishness has allowed us to infer what we can about Old Assyria from the tablets of its merchants hundreds of kilometres away. Houses in the Assyrian quarter of Kanesh looked just like the Anatolian, but the people who lived in them spoke Assyrian, worshipped the god Ashur, and were tried in Assyrian courts. Relations with neighbours were cordial, despite the fact that the evidence of the Kanesh archives suggests an Assyrian superiority complex vis-à-vis their neighbours.[9]

The *kāru* guaranteed the survival of an Assyrian economy engaged in 'commerce without an extensive productive branch'.[10] Having few industries or natural resources, the 10 000 inhabitants of the city of Ashur could not compete as unit producers with Sumerian and Babylonian weavers, farmers or cattlemen. Trade provided a solution, as the merchants of Ashur took over a middleman role linking the Gulf, Black Sea and eastern shore of the Mediterranean.[11]

Assyrian *kāru*, receiving goods by boat and caravan from the Sumerian–Babylonian trading posts to the south, shipped them to other Assyrian *kāru* and trading posts in Syria and Anatolia. This trade, though in private hands, was nevertheless strictly controlled. Unable to compete with the textile workshops of Ur, Larsa, Isin and Babylon, Assyrian merchants established a *kārum* at Sippar, through which they purchased vast quantities of fabric and clothing for resale to thousands of Anatolian buyers. Protectionism was rampant. Even though Babylonian, Sumerian, Akkadian and Elamite traders might enter Assyria to sell their wares, no foreign merchants were permitted to form *kāru* on Assyrian soil where they would be permitted to disturb the latter's tightly-knit trade routes across Mesopotamia.[12]

Overland trade between Ashur and Kanesh still travelled via donkey-caravan as it had for a thousand years in a simple but effective system. Once given a bank loan to cover their expenses, the drivers sealed packages of textiles and other Sumerian goods, along with clay tablets of lading. The seals were to be broken only when the caravans reached Kanesh. The journey, lasting about eight weeks, was dangerous and caravans usually numbered less than 20. Traders faced bad roads, bad weather, wild animals, brigands and taxation by several jurisdictions.

Assyria's entrance into world trade and politics came when state enterprise and royal power were, to some degree, giving way to capitalist initiative and private authorities like the *kārum*. Old Assyrian rulers and merchants 'fashioned a highly organized commercial enterprise, an international import-export business in the fullest sense'.[13] By the time of the Old Assyrian kingdom, business institutions in Mesopotamia were professional, international and a serious force in Near Eastern politics and society.

Kanesh, goal of the caravans, served as the major distribution centre for Assyrian goods, whence they were sent to smaller *kāru* under Kanesh's jurisdiction. Copper and silver from the *kāru* near the Taurus mines was exchanged for Assyrian tin and Babylonian textiles and garments. The latter brought profit margins of at least 100 per cent, which more than made up for the hazards, overhead costs and tolls levied on the northward journey. Returning to Ashur with their ingots of copper and silver, the mobile traders repaid their loans, pocketed their profits and swapped half their silver for fresh tin and textiles.[14]

The Assyrian *kāru* fascinate economists and historians through to our day. Those who set them up built better than they knew. A close examination of these business colonies and the networks they made up shows that they formed part of *history's first recorded multinational enterprises*. Based upon merchant-princes and their families, the firms that operated in Ashur, Kanesh and the other Assyrian settlements had head offices, foreign branch-plants, corporate hierarchies, extraterritorial business

> By the time of the Old Assyrian kingdom, business institutions in Mesopotamia were professional, international and a serious force in Near Eastern politics and society

law, and even a bit of foreign direct investment and value-added activity. Goods and money moved from Ashur to subsidiary offices in Kanesh and on to the branch offices beneath them as well as the other way.

The first recorded multinational: the saga of Pusu-ken

The faces of Pusu-ken of Ashur and his family give life and texture to the wider story of Assyrian business at the dawn of history. They are believed to have lived in the reign of King Ikunum, not long after 1900 BC, and were among the first generation to take up residence in Kanesh.[15] The business was very much a family concern. Lamassi, Pusu-ken's wife, dwelt in Ashur, managing the business when her husband visited the family offices in Anatolia. Their four sons, Suejja, Ashur-muttabbil, Buzazu and Iku-pasha, and their Assyrian and Anatolian wives became permanent residents of Kanesh.

Pusu-ken was a very important figure in Assyrian society and he corresponded frequently with the king. His firm was an early example of a family-based transnational business network. The dealings between Pusu-ken and Lamassi in Ashur and their sons far away in Anatolia also show an *internalization* of business dealings, goods and money being shipped within the structure of a single firm. This did not prevent disputes from arising within the ranks of a family enterprise. Pusu-ken's sons brought a dispute over his will before the city-assembly of Ashur, showing that a breakdown in trust was possible even in family firms.[16] A relevant ancient Arabic saying, 'Tahababu wa-tahasabu', admonished that friends and family members ought to love and trust one another, but nonetheless put their transactions in writing: 'Love each other, but make accounts with each other.'[17]

Pusu-ken did not travel a great deal, but relied upon his family connections to manage a large staff of employees or subordinates in Anatolia. Non-Assyrian natives were limited to menial and peripheral jobs.[18] In contrast, Assyrians residing in Anatolia were allowed the same rights and status as if they had resided in Assyria proper, in a manner many of today's business expatriates will recognize.[19] Evidence is found in the cuneiform tablets of business people from various ethnic origins, including Syrian and Eblaite, suggesting the possibility of a multicultural workforce.

Financing of the enterprise was provided by a partnership arrangement called a *naruqqum*, a capital fund of several investors to provide a ready cash flow for foreign trade. The merchant Amur-Ishtar invested 4 pieces of gold in a partnership with 14 others who contributed another 26. Amur-Ishtar contracted to trade with these 30 gold pieces, a fair sum, for a period of 12 years. The partners contracted for the distribution of profits and provided a penalty for early withdrawal of funds from the investment pool. This is suggestive of a very rudimentary form of stock market complete with shareholders', shareholders' rights, a long-term perspective and obligations and a 'professional manager'. In this case the manager, Amur-Ishtar, received one third of the profits, a handsome reward, even by today's standards.[20]

Assyrian importers and exporters faced the same frustrations as modern businesspeople in dealing with government regulations. The assembly of Ashur imposed strict controls on the import of textiles from Anatolia, and merchants such as Pusu-ken were fined for trying to get around them.[24] There was no escaping the long arm of the state regulators. Yet he and his backers no doubt felt that their extensive foreign operations were worth much more than the trouble.

Babylonia

The colonies of Kanesh vanished from the historical record at the same time as the Old Assyrian empire was overthrown by the Amorite dynasty at Babylon, a dynasty made famous by the exploits of Hammurabi. Quickly overrunning the lucrative cities of Sumer, the Babylonian armies soon absorbed Assyria as well. Records survive from the Old Babylonian kingdom at Sippar showing that the business and trading practices of Hammurabi and his successors closely resembled those of their Sumerian predecessors. Babylonian *tamkāru* took over the caravan routes across Iran to Afghanistan.

> This lively Babylonian trade remained a mixed enterprise. The crown and private merchants each contributed 50 per cent of the capital investment

Hammurabi's ships sailed down the Arabian Gulf to Dilmun, Arabia, East Africa and the Indus valley. This lively Babylonian trade remained a mixed enterprise. The crown and private merchants each contributed 50 per cent of the capital investment.

As already mentioned, relations between king and nobility, including *tamkāru*, remained on a feudal basis in which nobles and merchants received land grants in return for military and other forms of homage, a system anticipating that of medieval Europe. Profits from royal herds and lands contracted out to *tamkāru* were subject to crown royalties. As was the practice in both Sumer and Assyria, crown and temple sought to control prices. Perhaps not so surprisingly, these early investors faced difficulties similar to those of today – prices and income policies were always tenuous, black markets thrived and the issue of true market value was a concern then as now.[22]

Following the death of Hammurabi (either 1750 or 1584 BCE depending on the chronology one adopts), the Babylonian Empire contracted. Parts of Sumer became temporarily independent. Assyria slipped under the control of the warlike Mitanni to the north. For the rest of the second millennium before Christ, Babylon passed under the rule of a foreign dynasty, the *Cossaei Kahshu* or Kassites from western Iran. The Kassites ruled southern Mesopotamia for some four hundred years, replacing the older Sumerian city-states with a unified Babylonian nation-state. This arrangement with Babylon as the pivot was to last until the Persian conquest of 538 BCE. The tablets of Nippur and references from the Egyptian diplomatic archives of El-Amarna show that Kassite Babylonia followed in the pattern of trade and economy charted by Gilgamesh, Sargon, Ur-Nammu and Hammurabi. Babylonia, as it was now called, remained a major player in world affairs and the valued trading partner of Egypt's powerful Eighteenth Dynasty.[23]

This resurgence of Babylonia both revived the Gulf trade and restored prosperity to what is now southern Iraq. Danish archaeologists uncovered evidence of a form of foreign direct investment in the shape of a royal *kā rum*, administered directly from Babylon, centred at a Kassite fortress planted on Bahrain, in the heart of the Gulf. As for the British and the French after them, the goal was to control the lucrative maritime trade of the region. Further north, the impressive island fortress of Dur-Kurigalzu, planted near Baghdad, sought to control the mountain passes to the east. The overseas trade to Asia was now given a boost by utilising the horse, a significant advance on the slower-moving donkeys. By the 1200s BCE, the horse-drawn chariot had become the decisive weapon in war – the Late Bronze / Early Iron Age equivalent of the tank or aeroplane. Any nation with access to the regions of Iran, where such horses could be bred and sold, would possess an important advantage making it a strategic necessity for ambitious kings to control the mountain passes flanking the land of the Two Rivers to the east.

The Late Bronze Age (1550–1250 BCE) was a Golden Age for world trade and culture. Champion horses and the exotic spices of the East flowed from Babylonia to Egypt while copper from Cyprus, ivory and gold from Africa flowed into Babylonia from the south and west. The Mesopotamian models of mercantilist business endured as well, ready to be handed on to the energetic traders of yet another epoch. *Tamkāru*, both royal and private, continued to play a political as well as a commercial role. Private and public enterprise did not just coexist. They were so interwoven as to be virtually indistinguishable. Bronze Age corporatism!

NOTES TO CHAPTER 4

1. passim. Garelli, P. (1963) *Les Assyriens en Cappadoce*. Paris: Librarie Adrien Maissoneuve, 200.
2. *Ibid.*, 58–9.
3. Postgate, G.N. (1992) *Early Mesopotamia: Society and Economy at the Dawn of History*. London: Routledge, 212–3.
4. Hallo, W.W. and Simpson, W.K. (1971) *The Ancient Near East: a History*. New York: Harcourt, Brace and Jovanich, 63; Gurney, O.R. (1952) *The Hittites*. London: Penguin Books, 82; Orlin, L.L. (1970) *Assyrian Colonies in Cappadocia*. The Hague, 7–8, 23–5.
5. Özgüç, T. 'Early Anatolian Archaeology in the Light of Recent Research'. Anatolia, VII (1963), 2–3, 6; 'The Art and Architecture of Ancient Kanesh'. Anatolia, VIII, (1964), 28; Emre, K. 'The Pottery of the Assyrian Colony Period According to the Building Levels of the Kanis Karûm'. Anatolia, VII (1963), 87–91.
6. Hereafter the dated cited are traditional unless otherwise stated. The super-law dates given by historians such as Peter James and David Rohl, which are 200–300 years lower, are generally rejected by the broad academic community.
7 Larsen, M.T. (1976) *The Old Assyrian City-state and its Colonies*. Copenhagen: Akademisk Forlag, 235–41.
8 Orlin, L.L. (1970) *Assyrian Colonies in Cappadocia*. The Hague, 51–2.
9 Veenhof, K.R. 'Some Social Effects of Old Assyrian Trade' in (1977) *Iraq*, 39, Part 1: 109–18.
10. *Ibid.*, 115.
11. *Ibid.*
12. *Ibid.*, 111–2; Larsen, M.T. 'Partnerships in the Old Assyrian Trade' in (1977) *Iraq*, 39, Part 1, 119–20.

13. Orlin, L.L. (1970) *Assyrian Colonies in Cappadocia*. The Hague, 24.
14. Saggs, H.W.F. (1984) *The Might that was Assyria*. London: Sidgwick and Jackson, 30–3; Orlin, L.L. (1970) *Assyrian Colonies in Cappadocia*. The Hague, 52–8; Larsen, M.T. (1977) 'Partnerships in the Old Assyrian Trade' in (1977) *Iraq*, 39, Part 1, 119–20.
15. This section on Pusu-ken and his life is adapted from Larsen (*The Old Assyrian City-state and its Colonies*) who draws on the work of various archaeologists.
16. Goitein (1967) *A Mediterranean Society*. Berkeley, CA: University of California Press.
17. *Ibid.*
18. Orlin, L.L. (1970) *Assyrian Colonies in Cappadocia*. The Hague, 52–8; *see also* Lasswell, H. and Kaplan, A. (1950) *Power and Society*. New Haven.
19. Orlin, L.L., *ibid.*
20. Larsen, M.T. (1976) *The Old Assyrian City-state and its Colonies*. Copenhagen: Akademisk Forlag, 95–6.
21. *Ibid.*
22. Kuhrt, A. (1994) *The Ancient Near East, c. 3000–330 BC*. London: Routledge, Volume I, 111.
23. *Ibid.*, 195.

A deeper understanding of social capital

A concept that is currently receiving considerable attention in knowledge management circles is that of *social capital*. But the notion that wealth and value can be derived from contacts, connections and the ability to work well with others is age-old.

For example, the growth and triumph of Phoenician business networks was in large part due to the tight, honour-based relationships between firms, subcontractors and the public sector, as well as branches within a single firm. In ancient Rome, firms that combined the capital and expertise of a score of partners, known as *socii*, enabled international banking, transactions and investments on a scale previously unheard of. Roman firms had to rely upon 'a network of dependants, associates and contacts, carefully and systematically developed over time'.[1]

The most striking instance of the importance of social capital in Roman enterprise occurred with the *publicani* of the later Roman Empire. To compete in highly varied and disparate markets, they had to be radically flexible. To this end these enterprises maintained no permanent labour, and a very small cadre of permanent staff – in effect they were the first virtual enterprises! Their true assets were their business and management expertise and, most importantly, a vast network of connections with skilled miners, tax professionals, arms makers, shipbuilders and many others. The profitability of the firm was a direct consequence of its social capital.

However, many of these societies had a much broader notion of the value of social capital, which for them was not simply an instrument of maximising profit, but also an encompassing harmony that was an end in itself. For it was only from within the divine order of creation, nature and the community that the enterprise itself derived any value. The contemporary return to the importance of relationships, community and trust for the long-term health of a firm is a variation on a very ancient theme.[1]

1. Knowledge Management Review, Jan–Feb 2000.

5

The multinational becomes intercontinental

Ugarit and Tyre: 1400–600 BCE

B Y 1500 BCE the Middle Bronze Age was being succeeded by the Late Bronze Age. Mesopotamia was dominated by Babylonia, Asia Minor by the Hittites, and Egypt by its New Kingdom of expansionist Pharaohs who still operated a 'socialist' palace economy. A similar system prevailed among the Minoans of Crete and the Shang kingdom that was taking form in China. The collapse of the Harappan cities in India greatly reduced much of the Mesopotamian–Indian trade and the Kassite rulers who replaced Hammurabi's dynasty still maintained merchant colonies in the Gulf.

By the year 1000 BCE, a new trading power would begin to spread its markets across the Near East and eventually the Mediterranean. Within three centuries the merchants of Tyre would manage a multinational empire spreading from Cadiz in Spain to Babylon. The impressive achievement of the sturdy longboats and galleons of Ugarit, Sidon, Byblos and Tyre foreshadowed the much later voyages of the Vikings, Portuguese, Spaniards and others. The long sea voyages of these Canaanites in navigating, exploring and even colonising the isles and coastlines of the known Western world were driven by one single objective – to secure their well-organized network of trade and investments, a mercantile empire that spanned three continents. Borrowing from earlier Mesopotamian models of managed enterprise, the merchants of Tyre would push beyond these methods to create the first multinational trading hierarchy, and one of intercontinental proportions to boot.

The small city-states of what is now Lebanon and Syria were ideally suited by climate, geography, location and an inherited business savvy to assume the mantle of the vanished traders of Ebla. Some, like Byblos, were under Egyptian vassalage; others, like the northerly realm of Ugarit, did homage to the Hittites in return for access to the vast resources and markets of Anatolia. Ugarit's geographical position offered its merchants the advantage of location: what in business terms is called a *country-specific advantage.*

Ugarit

The world of the Phoenicians began to come to life in 1928 when French archaeologists digging at the site of Ras Shamra uncovered the metropolis of Ugarit. The remains of two-storey houses, business quarters, temples and a huge royal palace were quickly found. Within the palace, the French discovered a body of clay tablets written in a Semitic tongue akin to Hebrew that shed light on all aspects of fascinating Canaanite life. The cuneiform business records found among them offered a picture of an emerging business culture not unlike that of Mesopotamia.[1]

> Ugarit's geographical position offered its merchants the advantage of location, what in business terms is called a country-specific advantage

The merchants of Ugarit, as well as those of Byblos, Sidon and Tyre, and of ancient Israel, were ideally located at the very place where the trading spheres of Egypt, Babylonia and the Hittite realm intersected. Goods moving from Babylon to Greece either had to pass through Phoenician ports or move on roads that passed close to Phoenician territory. The same was true for trade between Anatolia and Egypt. With an increasingly urbanized population, with excellent harbours, an ample supply of lumber and a highly skilled and educated population, the cities of the Levant were ideally suited to develop a trade-based maritime economy of the kind later characteristic of Britain and Japan.

These huddled city dwellers had little access to already scarce grazing land for donkeys and horses. Timbered hills typified by the famed cedars of Lebanon made shipbuilding far more cost-effective and promised far more trade advantages – the theory of comparative advantage with a vengeance! Others might grow food and make war, but Ugarit and her sisters would sell them the metals and even the tools, growing rich and powerful in the process. With its face to the sea, Ugarit 'developed several

Ancient sources, modern insights

4000 YEARS OF KNOWLEDGE MANAGEMENT

Phoenician secrecy: in ancient Phoenicia, the process of using Mediterranean shellfish to make their famous purple dye created a highly coveted niche garment industry. This secret process was kept as solely tacit knowledge and passed down from generation to generation. Revealing this process to outsiders was invariably punished by death. They certainly understood the value of protecting their knowledge assets!

Precious knowledge: in ancient seafaring enterprises, it was not blind daring or brute force that created wealth. More likely to prove profitable was knowledge of foreign customs, prevailing winds and the whereabouts of pirates.

The first virtual corporation: faced with fierce market competition and variable markets, multinational enterprises in the Roman Empire had to be lean and flexible. While the firms provided capital and management, they could rarely afford permanent, organized labour. These companies had two main assets: their business expertise and their network of connections. They efficiently used social capital.

industries and crafts which were of purely maritime character, such as purple dye manufacture, and shipbuilding'.[2]

The merchants and neighbours of Ugarit quickly seized the opportunity to become strategic brokers and middlemen in the trading system of the Bronze Age. Vast trading fleets hewn from the forests of Lebanon sailed between Egypt and Cyprus and Canaan and along the Cilician coast of the Hittite Empire. Trade flourished! Grain grown in Egypt or Babylonia was sent to the Cypriots and Hittites in return for precious copper and other metals, commodities efficiently processed in Phoenician workshops or shipped by caravan and reed boats to Babylon, Sippar, Ashur and further east. Kassite horses were sold to Egypt while Egyptian ivory was sold to Mesopotamia, Elam and Hatti. Imported into Ugarit's harbours from the mines of Cilicia and Cyprus, copper and precious metals were distributed to guilds of merchants and traders by the harbour master. The profits and royalties paid to the crown were then reinvested, quite often into the construction of even more efficient seagoing vessels soon organized as mercantile fleets. The volume of trade escalated as international commerce flowed back and forth through the harbours and roads of the Phoenician trading mart.

> With an increasingly urbanized population, with excellent harbours, an ample supply of lumber and a highly skilled and educated population, the cities of the Levant were ideally suited to develop a trade-based maritime economy of the kind later characteristic of Britain and Japan

In this dynamic and stable new trading system, subsidiary industry flourished. In scores of cities and towns guilds of highly skilled craftsmen, most of them now self-employed, beat and smelted the raw copper and tin for resale as tools, weapons or decorative items. The gold and ivory of Egypt were turned into finished products shipped by caravan to Mesopotamia via Carchemish or north to Hatti or back to Egypt. Factories sprang up along the Mediterranean basin, the home of the *murex* shellfish, from which the famous and much-coveted Phoenician purple dye was made.

Not surprisingly, a highly specialized Phoenician garment industry was born, which exported over a thousand different items to Thebes, Troy, Rhodes, Hattusas, Babylon and every exotic bazaar that Canaan's zealous exporters could reach.[3] These small companies had a specialized knowledge that would help them reap rich profits for a time span measured in centuries.

Ugarit's texts show that the Phoenicians organized a system of mostly privately owned but royally managed production and commerce not too different from what we have seen in Sumer, Babylon and Assyria. This system of managed trade foreshadows, interestingly, the 'guided marketplace' of modern-day Japan.[4]

The Japanese parallel

While a full description of the Japanese system belongs elsewhere and there are profound differences between it and that of an ancient city-state, a student of international business history might see some similarities in both cultures:

1 Boundaries between public and private personnel and sectors were/are quite fluid.

2 Warrior aristocrats, soldiers and sailors were/are also merchants, participating in overseas commerce.

3 Major merchants and business organizations formed relatively permanent subcontracting relationships of honour-bound loyalty directly derived from a culture of landed feudalism.

4 Crown, aristocracy, navy and business formed an interlocked system of managed commerce. Private profit and market considerations were then and are now viewed in terms of the overall geopolitical military and strategic considerations of the nation or city-state as a whole.

In Phoenicia, as in all ancient Near Eastern societies, the boundaries between public and private enterprise were always hard to fix. The Phoenician equivalent of the *tamkārum*, or merchant-prince, was called a *mkrm*. A *mkrm* could be either private or a crown-sponsored trader, and was often both. Phoenicia was, like Japan, an industrial–feudal society. Trading abroad on behalf of his prince or king, the *mkrm* was awarded a rich landed estate, which often became hereditary.[5]

The records of Ugarit tell of two important merchants, Abdihaqab and Sinaranu, who served their prince, Niqmepa, in return for being given hereditary ownership of houses and fields. Sinaranu served as a crown real estate agent and became the richest man in Ugarit. Sinaranu also owned his own shipping fleet that plied the Aegean under royal protection.[6] Goods imported by Sinaranu's firm went directly to the prince and not to the royal inspector or harbour master as in the case of independent merchants. Sinaranu also served as the prince's tax collector, and subcontracted this duty out to more local merchants in each region of the principality who operated as his vassals, collecting the taxes in each village and town.[7]

Neither royal nor private merchants in Phoenicia worked as lone entrepreneurs, but traded as members of interrelated guilds. Overseas commerce was dominated by an assembly of merchant-princes. One thinks of the present Japanese Diet in which many deputies are members of or clients to the country's major firms. The Phoenician contract of *tapputu* was an early form of international business partnership. Guilds or individual merchants in one principality pooled capital and resources with those in neighbouring principalities to finance trade in Egypt, Greece, Mesopotamia or Anatolia. Sometimes these arrangements were on a very large scale, with the prince himself and his royal merchants becoming involved. This suggests an early version of the long-term partnerships found between Japanese trading and manufacturing firms.[8]

Similarly, the princes of the maritime city-states supported, oversaw and often organized their individual and collective overseas ventures. An expedition sponsored by the ruler of Byblos included some 540 shekels of silver, 50 of which were carried in the king's own personal ship. Crown investment into such ventures led to joint projects in shipping companies, which resembled ancient versions of Sumitomo. The harbour master and his boss, the vizier, did the day-to-day overseeing of foreign trade in a manner not unlike the directors of Japan's post-war Ministry of International Trade and Industry, the famous MITI. The strategic industries such as copper, lumber and shipping that remained were under heavy state control.[9]

Princes and royal merchants commanded the fleets shipping grain from Egypt or the Levant to Cyprus, and copper from Cyprus to the mainland. Royal merchants then distributed the copper to customers and transshippers in the harbours of Ugarit, Byblos, Sidon and Tyre. This highly desired metal was a prime stimulus for the growth of Phoenician merchant fleets. Oil was also a royal monopoly. Merchants well acquainted with their wharves and the lively mix of nationalities that a harbour attracts provided princes and viziers with intelligence on market conditions overseas.

Foreign merchants – Aramean, Hittite, Egyptian and Mesopotamian – trading in Phoenician ports faced a primitive version of non-tariff barriers. *Ubru*, as they were called, were forbidden to leave their foreign business quarter, enter the residence of native traders or conduct business without strict supervision from the harbour master. Phoenician merchant-princes played military, especially naval, roles like the Samurai of Meiji Japan who became directors and agents of trading and manufacturing corporations.

Ties between business and the navy in Phoenicia were very strong. Uniting in huge convoys, sometimes of 100 or more, round galleons and slender warships protected their traders and each other from storms, reefs and pirates. These vast armadas were set up along feudal military lines with admirals serving as princes and traders as well as sailors. The best captains became a new naval aristocracy, in which titles, fiefs and capital were bestowed upon them in the manner of domestic nobility.

> Phoenician merchant-princes played military, especially naval, roles like the Samurai of Meiji Japan who became directors and agents of trading and manufacturing corporations

For the Phoenicians, commerce, trade and investment represented a form of war by other means. The capture of markets became as valuable as the ability to make weapons and win battles, and was in fact directly related to it. From this, it was only a short step to the effective organization of Phoenician commerce along military lines. Merchants were often murdered on ventures, causing trade, war and diplomacy to be inextricably linked. A whole body of treaty law supervized international merchants, who often served in royal diplomatic corps. According to A.F. Rainey, 'Commercial, diplomatic and military activity went hand in hand.'[10]

Tyre

By the time of David and Solomon, around 1000 BCE, as the Bronze Age was giving way to the Iron Age, the profitable shipping firms of Phoenician princes dominated Levantine commerce. Prosperous as they had been, the merchants of Ugarit, Byblos and Sidon were now upstaged by the island traders of Tyre, destined to become the greatest Phoenician city of them all.

Situated just off the Lebanese shore, Tyre's harbour, surrounded by reefs and hewn out of rock, protected her teeming fleets from storms and enemy vessels.[11] The city seemed destined for the epitaph provided by the prophet Ezekiel: 'Thou didst enrich the kings of the earth with the multitude of thy riches and of thy merchandise' (Ezekiel 27:33).

Tyre's ascendancy was aided by the decline of Egypt, Hatti and Mitanni and the consequent freedom of the Phoenician cities. The armies of King David of Israel ensured not only Tyrian independence, but also a favourable climate for her commercial expansion. This took place in three stages, as Tyre became first a Levantine, then a Near Eastern, and eventually an intercontinental power (see Table 5.1).

Table 5.1 Tyrian commercial expansion, 1000–600 BCE

1000–900 BCE:	Trade partnership with united Israel to exploit Red Sea routes.
900–800 BCE:	Trade with and investment in Northern Israel, Cyprus, Syria and Anatolia to exploit Assyrian trade.
800–600 BCE	Trade and investment spread to central and western Mediterranean as Assyrian financier and supplier.

The remarkable expansion of Tyre began with Ahiram I, the famous Biblical Hiram, whose grand partnership with Solomon won Tyre access to the rich caravan routes linking the Euphrates, the Levant and Arabia, which were under Solomon's control. The building expertise and luxury goods of Hiram's merchants were exported to Israel in return for wheat, copper and silver. The Bible makes it clear that crown merchants remained the central agencies of Tyrian investment. Solomon's own words allude to a royal business partnership: 'My servants shall be with thy servants; and unto thee will I give hire for thy servants according to all that thou shalt appoint' (I Kings 5:6). Israel and Tyre merged their trading companies in a multinational partnership that extended into the Red Sea and even the Indian Ocean, 'aimed at opening up a new market, the Orient'.[12] From Ezion-Geber (Eilat) the fleets of Hiram and Solomon

> Prosperous as they had been, the merchants of Ugarit, Byblos and Sidon were now upstaged by the island traders of Tyre, destined to become the greatest Phoenician city of them all

imported gold, silver, ivory, peacocks, apes and precious stones from Arabia, Somalia and India.

The Hiram era was succeeded by one in which Solomon's realm split into two warring kingdoms ruled from Samaria and Jerusalem, abandoning the overland trade routes, and the kingdom of Assyria under Ashurnasirpal II began to march westwards, terrorising the Aramean lands with a policy of 'calculated frightfulness'. Tyre needed a new strategy, and a usurping priest of the god Melqart, called Itobaal I (891–859 BCE – the Ethbaal of I Kings 16:31 – provided one.

Itobaal merged Tyre, Sidon, Byblos and Arvad into a single state. His next step, in creating a single Levantine power strong enough to resist Assyria, was to try to incorporate the northern House of Israel, ruled by the dynasty of General Omri. Itobaal's daughter, Jezebel, was married to Omri's son Ahab. Tyrian merchants, craftsmen and priests flocked into Israel. Archaeological sites of the tribal territories of Asher, Zebulun, Issachar and northern Manasseh suggest the presence of Tyrian merchants trading the wares of Itobaal's workshops and the precious copper of Cyprus for Israelite grain. Itobaal directed a tightly organized network combining public enterprise projects, international subsidiaries and complex trading partnerships. Other Tyrian merchant colonies were founded in Syria and Cilicia, on the road to Asia Minor. Political turmoil in Israel and the continued expansion of Assyria would soon force another strategy upon the merchants of Tyre.

ITOBAAL

A LESSON IN THE CONFLICT OF BUSINESS CULTURES

IN 891 BCE a new king came to the throne in Tyre, Itobaal I. King, priest and manager rolled into one, Itobaal pursued a very ambitious business strategy designed to make Tyre the number one commercial power in the Near East. Merging the other Phoenician cities of Byblos, Sidon and Arvad under his rule, Itobaal also planted merchant colonies in Syria, Cyprus and the northern kingdom of Israel.

Under Itobaal the Tyrian business establishment was a tightly integrated alliance of crown enterprises, private merchant-princes, guilds of traders and craftsmen, and navy admirals. Copper was imported from Cyprus, worked into manufactured goods in Tyre, and then exported to Israel in return for the wheat of Galilee and Samaria. The archaeology of Israel in the Iron Age shows good evidence of a Tyrian commercial presence both in Samaria, where Phoenician-imported ivory goods became status symbols and in other cities such as Megiddo, where guilds of Tyrian craftsmen also operated.

The business alliances over which Itobaal and his merchants presided were underwritten by a temple priesthood, which played an important role in Phoenician business culture. The temples served as banks and multinational distribution networks for Tyrian goods. The priests of Tyre's patron god, Melqart, served to notarise and regulate commerce. Most Near Eastern merchants exchanged gods when they made alliances or traded goods. Any nation doing business with Tyre embraced Melqart alongside its own Hadad, Ra, Chemosh, Ashur or Marduk. As long as most cultures were polytheistic, this practice worked fine.

Itobaal attempted the same strategy with the Hebrew kingdom of Israel, whose powerful ruler, Omri, commanded the chariot corps. An alliance and ultimate union with Israel would afford Itobaal an abundant food supply and augment his military power against the rising threat of Assyria. To secure the alliance in both business and politics, Itobaal married his daughter, Jezebel, to Omri's son and heir, Ahab. The worship of Melqart became the state religion in a kingdom in which the God of Abraham and Moses was still acknowledged in theory as the only true deity.

In attempting to import Tyrian business culture into Israel, Itobaal was, ultimately, to fail. The highly feudal business practices of Phoenicia clashed sharply with the 'Jeffersonian' tradition of independent yeoman farmers found in Israel. While most Israelites for a time embraced the worship of Melqart, which was enforced by state decree, the ministry of the prophet Eliyahu (Elijah) exposed a growing discontent that would eventually lead to a military coup in 841 BCE by the nationalist general Jehu. Itobaal's refusal to understand the nature of Israel's economic and religious culture doomed his alliance, writing a lesson for those who might still adhere to a 'one size fits all' approach to international management.

Tyrian business becomes intercontinental

The rise of the Assyrian Empire was a terrible danger and a wonderful opportunity for the merchants of Tyre. Tiglath-Pileser III and his successors overran the entire Levant, including Phoenicia. Tyre, though, was permitted to keep her independence, for she was far more profitable to the warriors of Nineveh (Assyrian capital from eighth century BCE) in that condition. The Kings of the Four Quarters of the Earth needed new iron weapons and chariots to conquer their empire, grain to feed it, and hard silver currency to finance it. Just as a free Switzerland was useful to Hitler and a free Hong Kong to Mao, so a free Tyre, with all of her markets and business expertise, was indispensable to kings like Sargon II, Sennacherib and Esarhaddon. It was much more profitable, they reasoned, to use Tyre as a banker and a supplier than as a conquered territory.

As Nineveh took control of Tyre's Asian markets, the latter's kings and merchants adjusted their strategy accordingly. Even from the time of Itobaal, the westward march of Ashurnasirpal II and Shalmaneser III was a warning that Assyria was the wave of the future, and that Tyre had to adapt. Tyre adapted with a vengeance, bringing about her greatest commercial expansion.

Itobaal's heirs, Balmazzer III (846–841 BCE) and Mattin (840–832 BCE), faced not only Assyrian control of the overland routes to the mines of Anatolia, but an insatiable Assyrian demand for bigger and bigger shipments of metals. With the Israelite granary in political turmoil and access to Anatolia's mines impaired, the rulers, priests, merchants and sailors of Tyre embarked upon a search for markets and resources in the only direction still open to them. In 814 BCE, the settlement of Carthage was planted in Tunisia, followed by the sister African colonies of Utica and Hadrummeto. These were designed essentially to provide Tyre with a new source of grain and other foodstuffs. In the heart of the Mediterranean itself, other colonies were founded on Malta, Gozo, Lampedusa and Pantellaria. An important post was erected on the island of Motya, off the north-west coast of Sicily, and a similar settlement placed on the island of Sulcis, off the south-western shore of Sardinia.

Tyre's merchants, meanwhile, sailed beyond the central Mediterranean to discover and exploit their most significant investment opportunity. In approximately 770 BCE an expedition of Tyrian priests and businesspeople made landfall at the mouth of the Guadalquivir. Erecting a temple to

Melqart, these Phoenicians founded what would eventually become the modern city of Cadiz (known as Gadir or Gades in classical times). The land of Tarshish, in southern Spain, possessed the richest deposits of silver known to the ancient world. The native Iberians had been working them with their crude implements for centuries. The Phoenicians, journeying up the river, now had access to the silver mines of the region of Huelva.

Soon, there were some sixty mines operating in the region, chief of which were those that lay on the shores of the Rio Tinto, so named because the river itself was discoloured from the enormous deposits of silver and copper. During the 1960s and 1970s two Spanish engineer-archaeologists, Antonio Blanco-Freijeiro and J.M. Luzón, excavated the Rio Tinto mines. Not far from an enormous slag of silver some 1500 metres long and 500 metres wide, they uncovered the workshops and furnace of the miners, along with Tyrian pottery and new iron tools. The strata of the region showed that the arrival of the Tyrian jugs coincided with an enormous growth in silver production some time after 800 BCE.

The native Spaniards continued to work the mines and, with the help of Phoenician iron tools, their production grew enormously. Most of it went to their new customers. Huge shipments of silver and copper sailed down the Rio Tinto to the furnaces of Huelva, where they were processed into ingots before being shipped on to Cadiz. Other shipments went overland from the mines of Aznalcóllar near Seville to an alternative processing centre at San Bartolomé de Almonte and thence to Cadiz.

Once it reached Cadiz the bullion was loaded on Tyrian galleys to be shipped across the Mediterranean. The ingots were often unloaded at the warehouses on Motya and Sulcis for further value-added processing before being sent on to Cyprus. The water and land routes from the mines to Cadiz did not compete with one another but were part of a single Iberian–Phoenician consortium that supervized the shipping and processing of the ore.

Melqart, CEO

The maritime capitalism of Tyre was a variant of the 'temple capitalism' that had already existed for two millennia in the Near East. Religion and commerce were closely wed in these societies where gods and goddesses were sometimes portrayed as merchants. Temples were centres and protectors of trade, and deals were ratified under the watchful eyes of both priests and religious statues. Fear that the gods would punish fraud and breach of contract allowed priests to standardise weights and measures and act as notaries. Temples served as banks and warehouses – neutral storehouses that attracted private depositors of silver and other goods. What Canaanite, after all, would want to default on a loan to the priests of a dreaded storm-god, who might withhold prosperity and rain?

The role of temples in Tyre's strategy of international commerce cannot be overestimated, as guilds and merchants communicated with them. Well-organized and tax-exempt, temples enjoyed a competitive advantage over private firms even as they used their capital. Guilds of Tyrian merchants abroad would first erect a temple to their supreme deity, Melqart, as heavenly sanction and earthly direction for their international investments and local partnerships. If Cypriots or Iberians could then be persuaded to incorporate Melqart into their pantheons, this would help cement close business relationships. If the secrets of shipbuilding, bronze, iron and markets belonged to Melqart, to be strictly guarded by his priests, the transfer of those secrets went hand-in-hand with the adoption of his worship by Tyre's customers. References to Melqart in the places where his worshippers settled would thus 'signify the impact of a new technology'.[13]

> The more international temples expanded, the more they took on some of the structures characteristic of modern multinational corporations

The more international temples expanded, the more they took on some of the structures characteristic of modern multinational corporations.

Egyptian, Sumerian, Assyro-Babylonian, Hittite and Greek cults often had 'branch temples in several cities'.[14] Canaanite religion would follow suit. Local sanctuaries were in communication with main centres and the financial connections of one temple to another were quite strong. Often large amounts of capital and goods would be transferred among them. The temple hierarchy of Tyre would soon be an export as much as Phoenician dyes, lumber, pottery and tools. And so, in Phoenicia at the dawn of the Iron Age, a multinational religion in which the gods themselves were traders provided, along with the crown, important advantages of internalization in dealing with an ever-widening circle of foreign business relationships and markets.

According to Phoenicia expert Professor Maria Eugenia Aubet, the huge temple of Melqart in Cadiz oversaw the venture in its region, as did the smaller shrines in Sicily and Sardinia in theirs: 'the first Tyrian colonies in the west ... started ... as sanctuaries administered by a priestly group directly linked to the interests of Tyre'.[15] The massive Spanish shrine was, at the same time, itself subject to the Melqart temple in Tyre, from which it derived its architecture, decorative patterns, twin columns, three sacrificial altars and eternal flame. A huge administrative building housed a powerful Melqart priesthood destined to remain in the hands of a few aristocratic families.[16] As representatives of a deity worshipped as the supernatural King of Tyre, the Melqart priests of Gades exercized an immeasurable control over Ibero-Phoenician business. The temple became the commercial, as well as religious, bond between Gades and Tyre as both guarantor of honest exchange and source of finance capital:

> 'In distant places where he [Melqart] possessed a temple, his function
> was a very concrete one: to ensure the tutelage of the temple of Tyre
> and the monarchy over the commercial enterprise, thus converting the
> colony into an extension of Tyre; and also to guarantee the right of
> asylum and hospitality which, in distant lands, was equivalent to
> endorsing contracts and commercial exchanges.'[17]

Once again the focal point of the Canaanite diaspora, this time on a grand scale, the Cadiz temple used fear of Melqart to regulate both society and marketplace. Keeping a register of all transactions, the priests had supreme authority in business matters, enforcing honest deals and consistent exchange rates, weights and measures. As in Tyre, Motya and Sulcis, the temple itself played its part in a precise political and economic strategy. Phoenician shippers and traders burnt sacrifices to Melqart as protector on their long voyages from Gades to Tyre. Soon after the foundation of their new island temple, the worshippers of Melqart journeyed up the Guadalquivir relying upon the renown of their supreme baal to help persuade the natives to join in a permanent multinational business arrangement. As in the East, the Phoenicians hoped that the Iberians, in becoming trading partners, would assimilate not only Tyrian technology but Tyrian religion as well, admitting Melqart and Astarte to their native pantheons.[18]

The Tyrian overseas operations were the closest thing to real multi-nationals yet to exist in antiquity. They bought raw materials, turned them into finished goods (value-added production) and distributed them through permanent trading and manufacturing establishments in distant countries (foreign direct investment), all within the frame of a vast network of crown, temple, navy, private companies, private subcontractors and foreign partners:

> 'The structure of the Phoenician settlements was linked with the homeland mercantile "companies", in a family-based organization, which might have been operating in towns like Ugarit or Tyre. Some of these "companies" possessed large numbers of ships ... [which] would provide the capital for their trading activity ... as sponsoring and protective private institutions. It was indeed a private enterprise, owned by traders, who organized their workforce, ships and voyages. The traders seem to have had a high status and an equally high political rank, based on a kinship organization ...'[19]

Tyre's overseas colonies, according to archaeologist Richard Harrison, truly functioned as branch-plants and foreign subsidiaries in a multinational setting:

> 'The pattern of Phoenician trade was linked to specialist production centres, connecting different areas and political systems which otherwise would not have been drawn together, and establishing a rate of exchange much to their own advantage. They could do this fairly easily since they had a monopoly on both the specialized manufactures that everyone desired, and the marine transport, so they could stimulate demand where they chose to do so ... The traders worked through a system of Phoenician family firms, who had representatives in their home town in the eastern Mediterranean as well as in their new markets and factories; they owned their own ships, too, and were prepared to take risks which their overlords could not well calculate, or were unwilling to do, and so profited greatly.'[20]

If there was a head office for the entire Mediterranean operation it was situated in the city of Kition in Cyprus, still the major source of copper in the region. Kition, with its Melqart temple and warehouses, became the model for all the later overseas colonies. The island of Cyprus held a number of other Tyrian settlements, no doubt under its jurisdiction, each filled with guilds of craftsmen working the copper both from Cyprus and from Spain.

By 700 BCE the Tyrian royal and business establishment managed a commercial empire that stretched the entire length of the Mediterranean and even beyond. The Cyprus/Mediterranean operation was but the western division of Tyre, Inc. An eastern network supervized the distribution of silver and other goods to the hungry markets of the Assyrian Empire. Donkey-caravans and boats carrying wheat, metals and textiles linked the Tyrian settlements in Syria, Nineveh, Halah, Ashur and Babylon with the island merchant city. Even in the heart of Assyria itself, tablet records show that much trade was in Tyrian hands.

Never conquered by Assyria, Tyre prospered until her chief customer was replaced by the Chaldean Empire, founded by Nebuchadnezzar, which attacked Tyre, conquered its mainland territory, and began the city's slow decline. Reorienting her trade eastward, Tyre would slowly abdicate control of her western network to her chief colony, Carthage. In the meantime, the whole managed system of Near Eastern commerce would find a new challenge from the first free-market system in history.

NOTES TO CHAPTER 5

1. Kuhrt, A. (1994) *The Ancient Near East, c. 3000–330 BC*. London: Routledge, Volume I, 300–1.
2. Linder, E. 'Ugarit, a Canaanite Thalassocracy' in Young, G.D., ed. (1981) *Ugarit in Retrospect: Fifty Years of Ugarit and Ugaritic*. Winona Lake, Indiana: Eisenbrauns, 32.
3. *Ibid.*, 38; Kuhrt, A. (1994) *The Ancient Near East, c. 3000–330 BC*. London: Routledge, Volume I, 302.
4. For more detail see Moore, D. and Lewis, K. *Business History*, April 2000.
5. Heltzer, M. 'A Recently Discovered Phoenician Inscription and the Problem of the Guilds of Metal-Casters', in (1983) *Atti del I congresso internazionale di studi fenici e punici, Roma, 5-10 Novembre 1979*. Rome: Consiglio Nazionale della Ricerche, Vol. I, 123–5.
6. *Ibid.*, 136; Linder, E. 'Ugarit, a Canaanite Thalassocracy' in Young, G.D. ed. (1981) *Ugarit in Retrospect: Fifty Years of Ugarit and Ugaritic*. Winona Lake, Indiana: Eisenbrauns, 35.
7. Rainey, A.F. (1963) 'Business Agents at Ugarit' in *Israel Exploration Journal*, Vol. 13, 316–7; Heltzer, M. 'A Recently Discovered Phoenician Inscription and the Problem of the Guilds of Metal-Casters' in (1983) *Atti del I congresso internazionale di studi fenici e punici, Roma, 5–10 Novembre 1979*. Rome: Consiglio Nazionale della Ricerche, Vol. I, 136; Linder, E. 'Ugarit, a Canaanite Thalassocracy' in Young, G.D., ed. (1981) *Ugarit in Retrospect: Fifty Years of Ugarit and Ugaritic*. Winona Lake, Indiana: Eisenbrauns, 35.
8. Heltzer, M. 'A Recently Discovered Phoenician Inscription and the Problem of the Guilds of Metal-Casters' in (1983) *Atti del I congresso internazionale di studi fenici e punici, Roma, 5–10 Novembre 1979*. Rome: Consiglio Nazionale della Ricerche, Vol. I, 140–2.

9. *Ibid.*, 32.

10. *Ibid.*, 315.

11. Aubet, M.E. (1996) *The Phoenicians and the West: Politics, Colonies and Trade*, trans. Turton, M. Cambridge: Cambridge University Press, 27, 29–32, 35.

12. *Ibid.*, 36; I Kings 9:26, 10:22, 49.

13. Aubet, M.E. *ibid.*, 10.

14. Silver, M. (1995) *Economic Structures of Antiquity*. Westport, CT: Greenwood Press, 32.

15. Aubet, M.E. (1996) *The Phoenicians and the West: Politics, Colonies and Trade*, trans. Turton, M. Cambridge: Cambridge University Press, 235.

16. *Ibid.*, 218–20, 230–3.

17. *Ibid.*, 234.

18. *Ibid.*, 325–6; Silver, M. (1995) *Economic Structures of Antiquity*. Westport, CT: Greenwood Press, 6–10.

19. Gamito, T.J. (1988) *Social Complexity in Southwest Iberia: 800–300 BC: The Case of Tartessos*. B.A.R. International Series, 439. Oxford: B.A.R., 54.

20. Harrison, R.J. (1988) *Spain at the Dawn of History: Iberians, Phoenicians and Greeks*. London: Thames and Hudson, 42.

6

Birth of free enterprise

The Aegean market revolution: 1000–336 BCE

NEBUCHADNEZZAR of Babylon's 13-year siege against Tyre had dealt a crippling – though not fatal – blow to the great Phoenician trading empire. As well as the alphabet of 22 letters, the Phoenicians had improved the internalized 'top-down' model of business expansion through god-kings, merchant-princes and temple priests. They had continued to improve the size and scale of the first multinational enterprises to flourish in Kanesh, Dilmun and Ugarit.

An alternative business model, based upon small, independent enterprises, was to take shape in the Aegean. Working in a politically freer and less urbanized world, the traders of Greece forged history's first free-market economy. They effectively bypassed the strictures of the Eclectic Paradigm, which postulates the three factors of ownership, location and internalization advantages as crucial to foreign and overseas economic advantages. The merchant sailors and entrepreneurs of ancient Greece worked the area of the Black Sea and established ventures across the Mediterranean without the help of large corporate hierarchies or skilful internalized operations. The Greeks gave the world the first true entrepreneurial business culture, an economy dominated by independent traders. It reached its full maturity in Athens of the 5th century BCE with its flourishing overseas trade, private banks and relatively free capital markets. The Athenian model, in spite of its indispensable agrarian roots, represented an economic system that was a precursor of the Anglo-American consumer and shareholder capitalism of our own day.

But in the beginning, the Aegean was even less capitalist than Assyria or Phoenicia. The Bronze Age Minoan civilization of Crete was much more like Egypt with its state-run palace economy, and the same was true on a smaller scale of the first recognizable Mycenaean tribal kingdoms on the Greek mainland before about 1100–1000 BCE.

By the time of the *Odyssey*, some time after 700 BCE, Homer portrays a time in which the aristocrat and the tribal economy are being challenged by a new world. This new world is not to Homer's liking, for it is full of petty hustlers and swindlers. Far more than in the Near East, Greece is a land of self-sufficient families and rural communities who are a lot freer than their Assyrian and Tyrian counterparts. The petty tribal rulers who govern these yeomen are very careful not to tax or push them too far, lest they lose their fragile power. Jeffersonians in the Bronze Age!

> The Greeks gave the world the first true entrepreneurial business culture, an economy dominated by independent traders

Homer despises the new merchants he sees, but he certainly is well aware of their dealings and practices, which are described here and there in the *Odyssey*. The goddess Athena even poses as one, in order to hire a good ship and crew of sailors for Odysseus. When the aristocratic warrior-hero sails to the fictitious city of Phaiakia, located in Asia Minor, he finds its people already engaged in making trading their calling. Later on, the wandering Odysseus is mistaken for a rootless, greedy merchant, something Homer holds in utter contempt. Homer's greatest dislike is reserved, however, for the Tyrians who cross the Aegean with their wares and are the very epitome of crookedness itself.

The Iron Age

Behind Homer's lament for a bygone age of heroes lay a social and economic revolution propelled by new technology as well as Greece's deepening involvement in the international economy. The use of iron to make knives, tools and weapons began in Cyprus around 1200–1050 BCE and quickly spread westward to Greece as well as eastward to Phoenicia and Assyria. The Tyrians would soon spread it to Spain and, in league with the Greeks, to North Africa and Italy, where they would help jump-start the economies of Carthage and Rome.

Iron would permit the diffusion of civilization away from its cradles along the Nile, Euphrates, Yellow and Indus rivers. Iron swords were much stronger and cheaper than those of bronze, and cut through them easily. The Assyrians used them to equip their huge armies. Most Bronze Age cities still flourished in Asia near rich soil or where irrigation was plentiful. Iron ploughs and tools would now make it possible to cultivate drier, poorer soil and thus populate and urbanize more of Europe, Central and East Asia, and Africa.

By 850 BCE the Greeks were not only making iron knives, swords, hoes and other implements but were helping to spread them to others as they were drawn into Tyre's Mediterranean economy in the role of customers and independent partners. The first Greeks to enter the world of Iron Age commerce were the traders on the large lizard-shaped island of Euboea, which sprawled off the north coast of Attica. Tyrian and Cypriot merchants docking at the ports of Lefkandi, Chalcis and Eretria brought knowledge of iron and the phonetic alphabet and took back Euboean pottery, which found its way to the markets of Al-Mina in Syria. Greek goods went east, but Greeks bearing goods went west, in league with their Tyrian trading partners. Settling on the island of Pithekoussai, off the coast of Italy not far from Naples, thousands of Euboean metal-workers and traders helped stimulate the Iron Age in Etruria and, eventually, Rome.

Much more than the Phoenicians, the Greeks went abroad as private individuals (such as Menelaus, as described in the *Odyssey*), operating as independent agents buying on a contractual basis and bringing their profits back to Greece along with the all-important iron ore and prestige goods.[1] Menelaus was portrayed as owning a number of ships employed in trading-voyages across the eastern Mediterranean:

'Much did I suffer and wandered much before bringing all this home in my ships when I came back in the eighth year. I wandered to Cyprus and Phoenicia, to the Egyptians, I reached the Aithiopians, Eremboi, Sidonians and Libya where the rams grow their horns quickly.'[2]

And so Greek commerce became fixed in its historic pattern, 'informal [and] entrepreneurial in a world which provided security neither of contracts nor possession, and bringing an erratic and unpredictable return'.[3] Iron-working enterprises and the Euboean overseas carrying trade spurred the market revolution in the Aegean. 'It is perhaps not extravagant', says Professor James Redfield, 'to think that the trade route fuelled the whole Greek economic take-off in the mid-8th century BC.'[4]

Lessons of the Greeks

HUBRIS – PLANTING THE SEEDS OF OUR FUTURE DESTRUCTION

From Edward Gibbon's *Rise and Fall of the Roman Empire* to Paul Kennedy's more recent *Rise and Fall of the Western Powers*, many are fascinated by the way empires come to prominence and then, in time, are pushed aside, violently or otherwise, by a new power.

We also see this rising and falling occurring with firms; the fortunes of IBM have graced many covers of *Fortune* – in the 1970s and 1980s as being among America's most admired firms and in the early 1990s as a warning to all. In the computer industry we have witnessed a procession of strong players who fell to the wayside. In the 1960s there was the BUNCH and IBM; of the BUNCH (Burroughs, UNIVAC, NCR, CDC and Honeywell), none remains in its original form. In more recent times DEC, a dominant player in the 1980s, was bought by new player Compaq not many years after its peak. Though it has survived as one of the dominant players in this most global of industries, IBM provides a salutary lesson about the dangers of being blinded by your own success – a lesson, it appears, that many in the industry largely spawned by IBM have not learned.

Danny Miller of Montreal's HEC makes this point drawing on Greek mythology in his provocative book *The Icarus Paradox* (New York: Harper Business, 1990). Icarus was the figure who was punished for his hubris of using a pair of wings constructed by his father Daedalus and flying too close to the sun. Miller draws a compelling analogy to firms that get caught in the trap of believing that their successful business models of the past will continue to deliver in the future.

One of us joined IBM in the late 1970s and recalls seeing flip-chart diagrams drawn by IBM executives to demonstrate IBM's enviable record of decades of 15 per cent growth a year. The implication was that the new generation of IBMers merely had to learn well the IBM way to emulate this success. The problem was that a more turbulent time came and IBM was ill prepared to adjust, let alone radically rethink, its way of doing business. The reason, as Miller points out, was that its very success, for several generations of IBMers, had narrowed what IBM focused on, what behaviours it rewarded and whom it hired. The net result was a culture and organization that were admirably suited to deliver in a world that changed at a slow rate. However, when its environment changed, its momentum of profits, which took a few years to fall off, and its track record blinded it to the need radically to reform its business model. It took a deep pool of red ink to convince IBM that the day of reckoning had arrived. Successful organizations – and who doesn't want to be part of one? – face the danger of waiting too long on the S-Curve of Change (see diagram). When should organizations change? At point A,

S-Curve of Change

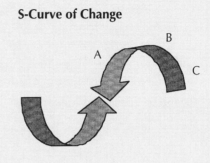

when they are enjoying success and have resources to spare and profitability that they can invest in change initiatives. However, few do, because they find it very difficult, if not impossible, to convince stakeholders that they need to change, 'If it ain't broke, don't fix it!' Many firms finally recognise imperatives for change at B, too late but better than C. It is often the most successful firms that wait till C, blinded by their success to what is happening in their market.

Do we learn from the rise and fall of titans like IBM? Most don't, but an encouraging number do. Microsoft seems to have, thus far, developed a culture that allows itself to turn rapidly, as it did when it realized that it had badly underestimated the impact of the Internet. IBM seems to have learned some profound lessons as well, though at the cost of tens of thousands of terminated positions. Not an easy thing for those personally involved. In both these cases a dominant CEO appears to be the means by which these firms have had the courage to overthrow the past; though a 'burning platform', as management consultants call it, of a sea of red ink for IBM and massive publicity about the Internet for Microsoft helped him gain the support of the mass of employees.

Putting aside the 'great man' theory of change, we argue that it is this ability to cast aside old business models at an increasing rate – what academics call strategic flexibility – that firms must develop in the 21st century or be in danger of being cast on the rubbish heap of corporate history. The firm must go into the very way it operates, is organized and is led in order to reach this goal of strategic flexibility. We can no longer rely on the corporate saviour alone. The world of globalization, e- and m-commerce, and economic turbulence calls for more.

The sharp-eyed traders that Homer described and despised reshaped the very map of Greece herself. Iron ingots flowed into Greece from Italy, where smiths turned them into hoes and ploughs. This enabled the peasants of Boeotia, Euboea, Attica and the Peloponnesus to grow more wheat. In a classic prefiguring of other industrial revolutions elsewhere, Greece itself was able to support more people, and the population of the Greek world began to rise slowly in the 8th century. New communities began to dot the shores of the Attic peninsula: Eleusis, Palaia, Kokkina, Anaphlystos, Myrrhinous and Marathon, all springing up near a coastline more and more free from the dangers of piracy. The 5th-century historian Thucydides hinted at this remaking of the Greek landscape:

> *'The cities which were founded in more recent times, when navigation had at length become safer, and were consequently beginning to have surplus resources, were built right on the seashore, and the isthmuses were occupied and walled off with a view to commerce and to the protection of the several peoples against their neighbours.'*[5]

New towns sprang up near Corinth and across the Aegean in Ionia. The pattern was the same – first the outside wall, then houses, local shrines and the apportionment of farmland. The archaeology of Greece in the 8th century BCE shows a surge of building activity and a growing density of sites, particularly around Athens, in north-west Crete and on the Peloponnesus.[6]

Pithekoussai was the forerunner of the grand age of Hellenic colonization, which gained momentum around 750 BCE and lasted for about two centuries. Colonies of settlers from Corinth, Sparta, Megara, Chalcis, Eretria, Phocaea, Miletus and other Greek cities were founded in southern Italy, Sicily, Libya and Egypt, and eventually along the northern and southern shores of the Black Sea. Significantly, these settlements of Hellenes were sovereign communities of *individuals* who migrated abroad in search of land or profit. The Greek merchant settling in Naucratis in Egypt or Syracuse in Sicily traded on his own, not as part of a temple or princely hierarchy. The Greek farmer abroad began to raise his own wheat, causing his competitors at home to seek new markets by growing vines, oranges and olives.

The *polis*, tyrants and a money society

The coming of free enterprise and iron-working would also help democratize some of the Greek cities. Big armies with chariots were a Mesopotamian phenomenon; in Greece citizen soldiers called hoplites fought on foot in massed ranks with their new iron swords. Every farmer or small trader mattered in these ranks, and every one of them could afford a bronze helmet, a breastplate and an iron sword. Limited government in Greece went hand-in-hand with limited warfare. Wars were short, usually small, and fought over land, not religion or conquest.

> It would be wrong to picture Greek capitalism as a totally freewheeling system of *laissez-faire*. Such did not exist then and does not exist today.

By Homer's day, the old tribal kingdom was giving way to a revolutionary new form of political organization called the *polis*, from which we have the word 'politics'. Mesopotamia had big kingdoms, Syria and Phoenicia medium-sized principalities, Egypt a centralized statist monarchy. The Greeks, including the islands of the Aegean, the Ionian cities of Asia Minor, and the overseas colonies, were soon divided into over 1500 independent *poleis*, most with an average population of 5000. The *polis*, with its codified rule of law, enshrined equality of justice for its *citizens*. For the first time, people were bonded together in a civic, as opposed to a purely tribal, union. A small community ruled by an oligarchy of rich farmers and traders governed by the rule of law was destined to be far less intrusive and hostile to free enterprise than the massive monarchies of the East.

The rise of the *polis* was followed by two more developments in the 7th and 6th centuries BCE that further accelerated the transformation of ancient Greece into the world's first true market society. In city after city, hoplite armies hired and equipped by men of capital began to depose rural oligarchies in favour of a new type of leader called the tyrant. Usually outcast aristocrats, the tyrants were, or often became, successful entrepreneurial business leaders. Once in power, they usually helped promote commercial development. The term 'tyrant' has a different meaning today from the meaning it had at that time. The tyrants of 700–500 BCE were strong leaders, but not necessarily harsh or oppressive. The term acquired this negative connotation much later, in the Athens of the 4th century BCE.

Another by-product of trade expansion and iron tools was the rise of coined money. For centuries, Assyrian, Babylonian and Anatolian merchants used ingots of silver or even gold in their commercial dealings. Around 700 BCE, however, the ruler of Lydia began to use iron tools to inscribe his royal trademark on a piece of gold-and-silver alloy called electrum. The idea of coined money caught on quickly, spreading across Asia Minor, then throughout the Aegean, and eventually to Athens and the rest of the Hellenic world. The owl-faced Athenian *drachma* would become the functional currency, the dollar of Hellendom.

Money would further commercialize Greek life, although barter was far from dead. Soon goatherds were haggling with their customers as the law of supply and demand began to work on a bigger and bigger scale. After 600 BCE, Greece was well on the way to becoming, on a small scale, the world's first real consumer society, and one that was increasingly competitive. The potters of Attica were now advertising their own individual brands, creating a marketing image and targeting specific overseas markets, be they mass or specialized.

It would be wrong to picture Greek capitalism as a totally freewheeling system of *laissez-faire*. Such did not exist then and does not exist today. Restraints were built into the system, but they were somewhat different from those in the Near East. The centralized hierarchies of 'temple capitalism' were, by and large, absent and priests had less control over transactions. Temples and oracles such as those at Delphi, Delos and Dodona served as business centres, but most Greeks worshipped at their own small shrines.

> The new Greek deism, in which the gods and goddesses kept hands off human affairs, was an indirect outgrowth of the market revolution

Religion in Greece was, to some degree, itself becoming entrepreneurial. Some cults were owned by private families; others were the creation of travelling evangelists and independent shrine owners. Most Hellenes remained devout worshippers of Zeus, Athena, Hermes, Apollo and Hephaestus. A small intellectual elite, though, was being led to question the entire supernatural world-view. Homer senses this in his portrait of Telemachus. As Greeks began to trade abroad and encounter the beliefs of Canaanites, Scythians, Lydians and Etruscans, some of them, like the poet Xenophanes, began to question the sovereignty of their own deities.

The new Greek deism, in which the gods and goddesses kept hands off human affairs, was an indirect outgrowth of the market revolution. Thales of Miletus, trading in wheat, began to study astronomy and the tides in the hope that a better understanding of navigation and the weather would help ensure safer, quicker and more lucrative voyages to the wheat markets of Scythia. Predicting an eclipse, Thales began to believe, like Newton, that the world operated by natural laws instead of the whims of Olympus.

As the rich became richer and some of the poor poorer, some began to take the next step. If Zeus did not intervene in the laws of nature, it is likely he did not intervene in the affairs of human beings, who must now build a society based upon virtue and reason. Reason dictated the intervention of the *polis* to ensure fairness in the market and stability in society and, in the case of Athens, the replacement of tyranny and oligarchy with a limited form of democracy around 510 BCE.

The climactic wars between the Greeks and a Persian Empire that hoped to conquer them pitted the princely/priestly hierarchies of the Levant and Mesopotamia against Greek independent enterprise

> The climactic wars between the Greeks and a Persian Empire that hoped to conquer them pitted the princely/priestly hierarchies of the Levant and Mesopotamia against Greek independent enterprise

The admirals and merchant-princes of Tyre and Sidon lent their fleets to the Persian invader, hoping to sweep all Hellenic competition from the seas. The Greek cities in Asia Minor, Phocaea and Miletus were ravaged, ensuring that 'one of the largest Ionian shipping centres collapsed to the advantage of Phoenician traders'. For a while the eastern Mediterranean 'once again became a Phoenician lake'.[7] Tyre's original trading sphere was temporarily restored.

In 480 BCE, Xerxes, supported by a combined Persian–Tyrian fleet, marched a vast army through Thrace, overrunning most of Greece, pillaging Athens, and wiping out the Spartan defenders at glorious Thermopylae. Greece was saved by the 'wooden walls' of her new navy. Inspired by the orator Themistocles, financed by the Assembly and the silver mines of Laurion, the new Athenian *trireme* warships (three rowers on each oar) were made by private contractors. Luring the mighty Tyrian and Persian fleets to their destruction in the narrow channel of Salamis in 480, the Athenian navy doomed Xerxes' invasion of Greece.

The Golden Age of Athens

Salamis ensured that Europe, free of the threat of Asian conquest, would also be free to develop along the lines of market enterprise. The Hellenic model was here to stay as the Golden Age of Classical Athens now beckoned. The battle did for Athens what Trafalgar did for Britain. The Aegean was now dominated by an Athenian-led Delian League. Athens built and manned the triremes, which the lesser states paid for by accepting Athenian taxation and trade regulations. The League turned into an informal Athenian Empire, deterring invasion for half a century, with Athens drawing perhaps £125 million in tribute from her allies.

> Greek art pictured humanity on its own terms, in vital and realistic, freely flowing movement, more like secular people wished it to appear and not how the gods desired

Most Athenians had a strong financial stake in the new imperial economy, which brought unprecedented prosperity to many, if not most, Athenians. The prosperity of a number of the 40 000 voting citizens depended upon maintaining and financing the Delian fleet. Bustling Athens was never out of earshot of the clanging hammer and the relentless whine of the saw. Shipbuilders profited from the manufacture of triremes, merchants from selling timber and pitch from the Black Sea, bankers from financing their voyages with exorbitant loans, smiths from shaping and exporting large quantities of hoplite arms. Masons profited from building fortifications linking Athens and the Piraeus. Labourers of the poorer classes enlisted in the navy to row the triremes about the Aegean and made sure that those they elected to the Assembly appropriated the drachmas to maintain them.

Athens and her market system in the middle of the 5th century BCE reached the heights of power and prosperity. This was the age of Pericles, her skilled and judicious leader (born 495 BCE). The first free-market metropolis in history gave birth to the first democratic urban culture. Within the circle of private homes and small farmhouses clustered in the surrounding villages of Attica, the beginnings of urban Europe were already evident. Rows of open-air houses crowded along the narrow, twisting boulevards beneath the Acropolis. Everywhere there were signs of a confident people. The epitome of that swaggering optimism was the vast Parthenon and the other splendid buildings constructed by Pericles on the Acropolis towering over the growing, prospering city.

These extravagant structures – perhaps costing approximately £600 million in current terms – became the symbols of Athenian pride and glory during the Periclean age. The décor of the massive Parthenon, dedicated to Athena, proclaimed the message that the gods and goddesses of Olympus were on the side of Athens, even though the average educated Athenian worshipped them only at his or her convenience. The statues adorning the temple spoke volumes about a society that was more devoted to Athenians than to Athena. For centuries the peoples of the Orient and the early Greeks themselves had depicted the human form in stiff, idealized poses, of which the sculptures of Egypt were by far the best example. Now, the Classical Age took root. Sculptures of nude male athletes and warriors and women in fine robes with bent arms and toned torsos adorned the public works encouraged by Pericles. Greek art pictured humanity on its own terms, in vital and realistic freely flowing movement, more like secular people wished it to appear and not how the gods desired.

The centre of Greek culture after Salamis shifted from Asia Minor to Athens. Under Pericles (prominent between 463 and 429 BCE) the Hellenic market economy flourished in its most advanced form as a rising tide lifted all *triremes*. A few areas, such as the silver mines of Laurion, were state-run.

Wine, olive oil and wool underpinned the new luxury exports of Athens – finely glazed pottery and exquisitely crafted jewellery. Fifth-century Athens was agog with wealth and splendour; it was a time of confident moneymaking, not philosophising. Athens was confident enough – like Victorian Britain – to embark on a virtual free-trade policy. Here, unlike in Sparta, thousands of *metics* (immigrants) were welcomed and encouraged to transact the business occupations disdained by many native-born Athenians who remained hoplite farmers at heart. Most important, company managers and traders were not Athenian citizens and many were not even Greek.

The Athenian business world was, unlike any other of its time, organized mainly by market forces and the rule of law. Busy traders on a typical day sailed into the harbour of the Piraeus where officials inspected their wares and levied a 2 per cent toll. Harbour agents then charged the merchant or his agent for the use of dock facilities. Avoiding the naval harbours, trading vessels then docked at the business wharves, the longest of which were reserved for the grain ships. The visiting trader next had to deal with the middlemen and the local grain inspectors.

Near the wharves lay the shops of an emerging consumer society selling pottery, fish, naval stores, textiles, ivory from Africa, furniture from Asia and meat from Sicily. 'The wares of the whole world', boasted Pericles, 'find their way to us.' Throughout the summer the bazaar was the scene of hundreds of deals among the squabbling small traders and money changers who formed the backbone of the Athenian economy. 'Fish! Fish! Get your fish here!' 'An exquisite robe from Carthage. How can you refuse?' In the *agora* (market-place) one could, quipped a cynical poet, buy anything under the sun: 'turnips, pears, apples, witnesses, roses, peddlers, porridge, honey-combs, chickpeas, lawsuits ... water-clocks, laws, indictments'. With the coming of autumn, merchants closed up shop until spring.

For almost two centuries Athens, with its wonderful harbour, free society and stable currency, seemed like the centre of the world. Her silver *drachmas* – Athena on one side, her distinctive owl on the other – remained the sterling of the eastern Mediterranean two centuries after Pericles. Grain was king. Every summer independent traders made about 800 voyages from Pontus to feed 200 000 to 300 000 Athenians. Imported cereals and fish were still in great demand, which explains Athens' aggressive ways with her Delian partners.

> The first directors of Lloyd's of London would have understood Athenian arrangements. The Athenian economy was infinitely more risk-oriented than the Tyrian, having no internalized private–public structure to absorb losses

Athens sent no organized merchant flotillas, based on the Tyrian model, to patrol northward from Athens through the Hellespont. Hellenic traders sailed alone, writing out individual contracts with shipowners, bankers and middlemen.

Borrowing *drachmas* from a banker at interest rates of 20–30 per cent for five months, many traders used the loans to charter a ship. An owner's vessel could stand as collateral, and sometimes his cargo filled the bill. The first directors of Lloyd's of London would have understood Athenian arrangements. The Athenian economy was infinitely more risk-oriented than the Tyrian, having no internalized private–public structure to absorb losses. The trader might lose his life, the shipowner his vessel, the banker his loan.

Once the ships actually sailed, they faced other challenges. Those on the Pontus route had to fight northerly winds all the way to Scythia (but were guaranteed an easy ride home). Those bound for Egypt had an easy ride south but had to buck mighty headwinds back to Athens. The western route to Sicily meant a tail wind on one side of the Peloponnesus and a head wind on the other. Even if he arrived home safely, the adventurous sea trader was by no means assured a profit. Grain prices in Greece were by no means fixed and, if deflation ensued, a merchant could finish with a loss after repaying the banker and ship owner.

While the Athenian economy anticipated Anglo-American capitalism, classical Greece was not a modern urban society. The independent farmer remained supreme as did traders such as agricultural labourers, gardeners, oil and walnut peddlers, donkey and mule drivers, potters, builders, carpenters, cooks, bakers and porters. Rooted in these small enterprises, Hellenic industrial life had less in common with the factory system of modern times than with the re-emerging custom-made production of the post-industrial era.

Athenian capitalism knew no factories on a scale that Charles Dickens would recognize. Shield factories, the biggest, employed about a hundred slaves. Athenian capitalism remained individualistic to its core. Most businesses employed but two or three people. The state maintained a *laissez-faire* attitude as far as wages and working conditions were concerned. Everyone in the Periclean age believed that the market itself and personal relationships based on virtue and intelligent self-interest would enable the system to operate.

The Peloponnesian War and the rise of Athenian bankers

Brilliant and dazzling as it was, the free-market revolution in the Aegean would eventually lose its lustre as the glory of Athens began to wane. In 431 BCE ancient Greece was plunged into the most terrible war in its history. The Peloponnesian War of 431–404 ranged Athens and its allies against the states of the Peloponnesus, led by the conservative oligarchy of Sparta. The causes of this war were geopolitical far more than commercial, although access to grain was an important factor. In a long struggle (the Athenian army and navy suffered from bad leadership and flawed strategy) the Athenians were eventually defeated and the Athenian Empire was dissolved.

Defeat in war led to a further revolution in Athenian business values. Business, still frowned upon by many, had redeemed itself in the Periclean age because it enhanced Athenian democracy and military power as well as human progress. Now, Greek writers began to have second thoughts about what the marketplace had wrought. The plays of Aristophanes symbolized a longing for a return to the simplicity of the rural life. In *The Frogs* (written 405) Aristophanes lamented the commercialization of his Athens by comparing the value of his fellow citizens to that of their coinage. Men needed to be content with what the gods had ordained: marriage, sacrifice and agriculture over trading, industry and a vanquished empire. To think that one could defy the natural agrarian order given to humanity by the gods through an economy based on human will and self-assertion was unnatural and even blasphemous.

The loss of empire, markets and tribute strained Athenian tax and welfare systems and the spirit of democracy itself. Greece was now looked upon as a decaying farm whose owners were weak and old and unable to pull up the weeds. The seeds planted by Aristophanes continued to germinate, watered by Plato and Aristotle. Democrats, tyrants and merchants were ridiculed. Aristotle in his *Politics* praised the hierarchical system of Carthage, to which we will shortly turn. Plato (who never had to meet a payroll!) advocated a utopian managed society run by philosophers who would not own property or engage in business.[8]

> Plato (who never had to meet a payroll!) advocated a utopian managed society run by philosophers who would not own property or engage in business

Business and the free market continued to flourish in Athens even in her decline. Private banks became the most advanced Athenian economic institution in the 4th, not the 5th, century. With the silver mines depleted and the empire gone, the Athenian tax burden on disclosed property became unbearable. Athenian merchants were not gleeful taxpayers and they entrusted their liquid assets to private banks where they might be hidden from the scrutiny of the tax collector. Bankers made loans in secret and were able to publicly shield the identity of their depositors, many of whom, like the orator Demosthenes' father, invested in maritime loans and privately reaped the benefits.[9]

Athenian bankers operated in a society that did not recognize the corporation as a legal person. The Greek tradition of independent enterprise frowned upon Athenian citizens' performing servile work. Slaves and dependent family became natural employees and even heirs for Greek bankers while free employees might set up their own rival businesses.

PASION: SLAVE ENTREPRENEUR

No story better shows the rags-to-riches possibilities of the Athenian economy than that of its most famous banker, Pasion (d. 370 BCE). Pasion was not a Hellene but a *barbaros* (barbarian) sold into Athenian slavery from his homeland. Unlike many unfortunates who wound up in the mines, Pasion, when he was brought to Athens, wound up as the property of the bankers Antisthenes and Archistratus. Pasion's career started ingloriously. He would have to carry heavy sacks of drachmas for Archistratus. His diligence, however, soon promoted him to working Archistratus' money-changing table in the Piraeus. Here Pasion had to deal with merchants coming and going between Athens and the outside world. Perhaps Pasion had an accounting background prior to his capture, for he was very shrewd. Being able to spot a dishonest trader or a poor investment, Pasion saved his owners a great deal of money. He was so trustworthy and indispensable that Archistratus eventually made him a free man.

Pasion not only became a free man, but also eventually inherited what he would turn into the most prestigious and reputable bank in Athens. Pasion lent not only to merchants but also to military and political figures.

As one of history's first professional bankers he not only guarded deposits but also wrote bank drafts that allowed seafaring traders to transfer funds to banks in Scythia, Libya, Asia Minor or Italy. Pasion reaped huge profits from the interest on shipping loans from all these traders.

Banking in Athens was a personal affair among networks of personal trust. Pasion became not only lender but also personal confidant to the son of Sopaios, who later accused him of fraud. The trader Timosthenes was a customer, as was the Athenian general Timotheos.

Shipping was not Pasion's only investment. As his wealth grew, he began to put money into his own shipping firm and opened a munition factory from which he gave the hoplites of Athens a gift of a thousand shields. He was even more generous to the navy, paying for five Athenian triremes. The Assembly responded by granting Pasion Athenian citizenship. The banker quickly took advantage of his new status with major investments in real estate.

Despite Pasion's reputation for integrity, he was, late in his career, accused of major fraud by the son of Sopaios and was found guilty by a jury in a case related in the *Trapeziticus* of Isocrates. On his death, Pasion turned his enterprises over to his own former slave, Phormion, who married his widow to preserve the family connection.

All Athenian banks and businesses were considered personal enterprises with no legal existence apart from their owners. Some examples were the bed-making shop of Demosthenes' father or the shield factory of the banker Pasion. Money on deposit with a classical Greek bank was said to be on deposit with the banker. There were risks galore! Bankers like Pasion tended to mingle their deposits with their own personal funds, which meant that a bank failure would ruin everyone. Greek banks were often managed out of owner's homes, just like many other enterprises. Little equipment was needed: perhaps a table, a scale, an abacus and papyrus rolls. Unlike his shield shop, Pasion's bank had little value apart from the considerable money that passed through it.[10]

Banking in Athens became highly personal as bankers formed networks of friends with whom they could deal. Pasion became not only lender but also personal confidant to the son of Sopaios. The overseas trader Timosthenes was not only a customer of Pasion but also a close friend and business partner of Pasion's own slave, Phormion. The general Timotheos borrowed cloaks, bedding and other items from Pasion's bank to entertain visiting dignitaries.[11]

> In Tyre, wealth, status and citizenship had to be inherited but in Athens even a barbarian slave might, possibly, become a powerful business manager

The careers of Pasion and Phormion reveal Athens as by far the most fluid, cash-based society that had yet existed. The free-market revolution supported most of the Greek accomplishments in letters, poetry and philosophy. In Tyre, wealth, status and citizenship had to be inherited but in Athens even a barbarian slave might, possibly, become a powerful business manager.

The Athenian economy operated on the liquid flow of cash. Impersonal dealings made in coin and bank notes made possible transfers of money from traders to bankers, to moneylenders and other traders. Commodity prices, no longer fixed as they were in Babylonia, fluctuated daily on the Athenian price exchanges, bringing into existence a class of speculators. Personal honour in business dealings did not disappear: it simply carried less weight than the credit rating of a client in this wide-open cash-based system.

The continuing importance of commerce in Athenian life is shown by the fact that the city was no longer guided by generals like Pericles but by financial experts like Eubulus and Lycurgus. A web of trade routes still criss-crossed the waters between Marseilles and the Crimea. Bankers, shippers and shipowners co-operated in using them to send every conceivable sort of product, especially the basic commodities of the ancient world: wine, oil and grain. Traders in Byzantium on the Bosporus cocked a wary eye at the crop in Sicily 800 miles away; rumours of a bad harvest in Egypt sent prices soaring on the exchanges of half a dozen Greek cities. At the centre of this hectic commercial activity stood Athens with its seaport town, the Piraeus.[12]

The Athenian *polis* endured, but its conservative political institutions – which still excluded foreigners, freedmen and slaves – were being undermined by rampaging market realities. These new factors that surcharged the day-to-day interactions of people in the Athenian *agora* were exposed by the 4th-century orator Demosthenes. Demosthenes described the not-so-subtle shifts. Sales and purchases were being conducted with the language of politics and war: the purchaser 'defeated' the seller whenever he bought something, and the seller who refused to take a bribe was likewise a 'winner' over the purchaser. Demosthenes' metaphors turned on the assumption that 'in commercial exchange there were winners and losers, just as in battles and bribery'.[13]

The fundamental change in these times, though, was that wealth and gain could now be secured in other, more exotic and exciting forms than household agriculture. Periclean Athens was pioneering a regime quite recognizable to our day, a time of free enterprise tied to banking, trading, mining and manufacturing. The older 'agrarian' ideals of equality and self-sufficiency were still preached, but they no longer corresponded to the way many Athenians lived. The city met this dilemma by moving towards democracy, accommodating the landless, building a large navy, and turning to the sea rather than subsistence farming as the source of national sustenance. These developments slowly undermined the old ideal of landed self-sufficiency.[14]

The brilliant Aegean experiment in free enterprise rested on strong foundations tied to economic expansion, military prowess, a growing population, and an increasingly able and diversified bureaucracy. Athenians under Pericles had learned to enrich themselves with both cash and capital in the new market order. Even as the economic solvents undermined traditional forms and values as the money machine cranked away, many, even among the hoplite orders, committed themselves to the open market. They became, in the process, self-made democrats willing to take up arms to defend the Athenian system against those such as Aristophanes who invoked a 'back to the land' ethic. Among the latter were philosophers such as Plato and Aristotle who favoured a return to oligarchy: 'Let the best people rule!' Athens faced the dilemma of extending the hoplite ideal to native-born residents but finding no way to incorporate the aliens, *metics* and others. Perhaps the city had aimed too high. It hoped to be both a *polis* and a Mediterranean power, retaining the values of the simple life while trusting their investments to the *agora*. In the end, the tension proved too great.[15]

While the Athenian experience represented the Greek market economy in its purest form, the experience of other Greek communities was somewhat different. In Thessaly, Crete and Sparta an economy not altogether different from that of the Mycenaean Bronze Age survived. Neither entrepreneurs nor chattel slaves flourished in these regions, which remained tied to a more feudal and manorial system. In oligarchic Sparta, for example, the men did not farm. The warrior class trained for battle while serfs worked the estates.[16]

The Greek model of independent household enterprise exemplified at Athens was the exception rather than the rule, though there were modified forms of it developing in Italy. In the Persian-dominated Near East, as well as in Carthage, the Oriental model of large estates and manorial serfdom prevailed.

Athens, which gave the world the idea of democracy, also gave the world a workable idea of free enterprise. Not surprisingly, entrepreneurial business would survive in Greece after both the Macedonian and Roman conquests. The independent agrarian base upon which the economy rested, however, would eventually wither away as a more hierarchical culture reasserted itself.

In spite of the Athenian decline, the Greek achievement was catalytic to the history of business. The free-market experience in the Aegean represented an impressive foreshadowing of Anglo-American free enterprise. The small private farms, low taxes and militia-style armies fostered a creed of rugged egalitarianism familiar to any American farmer living before 1860. In Athens, as in Britain and America, a broadly based form of constitutional government and a free-market business culture evolved. In an admirable way, the system worked! It encouraged productivity and rewarded innovation among captains of agriculture and industry.

Farm ownership introduced the idea that human excellence is fostered by individual – *not* corporate, *not* state – initiative. This original move towards privately held, intensive agriculture provided a surplus of food production in most areas. It freed a sizeable minority for commerce, small crafts and government bureaucracies.[17]

The end of the Athenian era

The end of the Athenian era was not long in coming. In 338 BCE the armies of Philip of Macedon subdued the most important Greek city-states, though a nominal independence under Macedonian overlordship was allowed. Within two years, Philip's son, Alexander, was to lead a unified force of Macedonians and Greeks on a march of conquest that placed most of the Near East under his rule. The Hellenistic age had begun! Greek democracy would be replaced by monarchical despotism and the free-market revolution in the Aegean would, in large measure, be transformed by the Oriental cultures among which it was to be planted.

NOTES TO CHAPTER 6

1. Redfield, J.M. 'The Development of the Market in Ancient Greece' in Anderson, B.L. and Latham, A.J.H., eds. (1986) *The Market in History*. London: Croom Helm, 41.
2. Homer, *The Odyssey*, tr. Lattimore, R. (1991). New York: Harper Perennial, iv. 80–5.
3. Redfield, J.M. 'The Development of the Market in Ancient Greece' in Anderson, B.L. and Latham, A.J.H., eds. (1986) *The Market in History*. London: Croom Helm, 43.
4. *Ibid.*
5. Thucydides, *History of the Peloponnesian War*, Books I and II, tr. Forster Smith, C. (1969). Cambridge MA: Harvard University Press, vii.
6. Osborne, R.J. (1996) *Greece in the Making: 1200–179 BC*. London: Routledge, 70.
7. Katzenstein, H.J. 'Tyre in the Early Persian Period (539–486 BCE)' in *Biblical Archaeologist*, Vol.42, no. 1 (Winter, 1979), 31.
8. Green, P. (1979) *A Concise History of Ancient Greece to the Close of the Classical Era*. London: Thames and Hudson, 134–6.
9. Cohen, Edward E. (1992) *Athenian Economy and Society: A Banking Perspective*. Princeton, NJ: Princeton University Press, 191–203.
10. *Ibid.*, 68–9.
11. *Ibid.*, 65–6.
12. *Ibid.*, 110.
13. *Ibid.*,120.
14. Hanson, V.D. (1995) *The Other Greeks: the Family Farm and the Agrarian Roots of Western Civilization*. New York: The Free Press, 365.
15. *Ibid.*, 387–90.
16. *Ibid.*, 391–2.
17. *Ibid.*, 398.

7

Overture to world economy

India, China and the heirs of Athens and Tyre: 331–146 BCE

W AR is cruel, rapacious and destructive, but under certain conditions it can be a boon for business, as in the 'military Keynesianism' of the 20th century.

A similar link between military expansion and the wealth of nations
existed in the final centuries of the first millennium BCE. The commercial
empires of trade, investment and liquid finance, pioneered by Tyre and
Athens, were inherited by Macedonia in the East and by Carthage and
Rome in the West. Thanks to Alexander the Great, the Hellenic market
revolution reached the borders of India. Transplanted to Africa, the
'managed' economy of Tyre and Sidon endured and prospered in Carthage
until it was absorbed by the most learned pupils of the Hellenic market
revolution: the Romans

The 200 years between the rise of Alexander the Great and the
destruction of Carthage and Corinth by Roman legions were a time of
conflict as old empires were shattered and new ones emerged. The feuding
states of Greece were united, not by a Greek but by a Macedonian, Philip,
whose son Alexander then went on to conquer the entire Near East as far
as the gates of India. Alexander's vast realm was divided after his death in
323 BCE, and the successor states of Ptolemaic Egypt and Seleucid Syria
encountered new powers based in Carthage, Parthia and Rome. A new
world, known as the *Hellenistic*, combined Greek enterprise with the much
older cultural legacies of Asia.

Alexander's armies seized vast amounts, some 180 000 talents, of gold
bullion from the palaces of Persia and released it into circulation. At a
single stroke the Near East became a money economy with the equiv-

alent of some £200 billion in circulation. Greek entrepreneurs settling in colonies from Egypt to eastern Iran soon provided the banking expertise to manage it.

The Hellenistic economies enjoyed healthy growth up to about 250 BCE as Greek merchants and *drachmas* spread across the realm of Alexander and its successor states. From 250 BCE on, though, a new round of wars and commotions disrupted the expanding markets and stifled demand for agricultural, mineral, forest and artisan produce. The Seleucids lost Asia Minor to the Attalids and Persia to the Parthians. Greece herself plunged into another round of fratricidal war among its various *poleis*. Natural disasters, civil strife, social unrest and a new epidemic of piracy further depressed business confidence in Rhodes and Corinth, the surviving economic motors of the Aegean. Six hundred per cent hyperinflation struck the Egyptian economy. In spite of this, its recuperative power remained quite strong, for other political events conspired to make Egypt the world's breadbasket. In the end, the lack of political unity rather than market failure would be the Hellenistic world's political doom.[1]

The Greeks could only partially transform the world they conquered. The long centuries of Mesopotamian-style 'temple capitalism' and the bureaucratic inertia of 30 dynasties of Pharaohs were too much to overcome. The thousands of new entrepreneurs had to operate in the midst of far older and more hierarchical ways of doing business. According to German economic historian Fritz Heichelheim, 'Hellenic individual private enterprise ... became generally embedded into the greatest planned organism of the ancient world, a contradiction indeed.'[2]

Egypt, the very centre of the Hellenistic economy itself, remained a thoroughgoing socialist state. The Ptolemies dictated what would be grown and where it would be grown, all grain being taken and sold by royal agents. Business taxes stifled dreams of independent commerce, being as high as 50 per cent on items such as olive oil. Traders coming to Egypt could not use their own money but had to convert it into the Ptolemaic 'ruble'. Bureaucrats were trained to supervise agriculture, register cattle, audit all village revenues, and ship grain on royal barges.

Practical as well as historical reasons ensured the survival of Near Eastern mixed and even multinational enterprise in the Seleucid realm of Syria, Iraq and Iran and that of the Attalids in Asia Minor. The tenacious merchant-princes of Tyre still played the game according to Dunning's

Eclectic Paradigm. Associations of traders and merchant shipowners arose in Egypt, Tyre and Sidon. Shippers headquartered in these ports opened permanent branch offices in Athens and Delos.[3] Hellenistic trade and commerce generally expanded with access to the sea. The local economies of the Ptolemaic, Attalid, Seleucid and Aegean worlds became more connected, but the new economic unity was often tenuous and 'hampered by the limitations and fluctuations of effective demand'.[4]

Apart from the few major cross-Aegean routes allowing Near Eastern merchants to invest in the Greek homelands, market weakness tended to limit commercial dominance in the eastern Mediterranean to one port at a time. The torch of economic opportunity passed from Athens to Rhodes, then Phaselis, Chalcis and finally Delos. Trade was much more governed by politics than by purely market considerations. In a largely agrarian economy plagued by incessant wars, inflation, government meddling and an epidemic of piracy, market failure became a far greater problem than in the days of Pericles.

> In a largely agrarian economy plagued by incessant wars, inflation, government meddling, and an epidemic of piracy, market failure became a far greater problem than in the days of Pericles

The result was that agriculture tended to become more self-sufficient. Egypt and Phoenicia, building upon their statist traditions, sought to bypass unreliable market conditions at home by spying out trade ventures overseas.[5]

International trade in the three millennia preceding Hellenistic times was, by and large, confined to the eastern Mediterranean. One *could* speak of a *regional* economy spreading from Britain and Carthage to Egypt, Persia and northern India. Events in China and the Indian Ocean, however, would make it possible to create the first *world* economy, encompassing Europe, Africa, India and the Far East. Once aloof and isolated, both China and southern India would now come into contact with the Mediterranean/Near Eastern trading network.

The *Arthashastra*: Indian supply-side economics

The Indian subcontinent enjoyed little contact with the Babylonian economy in more than the millennium following the collapse of the Indus-valley cities. Entering India from the north, the new Aryan-speaking settlers spread slowly eastward along the line of the Ganges. The lighter-skinned invaders, who worshipped gods such as Indra and Varuna, soon made themselves a ruling elite, reducing the darker peoples to subject castes.

There are almost no written or archaeological records of Indian life for a thousand years during what is called the Vedic period, named after the sacred text known as the *Rig Veda*. During this time, the outlines of Indian culture began to take shape, a culture far different from that of both the West and China. Indian thought has always been highly abstract and metaphysical, the language itself describing individuals as manifestations of certain categories. The gods and goddesses themselves were to be seen as manifestations of a force, the Brahman, that was the ultimate reality behind all things. Because life moved in endless cycles of death and rebirth, history was far less relevant than spirituality, and so it was not written.

> Because life moved in endless cycles of death and rebirth, history was far less relevant than spirituality, and so it was not written

The only written clues to Indian business come from what mattered most to the Indian mind: religious texts. Often vague and abstract in describing events, these texts do show India to have had a mixed economy not unlike the Near Eastern in which commerce played an important role. In the *Atharva Veda* (900–600 BCE) a hymn to the 'trader Indra' and the fire-god Agni implores the giving of riches: 'Successful for us be bargain and sale; let return-dealing make me fruitful ... successful for us be our going about and rising ... With what riches I practise bargaining, seeking riches with riches ...'[6]

The Vedas themselves alluded to some abiding contact with Persia, Assyria and Babylon, and this was confirmed by the Greeks. The Persian king Darius sent sailors down the Indus to explore the routes of trade, and some Indian merchants were trading peacocks to Babylon around 400 BCE. Alexander, as well, explored the Indus, seeking the best trade route between his empire and India.

Alexander's empire helped inspire the forging of a unified Indian state, a task begun by Chandragupta Maurya (322–298 BCE) and completed by Asoka (273–232 BCE), who conquered most of the subcontinent. During the Mauryan period, a work of Indian economy known as the *Arthashastra* was probably first compiled. The *Arthashastra* clearly showed merchant-princes and entrepreneurs flourishing in ancient India, as they did in Mesopotamia, under the watchful tutelage of the *rajahs*, or kings. Unlike their Ptolemaic contemporaries, Indian kings understood you had to create wealth before you could distribute it. Charity, desire and wealth were all important in life, but wealth was the foundation of the other two. It was the duty of the *rajah* to 'help his subjects acquire wealth and do good to them'.[7]

The handbook set forth a strong role for government in encouraging private enterprise and even an early version of supply-side economics! Supply-side economists such as Jude Wanniski preached the common-sense idea that higher taxes, beyond a certain point, produce less, not more, revenue. So did the *rajahs* of ancient India, whom the *Arthashastra* admonished to remit taxes whenever they could. Any official who reduced revenue consumed India's wealth, but any who doubled it would ruin the vitality of the nation and deserved severe punishment.

Taxation in India, as well as government's role, was heavy enough. The government encouraged mining, forestry, road building, irrigation and regulated weights and measures. Second to the *rajah* was his Director of Trade, charged with studying supply, demand and other market conditions. Government stores of merchandise were to be centrally managed, prices fixed, and dealers subsidized. Import–export traders were to be given a tax credit.

> Supply-side economists such as Jude Wanniski preached the common-sense idea that higher taxes, beyond a certain point, produce less, not more, revenue. So did the *rajahs* of ancient India, whom the *Arthashastra* admonished to remit taxes whenever they could

The Indian state encouraged business strategies designed to exploit its wealth, strengthen its defences, and pursue market advantages for it while denying them to its rivals. The key was for the *rajah* to ensure that the kingdom – in the case of the Mauryans, India herself – had more potential for economic growth than her enemies, allowing her to ignore them.

Market intelligence, including the use of merchants as spies, would play a vital role in business strategy: 'The merchant should obtain information en route as to market conditions and divert his merchandize to profitable markets, avoiding unprofitable ones.'[8]

Indian merchants carefully guarded their trading secrets from the West, until they fell into the hands of the Ptolemies. Under the tolerant reign of her first Buddhist *rajah*, Asoka, Indian merchants began to trade with the Hellenistic world. African ivory, conveyed by Arabian middlemen, journeyed up the Red Sea to the Egyptian crown merchants in the markets of Tyre, Sidon and Alexandria. This would provide a great opportunity for the Ptolemies, who began to import Indian goods delivered by Arabian merchants overland or via the Red Sea to Alexandria.

The royal merchants in Alexandria controlled all Indian, Arabian and African goods coming into Egypt or Phoenicia. Soon they discovered a vital market secret that would place them in the forefront of world trade: that of the monsoon winds that let ships cross the Indian Ocean far to the south of the Arabian and Persian shores. Both Indians and Arabs co-operated in 'keeping what they knew', according to maritime historian Lionel Casson, 'about the behaviour of these winds strictly to themselves' since 'neither was minded to divulge trade secrets to possible competitors'.[9]

This vital market knowledge fell into Western hands around 120 BCE when an Indian sailor described the monsoon to the explorer Eudoxus. Soon, Hellenistic merchants were meeting the westerly monsoon near the mouth of the Red Sea in May and riding it all the way to India, returning via the easterly monsoon, which began in November. Greeks set up shop in India, Indian shippers and agents in Alexandria, for the same winds brought Indian vessels to Egypt.[10]

The way was now open for a direct route between Europe and Asia in which India would play an all-important role.

China's 2000-year debate: Confucian socialism or Daoist capitalism?

While the bulk of the Indian trade was cornered eventually by Ptolemaic mariners, merchants in the Seleucid realm inherited the ancient Sumerian–Akkadian network. Wood, spices and other luxuries journeyed westward across Persia by caravan and the Euphrates from Mauryan India to Tyre, Sidon, Antioch or Ephesus. A second route reached Babylonia via the Persian Gulf whence camels and riverboats journeyed westward. The goods delivered via both routes now included silk from the Han Empire of China, which entered the international economy not long after 250 BCE.[11]

The first stirrings of both Chinese entrepreneurialism and Chinese philosophy took place during the Zhou (Chou) Dynasty. The Chinese state and creed, however, would be much less sympathetic to capitalism than the Indian. Nevertheless, entrepreneurial capitalism would flourish in a China in which either the state or the kin-group would be the fount of trust and authority, while temples or other forms of private and voluntary associations would have little importance.

Because China was a land of the concrete in contrast to India, a land of the abstract, Chinese historians such as Panku (P'an Ku) were able to record the lives of early Chinese merchants. Long-term planning in business enterprise was taught in the 5th century BCE by Chiyüan (Chi Yüan), who likened it to wise strategy in preparing for war. A ruler had to create wealth and power for his kingdom, making boats in time of drought, and wagons in time of flood: 'To anticipate what the future holds and act accordingly is the soundest principle underlying all rules.'[12]

Fanli (Fan Li), a compatriot of Chiyüan traded in Shandong (Shantung), where goods from all over China changed hands. Fanli, says Panku:

> 'bought, hoarded, or sold, depending upon the time and the circumstances. He relied on his own judgement and would not blame others whatever the result. Moreover, as a businessman of unusual ability, he knew whom he should entrust with responsibility and at what time he should buy or sell.'[13]

He accumulated 300 pieces of gold in two decades of trading, most of which he gave to his brothers and poor friends. The business, inherited by his children and grandchildren, eventually was worth tens of thousands of gold coins in assets.[14] Paikui (Pai Kuei) followed commodity prices carefully, buying when others sold and selling when others bought. He was not one for conspicuous consumption in food, clothing or other luxuries and lived no better than his workers or servants. When a profit-making opportunity arose, however, Paikui traded as if he were fighting a battle, setting an example for many later entrepreneurs:

> 'If a man is not intelligent enough to change with the circumstances, brave enough to make sudden and drastic decisions, benevolent enough to give whenever it is wise to give, or persevering enough to hold to what he believes to be sound and correct, he should not go into my field, the field of business.'[15]

The Chinese entrepreneur was as disturbing to the aristocratic ethic of Confucius as his Greek counterpart would later be to Plato. Confucius

MINTZBERG ON MANAGEMENT *CIRCA* 5TH CENTURY BCE

INTENDED AND EMERGENT STRATEGIES

ONE of today's best-known management gurus is McGill University's Henry Mintzberg. Right from the start he has been one of those academics who challenge conventional thinking. In his Ph.D. at MIT he followed around management to see what they actually did; the theory of the day was that they spent most of their time planning and thinking through strategies to take their organizations forward. What he found was far from what the textbook taught. Managers' days were filled with interruptions, were about firefighting and often consisted of short meetings in hallways.

From this early work Mintzberg went on to develop the important idea of emergent strategies. Much of strategic planning occurs in away weekends where executives gather and spend a concentrated two or three days working with a consultant to develop the long-term plan for the organization. The result is a three-ring binder that inevitably ends up on a shelf in the CEO's office and is never consulted again. One MBA student at Cambridge related how at one company he worked at someone had put a $100 bill in one such place and when they checked a year later it was still safely nestled in place! This type of corporate planning effort is what Mintzberg calls an intended strategy. The point he makes is that rarely, if indeed ever, does the strategy outlined in the three-ring binder come to pass. Events and competitors simply overrun the pretty diagrams and well-laid-out plans. He argues that a more realistic world-view of strategic planning is one in which strategy emerges out of the competitive day-to-day fray of the marketplace. It is the executive who is in the line of fire and who is intimately involved in the organization who develops the best strategy, not in an away weekend with a McKinsey consultant team, but on the run and in the heat of the battle. This is emergent strategy, strategy that comes from responding to opportunities and events.

In this chapter we have seen that these ideas of intended and emergent strategies are not new ideas. A proponent of planning was Chiyüan (Chi Yüan), who likened it to wise strategy in preparing for war. A ruler had to create wealth and power for his kingdom, making boats in time of drought and wagons in time of flood: 'To anticipate what the future holds and act accordingly is the soundest principle underlying all rules.'[17] In contrast, one of his contemporaries, Paikui (Pai Kuei), a highly successful Chinese business person of the 5th century BCE, captured well the idea of an emergent strategy: 'If a man is not intelligent enough to change with the circumstances, brave enough to make sudden and drastic decisions … or persevering enough to hold to what he believes to be sound and correct, he should not go into my field, the field of business.[18]

(551–479 BCE) enshrined duty, loyalty to family, self-restraint and unselfish public service, collectivist ideals that did not mesh well with the individualistic ethic of the entrepreneur: 'The gentleman understands integrity; the petty person knows about profit.' Taken to an extreme, Confucian ideals were downright anti-capitalist, even mandating that one sink into poverty to uphold them, something no Indian Brahmin would dream of. Kinship ties were even stronger in China than in Rome.[16]

Confucianism existed in creative tension with the older Daoist (Taoist) thought of Laozi (Lao-tze). The Daoist Zhuangzi (Chuang Tzu) ridiculed Confucianism as impractical altruism in the face of the realities of self-interest and the natural order. Would a sacred turtle, he once asked, rather be mummified and honoured or be dragging its tail through the mud? When one warlord boasted of his many virtuous Confucians, Zhuangzi suggested he execute anyone wearing Confucian garb who did not practise what he preached. Soon no one wore it. While Daoists were seldom acquisitive, their ideas of natural law would buttress the spirit of Chinese capitalism and even eventually inspire the French thinker François Quesnay and, through him, Adam Smith.

Zukong (Tz'u-Kung), a personal disciple of Confucius, illustrated the evolving debate between Chinese socialism and Chinese capitalism. A bureaucrat in the state of Wei, Zukong turned to money-making, enriching himself while other Confucian disciples starved in the gutter. Zukong owned scores of chariots and bestowed money and silk upon nobles. Confucius, though, was appalled: 'Is Hui [Yen Yuan] not close to being a sage even though he has little to eat? ... As for Tz'u, he has not followed what I taught. Whether he buys or sells, he always manages to realise the largest profit.'[19]

> Shi Huangdi was the Mao Zedong of his day, complete with Cultural Revolution

The Age of the Warring Kingdoms in which this debate took place was followed in 221 BCE by the unification of China under the fierce Qin (Ch'in) ruler Shi Huandti (Shih Huang-ti). Shi Huandti was the Mao Zedong of his day, complete with Cultural Revolution.

He smashed the warlords and linked China together with military roads, bureaucracy and standard weights and measures. His armies challenged the Huns and the Vietnamese. He erected the famous Great Wall, stretching 1600 kilometres from Gansu (Kansu) to the Pacific, at the cost of a million lives. In his war on China's traditions this revolutionary tried to standardize thought as he punished dissent by mutilation, slavery, burying and boiling alive, and dismemberment by chariots. Books were burned or hidden in official libraries and scores of Confucians were executed and laid in mass graves.

Sima Qian: China's Adam Smith

After Shi Huangdi's death China underwent a period of partial reform not unlike that under Deng Xiaoping. Under four centuries of Han rulers (save one interlude), the material achievements of the Qin were retained, their excesses were denounced, and Confucianism was made the state creed. Totalitarianism had created a new infrastructure but overall was bad for business.

Despite their Confucian orthodoxy, the Han were good for business. Products flowed back and forth between east and west and from the Yellow River to the Yangzi. The mountainous area of Shaanxi and Shanxi in the west produced lumber, bamboo, grain, hemp, flax and jade, served as grazing for horses, sheep and oxen, and was covered with hundreds of kilometres of copper and iron mines. Far away to the east, the Shandong coast was a source of fish, salt, lacquer and silk. To the south, the Yangzi valley produced cedar, gold, silver, lead and sandstone. The exchange of these products was an absolute necessity:

> In a climate of market reform, the Daoist Sima Qian articulated a primitive form of the philosophy of *The Wealth of Nations.* Who would grow China's food, make her tools, import or mine gold and silver for her coins, or obtain pearls and jade for her luxuries if everyone was a gentleman?

> *'All these products the Chinese love dearly. They are the materials for their food and clothing ... farmers raise crops; the miners bring forth minerals; the artisans fashion into articles what others have produced; and the merchants move raw materials as well as finished products to the market.'*[20]

In a climate of market reform, the Daoist Sima Qian articulated a primitive form of the philosophy of *The Wealth of Nations.* Who would grow China's food, make her tools, import or mine gold and silver for her coins, or obtain pearls and jade for her luxuries if everyone was a gentleman?

*'These activities have gone on and will continue to go on with or
without a government, and each person will do his very best to
obtain what he desires ... Each man ... seeks profits as water seeks
the lowest ground ... Wherever profit is, he does not wait for an
invitation, and he produces even though nobody has asked him to do
so. Does this situation not conform well to the principles of Tao? Is
it not a vindication of the soundness of the "naturalist" theory?'[21]*

Seeing as the producers – farmers, miners, craftsmen and merchants –
were essential to Chinese life, it was vital that they be given every
incentive to produce and earn a profit rather than conform to the
standards of the mandarin:

*'Under the circumstances the best thing to do is to leave people the
way they are, and the next best is to channel their materialistic
desires through reason. Less desirable is to educate them so that they
will reduce or lose such desires, and worse still, to use coercion to
achieve the same purpose. Of all the possible courses to take, the
worst the government can do is to join the people and compete with
them for material gains.'[22]*

Entrepreneurial capitalism had come to stay in China by the 3rd
century BCE. In the following century its trading contacts would, for the
first time, reach the West.

Carthage: African *keiretsu*

The Near Eastern model of management continued to thrive in the
western as well as the eastern Mediterranean. Left to their own devices
following the defeat of Tyre, the western outposts of Tyre gravitated to
the leadership of Carthage. From 550 BCE on, the Tyrian factories and
trading posts of Sardinia, Sicily and Malta, and even the mines of Spain,
became the foundation of Carthaginian economic power. The Phoenician
civilization became a Punic one.

In contrast to the individualistic capitalism of Athens, that of Carthage
was a direct inheritance from the temple-based naval capitalism of Tyre.
Carthaginian merchant-princes were sailors, managers, shippers and
fanatical devotees of both Melqart and the new deity Baal-Hammon. One
vast difference between Carthage and Tyre remained, and that was the

enormous role played by agriculture. Punic business leaders were often landowners as well. North Africa would, along with Egypt, become the granary of the Mediterranean world. While Greek traders peddled what the market dictated, Punic merchants specialized in bulk shipments of wheat, gold, incense, iron, copper, or African animals and dates.

As in Ugarit and Tyre, Punic enterprises such as mining and shipbuilding were run by a hereditary elite, which had strong political connections. As in some modern Asian systems, belonging to a rich family was a prerequisite for political power in a system ruled by a tight clique of princes and traders.

Mines, arms, factories and shipyards were state-run and capable of building 120 warships in a matter of two months. Gods, goddesses, priests and temples here were far more important economically than in Athens or the rising city of Rome. Temples were managed by a state board of notables and priests chosen from ruling families. Arms workshops flourished on temple land, and some temples, such as those of Eshmun, Reshef, Baal-Hammon and Melqart, were rich enough to own and manage entire communities.

How did the organized Punic economy work? The major centres were not independent communities on the Hellenic model but important nerve centres in a centrally directed system. No independent trader could finance such an enterprise; only the Carthaginian elite and state could do so. Every May convoys of galleys left Carthage and sailed east to Tyre and Sidon, no longer their masters but still their links to the markets of Asia. They then returned via Egypt and Libya, there to stock up on the goods of Africa. Other vessels sailed north from Carthage to Sardinia, Sicily and the Etruscan realm of Italy, with some vessels branching off to reach the Balearic Islands, the eastern coast of Spain and, eventually, Cadiz and Lixus in Morocco.

Having much to lose from market failure, the aristocratic managers of Carthage internalized their business organization under the protection of their admirals. With Greek and other pirates lurking along their arteries, the trading operations of the Punic Silver Fleet had to be well organized and planned. All Mediterranean routes had to be protected at the same time. Galleys were manned with marines and large warships made massive sweeps against pirates.[23]

Major trading operations under Punic 'maritime capitalism' assumed the form of a seaborne military campaign. This annual campaign affected the rhythms of everyday life in Carthage. Peasants who tilled the fields of Africa annually sent 24 000 of their number, once the spring planting was done, to row some 200 triremes. Returning from Spain or Tyre they would be back on their lords' estates in time for the autumn harvest. With an estimated population of 300 000, some 60 000 soldiers, sailors and marines were involved in these operations. This system of militarized commerce, which no freedom-loving Athenian would put up with, was destined to work fairly well in times of peace or brief war. Longer-term conflicts, though, strained the system. The huge apparatus and the largely agrarian economy that supported it became overstretched if full mobilization lasted more than two months, compelling Carthage to win wars quickly or obtain a compromise of peace.[24]

Carthage attained the peak of her power in the 300s BCE. Having failed to wrest control of all of Sicily from the Greeks, Carthage became an African as well as a Mediterranean power. Greeks were driven out of western Libya, and the Berbers of Tunisia, Algeria and Morocco were subjugated by the Carthaginian feudal system. Punic bases were beefed up in Malta and Sardinia and extended along the shores of Tunisia, Algeria and Libya. Leptis in Libya became the branch office in charge of trade in gold, ivory and animals from deep inside Africa. Caravans of Libyans on horseback crossed the Sahara to the south and west, working their way to the gold fields and ivory markets of Guinea and Niger. Inland posts and routes also reached overland to Egypt, well inland from the Greek Cyrenaica.[25]

Carthage also reached the gold and ivory of West Africa far west from Lixus in Morocco via the Atlantic. The most famous case of Punic market-seeking behaviour is recorded in the *Periplus of Hanno*, discovered in the ruins of Carthage by a Roman historian. Prince Hanno sent a massive fleet of triremes manned by 30 000 personnel down the African Atlantic coast. We do not know how far south he sailed, for the Punic business establishment may have doctored the account to confuse foreign readers and protect valuable market information. African markets this far south, however, could better be exploited on a smaller scale by traders who could come ashore or via the overland routes working through Libya.[26]

Himlico, possibly Hanno's brother, sailed another fleet up the Atlantic shore from Cadiz as far as Britain. Himlico's voyage was intended to establish direct access to the tin mines of Brittany and Cornwall. Given the huge growth in the Punic bronze industry in the 4th–3rd centuries

BCE and the intensity of Greek–Punic rivalry, it is logical to assume that the old Iberian tin trade down the Atlantic shore was now managed by Carthaginian executives based in Cadiz.[27]

Given their ability to monopolize access to and knowledge of the Atlantic, the merchants of Carthage based in Cadiz barred Greeks, Etruscans and Romans from passing through the Pillars of Hercules.[28] They were not always successful. One Roman captain posed as an ally and took his ship right into Cadiz. Having his own industrial spies he then shadowed a Carthaginian ship setting sail for the Tin Isles. Realising what was happening, the Punic skipper scuttled his ship on the Atlantic shore. In 310 BCE a Greek named Pytheas ran the Pillars of Hercules, sailing all the way into the North Sea, from which the Punic navy had excluded all competition: 'Never before had any Western navigator been able to sail so far north; Carthaginian commercial interests would not permit it.'[29] Looking for the mysterious Tin Islands, Pytheas also discovered that the North Star and Little Dipper were much higher in the sky than they were in the Mediterranean. This hinted to both Hellenic and Punic mathematicians that the earth itself was round![30]

Rome: family ties and the birth of 'legionary capitalism'

The rise of kingdoms in central Italy and their eventual unification by Rome was stimulated by the spread of the Iron Age and the Hellenic market economy to the boot-shaped peninsula. Both Etruscans and Latins emerge into history around 900 BCE. From 760 BCE Etruscan burials at Veii show the increased use of iron technology in the form of helmets, shields, swords and chariots. It is certain that the stimulus provided by the Greek presence in Pithekoussai accelerated the development of the Iron Age in Italy.[31]

> Roman life was, even then, based on an extended family and a powerful clan or *gens* system

Latin entrepreneurship was more family-oriented than its Greek counterpart and was differently shaped by geography. The vast ranges and poor soil of Greece reinforced the independence of the many *poleis* and their generally peaceful overseas expansion. The Apennines, in contrast, permitted Italians better overland communication and political unity, while the rich volcanic soil along the central Italian coastal plains of Latium and Campania became the prize over which many armies would fight. Romans held and gained farmland by overland military invasion instead of overseas expansion. Rome would live by the sword or face quick extinction.[32]

Rome before 700 BCE was a local trading centre at the junction of the Tiber and the roads leading between Campania and Etruria. Artefacts in Latin cemeteries hint at the business culture to come. Most bodies are buried without distinction, save for a few spears and swords interred with the better off. Roman life was, even then, based on an extended family and a powerful clan or *gens* system in which the values of a warrior society would be paramount.[33]

By 600, Rome was the largest fortified city in Latium, with a 'Spartan' warrior ethic. The political system of the Roman Republic, erected after 509 BCE, reflected and legitimized the warlike and familial character of Roman society. Rome's patrician oligarchy replaced monarchy not with a single tyrant but with a pair of elected *consuls*. The seeds of empire were present even then in the ability of a consul to assume unlimited emergency powers as *dictator* for six months. The ruling Senate represented landed patricians, and elected *tribunes* the plebeian orders of farmers, labourers and artisans. Business managers would one day emerge from the *equestrian* knights wealthy enough to fight on horseback.

Roman law was based upon the Twelve Tables of 450 BCE. This founding document of Latin jurisprudence enshrined limited government in the economic sphere, self-help and the all-important patriarchal extended *familia*.[34] The latter included all the slaves and dependents subject to the *pater-familias*. With no state to protect them, the weak sought inclusion in a powerful *familia*. Family property and enterprise were thus enshrined in Roman law far more than in Greek. The patriarch had the right of life and death over his extended family and, in return, was responsible for each of their actions.

> Roman law was based upon the Twelve Tables of 450 BCE. This founding document of Latin jurisprudence enshrined limited government in the economic sphere, self-help and the all-important patriarchal extended *familia*

As for the Roman state, it maintained a *laissez-faire* attitude to trading matters at sharp odds with that adopted by the merchant-princes of the Near East. Greek, Etruscan and Oriental traders in Rome were not excluded, regulated or taxed when they imported pottery from Attica or plied their trades of carpenter, smith, tanner, dyer and potter alongside their Roman counterparts.

To free markets and family patriarchy must be added expansionist militarism. Beginning in the mid-300s BCE the Roman Republic entered an era of constant warfare, during most of which Romans occupied themselves in search of land and booty.[35] The legions crushed one foe after another. Southern Etruria was subdued by 350, the Romans deporting many of the inhabitants, expropriating the farmlands, bypassing the centres with new roads, and occupying the coasts with Roman colonies like Cosa, future home of the Sestii, in order to cut off Etruscan centres like Caere, Tarquinia, Vulci and Populonia from their markets. The Etruscans, dying a slow death due to economic strangulation, eventually succumbed to Romanization.[36]

Rome's Latin rivals were subordinated in the Latin War of 340–338 BCE. The future political structure of the empire was now already present in embryo. Some states were annexed to Rome, others made protectorates or Roman allies. By allowing them to share in the spoils of future wars, Rome added their power to her own, integrating and Latinising first Italians, then Iberians, Africans, Greeks, Macedonians, Anatolians, Syrians, Gauls, Britons, Germans and Illyrians.[37]

Next came the warlike Samnites, followed by the Greeks in southern Italy. Three million people were now subject to Roman rule. Fifteen military colonies were founded between 334 and 263, as Rome could now call on an army of 60 000, twice the size of Alexander's.[38] The very face of Italy was transformed by the economics of the sword. Many Latin farmers sank into debt, but many others developed a vested interest in war, settling on conquered land that the Republic awarded them for their service. The private farm gave way to the patriarchal villas of Campania and other regions worked by thousands of Samnite, Etruscan and other slaves. Rome in the 300s became a slave-owning society.[39] Roman territory as a whole became more urbanized, the Roman countryside less populated: developments that would favour the growth of Roman business by concentrating capital and productivity.[40]

Between 350 and 250 BCE the city of Rome grew from 30 000 to 100 000 (she would eventually boast *one million* by the time of the empire). Roman maritime activity and trade became reality as a result of the wars of conquest. Rome built a small navy and exported her own pottery around the western Mediterranean. The first Roman coins bore the images of the

Roman military ethic: Mars, god of war, winged Victory, horses, or a laurel-crowned Apollo. These new coins were a declaration that the rulers of Rome now claimed enough power and prestige to consider themselves in the same league with the rulers of Carthage, Seleucia, Egypt and the other Hellenistic states. Rome would now challenge those states one by one, beginning with the formidable power of Carthage.[41]

Business cultures in total war: Rome versus Carthage

From 264 to 146 BCE Rome and Carthage fought each other in a series of wars not to be equalled in ferocity until modern times. These wars would utterly destroy Carthage while making Rome a world military *and commercial* power. Vast legions and fleets would become central to Roman life, paving the way for civil war and permanent dictatorship. The wars also would provide an enormous encouragement to a Roman capitalism that remained forever indebted to the legions and their wars for its full development.

War began over control of the strategic granary of Sicily, coveted by every power in the Mediterranean. Her previous enemies all having been land powers like herself, Rome now faced a seagoing foe that seemed to have enormous advantages. Carthage had resources, an advanced and internalized commercial system and an incomparable navy. Rome could only rely on the bravery and quality of her soldiers, her civic ideals and the adaptability of her generals and her entrepreneurs. In the end, these were enough to dethrone the Punic colossus.

The Carthaginians fought as mercenaries, the Romans as citizen-soldiers and citizen-sailors. Behind the warriors were the rising new Italian entrepreneurs, who overnight built a huge fleet of warships from nothing, working from a captured Carthaginian prototype. A culture in which independent enterprise and risk-taking were tolerated and encouraged could adapt itself easily to the task of not only copying but improving upon Carthaginian designs. This triumph of Roman entrepreneurship was recorded by Polybius:

> 'It was, therefore, because they saw that the war was dragging on that they first applied themselves to building ships ... [T]heir shipwrights

were completely inexperienced ... since these vessels had never before been employed in Italy. Yet it is this fact which illustrates better than any other the extraordinary spirit and audacity of the Romans' decision. It was not a question of having adequate resources for the enterprise, for they had in fact none whatsoever, nor had they ever given a thought to the sea before this. But once they had conceived the idea, they embarked on it so boldly that without waiting to gain any experience in naval warfare they immediately engaged the Carthaginians, who had for generations enjoyed an unchallenged supremacy at sea.'[42]

The Romans knew they were no match for Carthage's seasoned mariners, so their engineers turned the war at sea into a war of armies. Roman warships were fitted with an iron 'crow's beak', which they dropped on to the decks of the Punic vessels. Before the Carthaginian sailors knew what was happening, they were overwhelmed by nearly invincible Roman soldiers swarming over their ships. The First Punic War ended in 241 in a victory sealed by Roman capitalism. Rome was now a naval power, and one that held overseas interests for the first time, inheriting the Tyrian bastions of Sardinia and Sicily.[43]

With Sicily and Sardinia gone, Carthage prepared for the second round by entrenching its *keiretsu*-like system in Spain, now utterly essential to the Punic economy as a source of gold, copper, iron and silver. Ruling from Cartagena, the family of Hamilcar Barca (237–229 BCE), whose line included the famous Hannibal, continued the tradition of managed Punic enterprise. Vast amounts of gold and silver were extracted from mines extending from Rio Tinto in the west to newer sites such as Baebelo in the east. With these resources, Hannibal was able to hire a mercenary army claimed at 90 000 infantry and 12 000 cavalry, and a fleet of 50 warships, although those figures were slightly exaggerated. Many Iberians joined this army, not out of national feeling, but from a combination of financial motives and a strong sense of personal loyalty to the Barcids.[44]

War resumed when Hannibal's army, financed by an Iberian-based business network dating back to Tyrian times, crossed the Alps. Smashing one legion after another, Hannibal devastated Roman Italy, but the Romans under Scipio Africanus choked off his supplies and invaded Africa. Once again, Carthage's defeat was that of her business establishment. She lost Spain, and would soon lose her existence in a third and final war in 146 BCE.[45]

HANNIBAL AND THE BARCIDS

PUNIC ENTERPRISE

THE famous victories of the Carthaginian general Hannibal, who almost conquered Rome, might have established European civilization on a Near Eastern rather than a classical Latin foundation. Hannibal's power was made possible by the financial power of his family, the Barcids, who became the richest businesspeople in the realm of Carthage.

Following their defeat by Rome in the First Punic War, which ended in 241 BCE, the merchant oligarchy ruling Carthage, having lost Sardinia and Sicily, sought to consolidate its rule over Spain. The region was now indispensable to them not only for its foodstuffs but also for its valuable mines of gold and silver.

General Hamilcar Barca (237–229 BCE) marched into Spain to impose direct Punic rule on the inhabitants for the first time. Setting himself up as absolute ruler in what is now Cartagena, Hamilcar was soon succeeded by his son Hasdrubal in 229 BCE. Hannibal took over in 221.

The mines of Punic Spain were under direct Barcid supervision and even ownership. They no doubt continued the tradition of highly managed trade that was a hallmark of Carthaginian capitalism. Arsenals were state-run, as were many of the shipyards. Convoys carrying silver and wheat were well organized and co-ordinated by the Punic admirals. Temples, fleets and other public authorities underwrote the costs of doing business. Hannibal had resources such as these at his disposal when war with Rome was renewed. Able to hire an army that may have had as many as 90 000 men, plus 50 warships and large numbers of elephants, Hannibal marched over the Alps and into Italy, destroying both Roman legions and farms. Like many another commander throughout history, though, he failed in the end because he suffered from inadequate logistics. He could not supply his forces, allowing the Romans to neutralize his forces and achieve victory by invading Africa.

In the same year as Carthage was destroyed, Roman legions marching into Greece also destroyed Corinth. The western half of the Hellenistic world was soon destined to fall to Rome and that east of the Euphrates to the rising new power of Parthia. Far to the east and north, the armies of the Han Emperor Wudi (Wu-ti) were advancing deep into Central Asia, bringing the valued silk of the Orient. A world economy was in the making.

NOTES TO CHAPTER 7

1. Hanson, V.D. (1995) *The Other Greeks: the Family Farm and the Agrarian Roots of Western Civilization*. New York: The Free Press, 33–5.
2. Heichelheim, F.M. (1965) *An Ancient Economic History from the Palaeolithic Age to the Migrations of the Germanic, Slavic and Arabic Nations*, tr. Stevens, J., Leyden, Netherlands: A.W. Sithoff, 9.
3. *Ibid.*, 283–5.
4. *Ibid.*, 284–5.
5. *Ibid.*
6. 'For Success in Trade' in *Atharva Veda*, Book III, Hymn 15.1,4,6 from *Atharva-Veda Samhita*, tr. Whitney, W.D. (1905) *Harvard Oriental Series*, Vol. 7, Cambridge, MA: Harvard University Press, in McNeill, W. and Sedlar, J.W., eds. (1969) *Classical India*. New York: Oxford University Press, 10–11.
7. From the 'Arthashastra of Kautilya', Chapter 6 from (1962) *Essentials of Indian Statecraft Kautilya's Arthashastra for Contemporary Readers*, tr. Ramaswamy T.N. Bombay: Asia Publishing House, reprinted in McNeill and Sedlar, 19–20.
8. *Idem*, Chapter 31, in McNeill and Sedlar, 29–31, xxxi.
9. Casson, L. (1964) *The Ancient Mariners: Seafarers and Sea Fighters of the Mediterranean in Ancient Times*. New York: Macmillan, 186.
10. *Ibid.*, 185–7.
11. *Ibid.*, 178–9.
12. Panku 'The Merchants', 'Biographies of Merchants and Industrialists' in *Han shu*, roll 91, document 133, quoted in Li, D.J., ed. (1967) *The Essence of Chinese Civilization*. Princeton, NJ: D. Van Nostrand, 317.
13. *Ibid.*
14. *Ibid.*
15. *Ibid.*, 318.
16. Confucius 'The Gentleman', from the *Analects*, tr. Coyle, M. in Ebrey, P.B., ed. (1981) *Chinese Civilization and Society, a Sourcebook*. New York: Free Press, 13–14.
17. See note 12.
18. See note 15.
19. Confucius quoted in Panku 'The Merchants', 'Biographies of Merchants and Industrialists' in *Han shu*, roll 91, Li, document 133, Li, 317.

20. Ssu-ma Chien 'An Introduction to Economics' from 'Biographies of Merchants and Industrialists' in *Shih chi*, roll 129, in Li, document 132, 314–16, 315.
21. *Ibid.*, 315.
22. *Ibid.*, 314.
23. Demerliac, J.G. and Meirat, J. (1983) *Hannon et l'empire punique*. Paris: Les Belles Lettres, 194–8.
24. *Ibid.*, 202–5; '... as with any organization, this system had its advantages and its inconveniences ... thanks to it the Punic metropolis was able to mobilise, in a very brief time, in case of war, a force that was powerful and maintained in a very high degree of training and cohesion.'
25. *Ibid.*, 91–5; Tlatli, S.E. (1978) *La Carthage punique: étude urbaine, la ville. Ses fonctions. Son rayonnement*. Preface by Klibi, C. and Charles-Picard, G. Paris: Librairie d'Amérique et d'Orient, 241–5.
26. Soren, D. *et al.* (1990) *Carthage, Uncovering the Mysteries and Splendors of Ancient Tunisia*. New York: Simon and Schuster, 68–72. Hanno 'may simply have overreached his capabilities. To establish a far-flung network of colonies required a powerful support system, which he couldn't deliver' (*Ibid.*, 72).
27. *Ibid.*, 73; Fell, B. (1980) *Saga America*. New York: Quadrangle, 51–2.
28. Soren *et al.*, 74.
29. *Ibid.*, 60.
30. *Ibid.*
31. *Ibid.*, 302.
32. The geography of the Italian peninsula would help shape a very different history here from that of Greece. While the rugged mountains of Greece almost totally prevented overland communication and conquest, the mountainous geography of Italy encouraged her peoples to turn inward, not outward. Italy had few good natural harbours and a somewhat larger supply of good farmland, especially in the vicinity of Latium. These factors encouraged the Romans to expand overland instead of overseas prior to the 3rd century BCE. (Freeman, C. (1996) *Egypt, Greece, and Rome: Civilizations of the Ancient Mediterranean*. Oxford: Oxford University Press, 307.)
33. The early Latins named themselves, not after their cities like the Greeks (e.g. Plato of Athens), but after their *gentes* (clans). Latins would first give the personal *praenomen*, or first name, then the *nomen*, or clan-name (Freeman, 302). The 30 communities of the Latium plain were more ecumenical than the rather xenophobic Greek states. Having a common Latin culture they permitted any Latin gentile from any of their clans to share rights of marriage, citizenship and trade with members of any other Latin clan. (*Ibid.*, 308–9.)
34. Drummond, A. 'Rome in the Fifth Century, I: the Social and Economic Framework', in Walbank, F.W. *et al*, eds., *The Cambridge Ancient History*, 2nd edn., Vol.VII, Part 2 and (1990) *The Rise of Rome to 220 BC*. Cambridge: Cambridge University Press, 144–5.

35. Rich, J. (1995) 'Fear, Greed and Glory: the Causes of Roman War-Making in the Middle Republic' in Shipley, J. and G., eds., *War and Society in the Roman World*. London: Routledge, 44–6. 'The habit of constant war was as old as the Republic' (*ibid.*, 45).
36. *Ibid.*, 262–75.
37. Cornell, T.J. (1995) *The Beginnings of Rome: Italy and Rome from the Bronze Age to the Punic Wars (c. 1000–264 BC)*. London: Routledge, 348–9.
38. *Ibid.*, 380.
39. *Ibid.*, 333, 394–5.
40. *Ibid.*, 394.
41. *Ibid.*, 394–8.
42. *Ibid.*, 62.
43. Lazenby, J.F. (1996) *The First Punic War: A Military History*. Stanford CA: Stanford University Press, 61–80 tells the story of the Roman triumph at sea.
44. Scullard, H.H. 'The Carthaginians in Spain' in Astin, A.E. *et al.*, eds., *The Cambridge Ancient History*, 2nd edn., Vol.VIII (1989) *Rome and the Mediterranean to 133 BC*. Cambridge: Cambridge University Press, 20–43.
45. Lazenby, J.F. (1998) *Hannibal's War: A Military History of the Second Punic War* (Norman, OK: University of Oklahoma Press). 57–60, 66–9, 78–86 describe Hannibal's victories and strategies against Rome. The final Roman destruction of Carthage is treated in the same work of Lazenby on pages 243–6. See also Polybius, *Histories*, iii, 20–118 in Walbank, F.W., ed. (1979) *Rise of the Roman Empire*, tr. By Scott-Kilvert, I. London: Penguin Books, 197–176.

8

Rendering unto Caesar

Roman multinationals in a world economy: 146 BCE–476 CE

I‌N 146 BCE Carthage was a ruin and Hannibal was becoming a fading memory. By the first century BCE, a single economic order would prevail from the Atlantic to the Euphrates – what men would speak of long afterwards as the *Pax Romana*, 'the Roman Peace'. The Roman Republic and Empire ensured the spread of the free-market style of business across the Western world. In spite of this, vertically organized multinational enterprises, both public and private, existed in the Roman world to a greater extent than in classical Greece.

Many Roman enterprises possessed a familial character unknown in Greece. The large publican partnerships operated by Roman knights engaged in mass production, and even embodied an early form of limited liability. In this dynamic pairing of individual and integrated enterprise we first dimly recognize the form of future Western business culture.

Rome's total victory over Carthage had not made her the supreme Occidental power but gave her a full-fledged Latin commercial establishment. By 200 BCE, Rome's distinctive business culture was fully formed. Greek enterprise was grafted on to the extended Italian family structure, and Roman markets sprang less from free trade than from demand stimulated by incessant military expansion. The new business culture was reflected in the theatrical comedies of Titus Maccius Plautus (born *circa* 250 BCE):

> *Husbands gambling their fortunes away? Try*
> *the Stock Exchange. You'll know it by the callgirls*
> *waiting outside. You can pick up anyone*
> *You want to, at a price ...*
> *In the lower Forum*

You'll find the respectable bourgeois
taking their daily stroll ...
Below the old shops are the moneylenders,
The con-men behind the Temple of Castor,
The Tuscan Quarter is the red light district
Where you can make a living, one way or the other.[1]

The money that was beginning to talk so loudly in Roman life flowed from Rome's spreading ventures abroad as a *world*, not just a regional power. The legions marching into Africa, Iberia, Macedonia, Greece and eventually across Anatolia, Syria, Mesopotamia, Palestine, Egypt, Gaul, Germany and Britain vastly extended the market for Roman industry, trade and investment.

Rome's publican multinationals

Creation of a market encompassing the Mediterranean Basin and the lucrative contracts needed to sustain the legions encouraged the growth of enterprise on a much larger scale than that in Greece. Roman entre-preneurs began to expand the size of their partnerships, chief of which were the publican companies. These were giant partnerships, often family-based, which bid on government contracts to arm and equip the legions with clothing, shields, helmets and other weapons.

Apart from agriculture, war became Rome's biggest business. Some contracts were enormous. The legions grew from four to twenty during the Punic Wars and then settled at a permanent force of eight or nine – an army of close to 50 000 men. It cost three million *denarii*, or £20–40 million, just to clothe them. Even if the profit margins on military contracts were small, their sheer volume ensured a rich market for the *publicani*.[2]

The publican firms were formed as large partnerships that did not specialise in any given business endeavour. A given firm could farm taxes, make swords or build roads at different times. Their management and workforce were highly flexible: groups of partners would come together to carry out a contract and then disband. Lean and adaptable in the face of fierce market competition, they could afford little permanent staff. Permanent, organized staffs of skilled miners, tax professionals, arms makers, shipbuilders and others did, on the other hand, exist and these were likely to be bought and sold by the publican managers as they shifted from contract to contract.

Without formal corporation law, publicans were the first recorded examples of limited-liability corporations, considered to have a legal existence of their own if the firm's *manceps*, or CEO, were to die.

The *socii*, or partners, represented the shareholders and board of directors of the combined capital and expertise of the firm. Real executive power lay in the hands of the *magistri*. Beneath them lay the company's *decuriae*, or divisions, headed by other Roman knights of the Equestrian Order. The familial and other personal links among these knights ensured that the executives of the Roman firms, even while competing for the same contracts, were all part of a single network. At least in the last century of the Republic, 'The ties among all the companies were particularly close, so as to constitute a cartel.'[3]

> Without formal corporation law, publicans were the first recorded examples of limited-liability corporations, considered to have a legal existence of their own if the firm's *manceps*, or CEO, were to die

A publican company based in Rome, Campania or Tarentum operated through agents in places such as Delos, Pergamum, Ephesus, Laodicea, Alexandria, Massilia, Gades, Athens and Carthage. These officers, known as *promagistri*, represented the *socii* of the Italian firm in its overseas transactions and investments. *Promagistri* were not independent middleman contractors but full-paid employees of the Roman company in charge of keeping accounts, collecting taxes and sending reports to the *magistri* in Rome.

One such branch manager was Cicero's close friend Terentius Hispo, whose firm, one of Rome's biggest, held revenue contracts for Bithynia and Asia and supervized tens of thousands of employees. *Promagistri* such as Hispo held mandates not only for taxes and military procurement, but often for mail delivery as well. Banking was another function assumed by publicans in the century in which they dominated Roman commerce.[4]

Gnaeus Plancius was another in a long line of Roman executives defended by Cicero, who aligned himself in defence of property and against those such as Julius Caesar who appealed to the debt-ridden classes. The stiffness of competition for tax contracts caused Plancius and other managers in Bithynia, Asia and Cilicia to form a tight-knit cartel among the publican firms capable of monopolising tax collection in the Asian regions.[5]

Between 70 and 64 BCE, the Roman commander and rival of Julius Caesar, Gnaeus Pompeius Magnus, added Syria and Judaea to the Roman domain, bringing huge new markets and revenues for risk-taking publicans. Many made overnight fortunes, but rampant speculation soon led to a crash. The *socii* responded to such market problems in the same way Andrew Carnegie, J.P. Morgan and John D. Rockefeller did, with further association and internalization of their transactions in the next two years. 'We find', according to Professor Badian, 'companies getting together into a cartel ... and it seems to have been done quite openly and officially.'[6]

The Bithynian firm of Terentius Hispo formed an arrangement with an Ephesian firm to farm the grazing tax of both Asia and Bithynia. Taxes in Cilicia were probably farmed by another firm also closely linked to Cicero. The agricultural tithes of Bithynia, meanwhile, were collected by a consortium of companies linked to Pompey himself. At least in the realm of tax collection, cartelization in the most prosperous overseas region of the Roman world had supplanted the Hellenic

> The Roman firm based itself upon partnership and informal relationships between knights, freedmen, slaves and even senators

market economy. This was a significant step in which the companies 'got together, formed a joint company for the exploitation of the chief Bithynian tax, and ... [did] away with genuine competition.'[7]

Roman law allowed big companies such as this to grow. The Roman firm based itself upon partnership and informal relationships between knights, freedmen, slaves and even senators. It embodied the extended family as expressed in Roman society and law, representing, according to Professor John H. D'Arms

> *'the fundamental Roman social unit, the familia, enlarged and extended to perform functions far more complex than fulfilment of domestic needs. One such interconnecting web of relationships, among men of varied levels of rank and status, of varying degrees of closeness, and involving various types of expectations and obligations, the Romans knew as clientela'.*[8]

Roman knights at the end of the Republican period were investing everywhere, in Sicily, Africa, Gaul and, especially, Asia Minor. The Roman firms absorbed and incorporated the personnel, labour and capital of the older business cultures of the regions they entered. Many of the ships that bore their goods to and from Italy were made in the East, building upon Hellenic, Hellenistic and Tyrian seafaring traditions as well as Punic and Roman ones. Vessels from Alexandria, Tyre, Sidon, Cyprus, Asia Minor, Rhodes and Miletus not only supplied the navies of both sides in the Civil War but recaptured much of the eastern Mediterranean trade from southern Italian hands. Cicero himself noted that the Roman *negotiatores* (businessmen) of Asia employed Greek ships.[9]

The first European Union

The merging of business and military politics hastened the death of the Roman Republic. Having gained power and prestige through his conquest of Gaul, Julius Caesar mustered his legions and his own fleet to vanquish those of Pompey in 49 BCE. Having first championed and then betrayed the plebeian party, Caesar's aspirations to a *permanent dictatorship* quickly roused the ire of the Senate, whose agent, M. Junius Brutus, helped assassinate him on the Ides (15th) of March, 44 BCE.

The Ides of March were a prelude to a decisive round of civil war from which would emerge the Roman Empire. Caesar's adopted grand-nephew Octavian mustered his forces to rout the rebel fleet off Sicily in 36 BCE. Five years later he crushed the Egyptian-based forces of Mark Antony. Octavian's victories were due to the invention by his admiral, Agrippa, of grappling hooks fired from catapults, which allowed Octavian's marines to capture Brutus's and Antony's vessels.[10] Sea trade and sea combat had come a long way together.

Octavian, proclaiming himself Augustus Caesar, thus inaugurated the Roman Empire and the Pax Romana, which endured from 27 BCE to about 180 AD. Augustus and his successors presided over the further integration of a 'vigorous economic community of a size then hitherto unseen in the lands of the Mediterranean and Europe'.[11] A common currency, a coherent body of law and a well-organized infrastructure of ports and roads contributed to this integration as Rome continued to suppress piracy, establish order and control the commercial links of previous empires in Africa, the Aegean and the Orient. The torch was passed!

The Roman state played a key role in this first 'European' economy. Taxation of the rich provinces of Iberia, Asia, Syria, Egypt and Africa levied for the benefit of Italy and the frontiers compelled merchants to export. Legions in Gaul, Britain and the Near East, and by the Rhine and Danube, spent the tax-money on food, services and goods. New businesses serviced the legions, stimulating the economy from Spain to

Syria. People in the inner provinces became mass consumers and renters.[12]

The whole Roman Empire was now a single monetary economy in which the money supply in Italy, Gaul, Roman Germany, Illyria and the Near East expanded and contracted in tandem. The burden of taxation during the Pax Romana was also relatively low, taking only about one tenth of the average Roman's yearly earnings. Rome, moreover, was at that time a relatively free economy where anyone could peddle goods almost anywhere. 'Rome followed her policy of keeping all ports open to all trade,' according to Roman economic historian Tenney Frank. 'There were no monopolies, closed seas, or forbidden goods.'[13]

> With its own 'euro', the silver *denarius*, roughly equal to a day's wages (Matthew 20: 1–16), and a generally free internal market, Rome formed the original European Union

With its own 'euro', the silver *denarius*, roughly equal to a day's wages (Matthew 20: 1–16), and a generally free internal market, Rome formed the original European Union.

This union encouraged the growth of cross-border enterprises, many of which located in the city of Rome itself. Rome's one million inhabitants were a ready market for Italian and French wine, Spanish metals, Anatolian wool, Egyptian linen, Syrian glass and, as we shall see, a host of products from Africa and Far Asia.

The ports of Puteoli and Ostia became Rome's links to the world. Ostia became the centre for the Roman world's multinationals. A vast *piazza* housed the head offices of some five dozen companies, mostly headquartered in North Africa, Sardinia and Gaul. Puteoli harboured other overseas agencies, including one from Tyre. A Greek inscription from 174 CE found 'many a commercial agency in Puteoli', some of which, like the Tyrian, were part of larger internalized networks.[14]

The commercial expansion of Rome at first centred in Italy. In agriculture, the wine industry became Italy's main staple, as an economy managed by family and publican firms turned to slave labour for its manpower. Perhaps half of Roman Italy's population in the time of Augustus was servile. The peasant farm gave way to large villas clustered in the rich farm belt of Campania, Latium and Etruria in which agriculture became agribusiness and crop rotation, fertilization and irrigation immensely increased production, especially of wine, which Italian families like the Sestii exported to Gaul in large jugs called *amphorae*.

THE FIRM OF PUBLIUS SESTIUS

A ROMAN FAMILY ENTERPRISE

PUBLIUS Sestius, was one of Rome's most successful business managers. Publius inherited his wine business from his patrician father L. Sestius who, like his son, had also pursued a distinguished public career.

Publius himself entered public service in the middle of the 1st century BCE as a quaestor, an entry-level position of municipal authority. Soon, however, he rose to the office of tribune, where he was entrusted with the command of a body of soldiers. Publius used these soldiers in suppressing an uprising in Capua of conspirators loyal to the populist Catiline, who in 63 BCE had run on a platform of debt cancellation. The Sestii thus became identified in the eyes of Julius Caesar and his allies as supporters of property rights and potential enemies, an impression strengthened by his deep and close friendship with Marcus Tullius Cicero. When Caesar's minions accused Publius of corruption in a public trial in 56 BCE, the eloquent Cicero rallied to his defence, securing his unanimous acquittal.

The Sestii family firm operated for three generations from a villa on the west coast of Italy near Cosa, about 100 kilometres north of Rome. The Sestii soon grew rich from exporting the wine produced on their estates north to Gaul. Most of what we know about their trading activities has been deduced from the distribution of the big jugs, called *amphorae*, in which the Sestii shipped their wine. These jugs were trademarked with the initials SES or SEST.

Empty jugs were found near Cosa, but huge numbers of full ones have been discovered in the wrecks of ships off the French Riviera coast and others throughout southern and central France.

The discoveries, plus the accounts of his friend Cicero, point to the strong possibility that Publius and his family ran what we could call a Roman multinational. The Sestii seem to have had their own ships and hired agents in Gaul so that their wine went all the way from Cosa to their customers in Massilia (Marseilles) and Lugdunum (Lyons) in Sestian hands, with little contact with middlemen. Upon his death, Publius passed his firm to his son, L. Sestius Albianus Quirinalis, who began to diversify from wine into the selling of tiles. The building industry, booming in the time of Augustus, provided him with a new market.

SEST

SES

Mass production in antiquity

Manufacturing industries also began to prosper on a multinational pattern in the High (pre-200 CE) Empire. Roman manufacturing industry, originally small and geared to local markets, grew in scale and scope along with Roman dominion. Roman pottery, glassware, bricks, tiles, lamps and stone became humanity's first mass-production industries. They marketed such huge volumes of goods that they had to rely upon agents and middlemen.

Brick and tile industries were often integrated into the life and activity of villas. Potters got together in large partnerships, sometimes 200 or more, and shared the same kilns under the supervision of a joint manager. Some of the partners set up satellite workshops in nearby towns. The lamp industry was much more of an oligopoly, the markings on the lamps sold from Gaul to Asia Minor showing they were made in only a few places. The brick industry, which eventually produced the emperor Domitian, also concentrated in the villas. Lords and their *officinatores*, or managers, often supervized up to several dozen yards at a time. One of them, the Vindobona (Vienna)-based Decius Alpinus, operated a subsidiary in the French Alps through his slave Clarianus.

> Roman pottery, glassware, bricks, tiles, lamps and stone became humanity's first mass-production industries. They marketed such huge volumes of goods that they had to rely upon agents and middlemen

The Dunning model of multinationals was best followed by the marble industry of Asia Minor. Both Julius and Augustus Caesar became the best customers of an enterprise that before 100 CE remained essentially an entrepreneurial undertaking. After that time, emperors obsessed with grandiose building schemes worked the Egyptian and Anatolian quarries themselves or outsourced. The inscriptions on the big marble blocks shipped all across the Empire tell us that while the small quarries were as entrepreneurial as they had been under the Greeks, the big quarries were now Caesar's.

These inscriptions in marble also let us know that the Romans standardized, prefabricated and mass-produced their blocks and columns, and that the industries processed them in branch offices *en route* to their final destinations. The Roman marble industry, more than any other, was 'a commerce which can conveniently be summarized in modern technology: nationalization; mass production and stockpiling; a considerable element of standardization and prefabrication; the establishment of agencies overseas to handle specific marbles; and in some cases the availability of specialized craftsmen skilled in the handling of a particular type of marble.'[15]

> In spite of the prayers to Mercury, religion in general had little influence in the business dealings of a civic-minded practical people who separated temple and marketplace far more than the Carthaginians or even the Greeks

Marble from the major quarries was mined in bulk and stored in yards, sometimes for 200 years. This required a highly structured business able to weather the fluctuations of supply and demand. Two millennia before Eli Whitney, Henry Ford and the prefabricated homes of Levittown, marble columns were turned out in standard heights for Roman Italy and Africa.

Different models of caskets were also prefabricated for selected markets. Those made near Athens sold well in Greece and Italy; those hollowed and shaped in Asia Minor sold well in Egypt and the East. Sometimes, importing centres, like those in Ravenna, were also workshops, implying a value-added chain in a multinational organization of efficient business networks:

> 'These networks can only have operated through agencies established in some of the major importing centres; and although the resulting distributions do to some extent reflect traditional commercial patterns (as, for example, between Attica and Cyrenaica, or again between the Propontis and the Black Sea) they also show that the responsible organizations were powerful and efficient enough to secure a virtual monopoly in many areas. If we may assume (as I think we may) that such monopolies were based on price and efficient service, this in turn implies a very substantial investment in technical equipment and skilled personnel.'[16]

Roman attitudes to business, like those of the Greeks, were mixed. Trade on a small scale was seen as vulgar while the wholesale business, importing large quantities of goods from all parts of the world, deserved respect if it was accompanied by philanthropy and its profits enabled merchants to acquire landed villas. Seafaring commerce was praised if it proved one's

TRIMALCHIO

FIRST-CENTURY BOOSTER

As the Roman economy grew, new family firms that were not run by Equestrian knights prospered. Many of the patriarchs (and some matriarchs, like the mistress of Nero) who led them had a very different philosophy of business.

The *nouveau riche* family entrepreneurs of the Empire were scathingly parodied in the *Satyricon* of Gaius Petronius (died 66 CE). Gaius Pompeius Trimalchio is an ugly slave who rises by his own efforts to become a prosperous villa manager and international trader. He is Horatio Alger, George Babbitt and Gordon Gekko combined into one, a crass booster with a homespun philosophy of making money for its own sake. Trimalchio flaunts his wealth in a garish manner; he owns 'more farms than a kite could flap over'.[18]

Even the lowliest rag merchant embraces Trimalchio's self-help philosophy: 'Luck changes. If things are lousy today, there's always tomorrow. That's life, man.'[19] Trimalchio has utter contempt for the elitism of academics such as Livy or Plato who are 'takers' rather than producers. Practical learning in law, agriculture or business is another matter: 'There's a mint of money in books, and learning a trade never killed a man yet.'[20]

Trimalchio's planned epitaph shows little humility: 'He died a millionaire, though he started with nothing.'[21] He got rich by taking risks and others should do the same: 'Once I used to be like you, but I rose to the top by my ability. Guts are what makes the man; the rest is garbage.'[22] A slave inheriting his master's fortune, Trimalchio entered the wine business like the Sestii in real life. His first five ships sank but, undeterred, Trimalchio equipped and sent a bigger one. It paid off: 'No one could say I didn't have guts. But big ships make a man feel big himself. I shipped a cargo of wine, bacon, beans, perfume and slaves ... On that one voyage alone I cleared about five hundred thousand. Right away I bought up all my old master's property. I built a house, I went into slave-trading and cattle-buying. Everything I touched just grew and grew like a honeycomb. Once I was worth more than all the people in my home town put together, I picked up my winnings and pulled out. I retired from trade and started lending money to ex-slaves.'[23]

HE DIED A MILLIONAIRE, THOUGH HE STARTED WITH NOTHING

bravery as a good Roman, like this merchant of Brindisi: 'I have reached many lands ... nor do I fear that expenses will outstrip gains.'[17]

Roman merchants vied to convince others of their civic virtues in being thrifty and honest, paying taxes and helping the needy. The civic ideology of Roman capitalism, though, was often more rhetoric than reality. The poet Ovid describes merchants praying to Mercury to overlook greed while granting present and future commercial success: 'Only grant me profits, grant me the joy of profit made, and see to it that I enjoy cheating the buyer!'[24] In spite of the prayers to Mercury, religion in general had little influence in the business dealings of a civic-minded, practical people who separated temple and marketplace far more than the Carthaginians or even the Greeks.

Cadiz to Canton: world economy in antiquity?

The Roman Empire not only furnished the first example of a European economic union and a European currency but became an active player in a trading economy that, for the first time, encompassed the entire Eastern Hemisphere. For the first time, we can speak of a *world* economy, although it would not become a truly *global* economy until the Americas joined it after 1500.

Rome, having absorbed the Greek and Punic trading spheres into her own, now began to exchange her money and goods for the riches of India and China. At first trading with each other through middlemen in Central Asia, the Roman and Later Han Empires eventually traded with one another via India.

The Han became the Romans of the Orient. Like the Romans the Chinese were strongly based upon family and kin and created stable aristocratic empires with claims to rule all humanity. Roman Italy imparted its alphabet, law and, ultimately, the Catholic faith to all of Europe; Han China ultimately imparted its script plus Confucian, Daoist and Buddhist thought to Manchuria, Korea, Vietnam and even Japan, Tibet and Mongolia.

Han rulers fused the reality of Shi Huangdi's powerful empire with the traditions of the past, insisting that: 'China today is the same China as that of the ancient times' in which 'governing was perfect' and there was a sense of 'harmony and love between the governing and the governed'.[25]

Debate over the role of the market extended even into the Confucian establishment itself. To maintain the military establishment necessary to keep China secure, the Emperor Wudi (141–87 BCE) and his successors took the production of grain, iron, salt and liquor out of the hands of entrepreneurs and made them state monopolies. This was done, said the bureaucrats, in the interest of fair marketing, stable prices and revenue.

Oddly, the entrepreneurs found the strangest of allies in the most traditional of Confucian scholars. In 81 BCE these academics challenged the morality of government enterprise. In that year a group of Confucian scholars engaged the empire's Chief Minister in a written debate over the morality of government enterprise. To these scholars, Confucius had not cared that people were poor, only that they were content, moral and virtuous. The monopolies symbolized a money, not an agrarian, economy, which would lead peasants 'to shun duty and chase profit; soon they throng the roads and markets.' Trading and manufacturing were not the duties of the state. As far as military power was concerned, the Confucians insisted that if China had a benevolent, moral society, she would have no enemies. China, they said, was poor because farming was neglected. Still, they felt they were losing the battle, for 'even with all of the discriminations against commerce, people still do evil. How much worse ... if the ruler himself were to pursue profit.'[26] When gentlemen were greedy, the common people would follow: 'The government officers busy themselves with gaining control of the market and cornering commodities ... Quick traders and unscrupulous officials buy when goods are cheap in order to make high profits.'[27]

> For the first time, we can speak of a *world* economy, although it would not become a truly *global* economy until the Americas joined it after 1500

It was all well and good to talk this way, but China needed armies to defend herself and the state monopolies were the only way to pay for them. The Huns and other foes were too savage to be reasoned with, and true virtue lay in making China strong enough to resist them. State enterprise, said the Chief Minister, was as old as China itself. Without artisans and merchants, farmers would have no tools and no grain could be planted. It was therefore the duty of the empire to stimulate the growth of a market from which all would benefit:

'The ancient founders of our country laid the groundwork for both basic and secondary occupations. They facilitated the circulation of goods and provided markets and courts to harmonize the various demands.'[28]

If people were poor, it was because there were not enough artisans and merchants. The goods delivered by the market were needed to maintain millions of lives and depended upon merchants to distribute them as well as craftsmen to make them. This was why the ancient sages built boats and bridges and tamed cattle and horses to extend enterprise to all corners of China and why most people 'look to the salt and iron monopolies and the equitable marketing system as their source of supply.'[29]

Far more important in China's new role in the world economy was her silk industry, for it was silk that the Indians and Romans coveted above all else.

The Chinese were growing silk as far back as 1500 BCE. By Han times they had perfected the growing of silk into an art and a very lucrative business. The silkworms were watched throughout their life cycles, the long filaments of silk thread being extracted and then woven on looms into a fabric praised for its durability, comfort and beauty. More durable silk garments were made for the Han army.

> Far more important in China's new role in the world economy was her silk industry, for it was silk that the Indians and Romans coveted above all else

Most Chinese silk was made in the eastern provinces, although mulberry orchards, where the worms were tended, spread as far as Sichuan (Szechwan). Silk was shipped in bales about 50 centimetres wide and 9 metres long. The fabric, either white, dyed or embroidered, was valuable enough for an officer who earned 900 copper coins a month sometimes to be paid with two rolls of silk. In addition to silk, lacquerware in the form of bowls, boxes and other objects was a profitable Han export. These were made by both private entrepreneurs and government workshops. At first, lacquerware was made in red and black, but eventually many patterns and colours were available.

Chinese silk was already shipped to India through Burma and Assam long before Han times. When the Emperor Wudi sent his armies deep into Asia, making contact with the Parthians, a new overland trading route opened up. Establishing diplomatic relations with the Parthians, the Chinese gave their rulers silk as a tributary gift. Demand for the new cloth quickly became apparent, not only in the Near East, but also in Egypt, and eventually in Rome.

By the time of the Caesars, in the 1st century CE, Chinese silk and lacquerware were finding their way by caravan along the famous Silk Road. This route began at Changan, followed west along the Gansu (Kansu) Corridor in Inner Mongolia, skirted the mountains of Xinjiang (Sinkiang) and reached Turkestan. From there it would cross first Parthian and then Roman territory to reach the Mediterranean.

Chinese annals contain several references to their new trade with the West. The *Shiji* (*Shih-Chi*) speak of the first encounter with the king of Anxi (An-hsi, or Parthia). Sending a delegation of 20 000 horsemen to meet the Chinese, the Parthians established formal relations with the Han. The *Houhanshu* (*Hou Han Shou*) described the land of Anxi as vast and distant from China. When the Emperor sent his ambassador Ganying (Kan Ying) to reach the land of Tazin (Ta-Ts'in, or Syria), he reached what was, apparently, a port on the Persian Gulf where he was told of the dangers involved:

> 'The sea is vast and great; with favourable winds it is possible to cross within three months; but if you meet slow winds, it may also take you two years. It is for this reason that those who go to sea take on board a supply of three years' provisions. There is something in the sea which is apt to make men home-sick, and several have thus lost their lives.'[30]

Alarmed, Ganying turned back. There is no record of Han merchants' ever going that far west again. In reality, they had fallen victim to a clever piece of misinformation planted by the Nabatean traders who handled much of the commerce of the Parthian realm.

Parthia: the middleman

Little, sadly, is known of the marvellous Parthian Empire that arose on the ashes of the Seleucid kingdom in the 2nd century BCE. Partly descended from Scythian horsemen who settled in eastern Iran, the Parthians revolted against their Hellenistic overlords in 248 BCE. Under an aggressive later ruler, Mithridates II, these Zoroastrian nomads, who lived on horseback, elected their kings and tolerated all races and religions and carved out an empire that eventually included not only Persia, but also what had once been Babylonia and Assyria.

Most Parthian subjects lived on the land. Productive industry was minuscule, but trade became very important after the Seleucid collapse when 'the Parthians emerged primarily as middlemen, rather than as producers'.[31] Located between the Roman Empire on the west and India and China on the east, Parthia controlled the overland trade routes linking both India and Rome to China. As the story of Ganying shows, the merchants of Parthia were not eager to share their market knowledge with either the Romans or the Chinese. To do so would ruin their profitable careers as middlemen. According to the *Houhanshu*:

> *'The country of Ta-Ts'in (Syria) is ... situated on the western part of the sea ... Its territory ... contains over four hundred cities ... much gold, silver and rare precious stones ... corals, amber, glass ... gold-embroidered rugs and thin silk cloth of various colors. They make gold-colored cloth and asbestos cloth. They further have "fine cloth", also called "down of the water sheep"; it is made from the cocoons of wild silkworms. They collect all kinds of fragrant substances, the juice of which they boil into su-ho (storax). All the rare gems of other foreign countries come from there. They make coins of gold and silver. Ten units of silver are worth one of gold. They traffic by sea with Parthia and India, the profit of which trade is tenfold. They are honest in their transactions, and there are no double prices ... Their kings always desired to send embassies to China, but the Parthians wished to carry on trade with them in Chinese silks, and it is for this reason that they were cut off from communication.'[32]*

The Parthians separated their two customers lest the Romans and Chinese begin to compare prices.

Even though Rome and Parthia were often bitter foes, the Silk Road usually stayed open. The cities of Parthia along that route, both old and new, such as Hatra and Vologases, boomed and prospered. Many of the middleman traders hailed from the Syrian city of Palmyra, such as the caravan chief Taimarsu, known to us through an inscription from the year 193 CE:

> *'This is the statue of Taimarsu the son of Taima ... the caravan chief. It was raised to him by the caravan men who came up with him*

from Spasinu Charax, because he lent them 300 gold denarii of the old weight, and was agreeable to them. To honour him and his sons ... in the month Nisan, 504.'[33]

The prosperity of middlemen like Taimarsu would wane in the 2nd century CE as Romans turned more and more to the all-water route of the Indian Ocean, bypassing Parthia completely. Roman family firms likely set up their own permanent agents on Indian soil. They were in a good position to apply Professor Dunning's rules and internalize their operation. The Romans had *ownership-specific advantages* in shipbuilding, *location advantages* of ports on the

> The Parthians separated their two customers lest the Romans and Chinese begin to compare prices

Red Sea and *internalization* advantages in their experience in operating large-scale family firms.

We know much about the new Indian Ocean trade through the discovery of a 1st-century CE Latin book entitled the *Periplus* (Sailing Guide) *of the Erythraean Sea*. The *Periplus* describes the voyages of Roman ships from Egyptian Red Sea ports into the Arabian Sea. Hugging the Arabian coasts, they caught the south-west monsoons, which took them on a four-month voyage to the Indus valley or the southern tip of India.[34]

Roman Indian Ocean ships, up to 60 metres long, were sturdily constructed. Their incredibly strong hulls were fastened together by thousands of joints and supported sails designed for safety more than speed. Returning to Egypt via the calmer north-east monsoon, the big vessels brought huge amounts of Indian spices and Chinese silk. One shipment consisted

> Big cargoes sailing great distances in large ships could not be financed by the activity of a few small independent traders. This worked in favour of larger Roman family and partnership firms able to raise large amounts of money and employ overseas agents

of an estimated 1500–3600 kilograms of spice, 10 000 kilograms of ivory and 1600–1700 kilograms of textiles – a total of 131 talents, worth 1000 hectares of good Egyptian farmland. A Roman ship could carry anywhere from 150 to 300 such shipments.[35]

Big cargoes sailing great distances in large ships could not be financed by the activity of a few small independent traders. This worked in favour of larger Roman family and partnership firms able to raise large amounts of money and employ overseas agents.

SANUDASA AND THE *SARTHAVAHA*

THE HIGH-RISK ART OF INDIAN CAPITALISM

I N spite of the fall of Rome, India remained an important centre of international trade throughout late antiquity and into the Dark Ages. Under her 4th-century Gupta emperors she became the prosperous centre of an Indian Ocean economy that stretched from Byzantine Alexandria to Indonesia and even China. Like the cultures of the Near East, Indian business was a mixture of state-run and private enterprise.

Merchants in India's mixed economy were more socially respectable than in Confucian China, but not as venerated as in the Muslim world. Commerce was encouraged by Hindu writings such as the *Rig Veda* and the lawbook of Manu but was generally restricted to the *vaisya*, or trader caste.

One such *vaisya* was Sanudasa of the Ganges city of Kampa, in the north-eastern corner of India. The son of a merchant, he probably lived during the Gupta period. Having lost his family fortune through some unfortunate business dealings with untrustworthy partners, Sanudasa traded far and wide across land and sea to recover his personal and family fortune.

Sanudasa's career shows the central role of India as middleman in the world economy as well as the art of doing business in a low-trust, high-risk environment.

The business career of an Indian *vaisya* was often difficult and even perilous. The Indian *rajahs*, or kings, generally realized it was in their best interest to keep taxes at a reasonable rate, but such was not the case in times of war. Local tolls could often be onerous. The hazards of trading itself were also considerable, although the profits could be considerable enough to balance out the risks. Sanudasa traded by both land and sea. Leaving his home in Kampa, he joined one of the semi-annual caravans heading south through the forests and jungles of Bengal to reach the port of Tamralipti. Indian *vaisyas* never travelled alone; long-distance commerce on the subcontinent was too dangerous. The caravans became business enterprises in themselves, led by a *sarthavaha* who was one part soldier, one part manager and one part tour guide. Merchants joining up with him either risked everything and so often went along with their goods, or pooled their

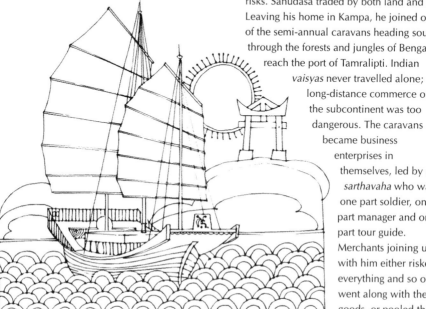

goods and capital in a travelling business alliance.

Sanudasa contracted to obey the *sarthavaha* implicitly if he hoped to reach his markets safe and sound. The caravan had many wagons and oxen and had to carry firewood, drinking water, rice and oil, becoming a self-sufficient community. Travel would only be undertaken by day; at night the carts were drawn up in a circle and campfires lit while men mounted guard. Organized brigands lurked in the jungle, as did warlike aboriginal tribes searching for sacrificial victims. Rivers had to be crossed by raft or using tree trunks, for India had no bridges.

If Sanudasa and his caravan crossed one of India's deserts he faced even more perils than in the jungles. Caravans faced hunger, thirst, wild animals, quicksand, poisonous plants and rumours of demons that would devour any wayward traveller. Caravans would stock up on water before heading out over the sand, camping during the day and journeying only by night. Merchants were in the hands not only of the *sarthavaha* but also of his land pilot who had to navigate by the stars. Sometimes the pilot would fall asleep, in which case the caravan would go astray, causing many to lose their money and lives in the wilderness.

On one occasion, Sanudasa's caravan was plundered and the cotton he hoped to sell in Tamralipti was burnt. Reaching the coast of Orissa, he formed a partnership with one Rudradatta. Sanudasa traded extensively by sea as well as land, sailing as far east as China and as far west as

Alexandria. Climbing on board a crowded India merchantman for a six-month voyage to Java, Canton or Alexandria was just as terrifying as crossing India, if not more so. Indian vessels were not as sturdy as the junks of their Chinese competitors or as swift and sleek as the Arab *dhows*. The coastal waters of India were often stormy, and ships could be swamped or their hulls breached quite easily. In cases like this, if Sanudasa were a devout Hindu, he would pray to the goddess Manimekhala, who was patroness of drowning sailors. Often the prayers of the shipwrecked were not answered in waters filled with sharks, giant turtles and pirates. Sometimes there was too little wind, causing the crew to sacrifice one of the merchants to appease the gods of the wind.

In spite of several accidents and being shipwrecked, Sanudasa survived to become a prosperous trader whose markets included not only India itself, but also Egypt, Central Asia, China, Indonesia and the rest of Southeast Asia. Trading the gold and textiles of the West for the spices of the East made him a wealthy man, for the estimated tenfold profits he reaped more than covered his losses.

Transporting goods between the Roman Empire and India could be done only in bulk once a year, for such trade 'required a formidable amount of capital' and was 'open only to large-scale operators'.[36]

Big Mediterranean *amphorae* and other artefacts found from the Punjab to the Coromandel coast near Sri Lanka tell us that India was a big market for Roman exporters. They traded their oil and wine for silk, wood, spices, animals, ivory, gems and other luxury goods. An exceptional concentration of Roman artefacts at the site of Arikamedu on the Coromandel coast hints at the presence of permanent Roman business agents in India.[37]

The excavations at Arikamedu, begun in the 1950s but continuing into the 1990s, found that Indians played a dynamic role even after the Romans came. The southern part of the city was a textile centre, the northern a port. The city began to flourish once the Romans arrived in about 50 BCE. Glassware found at Arikamedu and at the mouth of the Indus shows that the glass of Sidon and Tyre was a profitable cargo for Roman firms to carry. Unloaded at Roman centres on the west coast, it was taken by Indian middlemen to the east coast, and from there exported to China and the Far East.[38] All this evidence suggests that the finds at Arikamedu and elsewhere 'point', in the words of Lionel Casson, 'to the presence of a foreign colony, a group of Western merchants permanently established there'. [39]

Rome's Indian luxury trade was huge by the standards of its day. Over a hundred ships a year set out from Egypt, appearing in Indian records as the vessels of the Yavanas bringing gold and wine. Roman firms opened resident offices in Indian harbours 'anticipating by a millennium and a half the employees of Britain's East India Company'.[40] Embassies were exchanged between Rome and India as spices, silks, jewels and the luxuries of the East flooded into the Empire.

The flow of Asian imports did not go unnoticed in Rome. The Emperor Tiberius worried that the 'ladies and their baubles are transferring our money to foreigners'. Pliny the Elder claimed that imports from Arabia, China and India were costing Rome 550 000 000 *sesterces* a year.[41]

Decline and fall of the first world economy

Roman business culture in the first two centuries of Imperial rule set the stage for the future economies of Europe and America. The creation of a free market, large private firms, the issuing of shares and limited liability, mass production and business agents and partnerships – all were pioneered by the Romans.

Other legacies of Rome's threefold patrician/publican/plebeian approach to enterprise would also return: a common European currency, military Keynesianism, sophisticated levels of management staff and capital accumulation.

If one were looking for a term to characterize the commercial system of the Late Republic and the High Empire – one including both its military and familial nature – the best phrase might well be 'legionary capitalism': the ideas of the OLI framework of the Dunning Eclectic Paradigm, which would make little sense applied to the Euboeans, Corinthians, Milesians or Athenians (see Chapter 2). It would make better sense in the more partnership-oriented and internalized trade of the Roman world. The partnerships, internal hierarchies and use of overseas agents, which characterized the new Roman firms,

> Roman business culture in the first two centuries of Imperial rule set the stage for the future economies of Europe and America. The creation of a free market, large private firms, the issuing of shares and limited liability, mass production and business agents and partnerships – all were pioneered by the Romans

arose in response to the markets and opportunities provided by decades of constant and intensive warfare. A tentative model of the Dunning paradigm for Rome can be seen in Table 8.1.

Rome, mighty as she was, could not last forever. The story of her economic decline through inflation, corruption, and loss of market opportunities is quite extensive and can be summarized only very briefly here. The emperors who followed Marcus Aurelius lacked his stature. Facing both the Germans and the new Sassanid regime of Persia, which, after 226 CE became much more militant than the liberal Parthians, these Caesars had to maintain a huge military machine that became more and more of a political power. The 3rd century became a terrible time of political instability as at least a score of 'Barracks Emperors' followed one another. Business confidence declined as heavier and heavier taxes were levied upon a shrinking economic base. By the time of Diocletian (284–305) and Constantine (324–337) the Dominate, or Late Empire, was far less friendly to commerce than the Republic or the Principate of the Roman Peace.

Table 8.1 The Eclectic Paradigm applied to Roman business

Ownership-specific advantages

Hierarchy came more naturally in Rome, as Roman companies arose in a culture enshrining the primacy of the patriarchal and extended family in its *mores* and laws. Upon this familialism was imposed a powerful ethos from which Roman firms later developed under the direction of the *paterfamilias* or the equestrian knight. Partnership, family and military ties in these firms could then be extended to overseas markets.

Locational advantages

Given the large sums of money involved and the dangers of corruption and intense competition in the military contracting business, the presence of a resident branch office for an Italian-based firm near the legion encampments in Greece and Spain would ensure the proper completion of the contract. The mining and processing of resources situated overseas by Roman firms also necessitated a branch office in locations such as Anatolia and Greece.

Internalization advantages:

Publican firms dealing in large sums of money, large volumes of goods and large overheads thought it prudent to deal through their own agents in North Africa, Asia Minor, Spain and eventually, Gaul. The alternative of dealing through a middleman overseas involved additional costs and risks that might price the firm out of a very competitive market.

A brief recovery in the 4th century could not mask growing signs of long-term collapse. The countryside of Roman Italy became depopulated and war and disease took their toll on the entire Western Empire. Economic activity began to return to barter and subsistence as Germanic invaders and settlers moved in. In the Greek-speaking East, soon to be known as Byzantium, more prudent tax policies and a greater concentration of population and wealth slowed the decline. Egyptians, Syrians and others, though, began to reassert their own Near Eastern cultures.

The world economy of late antiquity began to unravel. In China, the Han Empire broke up into several warring states. Roman firms could no longer afford agents in India and their heirs in Constantinople were forced to rely upon the Ethiopians and southern Arabs as their middlemen. Most Indian trade fell into Persian hands and ferocious warfare broke out between Byzantium and the Sassanids. In the mutual exhaustion that would follow, the way would be open for a new force, inspired by a new pro-business creed, to create the greatest economic power of the Dark Ages.

NOTES TO CHAPTER 8

1. Plautus, *Curculio*, quoted in Arnott, P. (1970) *The Romans and their World*. New York: St Martin's Press, 78. The 'Stock Exchange' is Arnott's free translation of 'the basilica', (*ibid.*, 96, fn. 4).

2. Badian, E. 'Publicans and Sinners' in (1983) *Private Enterprise in the Service of the Roman Republic*. Ithaca, NY: Cornell University Press, 16–25.

3. *Ibid.*, 74.

4. *Ibid.*, 75–7. Roman companies varied greatly in size as well as profitability, the firm of Hispo being one of the largest. Sadly, historians still have very few hard statistics on trade and production for the Roman world.

5. Frank, T. (1940) *Rome and Italy of the Empire: An Economic Survey of Ancient Rome*, Vol. V, 346. Baltimore, MD: Johns Hopkins Press. Taxes on grazing and port trade in Sicily were collected not by the publicans, but by smaller firms that 'nevertheless constituted branches of a larger company of publicans' (*ibid.*, 345).

6. Badian, E. 'Publicans and Sinners' in (1983) *Private Enterprise in the Service of the Roman Republic*. Ithaca, NY: Cornell University Press, 106.

7. *Ibid.*, 107.

8. *Ibid.*

9. Cicero, *Letters to Atticus*, ii.16.4, referred to in Frank, T. (1940): *Rome and Italy of the Empire: An Economic Survey of Ancient Rome*, Vol. V. Baltimore, MD: Johns Hopkins Press, 356–7.

10. Casson, L. (1964) *The Ancient Mariners: Seafarers and Sea Fighters of the Mediterranean in Ancient Times*. New York: Macmillan, 206–8.

11. Wacher, J. (1987) *The Roman Empire*. London: J.M. Dent and Sons, 151.

12. The number of shipwrecks found buried in the western Mediterranean also documented the expansion of European trade. Out of 545 wrecks 20+ dated from before 400 BCE; 50+ between 400 and 200 BCE; a peak of 160 between 200 and 1 BCE; and almost as many, 130, between 1 and 200 CE. The number fell to 80 between 200 and 400 CE and to around 30 between 400 and 650 CE. Some 70 wrecks were of unknown date. (Keith Hopkins (1980) 'Taxes and Trade in the Roman Empire (200 BC – AD 400)' in *Journal of Roman Studies*, vol. 70, 101–25.)

13 Frank, T. (1940) *Rome and Italy of the Empire: An Economic Survey of Ancient Rome*, Vol. V, 357. Baltimore, MD: Johns Hopkins Press.

14. *Inscriptiones Graecae*, Vol. XIV, No. 830, in Lewis, N. and Reinhold, M., eds. (1966) *Roman Civilization, Sourcebook II: The Empire*. New York: Harper and Row, 196–7. The Tyrian council, in response, voted to continue the practice of subsidising the Puteoli office from the Tyrian agency in Rome. (*Ibid.*,198.)

15. Ward-Perkins, J. 'The Marble Trade and its Organization: Evidence from Nicomedia', in Darms, J.H. and Kopff, E.C., eds. (1980) *The Seaborne Commerce of Ancient Rome: Studies in Archaeology and History*. Rome: American Academy in Rome, 326; Dodge, H. 'Ancient Marble Studies: Recent Research', *Journal of Roman Archaeology* (1991), 4, 36.

16. *Ibid.*

17. *Corpus Inscriptionum Latinarum,* Vol. IX, Nos. 93337, 60 in Lewis, N. and Reinhold, M., eds. (1966) *Roman Civilization, Sourcebook II: The Empire.* New York: Harper and Row, 261.

18. Petronius, *Satyricon,* tr. by Arrowsmith, W. and quoted in Bailkey, N.M., ed. (1987) *Readings in Ancient History: Thought and Experience from Gilgamesh to St. Augustine.* 3rd edn. Lexington, MA: D.C. Heath and Company, 378.

19. *Ibid.,* 379.

20. *Ibid.,* 379–80.

21. *Ibid.,* 381.

22. *Ibid.,* 382.

23. *Ibid.*

24. Ovid, *Fasti,* verses 674–88, tr. By Cochrane, L.G. in Giardina, A. 'The Merchant' in *idem,* ed. (1993) *The Roman.* Chicago: University of Chicago Press, 267.

25. Ssu-ma Chien, 'An Introduction to Economics' from 'Biographies of Merchants and Industrialists' in *Shih chi,* roll 129, in Li, document 132, 13.

26. Ebrey, P.B., ed. (1981) 'The Debate on Salt and Iron' in *Chinese Civilization and Society: A Sourcebook.* New York: Free Press, document 7, 25.

27. *Ibid.,* 26.

28. *Ibid.,* 24.

29. *Ibid.,* 25.

30. Hsi-Yü-Chuan 'The Principal Account of Ta-Ts'in' in *Houhanshu,* Chapter 88, in Hirth, F., ed. (1966) *China and the Roman Orient: Researches into their Ancient and Medieval Relations as represented in Old Chinese Records.* New York: Paragon Book Reprint Corporation, 40–3. The compilation was originally published in 1885.

31. Colledge, M.A.R. (1967) *The Parthians.* New York: Frederick A. Praeger 77–8.

32. 'The Principal Account of Ta-Ts'in' in *Houhanshu,* Chapter 88, in Hirth, F., ed. (1966) *China and the Roman Orient Researches into their Ancient and Medieval Relations as represented in Old Chinese Records.* New York: Paragon Book Reprint Corporation, 40–2. We have omitted the verse numbers from the quotation.

33. Colledge, M.A.R. (1967) *The Parthians.* New York: Frederick A. Praeger, 81.

34. Casson, L. (1991) 'Ancient Naval Technology and the Route to India' in Begley, V. and Daniel De Puma, R., eds., *Rome and India: The Ancient Sea Trade.* Madison, WI: University of Wisconsin Press, 8–11.

35. *Ibid.,* 9–10.

36. *Ibid.,* 11.

37. Will, E.L. 'The Mediterranean Shipping Amphoras from Arikamedu' in Begley and De Puma, 151–6.

38. *Ibid.,* 117. E. M. Stern holds the presence of Mediterranean *amphorae* on the east coast above Arikamedu, along with glassware, as showing the possibility that Roman glass exported there 'was destined for transit trade with China', (*ibid.,* 117). The possibility of technology transfer may be indicated in the similarity of blue glassware products in India to slightly older ones from

Rhodes, suggesting that the 'technology ... must have crossed the Indian Ocean in the wake of the early Roman sea trade' (*ibid.*, 121).

39. Casson, L. (1991) 'Ancient Naval Technology and the Route to India' in Begley, V. and Daniel De Puma, R., eds., *Rome and India: The Ancient Sea Trade.* Madison, WI: University of Wisconsin Press, 10.

40. Casson, L. (1964) *The Ancient Mariners: Seafarers and Sea Fighters of the Mediterranean in Ancient Times* New York, Macmillan, 227.

41. *Ibid.*

9

Dark Age capitalism

Faith meets economics in the age of Muhammad and Charlemagne: 500–1000

USINESS in the Dark Ages? The very phrase 'Dark Ages' conjures up a picture of long centuries of grim poverty. It is 500 CE. The Roman Empire is dead and gone. Europe is overgrown with forests. Grass grows in the cities. Milan, Alexandria and Rome are partially destroyed. Illiterate tribal chieftains quarrel among the ruins and sally forth from wooden castles to wage unceasing warfare while serfs toil with crude ploughs to wrest bare existence from the soil. None but monks can read or write, and travel is unsafe. It is civilization's bleak nadir when life was nasty, brutish and short.

Much of this conventional picture of the Dark Ages is true, at least as far as Europe is concerned. Even so, business, even international business, did exist between 500 and 1000 CE. As historian Will Durant would write, every end contained the seeds of its own new beginning. The achievements of Greece and Rome were not entirely lost. Europe's Dark Age was the Golden Age of Islam, and China under the Tang would lead the world in civility and civilization. First Iraq and then Egypt became the centres of prosperous international economies that encompassed Africa and China. In an age when investment money was scarce and engaging in commerce was a high-risk venture, business was in the hands of small partnerships. The spread of popular forms of Christianity, Islam, Buddhism and Hinduism pinpoints this period as an age of faith. Effective capitalism, at least in the early stages, presupposes a system of basic morality. Thus the trust and sense of rights and values inspired by faith can become a potent economic factor. Faith, linked to strong family ties, allowed Dark Age businesses to invest, trade and even prosper. It is a story well worth the telling.

A series of dire crises after 180 CE had transformed the economy of the Roman Empire. Forced to defend its long frontiers against the growing Germanic tribes and the aggressive new monarchy of the Persian Sassanids, Rome had to spend increasingly large sums to supply her sagging legions. Power and wealth gradually shifted from Italy – the target of repeated barbarian invasions – to the regions around the Rhine, the Danube and the eastern Mediterranean. Ambitious generals made and unmade emperors and plunged the empire into instability. By the time of Diocletian, around 300 CE, taxes, inflation and increasing government intervention to restore order were beginning to cripple free enterprise in Rome. The empire's death-agonies would, nevertheless, be protracted. Fatal and demoralising were the outbreaks of plague that killed thousands upon thousands. By 500 CE the empire in the West had ceased to exist and much of the economy with it. After 200, Roman trading vessels were rarely seen in the Indian Ocean. Byzantium, Persia, India and Ethiopia kept commerce moving in the Indian Ocean, but no single power was able to dominate. After 600 this would change dramatically. Almost overnight the lands of the Near East would give birth to a dynamic new faith and religious world power whose shockwaves are still being felt to this day.[1]

The pro-business creed in Islam

As Rome spiralled out of control, Arabia, despite its inhospitable climate, found itself in a strategic position that allowed it to profit from the luxuries that flowed between the Mediterranean and India. The sharp-eyed traders of Jordanian Petra and Arabia Felix (at the south-east corner of the Arabian peninsula) trafficked in linen, glass and silk from Egypt and Syria. Indian traders brought silk and spices from Indonesia and China.

An Arab trading city in central Arabia, built on the site of Qaryat al-Fau, was uncovered in 1972. Qaryat flourished from 200 to 500 CE. Coins, temples, bazaars, tombs and even canals bore witness to its prosperity. Mecca was also a profitable shrine and marketing town. Twice a year, large caravans bearing incense, silk, glass and fabrics passed through it. These caravans were so large that entire tribes took part in the bargaining.[2] One of the merchants involved was a camel driver named Muhammad, scion of an illustrious family. Marrying well, the witty and imaginative young merchant became, in the words of Edward

Gibbon, an adept student of the book of man and nature. He retired to a cave for three years of contemplation. His visions, written in the *Qur'an* inspired a powerful new faith of uncompromising monotheism. Uncomfortable with Christian ideas of Trinity and incarnation, Muhammad's stress on good works and the relief of the poor underlaid a faith not inimical to trade and personal enterprise. Faith and life were not compartmentalized. Allah required total commitment of all Muslims, but that commitment provided plenty of room for business enterprise providing it was done honestly, fairly and with charity. While a Muslim could not charge usury, he could certainly enjoy the profits of trade and investments: 'O, you who believe, devour not your property among yourselves by illegal methods, although you may engage in trading by mutual consent. And kill not your people. Surely Allah is merciful to you.'[3]

> Faith and life were not compartmentalized. Allah required total commitment of all Muslims, but that commitment provided plenty of room for business enterprise providing it was done honestly, fairly and with charity

The Prophet's evangelistic fervour fell like sparks on dry timber. 'Either victory or paradise is our own' became an early war-cry. Muhammad's successors, the Caliphs, welded the Arab tribes into a formidable fighting force that wrested vast territories from Byzantine rule and conquered the entire Persian realm. Syria and Iraq were overrun by 638, Jerusalem by 640, and Egypt and Persia soon after. By 700 North Africa was under Muslim rule and by 750 the Caliphate governed from Spain to Turkestan. In their new possessions, the Arab rulers took over structures existing from antiquity. Many of the conquered became Muslims or survived as tolerated minorities within the vastest multinational empire the world had yet seen. The first Caliphs, the Umayyads, ruled from Syria until toppled in 749 by a descendant of the prophet's uncle. Abu al-Abbas staged an Iraq/Iran-based revolution that inaugurated the Caliphate of the Abbasids.[4]

This Abbasid Empire united the heritage of Iran, Mesopotamia and Egypt, bringing an age of Muslim glory that had both Persian and Arabian roots. Merchants had played an important role in the Abbasid revolution from the beginning and the new Caliphs responded with a very positive attitude towards making money.[5] The centre of the Muslim world rested in Iraq, the Land of the Two Rivers. For the first time, Muslims would take to the sea in earnest.

The Caliphate unified the Gulf and Red Sea routes under a common rule. Arab sailors and newly converted Persian traders flocked to India, Malaya, Sumatra and East Africa, and incorporated the old Iranian route to China in the Muslim sphere of international commerce. The Abbasid capital of Baghdad was chosen by the Caliph al-Mansur in 762 as an ideal location whence known-world trade could be managed. Goods could come down the Tigris from Egypt, Syria and Byzantium, while the goods of Asia could flow upstream: 'This is the Tigris; here is no distance between us and China. Everything on the sea can come to us ...'[6]

Sinbad the sailor: Muslim enterprise in legend

The quintessential entrepreneur of Muslim legend is Sinbad (Sinbad) of the *Arabian Nights*. While a fable, the story of Sinbad is very revealing of Islamic values. The text indicates the positive place of the businessman in Muslim culture, the role of faith and trust in the affairs of men and merchants, and the workings of the Arab proclivity to partnership. Sinbad knows that success depends upon the will of Allah, who 'enrichest whom Thou wilt, and whom Thou wilt Thou impoverishest'.[7] Sinbad sells his family estate and forms a partnership with other merchants. The partners sail across the Indian Ocean to a mythical locale composed of many islands, probably in Southeast Asia. Everywhere they go they trade, buying, selling and bartering. After being shipwrecked and losing his goods, Sinbad is saved by a King El-Mihraj, who promotes him to harbourmaster. The king makes Sinbad 'his superintendent of the seaport, and registrar of every vessel that came to the coast'. Like the biblical Joseph of old, Sinbad 'stood in his presence to transact his affairs' and became a person 'high in credit' with the king in 'intercessions, and in accomplishing the affairs of the people'.[8]

One day a ship arrives with unclaimed goods. Sinbad finds out that the goods are his own! At first the shipmaster thinks Sinbad is out to deceive him, but then Sinbad relates the details of his own voyage and shipwreck. Nothing was pilfered.

MUHAMMAD THE ENTREPRENEUR (569–632)

FOUNDER of one of the world's most extensive faiths, the Prophet Muhammad was also a very honest and successful businessperson. He was born in Mecca in the year 569 CE. Inhabitants of a city-state in the midst of a barren desert region, Meccans more than most other Arabs had to survive by trade and commerce. Members of Muhammad's tribe, the Quraysh, had for centuries earned their living as middlemen leading caravans from Yemen north along the Red Sea shore to Petra and then along the King's Highway to Damascus as well as to and from Bahrain and the Gulf.

Born into this world, the young Muhammad was orphaned at an early age. First his father Abdullah and then his mother died. By the time he was eight years old, Muhammad was being raised by his poor uncle Abu Talib. The young Muhammad had to work very hard to survive. Abu Talib, himself a struggling trader, took the boy with him in his caravans to Syria and employed him in his shop in Mecca.

By the time he reached his mid-20s, Muhammad already had a reputation as an honest and hard-working trader. He soon caught the eye of a widow named Khadijah, who had inherited her own business. She hired Muhammad to carry her goods to and from Syria. Driving his camels across the deserts of Arabia, Jordan and Syria, Muhammad quickly became a very prosperous and successful business agent. He and Khadijah soon married, and the marriage, brief as it was to be, was filled with genuine love and romantic attraction as well as being a lucrative business relationship. Muhammad also seems to have been a successful business partner in his own right. He and his partner, Saib, took turns

in journeying abroad while the other minded the business at home.

Muhammad's interest in spiritual matters began around the year 605. Not long after this, he began to receive the spiritual revelations that would form the basis for Islam. Believing in one just and transcendent god, Muhammad struck a balance between the physical and spiritual. Enjoying the material things of life and even reaping an honest profit were, according to Islam, noble goals, so long as they were done honestly.

Fleeing to Medina in 622, Muhammad was able to organise the first Muslim society, one remarkably human and progressive for its time. Medina had a written constitution, uniform administration of justice, freedom of religion and an economic policy based upon private property and encouragement of free enterprise mitigated by a social welfare system and prohibitions upon usury, cornering of markets and other monopolistic practices.

Muhammad created an entrepreneurial business culture that his successors would spread from Spain to the frontiers of China within a single century. Its emphasis on faith-based business alliances would shape medieval commerce not only in the Muslim but even in the Christian world.

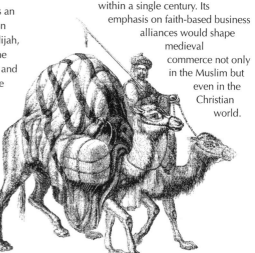

This tale suggests that a certain amount of trust existed in mercantile affairs that helped spur commerce. Sinbad returns to Basra and Baghdad a wealthy man with servants, *mamluks* (Turkish slaves) and African slaves. He could also now build himself a large establishment, with houses and many other possessions – a self-made man. Again and again Sinbad says he will not risk another ocean voyage, but the 'longing for the occupation of traffic ... and gaining my subsistence' causes him to cave in.[9] The expectation of tenfold profits eventually overcomes his doubts and those of his would-be partners in Basra and Siraf. On later voyages Sinbad first hires and then buys his own vessel, and forms a partnership with the chief merchants of Basra:

> *'I saw a great, handsome, lofty vessel, and it pleased me; wherefore I purchased it. Its apparatus was new, and I hired for it a master and sailors, over whom I set my black slaves and my pages as superintendents, and I embarked in it many bales. And there came to me a company of merchants, who also embarked their bales in it, and paid me hire.'*[10]

Sinbad's sixth journey takes him to Serendip, the main trading city of Sri Lanka and target of many an acquisitive Arab merchant lured by its jewels and spices. The ruler of Serendip makes Sinbad his personal ambassador to the famous Caliph Harun al-Rashid. Sinbad tells the Caliph of the splendour of the King of Serendip, who rules from an elephant and travels with 1000 horsemen clad in gold and silk. The Caliph sends Sinbad back to Serendip as *his* diplomat, in a manner similar to that of merchant-princes who served the kings of Babylon two millennia before. Sinbad is accompanied by many lesser merchants and is accepted by the king at once. Sinbad is obviously now a merchant-prince of great repute. The presents he brings to the King of Serendip are the chief exports of Abbasid Iraq; they include a horse with a jewelled saddle worth 10 000 *dinars*. Sinbad also gives him all kinds of Egyptian clothes made from flax, silks from Suez and Alexandria, and Greek carpets. A Horatio Alger hero could not have done better.[11]

Sumer reborn: the 'world' economy of Baghdad

Business was good. It would get even better, Dark Age or not. From 750 to 950 Abbasid Iraq and Iran were the engine driving an international trade that centred on the Indian Ocean. Sleek Arab ships known as *dhows* frequented the ports of Basra and Ubullah, carrying goods both east and west. The Persian port of Siraf, located in present-day Iran, excavated 1966–1973, became a trade metropolis on a desert shore.[12] Archaeologists uncovered six levels of artefacts at Siraf, which conveniently sketch the Caliphate's rise and fall. The pottery finds at Siraf indicated a tremendous growth – first increasing tenfold and, after that, sevenfold again – of Islamic Indian Ocean commerce. The trading customers were Africa and China. The bottom two levels date from pre-Abbasid times and have 4000 pottery fragments. These reveal that trade between Iraq, Siraf and India was not terribly extensive, at least at first. Coin deposits date levels three and four to the 8th century. There are about 40 000 sherds in each level, often next to Chinese ceramics. In the fifth level, covering the late 8th and early 9th centuries, the pottery finds explode to over 270 000 and the number and diversity of Chinese ceramics has dramatically increased. In the final level, ending around 850 CE, the number of pottery finds drops off sharply to about 44 000 amidst evidence of an enlargement of the city's mosque.[13]

Table 9.1 Excavation at Siraf

Level 6: 825–850:	44 000 sherds. Decline of trade and enlargement of mosque.
Level 5: 815–25:	271 000 sherds and many more Chinese ceramics. Full extent of Chinese trade.
Level 4: 775–815:	41 000 sherds and Chinese ceramics.
Level 3: 750–775:	44 000 sherds and some Chinese ceramics. Abbasid Caliphate founded; trade with India and China expands.
Levels 1–2: before 750:	4000 sherds; limited trade with India.

While Europe struggled out of the depths, the new Muslim metropolis of Baghdad on the Tigris and its environs stood at the centre of known-world trade. The ghost of Babylon – not far up the Tigris – seemed to hover over the emerging prosperity of Baghdad. The ancient Land of the Two Rivers was once again a commercial powerhouse and, with the possible exception of Canton, the most dynamic economy of the Dark Age world. No other city enjoyed such favourable location business advantages. If ever 'a route had proven comparative advantage, this was it', said historian Janet Abu-Lughod.[14] Eliahu Ashtor spoke of 'a true economic miracle, performed under the guidance of the Abbasid Government'.[15] Realms once divided between Christian and Zoroastrian belief-systems formed a single market unified by Islam. Not only luxuries but food, textiles and other mass-market goods were traded in the most distant places: grain from Iraq; olive oil and wool from North Africa; fruit and sugar from Syria; cattle and textiles from Central Asia; carpets from Armenia; and linen from Egypt.[16]

Muslim traders are first mentioned in Chinese records in 671 and appear in the following century as important shipowners in Canton. In 851 a merchant named Suleiman left a description of the Muslim trade routes of the Indian Ocean. Arabs and Persians sailed along the coasts of Iran and India to Malabar, Sri Lanka, Nicobar, Malaya, Malacca, Cambodia, Vietnam and Canton. Perhaps 200 000 Muslims and others lived in the Canton region as traders and artisans. The account of Yo K'o of the Arab agent P'u, written after 1200, retrospectively illuminates these early interactions between Chinese and Muslim:

> *The "sea barbarians" lived side by side with the Chinese in Canton and the most powerful of them was a man named P'u. Mr P'u, a white barbarian, came from Chan-ch'eng [Vietnam] where he was reported to be a man of great importance. On his way to China, he encountered a heavy storm; and fearful of the sea, he requested his employer to let him stay in China as a commercial agent so that he did not have to risk his life on the stormy sea again. His employer agreed to his request.'[17]

The P'u family became resident in Canton for a long time and their prosperity flouted the limits permitted merchants by the emperors. Since the local government was interested in encouraging more foreign investment and the P'u were foreigners, it did what many states eager for hard currency did – it looked the other way. Still, the robust faith of the Muslim merchants presented a culture-shock to their Chinese clients. For Muslim traders, faith and works went hand in hand.

The heyday of Abbasid prosperity – from about 750 to the capture of Baghdad by the Mongols in 1258 – was fostered by a huge expansion in the money supply. When Arab armies plundered the monasteries of

Byzantium, the tombs of Egypt and the royal treasuries of Persia, they released enormous quantities of gold into circulation. Even more gold came from African mines deep in Nubia, Niger and Senegal.[18] Camel caravans carried impressive quantities of West African gold across the Sahara to Morocco, Algeria, Tunisia, Libya and even Egypt. Predictably, the indiscriminate release of new gold reserves triggered inflation. Labourers found their gold *dinars* buying less wheat and fewer oranges, but enterprising merchants invested the new coins in expanding businesses.[19] The high quality of the new Abbasid coins made them the international currency of the day. Instead of saving their money, Muslims became consumers and investors. Interest in the Arab world was pegged at 10 per cent, half that of some European towns.[20] The trans-Saharan African trade was a lucrative one, indeed, given the cheapness of the salt, copper and textile products Arabs traded back to Africans for their gold and slaves. Arab enterprises set up permanent business offices with agents in several West African cities.[21] All major towns of the 10th and 11th centuries in Ghana and Sudan and on the Niger hosted Muslim merchant quarters. Although Maghrebian merchants from Algeria, Tunisia and Morocco played a great role in the Sudan trade, one should take into consideration that many of them were agents of Egyptian traders. The trans-Saharan route was probably, to a great measure, under the control of Egyptian traders.[22]

International trade involves exporting, importing, joint ventures, some form of licensing, direct foreign investment and some form of reverse investment and countertrade. The Abbasids knew this well. Products originating in one part of the Arab world were easily available in the others. As a result, a standardization of consumer goods developed among the estimated 12–15 million people living in the Caliphate. Arab merchants and scholars, dwelling midway between a slumbering Europe and an India and China often unaware of the full implications of their creative inventions, became agents of cultural transmission. They were the nexus for the technical inventions and wisdom of the East to reach the West at just the right time to produce the modern age. The art of papermaking, for example, invented in China in the 2nd century CE and introduced from Samarkand to Baghdad by Yahya, the vizier of the eminent Harun al-Rashid (786–809), found its way to Italy and Europe in the 1100s. Arab traders also imported mulberry trees all the way from China to Tunisia, creating a Muslim silk industry. They brought Indian cotton to North Africa. Egypt's sugar industry got its start from the Orient. Irrigation, rice, oranges, lemons and apricots were introduced along Abbasid routes.

As importers and traders the Abbasids were second to none. Yet from its earliest days, the Arab Empire laid claim to being the greatest consumer society that had yet existed, dwarfing even Rome: 'From the late 7th century to the end of the 12th, the Arab empire functioned much like a free-trade area.'[23] Asian ceramics were introduced as far as Spain. The Frankish emperor Charlemagne owned an ivory chess set given to him as a present by Harun al-Rashid. The Muslims sent their Christian contemporaries rich fabrics, exquisite rugs and even an elephant. An intricate clock from Baghdad was looked upon as a mechanical marvel by dumbfounded Europeans. The Abbasid penchant for the finest rugs, cushions and curtains the Orient could produce was obvious at the Caliph's palace in Baghdad, a structure that occupied a third of the city. Our modern business parlance – especially in textiles – owes much to the Arab ascendancy and is a lasting testimony to the Caliphate's clout in world commerce: *chiffon, mohair, damask, satin, cotton, muslin, traffic, tariff, check, magazine.* These words would pass into the English language via Arabic.[24]

Trade and countertrade: known as the *muqarada*, the stable and reliable Muslim trading partnerships were prominent in an early 10th-century business manual, the writings of Abu al-Dimashqi, the *Guide to the Merits of Commerce*. The *Guide* is an amazingly shrewd analysis of Dark Age internationalism. It described three types of merchant: 'he who travels, he who stocks [and] he who exports'. Trade is carried on in one of three ways: 'cash sale with a time limit for delivery, purchase on credit with payment by installment, and *muqaradah*.'[25] In a *muqarada*, a small investor (let's call him Mahmoud) lends his money to a shipper, Hussein, who owns a swift *dhow* and voyages to Africa, India and China. In return, Hussein offers Mahmoud a share in the profits from Indian spices, African gold or Chinese silk. Mahmoud agrees to bear any losses Hussein will incur; Hussein escapes liability. Mahmoud risks the money, while Hussein trades on both their behalves, directs the voyage and risks his life as well as his labour. Both of their resources, however, are now pooled. If other merchants – Hassan, Ali, Faisal or Harun – wish to contribute capital to the

> The Arab Empire, laid claim to being the greatest consumer society that had yet existed, dwarfing even Rome

OTHERE THE VIKING AND THE BIRTH OF 'CO-OP' CAPITALISM

THE very mention of the word 'Viking' has for a thousand years conjured up an image of a ferocious and barbarous people sailing forth from the coasts of Norway, Denmark and Sweden to burn Europe's cities and cathedrals, plunder its treasures and carry off its people as slaves. Such a picture, while true enough, is incomplete, for scholars are now taking a new look at the Vikings as successful capitalists who may have done as much to revive Europe as to destroy it.

The records of King Alfred's court mention two Viking traders who lived in Halogaland in the far north of Norway. Othere was a herdsman who owned 600 reindeer, 20 cattle, 20 sheep and 20 pigs, and ploughed the sparse Norwegian soil with his team of horses. Much of his income came from the tribute he received from his Lapp neighbours. The rest came from trading in furs and the walrus tusks of the Arctic waters, which were a valuable source of ivory.

Othere's enterprise involved a lot of dangerous travel and risky resource seeking. Once, in search of walrus and furs, he sailed north along the Norwegian coast, rounding the North Cape and exploring the White Sea, making landfall near what is now Archangel. Most of Othere's voyages were to the south, where he would take his pelts and tusks down the Norwegian coast to the Danish emporium of Hederby or the Frisian emporium of Dorestad. Here Othere would meet traders from most of Frankish Europe. In return for his fish, furs and ivory Othere would bring home glassware and silver coins.

Othere would also journey clear across the North Sea to trade at the court of King Alfred in Wessex. His Swedish counterparts undertook voyages that were even more risky. From their own emporium at Birka, not far from the site of Stockholm, Swedish Vikings crossed the Baltic, setting up trading posts in Novgorod, near St Petersburg, and then heading overland to the Volga where they met the overland silk trade. From here they followed the Volga to the Caspian and eventually brought their furs and wares to the markets of the Caliphate. An alternative route led from the trading post of Smolensk down the Dneiper to Constantinople. In return, the Swedes brought back slaves, spices, silk, gold and silver as well as the other luxuries of the Orient coveted by winterbound Nordic chieftains.

Viking trade was risky. Many Swedes erected rune stones in memory of loved ones who had gone south seeking their fortunes, never to return. The traders

Siguid and Vitgeir fell in Novgorod, Assur in Byzantium, the sons of Rodvisl and Rödolf in Latvia and Romania. Harald died seeking silk on the Volga.

Those who made it safely to a foreign port invoked Wotan, Freya and Thor for commercial success. Upon arrival, the pre-Christian Viking trader would bring his meat offering to a resident temple and, bowing himself before wooden images of Norse deities, would offer the food. If business were bad, he would continue to bow in the hope it would get better. If business was good, he bowed in thanksgiving. Like the Arabs with whom they traded, the Vikings were pioneers in developing business partnerships and alliances among themselves. Their trade was so profitable that the kings of Denmark, Norway and Sweden taxed and regulated it quite heavily. In response, by 1000 the Viking traders had formed trade associations to reduce market risk. In one sense, these were the first Nordic co-ops. They grew out of tribal and religious communalism and ritual banquets. Remarkably egalitarian and democratic for their day, the Viking guilds operated by consensus and provided traders such as Othere with emotional and financial support on their long and perilous voyages. Viking merchants now often traded together under the umbrella of their guild. The associations also served an insurance function if one were shipwrecked or enslaved. They protected one another's goods and their agents dealt directly with various royal authorities.

The prosperous Nordic trading networks of the Dark Ages, stretching from England to Russia and even beyond, for a while, to China and even Iceland, Greenland and the New World, revived business enterprise in much of Northern Europe. Without it, the growth of towns and the monarchies of Scandinavia and even England would have taken much longer.

It is interesting that, even today, much of the European Union's revival after years of stagnation is being driven by Nordic firms like Nokia whose high-tech alliances and networks are joining Europe through telecommunications and m-commerce much as the Vikings did through trade. See Lund, N. ed. (1984) Two Voyages of The Court of King Alfred: The Venture of Othere and Wulfstan together with the description of Northern Europe from the Old English Orosius Yole, UK, William Sessions.

partnership, perhaps Hussein can charter a second ship and voyage all the way to China instead of merely to Sri Lanka.[26]

Private merchant adventurers formed the backbone of much Abbasid wealth and commerce. Public and private monopolies traded alongside these small partnerships, particularly in the weightier primary commodities of wheat, timber and iron. The participation of princes in commerce, however, was criticized in the *Muqqadimah*, written by Ibn Khaldun, one of history's first sociologists.[27] Though the investment climate for merchants in Iraq was better than that of China or India, market freedoms and property rights were far from absolute in Baghdad and the vicinity. Unlike the feudal traders of Europe, where more localized governments were limited in their economic impact, Muslim merchants could find their businesses expropriated by a revenue-hungry Caliph.

The tax farmers of Baghdad and beyond were as powerful and unscrupulous as those of ancient Rome. Some became well known and feared plenipotentiaries, not unlike the Inland Revenue and IRS today. Ali bin Ahmad ar-Rasibi ruled the Gulf shore of Iraq and Khuzistan; Hamid al-Abbas held sway in northern Iraq before becoming vizier. The Baridis of Basra became governors and generals. Becoming a Muslim tax farmer was so costly that only wealthy merchants could afford to buy the office. A contract to be able to levy taxes on one or more provinces cost anywhere from 200 000 to 700 000 *dinars*. The rich Persian areas of Fars and Kirman sold for 10 million. Once they were in control, the tax farmers could, and often did, plunder the peasantry almost at will. They themselves, however, in spite of the astronomical profits they reaped, could be subject to the ravages of the *musadara* (forced public contribution) at any time. Rough justice prevailed. The estates of Hamid, worth over 2 million *dinars*, were seized in 923. Ten years later the Caliphate extorted 12 million from the Baridis.

Often, social unrest would take what the taxman did not. Southern Iraq and western Iran were filled with thousands of East African slaves toiling at bare subsistence level. In 869 they revolted against their masters, starting a civil war lasting 14 years. The revolt was concentrated in the port cities of the Gulf, where it wreaked havoc on overseas commerce. It took the entire Caliphate to crush the revolt, and the Caliphate would never be the same. The Golden Age of Harun al-Rashid was over. Iran, Syria and Egypt set up independent regimes. The Caliphs of the late 9th and early 10th centuries spent lavishly on new palaces and even a new capital, Samarra, not far from Baghdad. The treasury was bankrupt and the tax farmers levied ever-tighter exactions on an ever-shrinking revenue base. In the 11th century the Seljuk Turks invaded the Near East. Baghdad, while still prosperous, was a shadow of its 9th-century glory. Iraq's decline worsened after 1258 when the Mongols overran what had once been the heartland of the Abbasids. Gulf ports such as Qais (Kish) and Hormuz were, however, still flourishing and attempted to capture some of the trade still flowing through Siraf.[28]

Faith-based partnerships: the Fatimids

'The Moving Finger writes, and having writ moves on' was part of Arab wisdom literature. True to type, beginning in the 10th century the centre of the Muslim economy began shifting to Egypt, which now controlled the sea routes to India and China.[29] In 969 revolutionaries of the Ismaili sect known as the Fatimids seized power in Egypt and Syria. The Fatimids claimed descent from Fatima, the daughter of Muhammad and thus won the support of the Shiites, the largest dissenting sect in Islam. The Shiites believed that only lineal descendants of the Prophet could rule over Muslims and they were eager to turn against the Abbasids. Perhaps surprisingly, Jews and Christian Copts would occupy important positions in a tolerant Fatimid administration more market-oriented even than that of the Abbasids. Fatimid Egypt boasted minimal government regulation of industry and trade and a hard gold currency. Merchants based in the new Arabian power bases of Egypt and Syria could become profitable middlemen between the gold miners of Africa, the spice traders of India and the eager customers venturing forth from such up-and-coming port towns as Amalfi, near Naples. We know about Fatimid-era commerce thanks to hundreds of business records and letters preserved from Cairo. While the authors of these documents were Jews, their business culture was very similar to that of the Muslims.

The archives show a partnership economy resting on familial and religious ties. Sometimes these ties were strained. A letter from one Ibn al-Siqillî in Tunisia to Joseph ben Jacob Ibn 'Awkal in Fustat, Egypt, shows these ties being strained. Both are importing gems, flax, sugar, textiles, spices and woods from India and the Far East as well as silver from Spain and gold from Africa. Siqillî is angry with Joseph, who accused him of pocketing some of the latter's earnings.[30] Though he has not yet received anything from the silk they were planning to sell, the Tunisian will send Joseph 75 of his own *dinars* to protect his own reputation: 'I acted thus because of my esteem for you and because of your illustrious position, your noble character, and piety. All I ask is that you act with respect to my goods sent to you in the same manner as I acted with your goods sent to me.'[31]

Much Fatimid-era trade was in the hands of great family partnerships with numerous connections. Two of these were the Tustarîs and the Tâhertîs, who dealt in robes and other luxury clothing. Their correspondence shows that not only family ties but factors of religious trust entered into deals among Jews and between Jews and Muslims as well. Mûsa, the patriarch of the Tâhertîs writing to Abû Sahl, the patriarch of the Tustarîs, urges him to send the family merchandise on a trustworthy Arab camel-caravan between Tunisia and Egypt.

The courtliness and civility of the Fatimid dynasty, whose adherents and trading regime stretched from Morocco to the Red Sea, represent a high-water mark for mercantile capitalism. Ideally, capitalism has been seen by its defenders and formulators as a system of voluntary human relationships: one in which people exchange within a legal framework that prohibits force, fraud, theft and extortion. The Fatimid documents reflect some of these high ethical standards and in some ways show the Arab ascendancy in world affairs at its best. Success in commerce paved the way for Arab-based revivals of learning and philosophy. The gentle pessimism and soft poignancy of their best writings reveal a culture that took time from pressing business affairs to reach occasionally the sublime. The *Rubaiyat of Omar Khayyam* still speaks to us today:

> *We are no other than a moving row*
> *Of Magic Shadow-shapes that come and go*
> *Round with the Sun-illumined Lantern held*
> *In Midnight by the Master of the Show.*

The world economy seldom pauses long for poetry. The Fatimid caliphs also controlled the holy city of Jerusalem, theological storm-centre for three great religions – Judaism, Christianity and Islam. As Christian Europe began to flex its muscles at the beginning of the second millennium, the clash between Arab culture and rising Western military power would come, when it came, in the form of the First Crusade (1095).

Europe stirs

Richard the Lionheart. Godfrey of Bouillon. Frederick Barbarossa. These paladins of the Third Crusade in 1189 have left names that ring in history. They offer evidence that by the 1100s, and well before that, the heart of Western Europe, that great stretch of fertile land running from Rome to London and from Bremen to Venice, had survived the collapse of Roman civilization. Indeed, economic life had never died out in the turbulent period after the barbarian invasions of the 500s. Commerce would never completely falter even in the Dark Ages. Roman prosperity vanished in the 5th century, but some trade continued to pass through southern France. Through rich and thriving ports such as Marseilles, Narbonne and Arles, the economy of late antiquity carried on into the 7th century. Merchant ships brought Egyptian grain to Britain and tin to Egypt. When Justinian (527–565) reconquered North Africa, Italy and parts of Spain, this turn to commerce was strengthened. Local shops and warehouses clustered even more around Marseilles and independent traders carried goods to and from the hinterland. Most trade in this period, though, took place on a very small scale and over very short distances. The chief customers for the wheat, wine, oil, dates, spices and silk that streamed in from the Near East were the clergy. It was the monasteries that were to stir the embers of capitalism and prevent them from flickering out. What was happening?

The Church was the recipient of rich benefices and estates during the perilous times of the invasions and beyond. Those estates needed tending. Stewardship, after all, was a biblical virtue. Monasteries such as that of St Denis in the northern suburbs of Paris ran barges and trading caravans to branch warehouses in Aachen, Lyons and several other Frankish cities. Being a trader was not easy in Merovingian France (500–700). Brigands made the old Roman roads so dangerous that peddlers took to the back routes. They travelled in groups, stayed in monasteries-cum-motels and carried cash in bags around their necks for safe keeping.

Conditions worsened under the Carolingian rulers of France (emerging around 700) until the time of Charlemagne (771–814). These were distressing times. Towns and commerce shrank in France to the point where grass grew in the streets of Marseilles. The Church, however, addicted to the holiness of beauty, provided a thriving market for glass-makers, smiths and other talented artisans. The emerging feudal manor systems, fully sovereign by the late 9th century, were self-sufficient economic units. Originally organized out of military necessity in a time of civil wars and rivalries following the Carolingian collapse, the feudal system proved its worth against invading Muslims, Magyars and Danes in the 800s.

These stormy times helped coalesce Europe's characteristic social and economic model in the Dark Ages – the feudal system. Its name taken from the late Latin word *feudum*, 'fief', the lord–vassal relationship was the glue that held large sections of Western Europe together. The feudal system has had a bad press but in many ways it helped Europe get back on its feet after the Roman collapse. The Church was often there to arbitrate. A letter from Bishop Fulbert of Chartres to Duke William of Aquitaine, dated 1020, counselled the noble duke: 'The lord also ought to act towards his faithful vassal reciprocally in all these things. And if he does not do this he will justly be considered guilty of bad faith.' Thus, in a world that took the words 'Six days shalt thou labour' most seriously, the foundations were being laid for medieval prosperity. Armour was fashioned, swords were made, wool was raised, sheared and woven on the manors, peasants made shoes, cured meats and forged tools and utensils.[32] Soon there was a surplus, and where there is a surplus there is trade.

The trading networks of the Dark Ages became more regularized around 650. The conversion of the early Anglo-Saxon kingdoms put them into a trading network with the Merovingian rulers of France. Kentishmen in southern England traded luxuries with France while East Anglians traded with the Germans. Trading fairs were organized on the outskirts of Paris, along the Channel coast and in the Saxon kingdom of Wessex.[33] Coin discoveries at these sites show short-lived but important revivals in trading activity on both sides of the Channel. After 750 the order and stability provided by Charlemagne's military conquests helped trade even more.[34] Markets existed enough to be noticed but were still confined to fairs and a few commercial settlements organized and planned by the patrons and rulers.[35] London and Ipswich in England, Hamwih, Haithabu and Kaupang in Norway, and Löddeköpinge, Västergarn and Birka in Sweden sprouted as trading centres in sheltered inlets where boats could land easily.[36] Dorestad in the Netherlands was the chief commercial centre on the Rhine. Archaeologists excavating there uncovered a hoard of approximately two hundred gold coins, two-thirds of which date from the time of Charlemagne. Charlemagne, from his capital at Aachen, was bent on a full-scale revival of the Roman system. His officials, called *missi dominici*, tried to unite Europe and revive its trade in the absence of a strong bureaucracy.[37]

As early as the 9th century Rhenish and Anglo-Saxon capitalisms, both in their infancy, began to diverge. Charlemagne deliberately concentrated craft industries in Bonn, Cologne, Trier, Mainz, Frankfurt and Strasbourg, pioneering a tradition of state-directed enterprise that endures to this day.[38] The reviving markets of Saxon England encouraged merchants to locate on their own initiative. Around the 970s the first tier of English markets enjoyed a commercial take-off. York, Thetford, Lincoln, Norwich, Oxford and, of course, London, saw new wharves, shops, streets and other signs of real business activity. Pottery was among the first goods these towns bought, sold and traded. Potters spread from the major centres to secondary ones soon after 1000. Villages that had only farmland and monasteries became market towns.[39]

Thus a fledgling English free-market capitalism took root in the Saxon twilight of the 900s and 1000s. Markets flourish best where stable government provides the framework to do business. Under King Alfred the Great (871–901) and his successors, the internal market became more pervasive in England than in any other country.[40] Figures show that tribute paid to the Danes was £10 000 in 991. By 1018 it was £72 000 plus £10 000 from London, showing an eightfold growth in prosperity.[41]

> As early as the 9th century Rhenish and Anglo-Saxon capitalisms, both in their infancy, began to diverge. Charlemagne deliberately concentrated craft industries in Bonn, Cologne, Trier, Mainz, Frankfurt and Strasbourg, pioneering a tradition of state-directed enterprise that endures to this day. The reviving markets of Saxon England encouraged merchants to locate on their own initiative

By the late 10th and early 11th centuries the market economy would be a firm reality in England and on the Continent, especially in Italy and in Flanders. The concentration of coinage in fewer hands in Europe than among the Arabs tended to hinder market operations, though not to prevent very real economic growth. Slowly at first, Western Europe began to enter a *medieval* as opposed to a Dark Age economy. In the medieval period, business organization would become more sophisticated and world trade would again be a potent factor.

China's market revolution(1): the Tang Empire

The new world trading regime that was slowly emerging, dominated by the Muslims of Iraq and then of Egypt, increasingly centred on China. The histories of Europe and China present a curious parallel. While the consuls and Caesars had forged the imperial unity of Rome, the first true emperors of China, beginning with the despotic Qin and the more pro-business Han Dynasty, unified the Middle Kingdom, as the Chinese called their land, and initiated trade across the Silk Road with India, Parthian Iran and the Roman West. The collapse of Rome in the West was paralleled by the break-up of Han China in the East around the same time.[42]

By the 7th century, the Sui Dynasty reunited China after several centuries of division. Economic unification soon followed the political reorganization. Rising fortunes were epitomized in one of the greatest engineering feats of all time – the Grand Canal. The Grand Canal, constructed by thousands of labourers, joined the Yellow River and the Yangzi (Yangtse) in a single market. Goods and people could now travel between the north of China and the more tropical and relatively undeveloped south. The single Chinese market spurred the growth of all kinds of petty enterprises, and some not so petty, within China. The Tang Emperors (618–907) allowed merchants freedom to trade anywhere, not just in the wards of the cities where they resided. The very countryside of China itself was transformed. Family businesses spread across the land. Thousands of peasants in the Yangzi valley and elsewhere freed themselves from serfdom and became commercial traders and investors. Villages became markets and self-sufficient subsistence farms joined trading networks. By the year 900 the Lower Yangzi swarmed with new trading cities, commercial towns and rural markets. The transformation of China did not stop there. The fertile Yangzi was soon so crowded that those seeking farmland, markets and jobs moved even further to the south.

Under the Tang the south became China's new frontier. Few think of the Chinese as a pioneering people in the way we do of Americans, Canadians or Australians. For 3000 years, the northern plains around the Yellow River had been the heartland of Chinese civilization and settlement. The mountainous and jungle-covered regions of the south were still populated largely by native ethnic groups who were non-Chinese, the Chinese themselves preferring to remain settled on the richer river valleys to the north. The new market economy changed all that. Under the Tang the southern territories of the Chinese mainland absorbed one of the greatest mass migrations in history.[43]

The Tang were great patrons of the arts and education. The first printed book appeared in China in 868. China was leading the world in the civilized arts as the market revolution proceeded apace. A census from 606 CE showed that 23 per cent of Chinese households lived in the south and 77 per cent in the north, presumably north of the Yangzi. By 742 the population in the south had doubled to 43 per cent. The whole centre of gravity of Chinese civilization shifted. Regions such as Zhijiang (Chekiang), Fujian (Fukien) and Guangdong (Kwangtung), which included the present site of Hong Kong, grew enormously. The migration accelerated even more in late Tang times (i.e. the 9th century). Eventually 65 per cent of Chinese lived south of the Yangzi and the frontier of migration lay near the present Hong Kong and the Vietnamese border.[44]

The colonization of the Yangzi and south-east coast, where mineral resources were found in abundance, was profound. Together with the agricultural revolution and population growth, China's rulers vastly enlarged the scope of potential economic interchange. The growing productivity in the new southern regions stimulated demand, created an agricultural surplus and augmented the accumulation of both savings and capital. The market revolution was encouraged by other factors as well. The Empire loosened the restriction that each county could have only one market, located in its capital city. The official marketing organizations soon began to break down. Within towns, the old enclosed marketplace and walled barriers between wards gave way to a free market within the city and its suburbs. Commercial suburbs sprang up outside the gates of the old cities, while new market towns dotted the peasant countryside.[45]

In a curious symmetry, the centres of ancient civilization and the business cultures they fostered had fallen together and were getting ready to rise again. While energetic Muslim merchants held the balance of world trade, Europe grew in stability under rulers such as Charlemagne and Alfred the Great, and China's emerging market economy prospered as never before. The Dark Ages had become the seedbed of a medieval trading nexus that eventually would link the Old World in a dynamic and symbiotic international system.

NOTES TO CHAPTER 9

1. For a discussion of international business in these times, see Moore, K. and Lewis, D. (1999) *Birth of the Multinational: 2000 Years of Ancient Business History*. Copenhagen Business School Press.

2. Labib, S.Y. 'Capitalism in Medieval Islam', *Journal of Economic History*, Vol. XXIX. No. 1 (March 1969), 79–96.

3. *The Holy Book of Islam, Surat al-Nisa*, verse 29, in Labib, S.Y., *ibid*.

4. Roberts, J.M. (1993) *History of the World*. New York: Oxford University Press, 264–7.

5. Abu-Lughod, J.L. (1989) *Before European Hegemony: The World System AD 1250–1350*. New York: Oxford University Press, 217.

6. Tabari, in 923, quoted by Hourani, G. in Hodges, R. and Whitehouse, D. (1983) *Mohammed, Charlemagne and the Origins of Europe*. Ithaca, NY: Cornell University Press, 127.

7. 'The Story of Es-Sindibad of the Sea and Es-Sindibad of the Land', tr. by Lane, E.W., revised by Poole, S.L. in Eliot, C.W., ed. (1969) *The Harvard Classics: Stories from the Thousand and One Nights*. New York: P.F. Collier & Son, 235.

8. *Ibid.*, 239.

9. *Ibid.*, 261.

10. *Ibid.*, 273.

11. *Ibid.*, 292–5.

12. Hodges, R. and Whitehouse, D. (1983) *Mohammed, Charlemagne and the Origins of Europe*. Ithaca, NY: Cornell University Press, 132–41.

13. *Ibid.*, 146–7.

14. Abu-Lughod, J.L. (1989) *Before European Hegemony: The World System AD 1250–1350*. New York: Oxford University Press, 208.

15. Ashtor, E. (1976) *A Social and Economic History of the Near East in the Middle Ages*. Berkeley, CA: University of California Press, 77.

16. *Ibid.*, 76–8.

17. Yo K'o, 'The Arabs in Canton', *Ch'eng Shih* [History of the Ch'eng], roll 11, Li, Elements, Document 135, 323–5, 323–4.

18. The output of rich gold mines untapped by the Romans became 'one of the most important factors in the Moslem empire's economy'. Ashtor, E. (1976) *A Social and Economic History of the Near East in the Middle Ages*. Berkeley, CA: University of California Press, 80.

19. *Ibid.*, 80–1.

20. Ashtor, E. (1976) *A Social and Economic History of the Near East in the Middle Ages*. Berkeley, CA: University of California Press, 80–1, 85–6.

21. *Ibid.*, 100–1.

22. *Ibid.*, 101.

23. El-Mallakh, R. and D. 'Trade and Commerce' in Hayes, J.R., ed. (1983) *The Genius of Arab Civilization: Sources of Renaissance*. Cambridge, MA: MIT Press, 225, 227.

24. *Ibid.*, 229–30.

25. Al-Dimashqi quoted *ibid.*, 231. The boom of the 8th and early 9th centuries inspired the growth of a distinctively Muslim business class that pioneered in the realm of finance as well as production. Credit businesses were very active in the Abbasid realm during the 800s. While Frankish rulers struggled to resuscitate something resembling the old Roman monetary economy in the depths of Europe's Dark Age, the Arabs of Baghdad were taking the first steps to modern financing.

26. *Ibid.*

27. Ashtor, E. (1976) *A Social and Economic History of the Near East in the Middle Ages*. Berkeley, CA: University of California Press, 114.

28. *Ibid.*

29. Abu-Lughod, J.L. (1989) *Before European Hegemony: The World System AD 1250–1350*. New York: Oxford University Press, 213.

30. Goitein, S.G. (1973) 'An Angry Letter from Qayrawân' (ed. and tr.) in *Letters of Medieval Jewish Traders*. Princeton: Princeton University Press, Document 1, 29.

31. *Ibid.*, 31.

32. Thompson, J.W. (1966) *Economic and Social History of the Middle Ages*. New York: Frederick Ungar, Volume I, 209–17, 220–1, 228–9; Lebecq, S. 'Routes of Change: Production and Distribution in the West (5th–8th Century)'; Webster, L. and Brown, M. (1997) *The Transformation of the Roman World AD 400–900*. London: British Museum Press, 67–78.

33. Hodges, R. (1982) *Dark Age Economics: The Origins of Towns and Trade, AD 600–1000*. New York: St Martin's Press, 31–6, 41–4.

34. *Ibid.*, 44–6. The 9th century will witness the virtual demise of these two trading systems and emergence of vigorous regional trade.

35. *Ibid.*, 49–51.

36. *Ibid.*, 49–53.

37. *Ibid.*, 39–41.

38. *Ibid.*, 176.

39. *Ibid.*, 165–72.

40. *Ibid.*, 177–8.

41. *Ibid.*, 179.

42. *Ibid.*,184–5.

43. Shiba, Y. 'Urbanization and the Development of Markets in the Lower Yangtze Valley' in Winthrop Haeger, J., ed. (1975) *Crisis and Prosperity in Sung China*. Tucson, AZ: University of Arizona Press, 13–16.

44. *Ibid.*, 16–19.

45. Shiba, Y. 'Sung Foreign Trade: Its Scope and Organization' in Rossabii, M., ed. (1983) *China Among Equals: The Middle Kingdom and its Neighbors, 10th–14th Centuries*. Berkeley, CA: University of California Press, 89–115, 89–90.

10

Merchants of Venice, Inc.

Europe's road to the multinational: 1000–1450

EGINNING around 1000 CE, Europe was on the verge of revival. The steady rise in population and growth in new farming techniques acted as a stimulus to trade and innovation. An emerging continental economy encompassed the northern tier of states.

The European Middle Ages from 1000 to 1300 were not stagnant, morbid and backward, but far more dynamic than any period that had preceded them. The forests and swamps of the Dark Ages disappeared, population exploded, towns and universities sprang up, and water and wind were harnessed to power the first 'industrial revolution'. Serfs became peasant entrepreneurs. Markets replaced domestic production. Cottage industries gave way to factories. Faith- and family-based partnerships became sophisticated multinational business organizations.

This 'new' economy was driven by interconnected transformations north and south. Italy nurtured a revolution in trade and business organization; Flanders, with its rich soil and abundant waterways, spearheaded a manufacturing revolution in textiles that transformed the region from Paris to the Rhine into the perfect Italian market. Europe again became a productive force in an expanding medieval world economy before 1300. Though Europe's boom collapsed in the mid-1300s, the recession that followed led to innovations in management that would prepare the continent for its rise to global dominance.[1]

Faith-based partnerships:
Italy's crusader capitalism

During the 11th century Genoa, Venice and Pisa became the centres of a growing shipbuilding industry. The dragon-prow galleys constructed in busy Italian ports and financed by rich landowners frequented the Muslim shores of the Maghreb, much to papal chagrin. Venetians sailed into the Adriatic and the Aegean, and to Constantinople and the Levant. Italian galleys carried timber, iron and grain to exchange for the spices of the East.[2] The coming of the First Crusade, in which Jerusalem was captured by the armies of Europe in 1099, intensified this trade enormously. The Italian cities were the middleman for the wars of God.

By mobilising popular armies against the Infidel, Pope Urban II and his successors hoped to enhance their power and prestige against the German emperors. Knights, barons and peasants sought opportunities for free land, booty or remission from debt if they went on crusade. The Church promised it! Italy's sailors and merchants, who supplied the provisions and the naval power, looked on and set out to reap enormous profits in this medieval war economy.[3]

Genoa set up colonies in Jerusalem, Jaffa, Arsuf, Caesaria, Acre and the vicinity of Beirut.[4] Acre, on the shores of Palestine, was typical of such settlements. It was a self-contained community of warehouses, wooden dwellings, customs houses, churches, orchards and plantations. The familial element of Italian enterprises was much in evidence, with many of the agents in Constantinople and elsewhere being sons of Italian merchants. Marketing the family's goods abroad, they gained knowledge of Asian markets and experience in managing cargoes, and stepped into executive positions managing operations in Syria or Egypt. Italian merchants brought their wool, hemp, linen, iron and pitch to the customs house, buying silk, porcelain, ivory, spices, incense and other goods from an Asian trading imperium that stretched from Tyre to Canton. If their own goods did not cover the cost, they paid in Italian gold and German silver. The Genoese penchant was to act as intercontinental middlemen. Once in the spring and once in the late summer, the fleet left Genoa for Acre, stopping in Sicily, Crete, Rhodes and Cyprus.[5]

These Italian traders revived and modified Roman and Arab institutions of the partnership. The Genoese *commenda* and the Venetian *collegantia* closely resembled the Muslim *muqarada*. In an age where hierarchies were weak and trust limited, family and faith cemented business relationships among Christians, Jews and Muslims. Some merchants put up money; others made the voyages; profits were divided by agreement. A typical agreement was that made in August 1073 between the Venetians Giovanni Lissado and Sevasto Orefice. Sevasto and his heirs invested their money in partnership with Giovanni, who would sail for the silk markets of Greece:

> 'I, Giovanni Lissado of Luprio, together with my heirs, have received in collegantia from you, Sevasto Orefice, son of Ser Trudimondo, and from your heirs, this amount: £200 Venetian. And I myself have invested £100 in it.'[6]

Investing part of the partnership's capital in the vessel of one Gosmiro da Molino, Giovanni promised to garner the best return on Sevasto's money and all profits would be reinvested in the partnership. Contracts such as these usually listed the goods to be sold, but were often hazy on the destination. This was to allow the travelling partner much freedom of action, although the stay-at-home partner could recall him at any time. If goods were lost, each partner would bear the burden individually. The partnership was to be temporary, so long as both desired it:

> 'And with this capital we have acquired two shares in the ship of which Gosmiro da Molino is captain. And I am under obligation to bring all of this with me in taxegio to Thebes in the ship in which the aforesaid Gosmiro da Molino sails as captain. Indeed, by this agreement and understanding of ours I promise to put to work this entire capital and to strive the best way I can. Then, if the capital is saved, we are to divide whatever profit the Lord may grant us from it by exact halves, without fraud and evil device. And whatever I can gain with those goods from any source, I am under obligation to invest all of it in the collegantia. And if all these goods are lost because of the sea or of hostile people, and this is proved – may this be averted – neither party ought to ask any of them from the other; if, however, some of them remain, in proportion as we invested so shall we share. Let this collegantia exist between us so long as our wills are fully agreed.'[7]

The familial nature of the collegantia was fundamental. Extended family are brought in to guarantee any breach of the contract:

'But if I do not observe everything just as is stated above, I, together
with my heirs, then promise to give and to return to you and your
heirs everything in the double, both capital and profit, out of my
land and my house or out of anything that I am known to have in
this world.'[8]

Medieval partnerships such as these counted on religious and family
ties to guarantee agreement. Many such agreements were drawn up and
notarized by the parish priest: 'I, Domenico, cleric and notary, compiled
and certified this instrument.'[9]

One of the first prominent 12th-century Italian family partnerships was
that headed by the Genoese Guglielmo Embriaco. The Embriaci operated
two galleys supplying the armies besieging Jerusalem. Guglielmo was
given command of 30 ships and 8000 soldiers, with which he captured
a Muslim fortress, dividing the money and spices among his soldiers and
sailors. The business endured for three generations, until the Holy Land
fell to the Muslims. Nevertheless, Guglielmo's grandson became landlord
for the entire Genoese quarter of Acre.[10] Genoese partners faced ruthless
competition from their Venetian rivals. Venice had an advantage over
Genoa both in its geographic position and in its historic trading
relationship with Byzantium, which allowed Venetian partners most-
favoured-nation status in the form of reduced tolls.

European Tyre: the merchants of Venice

Venice itself fared much better. A leading (duke or ruler), doge Sebastiano
Ziani, was a wealthy patrician publican whose son Pietro had vast
holdings of farms, shops and mills in both Venice and Constantinople.
The Zianis played a major role in both Venetian and world politics, finan-
cially backing the Pope against the claims of the German Emperor
Frederick Barbarossa. All this strengthened the power of the Venetian
mercantile establishment. While Milan, Florence and other Italian cities
embraced more popular government, Venice would continue to be ruled
by an entrenched and autocratic oligarchy resembling that of Carthage,
Byblos and Tyre. Most importantly, Venice under Pietro Ziani, now doge,
became master of the Aegean and even Byzantium itself, after a naval
coup in 1204 that helped install a Latin pretender on the throne in

Constantinople. Venetian partners then expanded into the Black Sea just as the ancient Greeks had done.

Venice, like Tyre, was an island city having no fresh water, food or agricultural resources. Venetians, even more than Genoese, had to develop trade to survive. Like the Phoenician city-states, the Italian city-states 'gradually inserted themselves into the spaces between the dominant economies'.[11] Crusader Venice dominated the Aegean market, especially after 1204 when the Fourth Crusade installed a Latin emperor on the throne of Byzantium. Venice expanded her trading zone into the Black Sea region, where her merchants linked up with the traders of Genghis Khan's Mongol heirs. Italians imported silk, porcelain and Asian spices on an overland route not dominated by Muslims. Venetian policies of naval capitalism would have been familiar to the merchants of Tyre – expanding the fleet, defeating maritime rivals and planting trading posts:

> '*Venice ... would have to expand her merchant fleet and her navy, and turn her Arsenal, under construction from 1104, into an unrivalled power-house ... overcoming or by-passing competition [to] forge her own fiscal, financial, monetary, administrative and political institutions.*'[12]

Water, wind and horsepower: medieval Europe's 'industrial revolution'

Meanwhile, north-western Europe was changing from a world of Dark Age subsistence to one of cities, markets, mining, construction and textiles. With the adoption of the three-field system (one third sown with winter wheat; one third for spring harvesting; one third lying fallow) agriculture itself became more productive. A key factor in northern Europe's transformation was the harnessing of waterpower to create the first economy free from total dependence on muscle.[13] One Cistercian monk wrote: 'How many horses would be worn out, how many men would have weary arms if this graceful river, to whom we owe our clothes and food, did not labour for us.'[14]

The growth of monasteries along the streams of England, France and Burgundy from about 900 on provoked the spread of water mills, so that by 1100 north-western Europe was covered with mills. William the

Conqueror in 1086 counted 1 for every 50 English households. Each mill was run with two to five partners, bringing substantial returns that helped nourish the germinating seeds of capital gain. The importing of gear and camshaft technology from China let mills in northern Italy mechanise paper production. Cloth in Flanders no longer had to be painstakingly scoured by hand in rural homes but was woven in urban factories. In Paris, in a veritable industrial quarter, mills operated along the bank of the Seine near the Isle of Notre-Dame.[15]

The watermill tended to enhance the monopoly power of the miller, a feudal lord who forced peasants to use it at their own expense. The unscrupulous practices of millers was satirized in *The Canterbury Tales* of Geoffrey Chaucer:

> *Large tolls this miller took, beyond a doubt,*
> *with wheat and malt from all the lands about ...*
>
> *Whereon this miller stole both flour and wheat*
> *a hundredfold more than he used to cheat ...*[16]

Along with the watermill came the windmill, a portable year-round energy source (winds blew everywhere on the northern European plain). Their monopoly thereby threatened, lords used the political power of the state to enforce it. Jocelin of Brakelond describes how, in 13th-century England, Walter the Dean built his own corn mill, asserting that 'free benefit of the wind ought not to be denied to any man.' The Abbot Samson, however, tore the Dean's windmill down, seeing the threat market competition posed to his power. Merchants, he knew 'will throng to your mill and grind their corn to their hearts' content, nor shall I have the right to punish them, since they are free men.'[17] Free enterprise and private liberty were hereafter to be linked in Europe's history.

The Chinese horse-collar and shoulder-harness, imported to Europe and first applied in Carolingian times, did for farming what water and wind did for industry. The new harnesses fitted around a horse's shoulder and allowed it to pull carts and heavy ploughs of up to 5000 kilograms without choking the horse like the old Roman neck-harnesses. The horse could now become the tractor of the Middle Ages and they replaced oxen in northern Europe between 1000 and 1200, being 50 per cent faster and 30 per cent stronger.

The coming of horses and a warmer climate helped Europe adopt the three-field system of agriculture. A Frankish peasant of the 600s grew wheat on a two-field system, planting one field one year and leaving the other fallow, facing the very real threat of crop failure and starvation in a cold spell. The French peasant of the 1100s could rotate three fields on a larger plot of land, letting one lie fallow each year, planting winter wheat on the second, and spring oats on the third. He was in less danger of starving if his winter crop failed. He could afford a horse and perhaps, eventually, his freedom.[18]

Sheep were a more versatile investment. They did more for England's prosperity than anything else. They produced cheese, mutton, parchments and, most importantly, wool. English shepherds could reap 100 per cent profit given the insatiable demand in the new textile industries in Flanders and Italy. Cistercian monks, spreading throughout Western Europe from their Burgundian abbey of Cîteaux, turned shepherding into a multinational enterprise. These ascetic monks insisted on living in the wilderness by the labour of their own hands and turned to sheep-raising as the one activity most in line with their strict calling. Like the 'temple capitalism' of the ancient Near East, the transnational Cistercian network was very centralized. This network helped spread new mill techniques and ploughshares across the continent. English Cistercians dealt in wool, the French, Burgundian and German in wine. As the monasteries grew in number, the demand for wine used in Communion encouraged the planting of vineyards on lands once used to grow grain. Soon the vineyards of Cîteaux in Burgundy and Eberbach in Germany were exporting Clos-Vougeot and other wines to a general European market now able to afford and appreciate them.[19]

Able to feed more mouths, Europe grew from 42 million in the year 1000 to 70 million in 1300. England tripled in population, while France constituted a third of Europe's 70 million souls. Slavery vanished and feudal war declined, its energies directed outward in the Crusades. Besides textiles, mining and iron-production boomed so much that we could speak of a Medieval Iron Age, where iron completely replaced bronze for the first time. Without iron, knights and archers could not fight, horses could not be shod, waterpower machinery could not be made and stone could not be quarried. The convergence was dynamic and it sped the rise of talented artisans in the metal industry. Iron horseshoes and nails were often made by the thousands from raw iron imported from Spain, Normandy or Sweden. The new watermills, themselves crafted of iron, ran the hammers, bellows and intricate gears of the foundries. Beginning around 1250, the Cistercians, led by the abbey of Clairvaux, perfected Europe's first blast furnaces. This new molten-iron technology soon spread across eastern France.[20]

The cathedral- and castle-building boom of the 1100s and 1200s created a new labour-intensive construction industry. More stone was mined in France alone than in all of ancient Egypt! The Norman conquest of England added a new market for stone exporters while the French alone built 80 cathedrals, 500 large churches and 10 000 smaller churches. Blocks of Norman stone were shipped across the Channel by barge and then carted to Westminster Abbey, Norwich Cathedral and countless castles and town walls. With towns expanding, barons replacing wooden castles with stone, and popes and kings wishing to show their religious devotion, there would be no shortage of demand for brick, wood, stone or construction labour. The 12th-century revival of art and culture rested on a solid foundation![21]

Iron anchored the industry of the new Europe; silver secured its money supply. In the late 10th century, the first European lodes were uncovered in the Harz Mountains and in Saxony. Prospectors flocked into Germany, Bohemia, Austria and Italy to find more lodes. As in ancient Rome, the mines were sometimes owned outright by officialdom – the Holy Roman Emperors – and sometimes privately run. They were, though, underfinanced, and state ownership, control and royalties hindered entrepreneurs.

> The Age of Faith was also the Age of Fleece and Foundries

Mining itself was done in open pits or shafts until water- and horsepower drove pumps to drain the mines. Bellows and hammers also smelted silver and crushed stone. The silver discoveries of the late 12th and early 13th centuries allowed medieval Europe to continue to trade with the Near and Far East, import spices and other luxuries and finance its economic expansion well into the 14th century.[22] The Age of Faith was also the Age of Fleece and Foundries.

New opportunities expanded for transport workers. Thousands of independent owners made and drove carts and boats, charging by the load to ship grain or wine. Textiles still moved in caravans made costly by the upkeep of horses, the threat of brigands and tolls. Even when waterways did exist, transportation costs could be horrendous. English wool bound for Italy had to pay English customs, ship fees on the Atlantic and Mediterranean, and innkeeper, cartage and toll fees in France and

Italy. Private innkeepers, or *osti*, played a similar role to those in China, though more independent of state control: lodging and feeding charters, forwarding shipments, paying tolls and negotiating with princes.[23]

Shipping and shipbuilding industries operated on a large scale in terms of organization and operating capital. Like the Greeks and Romans, medieval shipbuilders worked on a contractual basis much more subject to forces of supply and demand than the building industry. Cathedrals were for worship, castles for defence, but cost-effective factors like speed, capacity and durability were more important in ships designed for turning fast profits. Shipbuilders along the northern coasts built their bulky round cogs in small yards on beaches near seaports. Even affluent Venice left shipbuilding to the private sector until the 1300s.

Italian shipbuilding was a heavy investment-oriented business, fuelled on the demand created by the Crusades. Genoese shipbuilders issued shares letting individuals eventually buy their own ships as owners or partners. Governments often became contractors as in Athenian and Roman times, and with the same cost-overruns we have today. Louis IX of France paid £7000 Genoese for vessels worth £2000 to Genoese shippers. The meticulous Genoese contracts, drawn up by accountants who recorded weights and values of the goods and receipts, levied no charges on small shipments if return cargoes were guaranteed. Ships on short voyages sailed alone, those on longer voyages in Phoenician-style convoys and, like the Phoenicians, according to intricate timetables.[24]

Accounting comes of age: the Italian multinational

By 1200 Italy's merchants were Europe's financiers and middlemen to the world. The southern commercial tier led by Venice, Genoa, Pisa, Milan, Florence and Barcelona met the northern industrial sphere of Bruges, Ghent, London, Paris and Lübeck. Some of these magnates created their own market spheres encompassing the North and Baltic Seas at the famous fairs of Champagne. By the 1100s the fairs, sponsored and regulated by the Counts of Champagne, were a premier business institution in Europe. Merchants from Flanders and Artois loaded their woollen cloth into horse-drawn wagons, while Florentines loaded the spices of the Orient on to their mule trains. These armed convoys braved snow, mountains, brigands and rivers in order to cross the Alpine passes along old Roman roads and reach the market towns of Champagne. Numerous centres along the way began to prosper as ferrymen, innkeepers and bridge builders took advantage of the growing volume of traffic.

These fairs were not merely annual events but operated year-round in six different locations in eastern France, including Paris and Troyes. Each lasted six or seven weeks. Jugglers, acrobats and troubadours entertained onlookers while traders from north and south arrived on donkey or horseback and settled in for the excitement that was there. For ten days Flemish merchants set out their textiles for Italians to bargain over, then the Italians brought out the spices and porcelain of India, Indonesia and China, giving the northerners a whole month to bargain over those exotic wares. Accounts were settled during the final week.[25]

A roaring success in the 11th and 12th centuries, the fairs were doomed in the changing climate of the 13th century, a period that saw the adoption of new techniques and forms of business organization. The fierce struggles of German emperors and Roman popes made the climate for Italian merchants ever more perilous. A Florentine manager could travel to Champagne only to discover his business gone upon his return. To solve the problem, trustworthy family members became permanent agents in Bruges, Ghent or London. Instead of sending coins across the Alps, paying more to ship them than they were worth, the Florentine could now go to a banker and purchase a *bill of exchange*. The bill operated like a modern bank draft and could be sent to his agent in Flanders to be converted into Flemish currency.

The bill of exchange was still only useful to big companies who had the collateral assets or reputation money changers demanded. It only worked in centres such as Bruges, Florence, London or Alexandria where credit was available, for the drawer was 'defined by his credit and his contacts'.[26] Deals were accompanied by cumbersome contracts of exchange drawn up by lawyers. Take the contract of January 1308 between Raniero Griffi, a partner in the Gallerani Company of Siena, and Vanne Guy, a partner in the Tolomei Company of Siena but living in Bordeaux. Raniero promises that he will pay the French equivalent of a thousand *florins* to Tolomei agents at the Champagne fair. The legalese is very thorough if not wearisome:

> *'In the presence of myself, notary, and the undermentioned*
> *witnesses, Raniero Griffi, citizen and merchant of Siena, partner in*
> *the company the Gallerani of Siena, in his name and in the name of*

*all the partners of the said company, for the exchange and the price
of a thousand gold florins which he has confessed and recognized to
have, in his name and in the name of the said partners and
company, had and received from Vanne Guy, his countryman and
merchant from Siena, partner in the Tolomei Company of Siena,
paying and counting in his name and in the name of the said
partners, has promized and agreed to the said Vanne and to his
partners and to each of them for all or to their representative or
proxy appointed for this reason, at the Lagny fairs currently being
held at Lagny, as just payment, two thousand one hundred and
twenty-five livres in small deniers tournois of which tournois one old
silver gros tournois is worth forty deniers or thereabouts.'[27]*

With more education and business expansion, transactions became
more secure. Lawyers' minutes were left at home and simple *letters of
exchange,* in double or triple copy, sent instead. Siena adopted the system
in 1225, Florence in 1201, Venice in 1350, and England, France and
Germany after 1400.[28] By 1465 letters were brisk and 'business-like' in
their wording, as in this letter sent from an Italian company in Valencia
to one in Bruges:

'In the name of God. 26 April 1465.
*Pay by this first letter of exchange within 75 days, made to Piero
de' Medici and company, 1564 ducats, that is 1574 phillippes for
the value paid to us, and put it, by you, in your account. Christ keep
you.*
Niccolò Manelli and Giovanni Chanigliani and company,
In Valencia
On the Reverse:
To Giovanni Salviati and Pietro da Rabatta and company,
In Bruges.
First.'[29]

Bankers and merchants kept track with a new system of *double-entry
bookkeeping.* Instead of simply writing down all receipts and expenses in a
single ledger, a merchant kept one book in his home office and another in
his agent's office in, say, Bruges. What was recorded as 'paid' in Florence
was recorded as 'received' in Bruges. Interest, depreciation, capital,
revenue and accrual, and a quick overview of profit and loss were also
recorded. Bankers could transfer funds from one depositor's account to

another's. Double entry also helped to keep one's foreign employees honest, as a manager had a record of his own to detect any fraudulent dealings.[30]

The new techniques allowed a giant step towards the modern multinational, with permanent Italian subsidiaries now more tightly managed than the merchant colonies of antiquity. Contracting with Venetians and Genoese to buy spices and porcelain in

> Bankers and merchants kept track with a new system of double-entry bookkeeping

Byzantium or Syria, Florentines shipped them *directly* to Flemish and English branch offices. The Peruzzi, Bardi and Accaiouli banking partnerships diversified after 1250 into multiple trading and manufacturing outlets, making their own woollen clothing instead of buying it from Flemish weavers. These multinational *supercompanies* tried to corner the European market in luxury fabrics by long-term planning and internalising operations. Using bills of exchange, Peruzzi agents in London paid Cistercians for raw wool years in advance, shipping it directly to Peruzzi offices in Florence. There, without ever seeing Flanders, it was dyed and finished for specialized markets throughout Europe, the garments being sold through the 14 Peruzzi branch offices.[31]

Table 10.1 Peruzzi company structure as of 1 July 1335

Chairman

Florentine operations	*Foreign operations headed by partners*	*Foreign operations headed by employees*
Banking	Naples – Donato Peruzzi	Southern Italy
Trading	Sicily – F. Forzetti	Cyprus
Textile manufacture	Avignon – F. Villani	Rhodes
Special accounts	England – G. Baroncelli	Sardinia
Charities	Bruges – Pacino di Guido Peruzzi	Tunis
	Paris – Filippo Peruzzi	Majorca
		Venice
		Pisa

The supercompanies evolved from mere partnerships into what Jean Favier describes as 'a more complex and fruitful structure: the *compagnia*', or as we know it, the company. Limited liability, dating from the

Romans, was now revived in the Italian firms of the early 1300s. Concentrations of capital became larger and more permanent, and investment separated from trading or banking. Agents became salaried governors and general managers. Even this new company-form was a family affair in medieval Italy. While the Peruzzi often rotated partners every few years, the family name ensured public confidence and brand quality.[32]

'Time is money': management restructuring and the Black Death

Supercompanies thrived into the early 14th century. The business climate of Europe, however, changed radically after 1300. The great boom inspired by the Crusades and Gothic cathedral-building gave way to the doleful years of the Black Death and its aftermath (1348–1350), a time when 'the Four Horsemen of the Apocalypse were anything but an abstraction'.[33] As Barbara Tuchman described the period, the four horsemen had become seven: plague, war, taxes, brigandage, bad government, insurrection and schism in the Church. Satan seemed triumphant. Religious and political upheaval, feudal war, upset weather, famine and the most terrible pestilence in history battered Europe. Winters in the north became unseasonably cold, wet and rainy while droughts affected the Mediterranean.

> Supercompanies thrived into the early 14th century. The business climate of Europe, however, changed radically after 1300

The trade routes linking Europe and Asia now transmitted bubonic plague both East and West, devastating China, the Muslim world and, finally, Europe. Entering via the Black Sea trade routes, the Black Death engulfed Italy in 1346 and spread northward along the routes of commerce to Flanders, Germany, France, England and even Scandinavia, Iceland and Greenland by 1352. Its recurrence throughout the 14th and early 15th centuries was horrific. Population growth was stunted for a hundred years. The political climate changed just as radically as the social order. Governments seeking to consolidate their power turned to autarky. Economic-warfare tactics were adopted, which even the Crusaders had shunned. England boycotted Flemish wool. France and Genoa attacked English shipping. English armies deliberately devastated the French countryside. Kings at war debased their coinage and sought to micromanage their marketplaces, imposing heavy new taxes and regulations on merchants with little regard to their impact.[34]

Europe's potential market shrank by at least a third. Commerce, demand, investment and income headed into a downward spiral. Neither supercompany nor *commenda* structures were suited for an age of pestilence, peasant and burgher revolts, currency crises, trade war and open conflict. Partnerships that depended upon alliances with trustworthy agents were devastated by the bankruptcies and plague that rocked Italy in the 1340s. By the 1380s Italian producers faced a depopulated market with too few workers to hire and too few customers. Market risks distorted business: 'It is difficult to imagine an era richer in uncertainty for businessmen than the fourteenth and early fifteenth centuries.'[35] In a period of 'creative destruction' – in some respects not unlike the 1990s, when vast numbers of businesses went bankrupt and 'downsizing' became a buzzword – new kinds of enterprise came to the fore:

> *'This "certainty of uncertainty" for business claimed many victims; but remarkably, throughout the era dozens of new businesses arose and flourished. When challenged, European business responded with a show of recombinant and adaptive force that preserved traditional business customs [but] arranged them into new organizational structures ... better suited to the changing environment.'[36]*

In a manner not unlike that of executives today, late medieval entrepreneurs facing higher risks turned to new techniques to control costs. This demanded not only more accurate accounting but 'more accurate measurement of time and of results. Determining the divisions of the workday was useful in helping mitigate the effect of higher wages but initially not as important in controlling costs as accurate measurement of results which entailed great emphasis on disciplined accounting, along with timely and *regular* reporting.'[37]

Western Europe's Catholic culture was more open to new innovations than the Orthodox world of Byzantium. In the Orthodox world everyone, including the church and local rulers, was subject to imperial control. Feudalism and the competing claims of powerful popes, priests, lords and towns permitted more autonomy and even liberal thinking throughout the Latinized West.[38] Inventions conducive to capitalism were able to take root where clergymen were more accepting of human progress, as the Cistercian experience proved. Europe in the 12th century was not hostile to science. Great thinkers such as Peter Abelard (1079–1142) and Gilbert of Tournai saw nature operating on the cause-and-effect principle with Christianity the foundation of knowledge in a widening world: 'Never will we find truth if we content ourselves with what is already known ... Those things that have been written before us are not laws, but guides. The truth is open to all, for it is not yet totally possessed.'[39]

> In a period of 'creative destruction' – in some respects, not unlike the 1990s, when vast numbers of businesses went bankrupt and 'downsizing' became a buzzword – new kinds of enterprise came to the fore

Giovanni di Dondi of Padua, trained in astronomy, medicine and logic, subscribed to this fusion of reason and faith. He and his entrepreneur father created one of the first mechanical clocks on which all 24 hours were uniform and equal. The di Dondi clock was the forerunner of many placed in the cathedral towers of northern Italy in the 1350s and 1360s. By 1400 most Catholic churches in Europe had one. Merchants wished to manage their time independently of the set routines of a progressive-minded clergy, which saw the need to do so. City life in Milan, Paris and elsewhere would now run by the hourly bells of the clock, not the routine of sunrise, sunset or the Mass. The happy result was that business was severed from the rhythms of nature, perhaps for the first time.[40] Accountants standardized money; clocks standardized time, and with timekeeping came timesaving, an innovation that would lay the foundation for Henry Ford and his assembly line. The result was predictable! After the year 1400 personal clocks spread to homes and businesses much in the manner of today's personal computer boom and, when the mainspring was perfected, portable clocks soon became valuable aids to traders and sailing ships.[41]

In a climate where merchants did all they could to avoid bad reputations, the new concept of risk management was quickly applied to business. Ancient and medieval merchants believed that both fate and profits were in the hands of God or the gods. Even the Greeks had no means of giving odds on what might or might not happen, for they 'lacked a numbering system that would have enabled them to *calculate* instead of just recording the results of their activities'.[42] The clumsy letter-numerals of Rome (I, II, III...) made basic arithmetic hard enough, let alone higher mathematics. Necessity was soon mother to a solution. The Arabs, borrowing a Hindu invention, digital numbers (1, 2, 3...) and the concept of 'zero', made it possible to create abstract equations, such as $4x = 4y + 20$.[43] Mathematics became a science of the abstract as 'Zero', according to author Peter L. Bernstein, 'blew out the limits to ideas and to progress.'[44] Now ordinary people, not to mention traders and managers, could write inconceivably large numbers using only the digits 0–9. By the early 9th century the Abbasid mathematician al-Khwarizmi formulated *al-jabr*, the science of equations, source of the modern term 'algebra'.

Soon Arabs and Persians were working with squares, square roots, cubes and even higher powers, the essentials of today's microelectronic revolution. Devout Muslims, they stopped short of probability theory and risk management that would emerge 'only when people believe that they are to some degree free agents'. This step they would leave to less fatalstic Europeans of the 15th century.[45]

The son of a Pisan consul, writing under the name of Fibonacci, entranced by his encounter with a visiting Arab scholar, journeyed around the Muslim Mediterranean learning all he could about the 'new' mathematics. Fibonacci's 1202 treatise *Liber Abaci* (*Book of the Abacus*) went far beyond anything extant by actually applying algebraic fractions, radicals and even quadratic and linear equations to the practical world of business. *Liber Abaci* showed Italian entrepreneurs, partners and managers how to use algebra in bookkeeping and in figuring profits, foreign exchange, weights and measures, and interest payments. For the first time, a technique existed whereby risk could be expressed in percentile or 'dollar-and-cents' terms, but it would not be until the 1400s that risk would be seen in terms of human error and calculation.[46] The results of all these ingenious advances were considerable. It was now possible for merchants to estimate the probability of losing cargoes on ships from Genoa to Bruges. Insurance underwriters in Genoa now computed risks and premiums for different kinds of voyages. Goods in armed convoys had low premiums, say 3 per cent, unescorted ships on shorter voyages perhaps 7 per cent or higher.[47]

Meanwhile, down in Florence things were hardly standing still. While Venetians and Genoese continued to use business partnerships, Florentine families such as the Alberti were forced to experiment with new forms of management when many of their partners died in the plague or suffered economic ruin. Founded in 1302 the Alberti partnership traded heavily in Flemish cloth and diversified into banking after 1315. The Alberti resembled today's AT&T. Hard times, beginning in the 1340s, caused the firm to split and resplit. From a centralized firm, Alberti made the transition to a large but highly decentralized family association. Exiled family members (Florence was famous for its exiles: Dante, for example) created new branches in Italy, Flanders, England, France, Catalonia, Spain, North Africa and the Levant. These 'baby Albertis' became independent firms linked by family ties, investment needs and other informal means rather than by a controlling hierarchy. The English branch, for example, had its own regional mandates for financing native sheep-herders and bringing the wool to Italy in its own ships. The parallels with our own day are astonishing. In a time of radically changing market conditions, centralized firms gave way to lean, decentralized business alliances. As a whole, Italian business in the late 14th century underwent an enormous amount of downsizing. According to Edwin Hunt and James Murray, most international business was now dominated by a number of independent entrepreneurs and 'relatively small family organizations operating in narrowly defined product or geographical niches'. These new firms were 'much more cautious and control-minded than their forbears, given the greater risks and more uncertain rewards that they faced'.[48]

Businesses such as those owned by the Datinis were very different from those of 100 or even 50 years before. Orphaned by the plague, Francesco Datini launched his trading business in Avignon in 1363, eventually relocating to Prato and Florence. By 1395 Datini companies established in Pisa, Genoa, Avignon, Barcelona, Valencia and Majorca dealt in a wide variety of goods and services. The Datini firms, like the Alberti, had a totally different structure from the Peruzzi company, one stressing the 'control, nimbleness, flexibility and risk management' needed to survive in the late 1300s.[49] This is summarized effectively in Table 10.2.

How was Datini able to manage and control all his partnerships? The key was with innovative and sophisticated methods of accounting, techniques that continued to improve throughout the century. Datini began by putting debits in the first half of his ledger and credits in the second, as shown in Table 10.3.

By 1393, however, he had learned a few things. His Venetian customers taught him to write down his debits on the left column of his page and his credits on the right, as shown in Table 10.4.

Table 10.2 From Peruzzi to Datini: new management styles in the 14th century

Peruzzi (early 14th century)	*Datini (late 14th century)*
Single legal entity	Series of independent businesses
Branches wholly owned by parent firm	Network of partnerships joined by Francesco di Marco Datini as dominant partner
Management by company shareholders partners and employees	Ownership and management by well known and loyal to Datini, including former employees

Table 10.3

Debits
Florence: 140 florins
Bruges: 280 florins
Antioch: 150 florins

Credits
Florence: 200 florins
Bruges: 360 florins
Antioch: 70 florins

Table 10.4

Debits	*Credits*
Florence: 140 florins	Florence: 200 florins
Bruges: 280 florins	Bruges: 360 florins
Antioch: 150 florins	Antioch: 70 florins

The old counting houses gave way to the new skill of accounting. It was now much easier to read the records and calculate profit and loss. All partnership ledgers now adopted this procedure whereby ledgers had to balance and statements had to be prepared every year. The Peruzzis had to balance their books only when they formed a new partnership. Datini could keep a much closer eye on his numerous partners. By dividing the financial reserves with his partners, Datini also minimized his risk of poor investment decisions. A 1382 partnership agreement with Boninsegna di Matteo of Avignon and Tieri di Benci of Avignon makes this clear:

> 'We, Boninsegna and Tieri, agreed with the said Francesco [Datini] that of the aforesaid sum, which belongs entirely to Francesco di Marco, the said Francesco must leave the sum of 3,000 florins of 24 sous each in their care, either in merchandise or in rents.

> 'The remainder, that is, 866 florins, will be deposited by us in his account, at the beginning of the year in cash, in deniers, so that we have under our care the sum of 3,000 florins. The said Francesco is content and wishes that Boninsegna and Tieri may trade in the way they see fit with the said merchandise entered in this account book, and with any other merchandise which may seem to them useful to trade in and profitable for the benefit of the said Francesco.'[50]

The results were dynamic. By the 15th century Datini's techniques were being copied by many Italian companies, who could now calculate a suite of capital gains, losses, reserves, deferrals, fixed versus liquid assets, depreciation, labour and production costs. Overhead expense in relation to product costs could be calculated by applied mathematical ratios. In 1318, the Del Bene company of Florence kept track of manufacturing and trading costs in the same book. By 1368 it had three books – one for raw wool, another for labour costs, and one for dyeing costs. The cost of producing any type or quality of cloth could thus be accurately estimated in advance, a sure advantage in the tough new marketplace.[51]

> The results were dynamic. By the 15th century Datini's techniques were being copied by many Italian companies, who could now calculate a suite of capital gains, losses, reserves, deferrals, fixed versus liquid assets, depreciation, labour and production costs

Thus, in spite of the severe crises of the 1300s, innovative and resourceful European businesses had given birth to flexible and resilient business institutions and valuable 'hands-on' techniques such as the company form, credit institutions such as the letter of exchange, and rudimentary risk and time management schemes. The systematising and simplifying of business procedures would be a boon for the next generation of merchants and managers. All this would play an even more important role after 1500 when the weakening of the medieval world economy finally abated. The Black Death and its apocalyptic *aides de camp* of famine, disruption and dislocation had done their worst. The discovery of the New World and the creation of the first truly global economy and its characteristic form, the joint-stock company, were ready to take centre stage.

NOTES TO CHAPTER 10

1. Braudel, F. (1992) *Civilization and Capitalism 15th–18th Century*, Volume 3: *The Perspective of the World*. Berkeley, CA: University of California Press, 91–101.
2. Gies, J. and F. (1972) *Merchants and Moneymen: The Commercial Revolution, 1000–1500*. New York: Thomas Y. Crowell, 33–4.
3. Thompson, J.W. (1966) *Economic and Social History of the Middle Ages*, Volume I, 3rd edn. New York: Frederick Ungar, 390–3.
4. Gies, J. and F. (1972) *Merchants and Moneymen: The Commercial Revolution, 1000–1500*. New York: Thomas Y. Crowell, 43.
5. *Ibid.*, 38–48.
6. Text of a Venetian *collegantia* contract between Giovanni Lissado and Sevasto Orefice drawn up in Venice, August 1073, from Evans, A.P., ed., *Records of Civilization: Sources and Studies Series*, no. LII; Lopez, R.S. and Raymond, I.W., eds., (1955) *Medieval Trade in the Mediterranean World*. New York: Columbia University Press, 176–7, quoted in McNeill, W.H. and Sedlar, J.W. *Readings in World History*, vol. VIII, McNeill, W.H. and Houser, S.O., eds., (1971) *Medieval Europe*. New York: Oxford University Press, 89–90.
7. *Ibid.*
8. *Ibid.*
9. *Ibid.*
10. Gies, J. and F. (1972) *Merchants and Moneymen: The Commercial Revolution, 1000–1500*. New York: Thomas Y. Crowell, 38–48.
11. *Ibid.*
12. Braudel, F. (1992) *Civilization and Capitalism 15th–18th Century*, Volume 3: *The Perspective of the World*. Berkeley, CA: University of California Press, 109.
13. According to Jean Gimpel, 'oil in the twentieth century plays much the same role as did waterpower in the Middle Ages'. Gimpel, J. (1976) *The Medieval*

Machine: The Industrial Revolution of the Middle Ages. New York: Holt, Rinehart and Winston, 2.

14. Clairvaux report quoted in Luckhurst, D. 'Monastic Watermills' in *Society for the Protection of Ancient Buildings*, no. 8 (London), n.d.: 6 in Gimpel, 6.

15. Gimpel, J. (1976) *The Medieval Machine: The Industrial Revolution of the Middle Ages*. New York: Holt, Rinehart and Winston, 11–17.

16. Geoffrey Chaucer, 'The Reeve's Tale' from *The Canterbury Tales*. Translated by J. V. Nicolson, Garden City, New York: International Collections Library, 109, 112.

17. *The Chronicle of Jocelin of Brakelond*, tr. (1949) Butler, H.E. London: Thomas Nelson, 59–60, quoted in Gimpel, 26.

18. Gimpel, J. (1976) *The Medieval Machine: The Industrial Revolution of the Middle Ages*. New York: Holt, Rinehart and Winston, 38–41.

19. *Ibid.*, 46–9.

20. *Ibid.*, 56–7.

21. Hunt, E.S. and Murray, J.M. (1999) *A History of Business in Medieval Europe, 1200–1550*. Cambridge: Cambridge University Press, 42–3.

22. *Ibid.*, 45–6. Gimpel, J. (1976) *The Medieval Machine: The Industrial Revolution of the Middle Ages*. New York: Holt, Rinehart and Winston, 59–63, 67–72.

23. Hunt, E.S. and Murray, J.M. (1999) *A History of Business in Medieval Europe, 1200–1550*. Cambridge: Cambridge University Press, 47–8.

24. *Ibid.*, 48–50.

25. Gies, J. and F. (1972) *Merchants and Moneymen: The Commercial Revolution, 1000–1500*. New York: Thomas Y. Crowell, 76–8.

26. Favier, J. (1998) *Gold and Spices: The Rise of Commerce in the Middle Ages*, tr. Higgitt, C. New York: Holmes & Meier, 216.

27. Text of contract 26 January 1308, *ibid.*, 224–5.

28. *Ibid.*, 226–7.

29. Text of contract 26 April 1465, *ibid.*, 227.

30. Hunt, E.S. and Murray, J.M. (1999) *A History of Business in Medieval Europe, 1200–1550*. Cambridge: Cambridge University Press, 62–3.

31. *Ibid.*, 106–9.

32. Favier, J. (1998) *Gold and Spices: The Rise of Commerce in the Middle Ages*, tr. Higgitt, C. New York: Holmes & Meier, 163.

33. Hunt, E.S. and Murray, J.M. (1999) *A History of Business in Medieval Europe, 1200–1550*. Cambridge: Cambridge University Press, 125.

34. *Ibid.*,125–8.

35. *Ibid.*, 149.

36. *Ibid.*, 149–50.

37. *Ibid.*, 151.

38. It is possible that even theology reinforced this divergence, for Greek theology taught that the Holy Spirit proceeded from the Father alone, while Latin theology insisted that the Spirit proceeded from both God the Father and God

the Son, which, together with the special veneration given to Mary and the saints, promoted a more pluralistic view of the Godhead, the universe and, therefore, the society.

39. Gilbert de Tournai, quoted in Gimpel, J. (1961) *The Cathedral Builders.* New York: Grove Press, 165, in *idem, The Medieval Machine,* 147.

40. Bernstein, P.J. (1996) *Against the Gods: The Remarkable Story of Risk.* New York: John Wiley and Sons, 16.

41. Gimpel, J. (1976) *The Medieval Machine: The Industrial Revolution of the Middle Ages.* New York: Holt, Rinehart and Winston, 159–60, 165–70.

42. Bernstein, 16.

43. *Ibid.,* 31–3.

44. *Ibid.,* 33.

45. *Ibid.,* 25.

46. *Ibid.,* 23–5.

47. Hunt, E.S. and Murray, J.M. (1999) *A History of Business in Medieval Europe, 1200–1550.* Cambridge: Cambridge University Press, 158–9.

48. *Ibid.,* 156.

49. *Ibid.*

50. Text of partnership agreement of 1 December 1382 in Favier, J., (1998) *Gold and Spices: The Rise of Commerce in the Middle Ages,* tr. Higgitt, C. New York: Holmes & Meier, 160.

51. *Ibid.,* 157.

11

China's chance

The enduring decree of heaven

CHINA under the Song (Sung: 960–1279), Yuan (Mongol: 1279–1368) and early Ming (1368–1644) dynasties was the most prosperous part of the medieval world economy. Her internal trade was far vaster than Europe's; European visitors were utterly astonished by the enormity of her cities and the inventions of her people.

The list of Chinese discoveries and inventions *in antiquity* is impressive: cast iron, steel, gyroscopes, compasses, waterpower and petroleum as energy sources, and seagoing ships with watertight compartments and multiple masts. During Europe's Dark Ages, China perfected block printing, mechanical clocks, primitive steam engines, gunpowder and rockets.

> China under the Song (Sung: 960–1279), Yuan (Mongol: 1279–1368) and early Ming (1368–1644) dynasties was the most prosperous part of the medieval world economy

China had an efficient civil service, printed books, progressed to the very edges of an industrial revolution, and eventually launched the most powerful navy in the world, which controlled the entire western Pacific and the Indian Ocean. She might well have ruled the modern age instead of Europe. What went wrong? The key lies in China's unique business culture, wherein extreme forms of state socialism and market capitalism existed side by side, and in the general crisis of the medieval economy itself.

The Chinese market revolution (2): the Song Empire

Under the peace and unity of the medieval Chinese Empire, food production and population mushroomed. Soon there was simply not enough land to go around. Peasants flocked to the cities putting tremendous strain upon communal resources. By the year 1000, Song China boasted the greatest mass market in the world. Enterprise spread from the cities to the countryside, affecting even the poorest of rural peasants. State monopolies of salt, iron, copper, coal, tea, porcelain, bricks and mineral production were revived and run by hereditary bureaucrats. Their operations were internalized. Copper coins became staple imperial currency, the circulation of which grew fivefold during the 11th century.[1] Taxes on grain financed roads, ports and canals, and grain was stored as a hedge against recurrent famine. The emperors fixed prices and exchange and interest rates, insured goods and enforced contracts, even as the economy as a whole became more privatized and market-oriented. Later dynasties would not be so interventionist.[2]

The 'socialist' economy of bureaucrats was now supplemented by family- and partnership-based business alliances. Song rulers attempted to control the market through merchant-princes as well as direct public ownership. Merchants would be recognized as brokers and charged with overseeing other businesses to ensure fair trading practices. Fairness, however, was often determined by personal dealings rather than a written legal code. 'Ties and fees to a particular broker, not a framework of even-handed laws settled disputes brought to such men.'[3] Brokers managed the market by deterring large partnerships and joint-stock firms from gouging or fixing prices. Song leaders accepted the market so long as desirable monopolies could be substituted for undesirable ones, while the petty entrepreneur was allowed to thrive. 'Accepting a national economy level of local trade but keeping incipient capitalism petty absorbed much official attention.'[4]

China's boom economy rested upon elaborate waterways such as the Grand Canal that bound the vast Chinese market together. Rice, grain and other crops grown in southern China, as well as silk, porcelain and copper were shipped by seafaring junks from the new ports of Guangdong (Kwangtung) and Fujian (Fukien) to Ningbo (Ningpo) on the Yangzi. There riverboats took them up the Grand Canal and other waterways, passing other boats bringing the silk, salt, incense and precious metals of northern

MANDARINS OR MARKETS?

CHINA'S 2500-YEAR DEBATE

Both socialism and capitalism have flourished in China and the creative tensions between them have shaped Chinese business culture for well over two millennia.

In the days of the Shang rulers (1700–1100 BCE) the state owned all the land and managed all enterprise. Farming was organized collectively and society ruled through communes called *zu*. The first capitalists appeared during the reign of the Zhou (1100–256 BCE).

Early Chinese records talk of the entrepreneur Fan Li who lived on what is now the Shandong peninsula. Fan Li bought, sold and relied on his intuition in following market conditions. Earning huge amounts of gold, he passed his wealth on to his children and grandchildren. The merchant Pai Kuei had a similar strategy, trading as if he were fighting a war, buying when others sold and selling when others bought.

The rise of Chinese capitalism was a worry to the philosopher Confucius (531–479 BCE), whose own ideals emphasized devotion to the state, family, duty and integrity at the expense of personal prosperity. When his pupil Zukong abandoned these ideals in pursuit of business success and became very rich, he was unsparingly condemned by the Master.

The philosopher Laozi (604–531 BCE), founder of Daoism, was just as unsparing as Confucius in his condemnation of acquisitiveness, the pursuit of material gain and naked self-interest. Paradoxically, however, the Daoist text known as the *Daodejing* (*Tao Te Ching*) contains a train of thought that fits well with the idea of free markets and limited government. The world, it said, would be a better place if people were left to harmonize themselves with the immutable order of nature. The best leaders were those whom the people hardly knew of. People would be more charitable if charity was voluntary. The world could not be controlled and one would make it a much worse place to live in if one tried to.

China heading in the opposite direction. A whole new class of specialized wholesalers congregated in the cities of the Yangzi valley. There, and in the new county markets, they traded fish, vegetables, firewood, sheep and other staples. Others specialized in tourism, becoming innkeepers commissioned by imperial favour. A semi-public, semi-private tourist industry grew up alongside that of the shippers. In smaller centres, rich farmers doubled as innkeepers for travelling merchants. In larger centres wealthy farmers served as middlemen. Once mere peddlers carrying goods on their backs, these sharp-eyed entrepreneurs soon became shippers, carrying the goods of others on their sampans and junks. As they prospered, many began to contract with their own middlemen.[5]

The Chinese style of business partnership, developed independently from those of Europe and the Near East, came into its own. Typical was that of the entrepreneur Qao Qing (Chao Ching) of Fujian or Guangdong. Qao's partnership included several friends and relatives and lasted for a decade, trading all the way up the Chinese coast to Manchuria. The profits were enormous, as recorded in the works of Qin Huaihai (Chin Huai-hai):

> *'He joined up with several persons from the same locality as himself and they went trading, sailing the seaways from Kwangtung and Fukien up to Shantung, coming and going across the seas, for more than ten years. He became extremely rich.'*[6]

Retiring to a monastery in response to his parents' wishes, Qao eventually gave his assets and profits to his partners. Qao's story reflects that of the conflict within medieval (and even current) Chinese capitalism. The prosperous market revolution of Song China grated upon many Chinese traditions. The rising prosperity of traders still clashed with ancient Confucian ideals of family, order and gentlemanly conduct and the more private asceticism of Daoism and Buddhism. Most Chinese partnerships were not as long-lived as Qao's. Usually a group of traders would sail on the same ship and put a member of their trading company in charge. Other partners would stay at home and entrust their goods or money to those who sailed, splitting the profits upon return. More wealthy entrepreneurs such as the Muslim Fo Lien, who owned a fleet of 80 junks, hired professional managers to trade for them. By the 14th century the emperors codified the different categories of merchants. The list has an astonishingly modern sound to it. There were: (i) sole proprietors: 'persons immediately in charge', (ii) managers, (iii) financial backers, and (iv) consortia and partnerships: a collectively owned 'system of voluntarily contributing ships'. An example of the latter is found in a 13th-century mathematical treatise, which describes a junk's bringing back aloes, pepper, tusks and other goods from India with the profits paid out in proportion to each partner's investments.

Chinese entrepreneurialism often depended upon 'harmonious hiring' whereby government forced private vessels to ship public grain, salt, wheat and silk along with the goods of the owner-merchant. Officials filled most of the space on the ships that they requisitioned with tax grain. Private traders filled the rest of the space. This practice likely saved many a petty merchant from the high risks of market failure.

The golden age of China's entrepreneurs

Song capitalism radically began to reshape one of the most traditional societies on earth. Civil servants lost their hereditary job-security and bought into the culture of conspicuous consumption, flaunting their silk, jade, pearls and mansions. The official Baohui (Pao Hui) describes the new money societies of riverboat and seagoing ventures of south-east China where 'all the people along the sea-coast are on intimate terms with the merchants who engage in overseas trade'.[7] Petty traders worked under the jurisdiction of larger merchants, foreshadowing the business alliances of the future: 'Large merchants gather what the lesser households have,' said the writer Yezhi (Yeh Shih). 'Little boats engage in joint operations with the greater vessels as the latter's dependants, going back and forth selling grain in order to clear a solid profit.'[8]

Song China carried family capitalism beyond anything practised by the Romans. *Patricorporations* based themselves upon extended families and households within which individuals had few rights. Wives, daughters and sons were often sold by family patriarchs. Chinese firms to this day are passed on not to professional managers but to family heirs. In a society where bureaucracy was strong and all other social groupings outside the family remained weak, the extended family was the best insurance policy against an intrusive government and harsh competition.

> *'Where each producer household's earnings threaten every other's,*
> *the long-term tendency ... is to dissolve ... human relationships in*
> *the impersonality of the market, where everything can be bought and*

> *sold. Such an economy breeds fear and distrust of one's neighbours in addition to that felt for autocratic authorities.'[9]*

Distrust of those outside the circle of kin deeply imbedded itself in Chinese culture. Nothing is more stigmatized in Chinese lore than the rootless beggar alone without property or family. Family farms and businesses provided security in a world where landless workers faced low wages and destitution, without welfare or pensions. Money itself became sacred in the popular religion of offering to ancestral spirits and rituals centred on becoming rich. Business itself became sacred in a Chinese society where even one's relatives had a price.

China's aborted industrial revolution

China's potential for world dominance lay in an iron and steel industry that had grown to gigantic proportions. By the 11th century China was producing 125 000 tonnes, almost a third of the 400 000 (metric) tonnes Britain would produce in 1820. Half of the production took place in the Hopei (Hupei) region, near the northern Song capital and much of it was handled by individual entrepreneurs. Some of the coal-burning foundries were true industrial-era factories. The complex at Qixun (Chi Tsun) employed 700 coal miners, 1000 ore miners, 1000 furnace workers, and consumed 35 000 tonnes of iron ore and 42 000 tonnes of coal to produce 14 000 tonnes of pig iron annually. Most of the production went into weapons: armour, swords, arrows and crossbows, but some went into making nails, ploughs and other farm implements. The writer Sosong (Su Sung) described a forerunner of the 1863 Siemens steel process: 'mixing the raw and the soft (cast iron and wrought iron), a metal is obtained ... called steel'.[10]

> Family farms and businesses provided security in a world where landless workers faced low wages and destitution, without welfare or pensions

Could a genuine industrial revolution have taken place in China under the Song? We will never know. The Song emperors had to abandon the Hopei mines and complexes following a Tartar invasion in 1127, aborting the industrial take-off.

More answers to the riddle of China's decline emerge when we examine her once enviable position in the world economy. Trading fairs in cities like

Hangzhou (Hangchow) combined the wholesale and retail commerce in goods flowing in and out of China from long-distance trading networks. A description of the autumn Medicine Fair of Zhengdu (Chengtu) was preserved by the 13th-century writer Duzheng (Tu Cheng). He catches the atmosphere of the press of the crowd as customers thronged to the gates in the earliest hours of the morning to pass through the arcades. Medicines, spices, herbs and leeches are laid out on mats and trays all over the ground, and the smell of ginseng, frankincense, aloe and sandalwood are everywhere: 'Merchants have buffeted the sea-winds and the waves, and foreign merchants crossed over towering crags drawn onwards by the profits to be made ...'[11]

> Trading fairs in cities like Hangzhou combined the wholesale and retail commerce in goods flowing in and out of China from long-distance trading networks

Merchants of the Muslim world especially treasured the decorative porcelain objects shipped 10 000 kilometres by sea from Guangzhou (Canton) through Sumatra and Malaya, Sri Lanka and India to the Gulf. At first, this trade would be carried in Persian, Arab and Sri Lankan vessels. Arab *dhows* lashed together with coconut fibres and commanded by captains who navigated by the stars billowed their triangular sails toward the exotic markets of Song China.[12]

The 'Middle Kingdom' of international trade

The Song responded creatively to the loss of northern industry by seeking overseas markets. The Emperor Gao Zong (Kao Tsung) actively encouraged foreign trade, letting his sages work out the contradictions this posed for Confucian gentlemen: 'Profits from maritime commerce are very great. If properly managed, they can amount to millions. Is this not better than taxing the people?'[13] Qen Qun (Chen Chun) and other sages now reinterpreted capitalism in such a manner as to be compatible with Confucian civic ideals: 'So long as one engages in profit-making when the business is proper and acquires a thing when the acquisition is correct, that is righteousness.'[14]

The Song expanded Indian Ocean trade in new junks that were the most seaworthy vessels in the world as the Chinese overtook the Arabs in naval technology. Chinese junks built with iron nails, oil caulking, watertight bulkheads, buoyancy chambers, floating anchors and rudders weighed up to 250 tonnes. They carried up to 600 tonnes of rice, lumber, porcelain, spices, silk and minerals or 10 000 pieces of porcelain goods. Sailing from Hangzhou they could reach Korea in five days and Vietnam in eight. Overseas commercial expansion and a much more active role in the world economy were within China's grasp. Merchants now set up Chinese colonies and business establishments overseas. Waiting for the next monsoon, many settled permanently in Indonesia, Vietnam, Cambodia and Korea.[15]

Where business goes, regulation soon follows. The Office of the Monopoly of Trade, set up in Kaifeng in 971, began to regulate the thriving new overseas commerce. Offices of Overseas Trade were opened in Canton, Hangzhou, Ningbo, Shanghai and half a dozen other cities. Hangzhou and Ningbo regulated the Korean and Japanese trade; Canton controlled the South-East Asian and Indian Ocean markets. Chinese junks were required to return to the ports whence they had departed. Profits were spread from the palace to the enterprising businesspeople. Imperial officials allowed tax farmers to charge customs duties and a 10 per cent tariff on the pearls, ivory and other imported goods and then helped themselves to a portion of the goods with public funds. The rest of the cargo was freely sold to the market.

The Chinese were guarded when it came to Arab and other foreign traders, who needed permits to transact business on Chinese soil, though their presence was encouraged. Certificates were issued allowing them to sell within China and to depart from China. Seapower was soon viewed as being as essential a defence to China as the army. 'A navy is of value,' said Finance Minister Zhang Yi (Chang Yi). 'To use our navy is to employ our strong weapon to strike at the enemy's weakness.'[16] Soon the Song navy grew from a few patrol boats to a force of 600 ships, including warrior junks with battering rams, catapults, guns and rockets. Despite their inbred faith in Chinese superiority, the intelligentsia of the Middle Kingdom now sought wisdom from 'barbarians' beyond the seas. The Song emperors encouraged research and development. They offered cash incentives for innovations in naval design. Chinese mariners studied Hindu and Arabian maths and geography, drew up more accurate charts and analysed the currents of the Indian Ocean, borrowing from centuries of Arab and Persian knowledge. Going far beyond their teachers, the Song soon invented a floating compass. They were on the way.

The new seagoing Chinese merchant fleets extended the reach of Song prosperity overseas. They made China the centre of the world economy. The Offices of Overseas Trade collected up to 300 000 to 500 000 strings of cash, some 3 per cent of the annual revenue. Junks sailed to the Malabar Coast of India and beyond to the Persian Gulf and Red Sea. Chinese copper coins and porcelains have been unearthed in Sri Lanka, East Africa, Egypt, the Gulf, Constantinople, Iraq, the Levant and India. Song copper coins became the international currency of the Far East, often being used to pay for the bulk shipments of Chinese ceramics, silk, porcelain and books. Paid for too were the spices and ivory of the Indian Ocean and the rare birds and flowers of Africa and South-East Asia to Japan, the Philippines, Indonesia and Malaysia. In return the Japanese traded silver, gold, swords and wood products; the Koreans, silver, linen, furs and medicines. Chinese silver, gold, silk, porcelain, rice, sugar and salt were very much in demand in Cambodia, Java, Malaysia and Sumatra. In return the Chinese imported spices, incense and aloe wood. Few official records of Song trade exist on which to determine whether China ran a trading surplus or deficit with its Asian customers. The mass exports of porcelain and copper coins must have brought China much profit, but it is possible that the huge imports of spices and incense, paid for by the southward flow of Chinese silver and gold, may have eroded or even erased that surplus. Even the Song emperors could not repeal the unrelenting law of supply and demand.

The Song Empire, too, had its deadly enemies. In spite of their pioneering the art of explosive gunpowder, the Song were overrun by the Yuan (Mongols) led by Genghiz Khan (1162–1227) in the 13th century. Overrunning the north and taking Kaifeng in 1233, the Mongols eventually captured Hangzhou in 1276. By 1279 the last Song heir was dead. Incorporating China into their Central Asian Empire, the Mongol forces simultaneously overran Iran, Iraq, Syria, Turkey and Russia, and menaced both Byzantium and the gates of Christian Europe. Kublai Khan was seen as the Gog and Magog of the biblical Apocalypse, and with small wonder.

Rule in the empire of the Yuan – larger even than the Abbasid Caliphate – was often harsh. Cities were sacked and then razed to the ground, and much of the Muslim world would never recover its former glory. Huge shipments of grain were brought in by Chinese seagoing armadas to feed the new Yuan bureaucracy. Grain shipments from southern China grew from 3 million to 200 million kilograms between

1282 and 1329. The lucrative carrying trade soon became the monopoly of merchants such as Zhuqing (Shu Ching) and Zhangxuan (Shang Tsuan), who dreamt of cornering the markets of South-East Asia as well. Extorting from both the government and the peasants with the help of enormous bribes and private armies, the two merchants were eventually tried for treason, but not before they inspired a Confucian anti-market backlash that would gain more momentum under the Ming Empire.

Yet even the power of the Yuan had its limits. In 1274 Kublai Khan sent an armada of 900 junks carrying 15 000 horses and 40 000 men armed with guns against Japan. They were routed by a typhoon. In 1281 the Khan assembled 4500 ships and 150 000 men, but once again the *kamikaze*, or divine wind, sent virtually the entire Chinese fleet to the bottom, and most of the army with it. The Yuan fleet had more success in extracting tribute from the Vietnamese and Indonesians and in projecting Chinese power into the Indian Ocean as far as Madagascar. Yuan traders were even stiffer competitors for Arab merchants than Song traders had been. They sailed forth in enormous four-mast junks with crews of 150–300. There were 60 separate cabins for merchants. This opulence and mercantile might was witnessed by a visiting European trader who served in the court of the Great Khan from 1275 to 1292. His name was Marco Polo.

Marco Polo's guide to the medieval world economy

Imprisoned by the Genoese as a Venetian prisoner of war in 1296, Marco Polo began to intrigue both his inmates and even his captors with stories of his 17 years in the realm of Kublai Khan. The Genoese were so fascinated that they allowed him to send for his diary. He began to dictate his account to his ghostwriter, Rustichello of Pisa. Polo's *Description of the World* was a glowing (but not always accurate) portrait of the Mongol superstate and the world economy over which it presided. Polo's stories fascinated both his jailers and his fellow prisoners. It painted a picture of Chinese cities much richer and more magnificent than anything Europe had to offer. Broad streets and avenues were lined with the splendid homes of the rich, and the palace of the Khan at Zhangdu (Shang Tu, or Xanadu) surpassed the Vatican.

This Cathay (as China was termed by Europeans), described by Marco, was far beyond Europe in every respect. The Great Khan could monitor and rule his vast possessions via a network of postal stations and riders not unlike the Pony Express. More boats passed along the Yangzi than on all of Europe's waterways. Polo described to rapt audiences the vast fleets of seagoing junks and the port facilities of Hangzhou and Zaitun (Amoy), which put Venice to shame. The cities were immaculate; they were paved with brick and stone and their all-important harbours were greater than those of Venice, Genoa and Pisa combined. The tall-mast junks brought back to China a hundred times more spices than was enjoyed by all of Christendom. And – innovation of innovations – the Chinese used paper money, which they printed from wooden blocks.[17]

Marco Polo was following in the footsteps of his father and uncle. They had first reached the East as a result of the political and economic rivalries of the Italian city-states in the 13th century. Niccolò and Maffeo Polo were Venetian merchants at a time when Venice dominated the trade of the Mediterranean. Even Byzantium, under a Latin emperor who had been installed as a result of the Fourth Crusade in 1204, was now a satellite of the Venetians. Their trading regime extended as far as the Black Sea. Between 1253 and 1260 the elder Polos sojourned in Constantinople, doing business with a well-connected older brother.

Niccolò and Maffeo, however, were well aware that business prospects for Venetian firms in Byzantium were not good. The exiled Greek emperor, backed by the Genoese, was planning a coup. Relocating to their branch office in the Crimea, the Polos found business prospects little better there but were soon attracted by the Mongol penetration of Russia, which offered the possibility of whole new markets. Now the Great Khan had unified and pacified Central Asia and made possible safer travel and trade between the Black Sea and China. Thus inspired, Niccolò and Maffeo headed eastward along the ancient Silk Route with their goods. They sojourned with Khan Barka of Bolgara and, when he made war on his Mongol rival Hulegu in Iraq, they pushed on further east to Bukhara, carting their goods in two-wheeled covered wagons. At Bukhara the Polos met an ambassadorial party of Kublai Khan, who persuaded them to come to China. The journey to Cambaluc (Beijing) took a year, but when the Venetians arrived, the Mongol emperor received them royally. Curious about Christian monotheism, Kublai Khan asked the Polos to serve as his envoys to the pope. The Polos left Beijing in 1266 and reached Venice three years later.

In 1270 Niccolò and Maffeo began their return to China. With them was Niccolò's 20-year-old son Marco. The Polos travelled through the Mongol-ruled Muslim world, hoping to reach China by sea. The caravan went through Iraq to Hormuz but, upon discovering that the Arab *dhows* there were too frail and dangerous to reach China, the Polos turned once again to what was becoming one of the world economy's classic overland routes. They headed past the ancient lapis lazuli mines of Afghanistan once so prized by the Sumerians, climbed the Pamir to Xinjiang (Sinkiang) and crossed the Gobi Desert to reach the palace of Zhangdu. The Polos spent the years between 1272 and 1292 in China. Eager to employ talented foreigners, Kublai Khan enlisted them as his aides and young Marco was given the chance to see many parts of the Yuan Empire. Marco's description of the entrepreneurial port of Zaitun (Amoy) is a gem of 'booster' writing and serves to highlight China's role in the medieval world economy:

> *'Zai-tun ... has a port on the sea-coast celebrated for the resort of shipping, loaded with merchandize, that is afterwards distributed through every part of the province of Manji. The quantity of pepper imported there is so considerable, that what is carried to Alexandria, to supply the demand of the western parts of the world, is trifling in comparison, perhaps not more than the hundredth part. It is indeed impossible to convey an idea of the concourse of merchants and the accumulation of goods in this which is held to be one of the largest and most commodious ports in the world. The grand khan derives a vast revenue from this place ... charges, including customs and freight, amount to half the value of the cargo; and yet upon the half that remains to them their profit is so considerable, that they are always disposed to return to the same market with a further stock of merchandize.'*[18]

Unwilling to risk life under Kublai's unpredictable successor, the Polos returned on a fleet of 13 junks headed for Vietnam, Sumatra and, eventually, Persia. The voyage highlighted the risks and dangers of international commerce in the world economy of the 13th century. Out of 600 people who set sail, only 18 reached Hormuz. The world to which the Polos returned after a 25-year absence was not a good one for Venetian business. Genoa was now in the ascendancy, the Greeks in Constantinople were less disposed to Venetian commerce, and the last crusader state, Acre, was now in the hands of the Egyptian Mamluks. Marco and his relatives had to return to Venice via Iraq, Armenia, Trebizond and Constantinople. The following year, Marco was captured in the war, but was released in 1299. Returning to Venice he ran the family business, married, bore three daughters, and died there in 1324.

Marco Polo made little money in China. He was one of the first 'booster' writers of the Western world. His greatest legacy, *The Description of the World*, would have a profound impact on Italian merchants seeking direct contact with the Far East to outflank Arab middlemen. By this time, European traders were running caravans from the Crimea along the Silk Road or from south of Trebizond on the Black Sea across Armenia to the realm of the Ilkhan of Persia. Hormuz was the vital embarkation point for India. The energetic Vivaldi brothers of Genoa set up trading stations on the Malabar coast in 1315, meeting the Chinese merchant fleet there just as the Romans had done long before. Soon there were enough Italians in Beijing to have an Archbishop of Cambaluc. The Genoese set up a warehouse in Zaitun. The Florentines even drew up a guidebook, *The Practice of Commerce* (1340), compiled by Francesco Pegolotti, a branch manager of the Bardi firm, as a guide for Italians now seeking to tap into the Asian market. Pegolotti advized traders heading east from the Sea of Azov to hire good interpreters and to allow the natives to take their women with them. The land route to China was perfectly safe according to Pegolotti, whose glowing accounts resemble modern travel writing:

> '*It is reckoned that a merchant with a dragoman [interpreter] and two menservants and goods to the value of 25,000 gold florins would spend ... if he wishes to economize, from 60 to 80 silver sommi; and for the entire return journey from Cathay to Tana [on the Sea of Azov], including expenses for food, and salary of menservants, and all [other expenses] connected with it, 5 sommi per pack load or [even] less.*'[19]

Issues of currency and exchange were not ignored:

> '*All silver which the merchants carry with them when going to Cathay, the lord of Cathay causes to be withdrawn and placed in his treasury; and to the merchants who bring it he gives paper money, that is yellow paper struck with the seal of said lord, that money being called balisci. And with said money you may and can purchase*

silk and any other merchandize or goods you may wish to buy. And all the people of the country are bound to accept it, and yet people do not pay more for merchandize although it is paper money. And of the said paper money there are three kinds, one being worth more than another according as the lord orders them to be worth.'[20]

Could China have ruled world trade?
The Treasure Fleet of Zheng He

The Italian–Chinese trading bonanza was secure! Or so it seemed. But in 1368, a revolt led by a commoner, Zhu Yuanzhang (Chu Yuan-chang, better known as Taizu: 1328–98), ended Mongol rule and led to the establishment of the Ming Dynasty. After a promising start, the Ming would eventually abandon the expansionist course of their predecessors. This would be the era of the Forbidden City and xenophobia. In an effort to revive classical Confucianism, the populist Emperor Zhu and his Ming successors reacted to a century of foreign humiliation and domination. They were also eager to correct the abuses of the unrestricted market economy. Slavery was abolished, large estates were broken up, and the prosperous regions of Guangdong and Fujian were subject to heavy taxation. Zhu concentrated power in his own hands, fragmented that of his generals, and turned tax collection over to municipalities instead of tax farmers. Under his successor Zheng Xu (Cheng Tsu, 1402–24), China once again flexed her military power, letting the Mongols, Vietnamese and even Japan know that she remained a world power.

Yet even Zheng was not averse to the profits of mercantile expansion. Indeed, in his reign China's political and economic influence reached its pinnacle, asserting dominion over the entire Indian Ocean. The principal weapon was the most magnificent navy yet to sail into the pages of history. From 1403 to 1407 the emperor supervized the labour of tens of thousands of trained craftsmen in huge dry-docks along the Yangzi and in other southern ports to build 1700 of the finest state-of-the-art junks and other vessels to outdo anything yet seen. The Treasure Fleet ships were about 130 metres long and 50 metres wide, among the largest ever, with watertight bulkheads, nine masts and a dozen square sails of red silk cloth. Each carried two dozen cannon with the capability to hit ships 300 metres away. The merchant-admiral Zheng He, appointed as commodore

THE TRADER P'U

AN ARAB COMMERCIAL AGENT

During the Middle Ages, many Arab and Persian traders employed permanent resident agents in Canton who would ship spices and porcelain back to the Gulf. One such trader was the 12th-century agent known only as P'u. Originally based in what is now Vietnam, P'u had become so fearful of the dangers of sea travel that he requested, and was granted, permission by his employer to settle permanently in Canton as a Muslim commercial agent.

The P'u enterprise in Canton soon became very wealthy in spite of Chinese governmental restrictions on foreign traders such as himself. Because the local officials wished to encourage more foreign investment, they tended to look the other way while P'u and his family amassed a fortune and built a luxurious mansion.

The Chinese writer Yo Ko described the ostentatious wealth accumulated by the Pu family. Their Chinese servants and employees were always tipped generously, while visitors to the spacious mansion were impressed by the manner in which the family patriarch loved to flaunt his pearls, perfumes and other valuables in front of his Chinese guests.

Being polytheists, many Chinese found the tall minarets and the prayers to a single invisible Allah difficult to understand. In Yo Ko's description, the 'white barbarian' traders spent all day praying in their tall pagoda, to a deity that no one could see, for the successful south winds that would bring the annual convoys from the West to China.

The account of Yo Ko hints at the low level of trust between Confucian bureaucrats and business in Song China, the culture shock between the native Chinese and their Islamic clients, and the strong role that faith played in Muslim commerce.

of the Treasure Fleet, set sail for Calicut, proving, to the chagrin of the reactionary Confucian sages who had counted on the Ming to oppose further globalization, that China was the heart and core of a world economy. The emperor was pleased: 'Now all within the four seas are as one family. Let there be mutual trade at the frontier barriers in order to supply the country's needs and to encourage distant people to come.'[21]

This formidable treasure fleet carried gigantic sailing charts demarcating Africa and India and offering elaborate navigational directions. Landmarks, pagodas and forests were clearly shown. Zheng's floating emporium traded silk and porcelain in Vietnam, then sailed on to Chinese colonies on Java, where they picked up consignments of spices before heading on to Sri Lanka and India. In Calicut, we are told, Zheng's officers would dicker with Indian brokers on the value of Chinese silk and porcelain versus Indian stone and spices – the Chinese using their abacus, the Indians their fingers and toes. They then joined hands to ratify their contracts: 'In such and such a moon, on such and such a day, we have all joined hands and sealed our agreement with a hand-clasp; whether the price is dear or cheap, we will never repudiate it or change it.'

Zheng's merchant fleet helped link and stabilize the vast Chinese trading regime. Later voyages would set up a commercial settlement for imperial merchants in Malacca, where Indian and other goods could be stored and reshipped to China. The fleet forcibly opened the markets of Sri Lanka in 1411. In 1414, Zheng voyaged into the Persian Gulf, to Hormuz, where the Chinese traded porcelain and silk for the precious stones and carpets of the Gulf. Zheng's fifth voyage, in 1417, took him for the first time into Africa. The Africans, who made an excellent market for Chinese porcelain, were nonetheless terrified by the guns of the huge fleet, and Zheng backed off only to return to Africa on his sixth voyage in 1421.[22] In 1431–1432 came the final voyage of the Treasure Fleet to Vietnam, Malaysia, Java, Sumatra, Malacca, Sri Lanka, Calicut and Arabia. Zheng, now in his sixties, died in Calicut. According to his biographer Louise Levathes, Chinese influence abroad was now at its peak, the emperor's writ stretching from Korea and even Japan to South-East Asia, India and even East Africa:

> *'From this lofty pinnacle China could have consolidated its position and become the dominant power in shaping the modern world. While Europe was still emerging from the Dark Ages, China, with her navy of giant junks, was poised to become the colonial power of the sixteenth century and tap the riches of the globe.'[23]*

How and why did China begin to retreat from her seeming destiny? There were obvious immediate causes. After Zhu Di died in 1424 a long period of political instability ensued. China fell into the hands of boy emperors and Confucian traditionalists. In 1449, a Ming emperor shut down both the Treasure Fleet and its shipyards. The Chinese now 'began to lose their technological edge over the West, never to regain it'.[24]

As so often happens, political chaos generated economic chaos. The tax base contracted from 45 to 20 million hectares. The Ming currency collapsed in a wave of inflation and China's neighbours quickly asserted their financial and political independence. The Ming withdrew more and more into parochialism and isolationism, abandoning Vietnam and Mongolia. Contacts with foreigners were restricted and closely supervized in a wave of xenophobic, anti-capitalist Confucianism. Soon, ambitious Europeans would learn of China's inward turn and would exploit it ruthlessly. The 16th-century missionary Juan González de Mendoza recorded the Ming débâcle:

> '[The Chinese] have found by experience [that] to go forth of their
> owne kingdome to conquer others, is the spoile and loss of much
> people, and expenses of great treasures, besides the trauaile and care
> which continually they have to sustaine that which is got, with feare
> to be lost againe; so that in the meane time whilest they were
> occupied in strange conquests, their enemies the Tartarians and other
> kings borderers unto them, did trouble and invade them, doing great
> damage and harme ... [So] they found it requisit for their quietnes
> and profite ... to leaue al [that] they had got and gained out of their
> own kingdome, but specially such countries as were farre off. And
> from that day forwards not to make wars in any place.'[25]

The ultimate tragedy of Chinese capitalism was that it became identified with a hated Mongolian dynasty and conflicted with the deeply held ideas of a powerful bureaucratic elite. The American experience with the Shah of Iran in the 1970s was a close modern parallel. Culture played its part. Businesspeople in Ming China had far less prestige than in Mameluk Egypt or in Christian Europe. Thus the most pro-business dynasty in Chinese history was also the most foreign. When the Mongol Yuan were overthrown by the Ming, capitalism became the victim of a reaction against all things foreign. The very things that were responsible for China's becoming the superpower of the Middle Ages – the acceptance of business enterprise, open contact with and toleration of foreigners at home and abroad, vigorous naval expansion and promotion of overseas trade – were now stigmatized. In the nationalist reaction businesspeople and merchants were labelled as 'un-Confucian' and 'un-Chinese'.

More recent historians such as Janet Abu-Lughod have found another cause for China's aborted world hegemony. In her mind, the Black Death, which ruined Arab power, also greatly affected China. Carried by the Mongols in the early 14th century, the plague ultimately spread as far as Fujian and Guangdong by the 1360s. The plague hit southern China far more than the north, fatally weakening the Yuan Dynasty and allowing the Ming to seize power. Once in power, the Ming moved their capital to Beijing (Peking) and sought to build up their economic and political power base in northern China. China's political centre was in the north but her economy was in the south. For a while, this worked. 'Two systems of external trade' complemented each other – the Silk Route across Central Asia terminated at Beijing; the Indian Ocean sea trade terminated in Canton and Hangzhou. Between 1250 and 1350, China, according to Abu-Lughod, was a 'crucial link between the land and sea trades and, in her domain of influence at least, became a formidable power in an increasingly integrated world system.'[26] By the time the Ming drove out the Mongols, the more entrepreneurial China of the south was decimated by the Black Death and the old Silk Route, blocked by the Mongol Tamerlane, was closed. The voyages of the Treasure Fleet would gradually yield diminishing returns, persuading the Ming to abandon the active quest for world power: 'The aberration of some two hundred years of southern port centrality to the economy ended and, with it, the chance for world hegemony.'[27]

China, the glorious China of porcelain, spices and gunpowder, was shut off from the era of European expansion, which would soon follow.

NOTES TO CHAPTER 11

1. 'Copper coins were circulated as legal tender, rising from 1.83 million strings around 1000 to 5.06 million strings in 1080. These measures unified China enough to allow the Song to rule for three centuries: Shiba, Y. 'Sung Foreign Trade: Its Scope and Organization' in Rossabii, M., ed. (1983) *China Among Equals: The Middle Kingdom and its Neighbors, 10th–14th Centuries*. Berkeley, CA: University of California Press, 89–115, 91–2.
2. Gates, H. (1998) *China's Motor: A Thousand Years of Petty Capitalism*. Ithaca: Cornell University Press, 22–8.
3. *Ibid.*, 28.
4. *Ibid.*: 'By checking the inherent tendency of free markets to produce ever-larger pools of capital, official policy encouraged the maintenance of an intensely competitive market for petty capitalists while retaining the power to monopolize that market for its own use.'

5. There was by Song times, after 1000 CE, a persistent legacy of public enterprise not unlike the temple and state capitalism found in the ancient Near East. Mandarin bureaucrats, army officials and Buddhist and Daoist monasteries coexisted with the small family enterprises and partnerships. The empire still ran the salt and tea trade as public monopolies as they had done for centuries. These public firms were exempt from certain taxes and enjoyed certain advantages over privately owned shippers. See Shiba, Y. 'Urbanization and the Development of Markets in the Lower Yangtze Valley' in Winthrop Haeger, J., ed. (1975) *Crisis and Prosperity in Sung China*. Tucson: University of Arizona Press, 13–33.

6. Kuan, C. *Works of Chin Huai-hai*, quoted in Shiba, Y. *Commerce in Sung China*, tr. Elvin, M. (1970). Ann Arbor, MI: University of Michigan Center for Chinese Studies, 27. The name and place of the publisher of these Chinese sources quoted in this volume are not given by Shiba.

7. Shiba, Y. *Commerce in Sung China*, tr. Elvin, M. (1970). Ann Arbor, MI: University of Michigan Center for Chinese Studies, 33.

8. Shih, Y. quoted in Shiba, Y., *ibid.* 34, 14. In addition to the umbrella arrangements, firms that represented early joint-stock arrangements were noted in a Song Dynasty legal digest of 1142: 'Merchants are forbidden to trade privately in tea and to cross the Huai River secretly in order to engage in private commercial exchange with merchants from the (Chin Tartar) North. Members of associations of partners ... joint capital partnerships ... or associations of members of the same trade without joint capital ... who carry information against smuggling shall not be regarded as committing any offence.'

9. Gates, H. (1998) *China's Motor: A Thousand Years of Petty Capitalism*. Ithaca: Cornell University Press, 34.

10. Quoted in Temple, R. (1998) *The Genius of China: 3000 years of Science, Discovery and Invention*; introduction by Needham, J. London: Prion Books, 68.

11. Cheng, T. cited in Shiba, Y. *Commerce in Sung China*, tr. Elvin, M. (1970). Ann Arbor, MI: University of Michigan Center for Chinese Studies. Shiba, Y. 'Sung Foreign Trade: Its Scope and Organization' in Rossabii, M., ed. (1983) *China Among Equals: The Middle Kingdom and its Neighbors, 10th–14th Centuries*. Berkeley,CA: University of California Press, 109.

12. Levathes, L. (1994) *When China Ruled the Seas: The Treasure Fleet of the Dragon Throne, 1405–1433*. New York: Oxford University Press, 34–6.

13. *Ibid.*, 41.

14. *Ibid.*

15. *Ibid.*, 106.

16. *Ibid.*, 42.

17. Gies, J. and F. (1972) *Merchants and Moneymen: The Commercial Revolution, 1000–1500*. New York: Thomas Y. Crowell, 114–15.

18. *The Travels of Marco Polo* [*The Description of the World*], Book II, Chapter 77, Marsden-Wright translation. New York: Orion Press, n.d., 253.

19. Pegolotti, F. *The Practice of Commerce: Traveling to China*, extract from Evans,

A.P., ed., Records of Civilization, Sources and Studies Series, Vol. LII, *Medieval Trade in the Mediterranean World*, Lopez, R.S. and Raymond, I.W., eds. (1955). York: Columbia University Press, 355–8, reprinted in McNeill, W.H. and Houser, S.O., eds., *Medieval Europe*. New York: Oxford University Press, 285.
20. *Ibid.*, 286.
21. Levathes, L. (1994) *When China Ruled the Seas: The Treasure Fleet of the Dragon Throne, 1405–1433*. New York: Oxford University Press, 101.
22. *Ibid.*, 145–52.
23. *Ibid.*, 142.
24. *Ibid.*, 177.
25. *Ibid.*, 180–1.
26. Abu-Lughod, J.L. (1989) *Before European Hegemony: The World System AD 1250–1350*. New York: Oxford University Press, 346.
27. *Ibid.*, 347.

12

A global economy

The age of the chartered trading company: 1450–1800

IN the year 1500, humanity stood on the threshold of the modern age. China's retreat from world naval hegemony was followed by the entry of first the Portuguese and then the Dutch, French and English into Asian waters. Spanish vessels crossed the Atlantic to exploit the resources of the New World. The result was the creation of the first genuinely *global* economy.

Midwife to this new economy was a new phase in business organization in which the corporate form would overshadow the partnership. As rival nation-states consolidated, a new era of managed trade began. The business cultures of Portugal, Habsburg Spain, Royalist France, Calvinist Holland and, finally, Tudor, Stuart and Hanover England were new variations on an old theme: Phoenician/Carthaginian naval capitalism. The newness came in the form of the chartered, joint-stock company, a semi-private, semi-public firm to which kings would grant monopoly power over vast sectors of the world's trade and of the world's geography. From this would come our first modern multinationals and professional business schools.

Harvard's David Landes traces Europe's rise to market economics and property rights. Europe was fragmented among competing nations, so that if Spain monopolized a large slice of the economic pie, one might turn to the Dutch as a trading partner. In this emerging mercantile system, competition was the life-blood of trade. Marxist-oriented 'world system' historians insist that Europe rose through forceful exploitation of the non-Western world. Andre Gunder Frank even now insists that Europe did not truly dominate world trade until after 1800! While Frank's extreme thesis is rejected by most historians, he nevertheless is on stronger ground in documenting the growth of the first truly *global*, as opposed to *world* (i.e. Eastern Hemisphere alone) economy. In 1691 the Englishman Dudley North observed, 'The Whole World as to Trade, is but one Nation or People, and therein Nations are as Persons.'[1]

Asia was bustling when Vasco da Gama rounded the Cape of Good Hope in 1497. The Portuguese acted as middlemen and investors as well as conquerors. Christopher Columbus and the Spanish and Portuguese conquests and settlements that followed him brought the Americas into the medieval economy at almost the same time, transforming it from a hemispheric to a truly global economy.

By 1550 Spanish Mexico was shipping thousands of tonnes of silver ingots to Spain and Europe. Two-thirds of European exports to Asia were made up of bullion. Between 1660 and 1720 bullion comprised around 90 per cent of the Dutch East India Company's yearly exports. The oriental route was still a prosperous trek. To the north of Byzantium lay the trade routes of Russia and Central Asia, to the west the trails to Europe via the Levant, to the south the routes to Arabia, Egypt and Africa, and to the east the way to the Indian Ocean and Far East. The Turks formed a land-bridge for the spice and silk trade. In return, the spices and porcelain of the East Indies and China were shipped westward to Europe and beyond to America, some of it coming across the Pacific via the Spanish domain in the Philippines.

> Christopher Columbus and the Spanish and Portuguese conquests and settlements that followed him brought the Americas into the medieval economy at almost the same time, transforming it from a hemispheric to a truly global economy

Competition in this First Global Economy was harsh. Textiles from the East Indies competed with those from Europe. Portuguese sugar traders from their Brazilian base had to vie with those of Java and Bengal. Chinese silk competed with Persian and Italian strands, Japanese copper with Spanish American. The prices of all these commodities were recorded on the Amsterdam Stock Exchange. The Dutch East India Company practised shrewd outsourcing tactics. Europeans could make or break their more confined competitors. The Dutch bought cheap sugar, coffee and other commodities in Brazil and the West Indies, depressing the economy of the Persian Gulf. A hinge of fate had turned.[2]

Crusader capitalism: the Genoese and Venetians

The First Global Economy grew from the ongoing rivalry of Genoa and Venice. Europe after 1450 inherited a host of mercantile techniques, from bookkeeping to early insurance policies. By 1500 feudalism was dead and the economy transformed 'from medieval exchange on terms set by custom and usage to market pricing based on negotiation between traders'.[3] As in Greece or Phoenicia, no one government could control access to all overseas markets. In the 1200s Venice dominated the Mediterranean for the next 80 years, until the Genoese were able to place an ally on the withering Byzantine throne. The 1300s belonged to Genoa until the Venetian fleet reversed the verdict in 1380. With the Mongols under Tamerlane blocking the Silk Road, Venice controlled the most secure route to Syria and Egypt. In the 1400s Venice towered over other Italian cities and became the richest city in Europe. With 150 000 people and 1.5 million subjects, Venice had a revenue of 1.6 million ducats. France, with 15 million people, collected only 1 million. By 1450, the merchants of Venice all but monopolized the major commodity trades of the Mediterranean: pepper, spices, cotton, grain, wine and salt. The doge's canny subjects invested 10 million ducats a year in trade, reaping an interest of 2 million and a profit to match – an enviable return on investment of 40 per cent.

The Venetian Empire foreshadowed the naval capitalism of the First Global Economy: 'Venice ... carved ... out an empire ... reminiscent, though on a very different scale, *of the Portuguese and later the Dutch Empires* in the Indian Ocean, a trading-post empire forming a long capitalist antenna; *an empire "on the Phoenician model", to use a more ancient parallel*' (emphasis added).[4] According to Fernand Braudel 'the whole of Europe was in Venice's hands'. He might have included the Mediterranean and the Black Sea as well. The Venetian economic sphere stretched all the way to the cities of Germany, England and the Levant, and linked up with the Muslim-held routes to the Indian Ocean, Sub-Saharan Africa and the Gulf from which spices, medicines and silk poured into the West. As in ancient Phoenicia, Venice could be very self-protective. Foreign merchants were restricted to their own quarters. Like the ancient Canaanites, the 15th-century Venetians pursued a conscious strategy of managed trade, although it was based upon partnerships, not merchant-princes. All exports and imports traded with Venice passed through her busy waterways. The armed convoys of Venice were the pride of her shipyards with some vessels weighing up to 300 tonnes.

Portugal, Spain and Holland sought to circumvent the Venetian monopoly with their own versions of Phoenician-style naval enterprise. Innovative tactics of fighting, investing and trading helped to even the odds with the Queen City of the Adriatic. Spanish and Portuguese galleons and caravels and Dutch *fluyts* were now sturdy and cost-effective enough to cross oceans. Discoveries of Galileo, Newton and others in astronomy and physics were applied to navigation.[5] Most Atlantic states in the late 1400s and early 1500s hired Italian navigators and merchants. Christopher Columbus and Amerigo Vespucci (Spain), Giovanni and Sebastian Cabotto (England) and Giovanni da Verrazano (France) became household names.

The Portuguese were the quickest to adapt Italy's prodigious market knowledge. Early in the 1400s Prince Henry the Navigator created an institute devoted to learning how to reach India by sailing around Africa. Among the prince's hired knowledge-workers were Europe's finest astronomers, map-makers and sailors. In 1418, Portuguese ships began to follow the ancient trail of Hanno of Carthage, sailing down the shores of West Africa. The new caravels had three masts, triangular sails, rudders, compasses adapted from the Chinese and the finest maps Italy could produce. They inched southward, reaching Rio de Oro in 1436, Cape Verde in 1446, Sierra Leone in 1460, the Gold Coast in 1481, the Congo in 1482 and the Cape of Good Hope in 1488. In 1497 Vasco da Gama rounded the Cape, reached Mozambique, Madagascar and Malindi in East Africa and sailed on to Calicut in India, a traditional trading port of the Chinese. Risks on these oceanic voyages remained high: da Gama lost two of his four vessels and two-thirds of his crew. The Indian spices he acquired, though, more than justified the risk and more than paid for the voyage.

European history's axis, dominated for two millennia by the Mediterranean, now shifted dramatically to the Atlantic. While Italy fell under the curse of fierce political wars between French Valois and Spanish Habsburgs, Portugal opened a direct sea route to India and Asia, wresting the spice trade from Venetian hands. The commercial dominance enjoyed by the Italian city-republics was doomed. Portugal developed a strong trading presence among the Indian, Chinese, Indonesian and other merchants of the Indian Ocean, which would last until the 1670s.

Booster literature like the *Suma Oriental* (*Account of the East*), penned around 1515 by the royal pharmacist and accountant Tomé Pires, described the economic opportunities of the East. Pires recognized that 'whoever is lord of Malacca has his hands on the throat of Venice'.[6] The writer lived in Malacca from 1513 to 1516 and served as his country's first ambassador to China, where he was imprisoned by a hostile Ming emperor and died. Malacca was the core of the Asian trading economy. Not only Portuguese but hundreds of Indian, Arabian and other merchants traded or had agents there. Cross-border enterprise in Asia was thriving. Gujaratis, the most expert traders of them all, like Italians in their knowledge of and dealings in merchandise, were settled everywhere in Malacca, along with Muslims from Aden and Hormuz.

Hindus possessed the best market knowledge, something those 'who want to be clerks and factors ought to go there and learn. [The] business of trade is a science in itself,'[7] a science Pires felt his country needed to acquire. 'They trade with the kingdom of the Deccan and Goa and with Malabar, and they have factors everywhere ... [T]here is no trading place where you do not see Gujarat merchants.'[8] Asian trade was highly interdependent: 'If Cambay (Gujarat) were cut off from trading with Malacca, it could not live, for it would have no outlet for its merchandise.'[9] Hindus and Muslims were an integral part of an abiding Indian Ocean network:

> 'Because those from Cairo and Mecca and Aden cannot reach
> Malacca in a single monsoon, as well as the Parsees and those from
> Ormuz and Rumes, Turks and similar peoples such as Armenians, at
> their own time they go to the kingdom of Gujarat, bringing large
> quantities of valuable merchandise; and they go to the kingdom of
> Gujarat to take up their companies in the said ships of that land, and
> they take the said companies in large numbers. They also take from
> the said kingdoms to Cambay, merchandise of value in Gujarat, from
> which they make much profit. Those from Cairo take their
> merchandise to Tor, and from Tor to Jidda, and from Jidda to Aden,
> and from Aden to Cambay, where they sell in the land things which
> are valued there, and the others they bring to Malacca, sharing as
> aforesaid.'[10]

Malacca linked the Far East with the Indian Ocean, distributing the spices of the Moluccas (Spice Islands) to China as well as to the Indian Ocean. This allowed merchants to reap a 30–50 per cent profit in the Cantonese market. The aggressive naval capitalism of antiquity, based on control of the critical trade routes, took on new life in the fleets and bases of Madeira, the Azores, Angola, Mozambique, Goa, Sri Lanka (1515), Ormuz, Malacca, the Moluccas, Macao (1557) and Brazil. The Portuguese navy and merchant captains in Goa, Malacca and Macao soon captured a large chunk of the middleman trade between the East Indies, China, Japan and India from their powerful Muslim and Hindu competitors after defeating the Muslim fleet off the coast of India in 1509. Lisbon's trade with India and the Spice Islands was a crown monopoly, all spices being sold through the India House in Lisbon.

Spanish naval capitalism was more militant. To bypass Venetian control, Columbus sailed out into the Atlantic along a route Carthaginians may also have tried. Ferdinand and Isabella underwrote Columbus's scheme to find an alternative route to the East Indies by sailing west across the Atlantic. The Court in Lisbon, its market intelligence honed to efficiency, knew that the Indies were just too far away, as Magellan would later discover. Shut out of most Asian markets, Spain found that her 'mistake' became her opportunity. Westward she looked and the land was bright! The gold and silver of Mexico and Peru became far more valuable than the spices of the Indies. By 1600 Spain ruled most of the Western Hemisphere, though the native populations suffered unspeakable horrors of disease and slavery. The New World's birth-pangs were needlessly severe. The brutal Spanish conquests would, though, fund the First Global Economy, a development that held out – still holds out – hope for the millions.

A handful of ruthless *conquistadores* in search of a legendary El Dorado nudged the soaring trajectory of world civilization. Gold and silver looted from the Aztecs and Incas was exported to Spain; spices from Indonesia and porcelain from China entered Europe through Lisbon. The conquest transformed global ecology along with the global economy. Horses, cattle, sheep, chickens and bees as well as bananas, coffee, sugar, wheat, barley, rice, turnips, cabbage, cotton and lettuce were introduced to the Americas. American corn and potatoes would eventually double China's farmland and triple its population, as well as that of Europe after 1750. Africans obtained corn, tomatoes, sunflowers, cacao, peanuts and pineapple, which eventually they would consume and export.[11]

Spain quickly moved into a position of potential world power based upon the vast new reserves of hard currency from the mines of Mexico and Peru, and a supremely powerful navy. Her boldest explorers were often soldiers as well. They carved out state-supervized trading colonies for controlling and monopolising the flow of silver, gold and the exotic tobacco and potato plants from the Americas. The cash bonanza, however, was paramount! Already in possession of most of Christendom's new money supply, the Spanish Empire grew mightier still when Charles I of Spain became Holy Roman Emperor Charles V in 1519. Now Austria, Hungary, Burgundy and much of Italy lent their support to the overspreading of the Americas. The Habsburg *world* empire of Charles V lasted 40 years but, in spite of its vast resources in agriculture, cloth and iron industries, and currency, it would crumble.

Spanish naval capitalism was not as sound as the Phoenician/Punic model it resembled, for its rulers were far more hostile to the enterprises that created their wealth and they dabbled incessantly in Europe's crises. Not least of these was the Protestant Reformation, initiated by the German monk Martin Luther in 1517. Charles V became the hope of the Catholic Counter-Reformation, and Spanish absolutism and Habsburg Catholicism encouraged neither independent thought nor business. In Spain itself, the more enterprising Jews and Moors had to convert or leave, taking their market secrets and commercial zeal with them. No hope for a market revolution in Madrid! Military might and politics meant everything; markets were ignored. Endless wars to unite Europe under the Catholic fold began to undermine even the dreams of El Dorado. Paid for by massive borrowing and taxation, the Counter-Reformation sapped Spanish enterprise and aborted economic growth. As it had done in the original Roman Empire, the tax burden fell on peasants and small proprietors least able to pay. Meanwhile, the tax-exempt 2–3 per cent of the population, most of them nobles, owned over 97 per cent of Spain's rich lands. Thus, in spite of the huge flow of bullion from the Americas, which rose from 1 to 9 million ducats a year between 1540 and 1590, Spain's extravagant rulers ensured that the mother country was always heavily in debt. The Spanish Habsburgs forgot the example of the mercantilist rulers of ancient Tyre and Carthage and practised instead the unfortunate paradigm of Minoan Crete and Pharaonic Egypt.

The Calvinist Dutch

Positioned at the centre of the Northern European take-off of medieval times, the Low Countries, especially Calvinist Holland, were more market-oriented than anywhere else in Europe save Italy. Cattle, wheat, tulips, beer and hemp were raised for the urban textile centres of Italy and Flanders. Like Ugarit or Carthage the Dutch mixed farming and commerce under an oligarchy of town merchants whose practical, 'works-based' religion was extremely conducive to enterprise. The Elect were marked by the signal favours and divine blessings of God. The Dutch worked at their own salvation, as Paul encouraged the faithful in Philippians 2:12–13. The sturdy Calvinist creed took seriously the injunction 'Six days shalt thou labour' and nurtured a religion ideal for the rise of capitalism. The charging of interest was seen as socially and morally good. Even more than Muhammad, Calvin placed divine approval on the creation of wealth, investment, industry and commerce. No religious system till that time so encouraged money-making.

> Even more than Muhammad, Calvin placed divine approval on the creation of wealth, investment, industry and commerce. No religious system till that time so encouraged money-making

Even before their national revolt in the late 1500s, Dutch traders exchanged Spanish silver from Mexico for the grain, timber and naval stores of the Baltic, paying for them with textiles, fish and dairy products from their own confined but productive realm. Amsterdam processed and exported the cloth and raw materials of other producers in a way recalling the Phoenicians of old. The Dutch showed religious toleration for Jews, Huguenots, Flemings, Walloons and other refugees with capital and the acumen to use it. Meanwhile the Stadtholder and his regents waged all-out commercial warfare on Portugal's Catholics. Dutch men-of-war descended upon galleons bound for Lisbon and Goa. Dutch admirals set up bases at the Cape of Good Hope in Surinam, the Moluccas, Java, New York and Brazil. Dutch commercial strategy concentrated on the East Indies and the Indian Ocean. The Dutch East India Company, chartered in 1602, was the Republic's principal trading weapon. Jan Compagnie, as it was called, one of the first multinational enterprises of modern times, wielded a power that few but the Phoenicians had brandished before them:

> *'The Portuguese king maintained a monopoly over the spice trade, but private individuals could invest in the trade effort. Private trade in non-monopolized commodities was carried on alongside the spice trade,*

*making use of Asiatic traders. The Dutch Company, in contrast, gained
a complete monopoly over the entirety of Dutch trade.'[12]*

Company officials exercized political and even military authority in areas
where money was invested. East India Company directors made war,
signed treaties, governed natives and secured fortifications. The Dutch
home office ruled the firm through its board of directors, the Heren XVII
or Seventeen Gentlemen. East India subsidiaries were run by a governor-
general with the jurisdiction and mandate ruthlessly to establish 'an early
and complete dominance over the production and distribution of spices'.[13]
Dutch East India marines invaded Tidore and Amboyna in the Moluccas
in 1605 and Java in 1606. Sri Lanka was next in 1638 and Malacca in
1641, leaving but Goa and Macao to the Portuguese. Through it all, the
Moluccas were the key strategic target for capital investment. The Sultan
of Ternate granted the East Indiamen a monopoly over the cloves of
Amboyna and the nutmeg and mace of Banda in return for military
protection. The company could be ruthless in the protection of its markets,
as the Sultan's subjects soon learned. For example, to protect its sources of
supply, the natives of Banda – an inexpensive labour market – were
deported and clove trees outside company control were cut down. Dutch
capitalism had its dark side.

In the fateful struggle with its competitors, Holland looked to her fleet
– more manoeuvrable and better armed than its Portuguese rival and
with better lines of communication. Dutch *ownership-specific advantages,*
i.e. better naval expertise and a more flexible management structure,
won over rigid Portuguese rivals whose 'inefficient and centralized
command' lacked men, ships, money, tactics and discipline.[14] In 1655,
the Portuguese neglected to occupy a strategic beach near Colombo,
letting the Dutch lay siege to the city. Generations of Dutch experience
with capital-accumulation in the Middle Ages paid off handsomely in the
crucible of a commercial war where: 'Portugal soon fell prey to the
poverty of its home base and to its need to import cereals, cloth and
manufactured goods,' as 'a mercantile bourgeoisie defeated an elite of
sea-trading aristocrats.'[15]

The Dutch East India Company reached its height under Johannes
Maetsuyker, governor-general from 1653 to 1678. The firm ruled in Java,
Sri Lanka and South Africa and vanquished England in three trade wars.
Holland's rivals were all but driven out of the Indies. Maetsuyker ran Jan

Compagnie through a combination of toughness, fairness and respect for the cultural sensitivities of the Sri Lankans, a race 'very sensitive regarding their personal dignity'.[16] The Heren XVII themselves ruled with little responsibility to company shareholders. Family members and friends were given executive positions in Java regardless of merit. Some, like the drunken poet Aernout van Overbeke, however, performed well, beating off attacks by English frigates during the war of 1672. The admiral-trader Rijkloff van Goens of Batavia (1619–82) rose quickly in company ranks from menial beginnings to become Maetsuyker's naval commander. By the 1670s he had driven the Portuguese, the English and the French from the East Indies. Van Goens believed force could resolve any trading dispute. Following his victories he became branch manager in Colombo, where he exercized a heavy-handed jurisdiction in Sri Lanka and Malabar. His freewheeling style did not help the company's reputation. His replacement in the Indies, Cornelis Speelman (1628–84) of Rotterdam, was a tactful manager, having served in Persia, Coromandel and the Indies, where he worked 16-hour days in Batavia Castle. Speelman pioneered the life of the effective executive. He sometimes dictated three letters at once and audited accounts with the precision, it is said, of a modern computer.

> By 1664 the Dutch East India Company, 'a colossal organization, comparable to one of the great multinational firms, when due allowance is made for differences in time, space, and demography', was at its apogee

Dutch power had its limits. Speelman needed an Indonesian army to capture the Spice Islands. Much Far Eastern trade remained in Asian hands. Maetsuyker admitted that: 'our own people can never compete successfully by sea or land against the Muslims, Chinese and other indigenous traders,' since the latter 'move round much more cheaply, and ... regulate their affairs better.'[17] Maetsuyker's failure in Taiwan reflected poor office politics, market intelligence and understanding of Asian business cultures. Taiwan branch head Frederick Coyet warned in 1662 of a Ming invasion; his council discounted the warning, then prosecuted Coyet when Taiwan fell. The Dutch fleets next tried to support the rising Qing (Manchu) forces in Manchuria, but could not communicate with them!

By 1664 the Dutch East India Company, 'a colossal organization, comparable to one of the great multinational firms, when due allowance is made for differences in time, space, and demography', was at its apogee. It deployed 140 ships and employed 25 000 workers.[18] A 1673 letter by Maetsuyker to the Heren XVII indicated that the company was making a lot more money handling trade among Asians than with other Europeans. The lesson was that 'interport trade should always be preferred over that with the fatherland'.[19] Branches in Persia and India were doing well, while militarized settlements in Sri Lanka and the East Indies were losing money. Competition was not always the lifeblood of trade in an age when the military and the mercantile kept pace with each other. No sooner had they cornered the European share of the spice market, around 1678, when the Dutch East India Company faced a new challenge from the English East India Company, a firm they had sorely underestimated. Investing in goods from Surat, Bengal and Coromandel, the English, a second-rate sea and trading power through much of the 16th century, doubled their East India Company's capital from what it had been in 1676.

'Imperial overstretch' and the struggle with Louis XIV of France were playing their part. Dutch commercial power was fading by 1700, the numbers and quality of their ships and sailors deteriorating. The Dutch East India Company manned 124 ships in Asia in 1674, but only 81 by 1704, and fewer and fewer of the crews were Dutchmen. By the 1680s the global economy itself began to shift as demand for spices began to fall for the first time in centuries. The Dutch had cornered the wrong market! Both the Dutch and the English East India Companies began to diversify into textiles. In the period 1674–1679 the Dutch imported 328 500 pieces, between 1704 and 1709, 819 000 pieces and between 1724 and 1729, 1.2 million pieces of finished Asian goods. India at first figured very heavily in this new trade. One third of Dutch Asian imports in 1697 came from Bengal alone. The Dutch sold these products across Europe, from Russia to Spain. Quite often they would buy Chinese silk in Seville, which Spanish galleons based in Manila had acquired from China and exported across the Pacific to Mexico. From there it was shipped to Europe in Spanish galleons. This was a world economy in spades!

By 1700, the market for Chinese silk, porcelain and tea was replacing the Indian. The English established a company branch in Canton in 1701. The Dutch, outmanoeuvred, were resupplied by Chinese middlemen from Guangdong and Fujian. The goods were then shipped to

Batavia (Java). The silver of Mexico, making its way clear around the world to Seville, Amsterdam and finally Batavia, financed access to this circular trade, a trading regime based on China where Dutch and other European merchants worked the local Canton markets. At the same time, Chinese junks coming to Batavia could still be paid in spices. The complexity was marvellous but subject to the vagaries of supply and demand.

What was happening was instructive for the developing history of multi-national business. Britain's locational advantage in Canton was under-cutting the Dutch lead in textiles. When the English East India Company set up shop in Sumatra in 1736, they acquired a major share of the Dutch pepper market. Unrest in Java and Sri Lanka and the harsh winter of 1740 stretched Holland's resources to the limit. The Heren XVII, still paying high dividends, ran up huge losses in the Asia middleman trade, and fell more heavily into debt while their management became more and more bureau-cratic. The company's collapse and dissolution took place in 1799 just after the British had captured Dutch possessions in India and South Africa. Dutch mastery of the long-coveted world spice market was, in the end, a hollow triumph. All that glittered was not gold.

Thus was closing an important chapter in the history of the first modern multinationals, where advantage accrued from 'cross-border transactions through sales or production branches in two or more countries'.[20] The volume of business was enormous even by modern standards, with hundreds of thousands of transactions recorded each year. The invoices of the 1600s circulating between the Dutch firm's East Indian office and the Heren XVII alone filled 500 hefty volumes. New techniques of adminis-tration were implemented to boost market knowledge, control, cost-cutting and risk reduction.

The Dutch and English East India firms inaugurated the age of the joint-stock company. Previously, individual merchants had come together under a government-regulated company along the model of the old medieval guilds. What was needed now was an association that could tap the resources of a given nation, organized in such a way as to attract the confidence of investors from the very small to the very great, thus securing a supply of ready capital as well as functioning as a risk-absorber.

The joint-stock company was an association of managed capital, not of individuals, who nonetheless bought shares in a certain venture and shared the profits and the hazards. The company brought businesspeople into contact with statespeople and monarchs at a time when the military had to protect far-flung investments. The resulting synergy sped the life of trade as the world entered the age of mercantile and commercial expansion. This amazingly flexible organization would cast a long shadow as parent of many other economic and political institutions. Virginia, Massachusetts Bay and the *Bank of England* began as joint-stock companies.

These new organs of business – the English Muscovy, the Hudson's Bay Company, the Royal African and the Dutch West India Company traded in 'virtually every known corner of the globe, from Russia to India, from Africa to Canada'.[21] Both the Dutch and the English East India Companies employed 350-plus executives in their head offices, more than most British multinationals of the 19th and even 20th centuries. Even Standard Oil in 1911 had only 1000 general administrators. The East India firms were *vertically integrated*. They carried out many of their operations within the firm, in the Near Eastern manner, rather than through contracts and markets, in the ancient Greek manner. Dealing through markets via fickle price mechanisms alone necessitated extra costs for market intelligence, negotiation and enforcement. Vertical integration worked much better. It was far cheaper for companies to buy goods in Asia and sell them in Europe with their own ships and sailors within their own controlled network, rather than be over-dependent on suppliers and transshippers every step of the way. The open market could be a perilous place in an era of more-or-less unregulated trade.

Internalization advantages would also flow from this attempt to escape the vagaries of supply and demand, or perhaps attempt to harness those dynamics. It took 18 to 24 months to buy goods in Asia, sell them in Europe, acquire goods in Europe and then sell them back to Asia. Distances were vast and communication slow. In these circumstances it became necessary for joint-stock companies to reinforce themselves from the top down. It now became much more cost-effective to rely on 'hierarchies of salaried managers'. Their job was to 'economize on the market', to 'collect and process information about different markets', then to draw up lists of commodities to be procured, in both Asia and Europe. The goal was to allow the companies to steal a march on raw market forces, 'as the means of equating supply and demand'.[22] Every ship of the English East India Company, for example, returned to London with ledgers giving meticulous details of what was in the Indian warehouses and what contracts had been signed. Future demand was then projected on the basis of past demand. In Europe, companies used the existing commercial networks to buy iron, wool, guns and gunpowder. Yet the Dutch and English East India Companies, importing far more from Asia than they exported, would plug into the existing Asian trading systems as middlemen, while protecting their own men and goods. All this served to '[reduce] the costs of transacting below those of market trading'.[23]

The English East India Company, chartered in 1600, run by a London Court of Governors, appointed by the shareholders, directed the business strategy of a lean, decentralized and efficient firm. The Company administered most of India with no more than 1000 agents, supplemented by hired Indian clerks and troops. Local officials with sweeping jurisdiction wrote monthly reports on conditions and problems to India House in London. Management hierarchies were still 'a flat hierarchy with few intermediate managerial grades', small and simple. There was still little in the way of middle management and the costs it entailed.[24] Yet, communication between London, provincial offices and the field was remarkably quick and efficient for its time.[25] The East India Company, starting as a trading firm, eventually assumed a jurisdictional role when the powerful Moghul Empire of India began to dissolve in the late 1700s. As local princes battled for control, Robert Clive, Warren Hastings and other freebooting adventurers saw their firms' markets facing grave danger. This forced them to assume the government of Bengal, Behar and Orissa.

As Governor, Clive hired all the Indian tax collectors, who became true specialists on Indian affairs. Clive and Hastings were forced to govern huge sections of India without the trained staff to do it. Management schools were set up by the firm in Calcutta, and an East Indian College was established in Hertfordshire. Haileybury, as it was called, was the first modern business school. Academic training was remarkably advanced and varied for an age in which management studies were in their infancy. Taught there were the necessities of accounting, business law, financial administration and history and political economy. Equally importantly, the trainees received a strong grounding in Indian and Persian literature and culture. Some of the professors came from India and the Near East. The average student body for the two-year programme was about 100, and the graduates joined not only the India administration but also the British army and Foreign Office. The Company thus became the first multinational systematically to create knowledge workers. These newly minted business graduates would prove to be in high demand as the British Empire expanded. There were, of course, criticisms of these new elites, some of them coming from Company officials themselves. Sir Richard Burton, a soldier and explorer, voiced a complaint that many MBAs and academically trained professional managers since the 1970s would hear incessantly. Rugged entrepreneurs criticized an alleged lack of real-world business experience. Burton felt that the Haileybury graduates 'read too much, had written too much', were 'too clever' in book learning and 'much too confident'.[26] Having to do business and govern a country at the same time – 'learning on the job' – may have been possible in the more slow-moving firms of ancient Ur, Ashur or Babylon, but they were hardly feasible under the strained conditions of the British Raj. Again and again, political and administrative decisions were being forced upon Company managers trained in business, not in war and diplomacy. It was proving hard to manage a subcontinent and run the store as well! Competitors began to gather strength. The Company lost its monopoly of trade in 1813, being forced to face market forces at a time when more and more governmental responsibilities were being thrust upon it.

In 1832, the Canton monopoly was also revoked, 'effectively shutting down the Company's commercial operations'. The deficit crunch meant that the Company could not afford to govern India.[27] After the 1857 mutiny, the British Government took over direct rule of India. The Company spiralled even further into decline and went out of business in 1874. The ultimate failure of the East India Company to make the transition from the world of managed trade to the free-market revolution should not dampen the wisdom expressed by Sir Robert Clive in the imperial heyday. Clive was thinking holistically. He saw the need to change the culture of the firm from one in which trading considerations were absolute to one in which an educated and efficient administration was needed. This was a profound shift in the developing philosophy of British mercantilism. *For the first time, the knowledge of how to run a company and organise it was as important as finding markets and cutting costs.* This innovative concept came too late to save the East India Company. It was, sadly, frustrated by poor management at the very top, which, encumbered by governmental priorities, had lost sight of the bottom line. The basic purpose of a joint-stock company must always be to turn a profit. Yet the East India Company had had its day and its day had been glorious. Despite its failure, it had foreshadowed the impending rise of other firms, some of them British but more and more of them American, German and Japanese, the last three seriously devoted to training and relying on a brave new class of professional managers.

> For the first time, the knowledge of how to run a company and organize it was as important as finding markets and cutting costs

But the maritime powers of North-West Europe were far from finished. There were lessons to be learned from the first world economy. In retrospect, the East India Companies were the first and most spectacular victims of changing market dynamics on a truly global scale.[28] The margin of error in the world economy would never be large. Dutch merchants and magnates, sidelined by risking everything on a single commodity, were too exhausted to enter the high-pressure race for world markets opening at the end of the 17th century. In this race, entry into which demanded human, capital and technological resources on a mammoth scale, the chief rivals would be France and Britain. By the mid 19th century Britain would be supreme in world trade. She would be in the forefront of a global economy based on the massive application of industrial technology and the ability to sell its wares around the world. In that respect, the British Empire would recall the naval capitalism of Tyre more than any other system. 'The workshop of the world' would depend very much on the tread of her keels.

NOTES TO CHAPTER 12

1. North quoted in Cipolla, Carlo M., ed. (1974) *The Fontana History of Europe*, Vol. 2, *The Sixteenth and Seventeenth Centuries*. Glasgow: Collins/Fontana, in Frank, 53–5
2. Frank, A.G. (1998) *ReORIENT: Global Economy in the Asian Age*. Berkeley, CA: University of California Press, 53–55, 75–84.
3. *Ibid.*, 72.
4. *Ibid.*, 119.
5. Rosenberg, N. and Birdzell, L.E., Jr. (1986) *How the West Grew Rich: The Economic Transformation of the Industrial World*. New York: Basic Books, 71–2.
6. Pires, T. quoted in Frank, A.G. (1998) *ReORIENT: Global Economy in the Asian Age*. Berkeley, CA: University of California Press, 58.
7. Pires, T. *The Suma Oriental*, ed. and tr. Cartesão, A. Works issued by the Hakluyt Society, Second Series, Nos. LXXXIX–XC; Vol. I, 41–7, 104, 107–9,

122–7, 174–5, 180, 182, 214–16, 219–20; Vol. II, 269–74 (n.p., Hakluyt Society, n.d.), reprinted in Lach, D.F. and Flaumenhaft, C., eds., (1965) *Asia on the Eve of Europe's Expansion*. Englewood Cliffs, NJ: Prentice-Hall, 17–31, 19.

8. *Ibid.*, 19.
9. *Ibid.*, 19–20.
10. *Ibid.*, 29.
11. Frank, A.G. (1998) *ReORIENT: Global Economy in the Asian Age*. Berkeley, CA: University of California Press, 60. In retrospect disease turned out to be the most powerful weapon of the *conquistadores*, wiping out the native peoples of the Caribbean by 1550. The smallpox brought by Cortes and Pizarro was equally brutal in devastating the civilizations of Mexico and Peru. There were an estimated 25 million Aztec and Maya in 1500, 1.5 million in 1650. All but 600 000 Andean natives survived from a population of around 9 million. In North America, a population of perhaps 5 million was reduced, ultimately, to 60 000. Multitudes of slaves were imported from Africa. Native cultures were suppressed and native populations in the Caribbean replaced by a mixture of Spanish and African (Cameron, 1993, 105–6).
12. Wolf, E.R. (1982) *Europe and the People Without History*. Berkeley, CA: University of California Press, 237.
13. *Ibid.*
14. *Ibid.*, 239.
15. Boxer, C.R. (1979) *Jan Compagnie in War and Peace 1602–1799: A Short History of the Dutch East India Company*. Hong Kong: Heinemann Asia, 239.
16. Maetsuyker quoted *ibid.*, 32. The Governor had his critics, who charged him with a cantankerous disposition, a condescending attitude towards those of lower class, fraud and spying on his junior clerks.
17. Maetsuyker quoted *ibid.*, 36.
18. *Ibid.*, 51.
19. Maetsuyker letter to Heren XVII, January 1673, *ibid.*, 46.
20. Carlos, A.M. and Nicholas, S. (1991) 'Giants of an Earlier Capitalism: The Chartered Trading Companies as Modern Multinationals', *Business History Review*, 62 (Autumn 1988), in Wilkins, M., ed. *International Library of Critical Writings in Business History*, Volume I: *The Growth of Multinationals*, Aldershot, UK: Edward Elgar Publishing, 450.
21. *Ibid.*, 455.
22. *Ibid.*, 459.
23. *Ibid.*, 463.
24. Witzel, M. (date unknown) *The Old School of Management*, Financial Times Mastering Management Review, 16–17.
25. *Ibid.*, 16–19.
26. *Ibid.*, 19.

27. *Ibid.*
28. *Ibid.*, 17. From 1772 on, 'the nature of the Company', according to Professor Morgan Witzel of the London Business School, 'began to change. No longer was it solely a commercial enterprise', but was now 'faced with the responsibilities of government, including administering justice and raising taxes.'

The Second Global Economy (1)

The 'Hellenic' free-trade world of the Pax Britannica: 1800–1931

THE Second Global Economy was inaugurated with the telegraph in 1844 and ended with the dethroning of the British pound in 1931. It witnessed the rise of global empires, rapid communication, free trade and new multinational forms of business management. This new economy would be industrial as well as agricultural.

Why Britain?

Britain's experience resembles that of some of the *poleis* of ancient Greece, separated from other centres by the seas, and developing constitutional government and free enterprise. Britain's economic thinkers, led by Adam Smith, would travel far beyond Hellenic ideas of natural law, formulating a conscious ideology of self-regulating markets.[1]

> Britain's economic thinkers, led by Adam Smith, would travel far beyond Hellenic ideas of natural law, formulating a conscious ideology of self-regulating markets

Though the Anglo-Saxons had eradicated Roman business culture, later kings, led by Alfred in the 800s, formulated a body of national law drawn from Celtic, Germanic and even Old Testament tradition quite conducive to property and enterprise. Eventually codified as Common Law, it provided for one's innocence until proven guilty, for trial by jury, and for everything to be permitted unless expressly forbidden. Norman kings gave England a unified market, and a long series of struggles established the supremacy of a landed gentry who, after 1688, controlled the House of Commons. The island kingdom had no large standing army able to crush that Parliament. Britain's gentry were less of a drain on the country's coffers than their far more numerous Continental counterparts, and had less aversion to going to business themselves. English Protestant religion was also conducive to free enterprise, for the idea of personal responsibility before God carried over into the economic sphere.

Britain, like Greece, was the constitutional exception in the surrounding world. A cost-conscious Parliament of gentry saw England's finances as England's, not the king's, creating a culture of fiscal responsibility. The Bank of England, a stable currency and an organized stock market provided the credit that financed Britain's rise to global power. The British Government could borrow money at only a fraction of the cost of its French rival. Policies were made by merchants, not against them. Limited government and a pro-business culture encouraged the growth of capital markets, transportation infrastructure and a deregulatory, entrepreneurial, individualistic approach to business organization.[2]

> Limited government and a pro-business culture encouraged the growth of capital markets, transportation infrastructure and a deregulatory, entrepreneurial, individualistic approach to business organization

London was already the magnet for Europe's growing financial markets. The Bank of England first issued notes in 1694. Together with the East India Company, the Bank of England was the leading joint-stock monopoly of the 1600s, although the Bubble Act of the 1720s soon erected 'a legal barrier against the joint-stock (or corporate) form of business organization, condemning most of its industrial and other enterprises to partnerships or simple proprietorships'.[3] This would actually encourage British entrepreneurs. England's freedom from big government, land wars and borrowing costs freed capital for investment in the infrastructure of turnpikes and canals vital to her industrial take-off. Every British market was soon linked via canal, river or harbour. Canals were run by the gentry; the dirt and plank turnpikes run by local farmers and merchants were rewarded with tax cuts. By 1770 England and Wales were covered with 25 000 kilometres of turnpikes where there had been only 5000 in 1750.

BOULTON & WATT

18TH-CENTURY MICROSOFT?

JAMES Watt (1736–1819) and Matthew Boulton (1728–1809) formed one of the most important business partnerships in history. The Scottish scientist Watt, inventor of the steam engine, could not have transformed society without the capital and business acumen of the Birmingham manufacturer Boulton.

The engine, invented by Thomas Newcomen at the dawn of the 1700s, was already in commercial use through much of that century, pumping water out of British coal mines. The Newcomen engine, however, was much like the giant computers of the 1950s and 1960s, being cumbersome, inefficient and rarely cost-effective. The use of steam power was very rare before the 1780s.

Watt, in the meantime, was a gifted Glasgow mathematician struggling to operate a business of his own without the right hereditary connections and a formal apprenticeship. Much as Henry Ford began by tinkering with cars or Bill Gates with computers, Watt earned his living by running a small partnership business on the University of Glasgow premises. Here he and his partner, John Craig, tinkered with the inventions of the day while earning a mere £600 in gross receipts. Like Gates, it is interesting that this early techno-entrepreneur serviced an academic market.

One of the machines Watt repaired in 1763 or 1764 was a Newcomen engine. He was quickly taken by the wasteful inefficiency of the machine with its up-and-down piston. A lot of heat and energy were lost. Watt envisioned a much more efficient machine with an airtight piston. If the engine were placed inside another casing, it would lose far less heat and steam and be much more economical to operate. Like the personal computer, it would be much more commercially profitable and affordable to operate.

Watt, however, needed capital and a ready market, which Matthew Boulton was able to provide. Inheriting a hardware business in 1759, the Birmingham entrepreneur quickly built it into the most prestigious firm in England. Boulton & Fothergill grossed £30 000 annually, turning out buttons, sword handles, metal boxes, chains and a multitude of other iron and even steel goods. Its factory in Birmingham's Soho district employed 800 workers. The firm was a living example of the new industrial capitalism. Workers and managers became more distant, jobs more specialized, managers more professional. Boulton's water-driven lathes and tools were state-of-the-art for their time.

An enterprise on the scale of Boulton's created a demand for new manufacturing technology. Watt's new engine satisfied that demand. In 1774 Boulton bought half the share in the patent for the Watt engine and erected one in his factory. It was a partnership not too different from that between the fledgling Microsoft and IBM. Boulton absorbed the costs involved in Watt's research, while Watt went on to improve his engine and by 1782 was able to develop the rotary engine, which would dominate railways, steamships and factories for a century.

By the 1770s mine owners were turning to Boulton & Watt to provide steam engines efficient and affordable enough to keep them in business, just as small businesses in the 1980s would turn to microcomputers and standardized IBM- or Macintosh-compatible software for the same reasons.

In order to make steam-engine manufacture profitable, Watt and Boulton were able to obtain a long-term guarantee of monopoly status from the British Parliament. Britain in 1774 was still a mercantilist society, and free-market ideas would not prevail until the 1840s. Without this guaranteed market, Boulton & Watt could have neither developed nor marketed their engines. Even in the 1770s entrepreneurs arose very quickly attempting to copy Watt's invention, as surely as they later attempted to copy Microsoft software or early IBM personal computers.

The marriage of business acumen and revolutionary technology in a single, dominant firm was as decisive then as it has been in our day, for the scores of engines manufactured by Boulton & Watt would lay the groundwork for the widespread commercial use of steam-power, leading to the further spin-off in the following generation of the railway.

The post-1750 British Industrial Revolution represented *the* critical turning point in world economic history. Business was now no longer confined to small and narrow groups in society, nor were inventions restricted to one occupation. After 1750, inventions were quickly applied to other industries, becoming *technologies*. The steam engine was first applied in mining, then in factories, locomotives and steamships. Building upon the water-and-wind revolution of the Middle Ages, the energy sources and factories of the new Industrial Revolution worked on a much larger and more powerful scale.[4]

Steam turbines dated from Hellenistic times and pistons from China after 400 CE. Thomas Newcomen in 1712 created a piston engine that drained mines and ran water wheels. In the 1770s and 1780s a more efficient engine was perfected by the Glaswegian James Watt. Watt's piston turned a rotating wheel just like a waterfall did, only more rapidly and efficiently. As a result, Britain would quickly lead Europe in the most efficient source of energy of the First Industrial Revolution. By

1820–1824 Britain produced 18 million metric tons of coal and lignite a year in contrast to only 2 million from the whole Continent combined.

Watt's engine quickly entered England's new cotton industry, which had no restrictive guilds and was open to new methods of production encouraged by awards given through the Society of Arts. The flying shuttle (1733) allowed one weaver to do the work of two. James Hargreaves' spinning jenny (1764) let one weaver run several spindles. Richard Arkwright's water frame (1769) was so big it had to run in the new factories, not in homes. Samuel Crompton's mule (1779) combined the jenny and the frame and by 1790 was running in factories powered by Watt's steam engines; by the 1820s power looms were weaving cloth in similar factories. With the rise in cotton weaving came a revolution in trade. England imported 500 tons of cotton in 1700, 2500 by 1770 and, after the industrial take-off, 25 000 in 1800. By 1860, raw cotton imports were up to 500 000 tons.

Britain also took the lead in heavier industry, as noted in the production of iron. By 1850, and even into 1880, Britain produced twice as much iron as the rest of Europe combined. The First Industrial Revolution was clearly a time of overwhelming British dominance, as outlined in Table 13.1.

Table 13.1 Annual output of pig iron (in million metric tons)[5]

	1820	1850	1880	1910
United Kingdom	0.4	2.3	7.9	10.2
France	0.2	0.4	1.7	4.0
Belgium	–	0.1	0.6	1.9
Germany	0.1	0.2	2.7	14.8
Italy	–	–	–	0.3
Russia	0.1	0.2	0.4	3.0

When it came to trade as well, Britain ruled the seas until the time of the Second World War (see Table 13.2).

Table 13.2 Merchant ships registered by country (in thousand tons)[6]

	1840	*1880*	*1910*	*1938*
United Kingdom	2 768	6 575	11 556	10 702
France	663	920	1 452	1 664
Germany	352	1 104	2 890	2 482
Belgium	23	75	191	272
Italy	–	999	1 001	2 039
Russia	–	468	723	1 273

Prophet of market capitalism: Adam Smith

The rise of industrialism in Britain was accompanied by Adam Smith's free-market ideology ultimately based on the Hellenic concept of natural law bolstered by the physics of Sir Isaac Newton.

Born in Scotland in 1723, Smith began to lecture and write on economics and moral philosophy from 1748 onwards. *The Theory of Moral Sentiments* (1759) denounced unrestrained selfishness pitting rich against poor and ruining commerce and productivity. People were naturally motivated by social approval as well as by ego and acquisitiveness. Within the context of this moral framework, Smith published *The Wealth of Nations* in 1776, which would radically reverse the thinking of centuries and become the most influential economic work of all time. Smith insisted that government should be minimal, confining its role to the defence of country, life and property, maintaining certain public works, and giving a minimal help to the destitute.[7] Real wealth lay less in land or bullion than in productive labour, for the 'uniform, constant and uninterrupted effort of every man to better his condition', based on self-interest, 'is frequently powerful enough to maintain

> The rise of industrialism in Britain was accompanied by Adam Smith's free-market ideology ultimately based on the Hellenic concept of natural law bolstered by the physics of Sir Isaac Newton

the natural progress of things toward improvement'. Acting out of self-interest, a merchant is nonetheless 'led by an invisible hand to promote an end which was no part of his intention'.[8] Supply and demand would affect prices and this would lead merchants to specialize in activities most profitable for them, and to efficient division of labour. Free trade and competition among merchants in all nations allowed everyone to buy grain and other goods more cheaply from other countries than they could from their own farmers:[9]

> 'It is the maxim of every prudent master of a family, never to attempt to make at home what it will cost him more to make than to buy ... What is prudence in the conduct of every private family, can scarce be folly in that of a great kingdom.'

Public companies and even private monopolies invited both irresponsibility and unprofitability:

> 'The agents of a prince regard the wealth of their master as inexhaustible; are careless at what price they buy; are careless at what price they sell; are careless at what expense they transport his goods from one place to another ... No two characters seem more inconsistent than those of trader and sovereign.'[10]

The ideas set down in *The Wealth of Nations* did not really come into vogue until the 1830s and 1840s. British industry matured and its managers were now an important political force. Their rise reinforced the mid-Victorian gospel of free trade and economic individualism. This gospel, through the writings of Samuel Smiles, greatly influenced English popular culture between the 1850s and 1880s. Watt, Arkwright, Hargreaves and Compton, men of punctuality, hard work and self-discipline, became heroes in an age of free trade and evangelical religion that did not believe society owed anyone a living. In *Self-Help* (1856), Smiles praised those who rose from poverty by their own efforts. Anyone could do the same: 'The spirit of self-help is the root of all genuine growth in the individual ... the true source of national vigour and strength.'[11] Government must never create dependency and destroy character, but confine itself to 'protection of life, liberty and property' for 'no laws ... can make the idle industrious, the thriftless provident, or the drunken sober'. Society can only be bettered 'by better habits, rather than by greater rights'.[12] *Self-Help* sounded a note of anti-intellectualism as old as Trimalchio. Real education came from the school of hard knocks in the workshop or factory far more than from Oxford or Cambridge, for 'a man perfects himself by work more than by reading' as 'life rather than literature, action rather than study, and character rather than biography ... tend ... to renovate mankind'.[13]

The repeal of the Corn Laws in the late 1840s, free trade between England and France in 1860, and a series of Continental pacts cutting duties on any European goods going to Britain helped inaugurate an era of free trade in Europe and eventually the globe. During the 1860s and 1870s Europe had the closest thing to a single market before the present era, its internal trade growing fivefold between 1850 and 1870 and doubling again by 1900.

A *British* global economy: the age of the free-standing firm

The Second Global Economy was forged not just by industry and free-trade policies but by a revolution in transportation and communications. One of the heroes praised by Smiles was George Stephenson, who in 1822 applied the steam engine to transportation by putting it on iron rails already used to haul coal from the mines to the foundries and wharves in Newcastle and Wales and along the Tyne. By 1825 Stephenson's first locomotive was pulling cars along iron rails and 1830 saw the first true rail line, that of Liverpool and Manchester. Railroads grew explosively throughout the following decades, making Great Britain the first truly mobile society in history. Between 1840 and 1850 Britain and then Europe laid the first major trunk lines. By 1850 Britain was covered with railroads and a thin web stretched across the northern European plain from Berlin to Paris. By 1870 scores of feeder lines covered Western Europe. Before 1870, Britain would lead Europe in amount of track (see Table 13.3).

The United States, of course, was on a par with Britain, and the same lines that brought settlers to the Midwest also brought American wheat to steamships and to Europe. Railways would link countries together, and swift new steamships would make continents closer than ever before. More importantly, the invention of the telegraph made it possible for merchants in England to communicate instantly with bankers or agents in Europe, America or even Asia as cables were laid not only across vast continents but even under the Atlantic and Pacific Oceans. It would become much easier for multinational corporations to operate and for large-scale British investments to be made in places like India, America, Canada or Australia.

In the 19th century large numbers of people and large amounts of capital circulated freely between continents without restriction. Britain led the world in manufacturing, trade and naval power, as well as in overseas colonization. The Second Global Economy was a *British* global economy, for London ruled, directly or indirectly, a full quarter of the world's land and its people before 1914. India, Burma, Malaya, East Africa from Capetown to Cairo, Ghana, Nigeria and other West African territories, Canada, Australia, New Zealand, Ireland, Newfoundland, Hong Kong and a multitude of island possessions were all under the British Empire. Much of Latin America and even China were in Britain's economic sphere. The scope of intercontinental trade grew 2500 per cent between 1800 and 1913, and over 60 per cent of this was European and heavily British.

> The Second Global Economy was based much more on industrialism and European imperialism than the First. For the first time, *global business cycles* appeared

The Second Global Economy was based much more on industrialism and European imperialism than the First. For the first time, *global business cycles* appeared.

In the 1600s or even 1700s famine or depression in London did not necessarily trigger famine or depression in Boston or Malacca. Now the web of railroads and telegraph lines, money transfers and growing inter-

Table 13.3 Railway track, 1840–1900 (in kilometres)[14]

	1840	1860	1880	1900
United Kingdom	2 411	16 789	28 846	36 004
France	410	9 167	23 089	38 109
Germany	469	11 089	33 838	51 678
Belgium	334	1 729	4 112	4 562
Italy	20	2 404	9 290	16 429
Russia	–	1 626	22 865	53 234

dependence in international trade meant that both booms and panics could, according to Thomas Friedman, spread around the world in a matter of hours:

> *'If you compared the volumes of trade and capital flows across borders, relative to GNPs, and the flow of labor across borders, relative to populations, the period of globalization preceding World War I was quite similar to the one we are living through today. Great Britain, which was then the dominant global power, was a huge investor in emerging markets, and fat cats in England, Europe and America were often buffeted by financial crises, triggered by something that happened in Argentine railroad bonds, Latvian government bonds or German government bonds. There were no currency controls, so no sooner was the transatlantic cable connected in 1866 than banking and financial crises in New York were quickly being transmitted to London or Paris.'*[15]

The growing interdependence of the world and the consequences of globalization were felt in agriculture. Before free trade, railroads, telecommunications and the opening of the wheat fields of the Americas and Australia, most nations grew their own wheat. After 1850, though, 'the world became', according to Canadian economic historian C. Knick Harley, 'a single market in bread grains'.[16] The railroad and the steamship combined to reduce drastically the costs of shipping American, Canadian and Argentinian wheat to European consumers. American railways based on new steel rails, faster and cheaper cars and locomotives, and an expanded volume of traffic across the United States, cut freight charges. It cost 33 cents a bushel to send wheat from Chicago to New York in 1874; by 1881 it was only 14 cents. Lower steel prices and new steel-clad ships driven by steam turbines and screw propellers crossed the Atlantic, Pacific and Indian Oceans in less time, with less coal and smaller crews. Refrigeration techniques allowed Europeans to import huge quantities of beef and mutton from New Zealand, Australia and the Americas. It cost 20 cents a bushel to ship wheat from New York to England in 1875 but by 1881 only 2 cents. To ship a ton of goods from Marseilles to Hong Kong in 1875 cost 200 French francs; by 1906 it cost only 70.[17]

New developments in milling between the 1860s and 1880s made the harder strains of American wheat more popular with European consumers. In areas like the American Midwest and, eventually, the Great Plains and the Canadian Prairies, the price of wheat began to rise at the same time as it began to fall in Europe. The result was that intercontinental trade in wheat grew fifteenfold, from 40 million bushels around 1850 to some 600 million bushels by 1914. Europe in 1914 imported 30 per cent of its wheat, Britain 75 per cent. As Table 13.4 shows, the huge growth of overseas wheat production created a global economy that was far better nourished but also far more interdependent, especially in the urban countries of Europe.

Table 13.4 Change in average wheat production and exports between the 1870s and World War I in millions of imperial quarters (1 quarter = 8 bushels)[18]

	Late 1870s		Eve of World War I	
	Production	Export	Production	Export
Russia and Danube	43	5.8	100	17.8
North America	61	13.8	112	26.5
India	28	0.8	46	6.8
Argentina	3	0.5	12	6.6
Australia	10	0	19	11.7
United Kingdom	10	n/a	7	n/a
Total	268		480	

Over £400 million flowed into Latin America by 1890, overwhelmingly in government securities and railways. Robert Stephenson built mine tramways in Argentina; Scottish miners and milkmaids brought mining and dairy expertise. Before 1860 most British foreign investment went to Europe and America; after 1860 it went to the Empire dominions: 12 per cent in the 1860s, 30 per cent in the 1880s, 40 per cent by 1929. By 1939 75 per cent of British capital exports went to imperial destinations, another 20 per cent to Latin America.[19] British entrepreneurs and partners settled in Buenos Aires, raised capital in Britain and then invested it in building rail lines. By 1913 Britain invested £4 billion abroad, but most was *portfolio* investment 'involving the acquisition of foreign securities without any control over the foreign institutions or companies concerned'. Recent research by Professor Geoffrey Jones and others, though, suggests that as much as 40 per cent may have been direct, involving the 'ownership and management of a foreign operation', which is important in a modern multinational company.[20]

The Second Global Economy made possible 'the initial era of the modern multinational enterprise'.[21] It was now possible to co-ordinate the operations of companies efficiently across oceans as well as land borders.

Orders could be placed, managers fired, market conditions examined and goods shipped in much less time in 1880 than even in 1820. According to Professor Mira Wilkins: 'The late nineteenth and the early twentieth century was the first period in world history when, owing to the transportation and communications innovations, it became possible to have meaningful business co-ordination, control, and influence over distance and ... frontiers.'[22]

Britain would be the biggest multinational investor in the Second Global Economy until its demise in the 1930s. Even after World War II she would remain second only to the United States. British emigrants set up free-standing companies, small multinationals without British home offices, in Asia and throughout the Empire. Free-standing firms, especially in Asia, dealt in indigo, jute, cotton, teak, river transportation and shipping. In many ways they filled the vacuum when the East India Company was dissolved. The new merchant houses had intimate local knowledge of their corners of the British Empire but also did business in London, Glasgow, Liverpool or Manchester. Retired senior partners would often return to the United Kingdom after having made their fortunes abroad. There they would continue to maintain business and advise those overseas. The most vigorous development of the free-standing agencies took place after 1860. Originally specialising in cotton and silk, the agencies began to diversify after Britain signed a free-trade treaty with France, France opened the Suez Canal and the India cable was laid.

The manufacturing of many new products and the rise of disposable income provided the demand and the market. Free-standing companies trading in coal, iron, gold, tea, rubber and petroleum formed a network

> The Second Global Economy made possible 'the initial era of the modern multinational enterprise'. It was now possible to co-ordinate the operations of companies efficiently across oceans as well as land borders

including Calcutta, Bombay, Madras, Burma, Persia, Malaya, Borneo, Java, Siam, Japan and elsewhere. While they played only a small role in the migration of British capital to Asia, the merchant houses did a great deal in building up the infrastructure: railroads, docks, harbours, etc. throughout Britain's colonies, dominions and protectorates. They furnished creditors for imperial banks and became creditors for many foreign businesses. Many even opened offices in Britain. By 1900 one third of the largest British Empire companies (generally capitalized at over £4 million) were agency houses in India, South Africa, Russia and Latin America.[23] Manufacturing in the British colonies was 'of small financial importance' compared to other activities and limited to local market needs for beer, soap and other such goods. These 'small-scale enterprises that did not depend for survival upon ties to technological developments or upon access to world markets' would set the tone for much of modern British business.[24]

Free-standing UK multinationals were very small in scale, often having just a board and a secretariat and owning a single mine or oilfield. Manufacturing multinationals of larger size and complexity with London home offices began to appear in the 1880s and 1890s. By 1914, 14 of the 100 largest British manufacturing companies had significant foreign direct investment abroad in the form of branch and subsidiary offices. Unlike the free-standing companies, these firms were true multinationals, managed from a home office in the United Kingdom (see Table 13.5).

Table 13.5 Major British multinationals in 1914[25]

British American Tobacco (Tobacco)	Lever Brothers (Soap)
Bryant & May (Matches)	Liebig Extract of Meat (Food)
J&P Coats (Cotton thread)	Nobel Explosives (Explosives)
Courtaulds (Synthetics)	Pilkington (Glass)
Dunlop (Rubber)	Reckitts (Starch)
English Sewing Cotton (Cotton thread)	Royal Dutch Shell (Oil)
The Gramophone Company (EMI) (Records)	Vickers (Arms)

Out of an estimated $14 billion in total foreign direct investment in 1914, Britain had perhaps $7 billion (including free-standing companies), America $2.5 billion, France $1.4 billion and Germany $1.2 billion. British multinationals were the most global of all, investing heavily in Europe, America and Australia.²⁶ Many of these firms dealt largely in consumer goods. The Gramophone Company, Courtaulds, Dunlop, Nobel and Vickers went into new technologies, generally invested in competitive high-income markets, and sought to circumvent tariff walls. Most of the consumer-oriented companies invested heavily in Canada, Australia and the other dominions, plus the USA; British American Tobacco and Coats heavily in Asia; and Shell in the USA, Russia, Indonesia, Mexico, Borneo, Romania and Egypt. Many of these firms developed special competitive advantages in technology or marketing. Courtaulds obtained a patent for viscose silk. The Gramophone Company and its successor, EMI, won markets in 19 countries by catering to local musical tastes. Vickers made arms not only for Britain but also Italy, Spain, Turkey, Japan and Russia. Lever exploited soap demands in the dominions. Shell, merging with the Royal Dutch Company in 1907, began as a free-standing company based in the Far East, acquiring oilfields in Romania and Russia where John D. Rockefeller would not go.²⁷

Plato's revenge: the aristocratic challenge to British entrepreneurs

By the 1870s a new generation growing up under global capitalism questioned the ethic of Samuel Smiles. An early influence in shaping the turn from entrepreneurial values was Charles Dickens (1812–1870), whose novels traced English life from the 18th century to the dawning of the collectivist age. The early Dickens saw problems with capitalists, not capitalism. *A Christmas Carol* (1843) satirized business ethics in the person of Ebenezer Scrooge. Scrooge, totally consumed with the bottom line, winces at the very notion of 'liberality'. Even love itself takes second place to his new commercial values:

> *'This is the even-handed dealing of the world ... There is nothing on which it is so hard as poverty; and ... nothing it professes to condemn with such severity as the pursuit of wealth.'²⁸*

Dombey and Son (1848) showed English family enterprise at the dawn of the free-trade era, where Walter Gay's uncle Solomon cannot cope with the new competitive world of globalization: 'competition, competition – new invention, new invention – alteration, alteration – the world's gone past me. I hardly know where I am myself, much less where my customers are.'[29] Hardly a customer now comes to Solomon's shop, for his marketing skills are as deficient as his dwindling market: 'Tradesmen are not the same as they used to be, apprentices are not the same, business is not the same, business commodities are not the same.'[30] The grim landscape of Coketown in *Hard Times* (1854) pictured the dark underside of the new capitalism and the self-help ethic that sustained it. The churches and chapels of Coketown are frequented by the middle class, not the factory workers who ignore the bells on Sunday morning and find solace in alcohol. Josiah Bounderby and Thomas Grad-grind, the two eminent business leaders of Coke-town, see the latter as shiftless and ungrateful whiners. Education in Coketown is maths-oriented and leaves little room for art or philos-ophy, as if a Trimalchio had written the curriculum. Young Sissy Jupe, a circus orphan who represents the humanity Dickens hopes to defend, is asked questions like: 'This schoolroom is an immense town, and in it there are a million inhabitants, and only five-and-twenty are starved to death in the streets, in the course of a year. What is your remark on that proportion?' and: 'In a given time a hundred thousand persons went to sea on long voyages, and only five hundred of them were drowned or burnt to death. What is the percentage?'[31]

> Like the later Athenians, many late Victorian and Edwardian Britons began to question the abuses of the market and reaffirm traditional agrarian and aristocratic ideals of *noblesse oblige*

Like the later Athenians, many late Victorian and Edwardian Britons began to question the abuses of the market and reaffirm traditional agrarian and aristocratic ideals of *noblesse oblige*.

English writers themselves began to see parallels between themselves and the Greeks: 'During the nineteenth century,' writes historian Frank Miller Turner, 'the perception of a close relationship between the political history of ancient Athens and Great Britain had emerged as an almost unques-tioned assumption for numerous British intellectuals.'[32] John Stuart Mill declared the Battle of Marathon (490 BCE) more important to English history than the Battle of Hastings; Lord Acton argued that the British were the inheritors of the Periclean ideal of an impartial constitution that protected the liberty of the individual and private property. George Grote's twelve-volume *History of Greece* (1846–1856) saw Athenian democrats as the first Victorians, evolving from royal absolutism to parliamentary democ-

BUYING 'CHINA'

THE FIRST GLOBAL ECONOMY AND THE RISE OF CONSUMER BRANDS

BY 1700 British importers began to profit handsomely from the rapid growth of a new mass market in the West for Chinese silk, tea and porcelain. The goods of China were now so esteemed in Britain and Europe that they became identified in the minds of consumers as superior brand names.

Company brands or trademarks like Coca-Cola, BMW, Xerox or Levi's are described by Morgen Witzel of the *Financial Times* as 'brand images associated with a product made by a particular company'.[36] They have existed from the time Hellenic potters and Roman merchants like the Sestii and Domitiani stamped their initials on their jugs and bricks, medieval Flemish guilds placed the mark of Ghent or Bruges on their products, and the Japanese branded their Samurai swords.

It was, however, in China, that brand names became a truly global phenomenon. Metalwork began to be branded under the Song. Demands for Chinese trademarks were first felt in the West in connection with the silk industry. From Roman times and in the earlier part of the Dark Ages, Chinese growers had a monopoly on silk production until Byzantine agents managed to smuggle the secret into the Mediterranean world. By the 13th century both the Italians and the Arabs had their own silk industries.

The coming of the First Global Economy would be a tremendous boon to the Chinese. British ships arriving in Canton and elsewhere quickly discovered that the silks of China were of far higher quality than their European imitations. Chinese silkworms lived far longer than European ones. Consequently, European consumers flocked to buy clothing and scarves made from silks of China, which were branded after the region in which they were grown, such as Suzhou (Soochow).

Demand for Chinese brand names soon spread to other areas after 1700. Drug makers like Lei Yunshang and Tongrentang, confectionaries like Kaizhi Zhai and brushes made by Yipin Zhai all became popular trademarks. By 1720 Chinese tea, branded by its various grades, was replacing both silk and spices as the mainstay of the East India Company's trade. British importers by the 1740s bought at least a million kilograms of tea per year. Tea, as we know, transformed British culture and even helped trigger the American Revolution when London tried to tax it. The Chinese brands, especially pekoe and souchong, were still valued much more than over the cheaper grades grown in Africa and India.

Porcelain goods were branded with the very name of the country itself. An important export from the Yangzi valley, even in Han/Roman times, the porcelain wares of the imperial kilns at Jingdezhen were much more expensive in Britain, Holland and Portugal than in China. The European mass market was insatiable, with 100 000 teacups and 40 000 pots, 10 000 teapots and a host of other goods being carried from Canton in a single ship.

[217]

European imitations such as Stafford and Delft were regarded as less desirable than the Asian originals. Just as photocopies are often called 'Xeroxes', porcelain goods became known as 'China'.

The East India Company and Chinese manufacturers and middlemen were co-operating in global custom marketing on the eve of the Industrial Revolution. The factories of Jingdezhen turned out dishes and pots tailored for British households, relying on wooden models sent to them by the East Indiamen through Canton middlemen. The crockery was then made in the factories of the Yangzi and shipped to Canton, where it was decorated, finished and branded by Chinese craftsmen under British supervision.

While these goods were considered lower-quality in China, this was not the case in Britain, where Western consumers were, in Witzel's words, 'buying not just tea or porcelain', but buying China itself'.[37]

ratic rule.[33] While Edwardian English Liberals and Labourites praised Athenian democracy, Tories like George Beardoe Grundy drew the lesson from Athens' decline that Britain should rely on her aristocrats, not her democrats. The welfare state, with its expanded rights of citizenship and tax-supported employment for these workers on juries or in the navy, Grundy argued, was costly and created an entitlement mentality.[34] Alfred Zimmern, however, looked at economics: to give much more attention to the role of economics in both Athens and Britain. Athenians and Britons were patriotic because their democratic welfare state improved their lot in life. Zimmern saw in Athens 'the most successful example of social organization known to history ... so arranged as to make the ... best of the human material at its disposal'. The Parthenon was a product not only of Phidias but also of 'the genius of the social system which knew how to make use of him'.[35]

Britain in 1914 entered its own version of the Peloponnesian War, a war of siege and attrition in which economics was as decisive as arms. Seapower enabled Britain to strangle Germany economically while the British invention of the tank eventually overcame the stalemate of trench warfare in the first major war of the industrial age. Germany, though, might have won in 1917 through her own unrestricted submarine warfare, had not the British adopted the old Carthaginian convoy system. The new interdependence of the global economy, which some thought would make war unthinkable, made it infinitely more frightful when it finally came. Britain emerged much poorer in 1918. Many overseas investments were liquidated, many free-standing companies sold. Free-market economics were less popular than ever in a time of economic contraction, and the country village and gentleman, not the hustler, became the centre of English values. During World War II historian Arthur Bryant insisted that the character of England had been set long ago by the yeoman farmer: 'Most of us today are town dwellers, yet there are very few of us whose great-great-great grandparents were not country folk, and ... our subconscious selves hark back to their instincts and ways of life.'[38] Importantly, even English businessmen now questioned the accumulation of wealth as an end in itself and came to adopt a paternalistic ethic. Samuel Courtauld, director of one of Britain's most successful multinationals, sounded like a veritable socialist:

> '*I believe that the worship of material values is the fatal disease from which our age is suffering, and that, if we do not eradicate this worship, it will inevitably destroy our whole society and not even leave us any business to discuss. We must steadfastly keep on reminding ourselves all the time that material efficiency is only a means and not an end.*'[39]

Many businesspeople in England imitated the gentry, absorbing the values of both the old landed and the new professional classes, whose values 'inhibited their quest for expansion, productivity, and profit'.[40] London financiers found it easier to merge with the gentry than northern manufacturers. William Morris, creator of what one day would be British Leyland, invented a popular car but was never idolized like Henry Ford. In contrasting aristocratic and commercial ideals, the British in the 20th century were unique. Neither German, French nor Japanese aristocrats and graduates had the reservations about capitalism that their British counterparts did, and Americans certainly had no such reservations. The shock of defeat in France in 1940 and in Germany and Japan in 1945 opened the way for the French technocrat, the German craftsman and the Japanese Samurai to reappear in the framework of capitalism seen as national as much as individual causes. In Britain, the absence of defeat permitted an overconfidence that permitted the survival of Late Victorian and Edwardian modes of business thought.

The British were to be pioneers in the new wave of multinational enterprise, but the true Age of the multinational would be in the 20th century, in which not only British but American and European transnational firms would prosper as never before. The New 'Hellenic' era of British commercial leadership would, in the process, give way to a new 'Pax Romana' dominated by large-scale American firms who, in turn, would be challenged by two rapidly rising powers whose commercial cultures resembled those of the ancient Near East.

> 66 Britain's original strength in the Second Global Economy became the source of her decline 99

The coming of the 'Great Depression', actually a series of stop go recessions between 1873 and 1896, stimulated protectionism in most countries, encouraging manufacturers in Britain and elsewhere to move around tariff walls by setting up multinationals on foreign soil. British firms would invest in Europe and Argentina, American firms in Europe and Canada, and Europeans largely in Europe itself (see Table 13.6). Free trade gave way to protectionism everywhere but in Britain. British industry was slow to adopt new technologies and economies of scale like its German and American rivals. Like Greece and Rome, whose technological progress was deterred by plentiful slave labour,

Table 13.6 Manufacturing subsidiaries by location, pre-1914 [41]

	US MNE 122 subsidiaries	UK MNE 60 subsidiaries	European MNE 167 subsidiaries
United States	n/a	3.3%	5.4%
Canada	27.0%	15.0%	1.2%
Western Europe	51.7%	21.6%	61.8%
Australia and New Zealand	1.6%	8.4%	0.6%
Japan	0.8%	3.3%	nil
South Africa	0.8%	5.0%	0.6%
Latin America	8.1%	26.3%	1.2%
Mideast	4.1%	3.3%	15.4%
Africa	nil	3.4%	0.6%
Asia	nil	3.4%	1.8%

Britain's existing investment in coal and steam deterred investment in electricity and petroleum. Britain's original strength in the Second Global Economy became the source of her decline.

It was 'following the path of least resistance' for British managers to redirect investment into China, Argentina or the Empire rather than modernising industries at home and trying to compete with giant German and American rivals.[42]

NOTES TO CHAPTER 13

1. The parallel between Britain and ancient Greece, fascinating as it is, has to be used, as must all the parallels in this book, with caution. England in its early stages was a centralized monarchy; Greece never was. The Industrial Revolution affected people far more than the Iron Age did. The ancient Greeks never developed anything resembling a multinational enterprise, while Britain did, although often in a much more free-standing form than elsewhere.
2. Cameron, R. (1993) *A Concise Economic History of the World, from Palaeolithic Times to the Present.* New York: Oxford University Press, 158.
3. *Ibid.*, 172.
4. Drucker remarks how between 700 and 1100 CE the invention of the stirrup created the medieval knight and the windmill created the urban craftsman. For the first time the water wheel and the windmill used power other than muscle. This was Europe's first machine age, empowering peasants and slaves to become craftsmen and burghers. The stirrup, water wheel and windmill spread rapidly throughout Europe, but 'the classes of the earlier industrial revolution remained European phenomena on the whole'. (Drucker, P. (1993) *Post-Capitalist Society.* New York: Harper Business, 23.) 'In China, in India, in the world of Islam, the new technologies had no social impact whatever.' (*Ibid.*, 24.) The social changes of this industrial revolution took almost 400 years to take effect in Europe. The social transformation of this medieval industrial revolution took almost 400 years to take full effect even in Europe. The transformation of society of industrial capitalism took less than a century in Western Europe. Capitalists and proletarians hardly existed in 1750; by 1850 they dominated the class structure in Western Europe. The transformation took 30 years in Japan from the Meiji Restoration in 1867 to the war with China in 1894. (*Ibid.*, 24.)
5. Cook, C. and Stevenson, J. (1987) *The Longman Handbook of Modern European History: 1763–1985.* London: Longman, 230.
6. *Ibid.*, 237.
7. Heilbroner, R. ed. (1986) *The Essential Adam Smith* New York: W. W. Norton & Company, 1–12.
8. Smith, A (1776) *The Wealth of Nations,* Book II, ch.3, Ibid. 241.
9. *Ibid.*

10. Smith, A. (1776) *The Wealth of Nations*, Book IV, ch. 2, Cannar, E. ed. (1937) New York: Random House, 771.
11. Smiles, S. (1856) *Self-Help; With Illustrations of Conduct and Perseverance*. Gutenberg E-texts, E-text No. 935, June 1997, ftp://sunsite.unc.edu/pub/docs/books/gutenberg/ etext97/selfh10.txt>, 27 October 1999.
12. *Ibid.*
13. *Ibid.*
14. Cook, C. and Stevenson, J. (1987) *The Longman Handbook of Modern European History: 1763–1985*. London: Longman, 235.
15. Friedman, T.L. (1999) *The Lexus and the Olive Tree: Understanding Globalization*. New York: Farrar, Strauss and Giroux, xiv.
16. Harley, C.K. (1980) 'Transportation, the World Wheat Trade, and the Kuznets Cycle, 1850–1913' in *Explorations in Economic History*, Vol. 17, 218–50, 218.
17. Stone, N. (1988) *Europe Transformed, 1878–1919*, 4th edn. London: Fontana Press, 23–7.
18. Harley, C.K. (1980) 'Transportation, the World Wheat Trade, and the Kuznets Cycle, 1850–1913' in *Explorations in Economic History*, Vol. 17, 228.
19. War, inflation and political turmoil of the 1920s increased the risk of market failure causing British investment to adopt a much more regional character. See Stopford, J.M. (1991) 'The Origins of British-Based Multinational Manufacturing Enterprises', in Wilkins, Mira, ed., *International Library of Critical Writings in Business History*, Volume I, *The Growth of Multinationals*, Aldershot, UK: Edward Elgar Publishing, 165.
20. Jones, Geoffrey (1991) 'Origins, Management, and Performance', in Wilkins, 252–3. During and after World War I foreign direct investment began to increase while portfolio investment declined. Fewer people migrated from the British Isles and many of the smaller expatriate firms ceased to operate, being purchased by American interests. By 1927 direct investment had risen to 20 per cent of British capital exports and this doubled by the time of World War II. [Stopford, 'Origins', in Wilkins, 165–7].
21. Wilkins, Mira (1991) 'European and North American Multinationals, 1870–1914: Comparisons and Contrasts', in idem, ed., *International Library of Critical Writings in Business History*, Volume I, *The Growth of Multinationals*, 53.
22. *Ibid.*, 52–3.
23. Chapman, S. 'British Free-Standing Companies and Investment Groups in India and the Far East' in Wilkins, M. and Schröter, H., eds. (1998) *The Free-Standing Company in the World Economy, 1830–1996*. Oxford: Oxford University Press, 202–17.
24. Stopford, J.M. (1974) 'The Origins of British-Based Multinational Manufacturing Enterprises' *Business History Review*, 48, 303–35, in Wilkins, M., ed. (1991) International Library of Critical Writings in Business History, Vol. 1, *The Growth of Multinationals*. Aldershot, UK: Edward Elgar Publishing, Article 6, 159–91, 162–3.
25. *Ibid.*, 172–3.

26. Jones, G. (1986) 'Origins, Management, and Performance', 252–5.

27. *Ibid.*, 171–8.

28. Dickens, C. *A Christmas Carol.* Gutenberg E-texts, E-text No. 92, <carol10.zipftp://sunsite.unc.edu/pub/docs/books/gutenberg/etext92/carol10.tx t>, 8 October 1999.

29. Dickens, C. *Dombey and Son*, Gutenberg, E-texts, E-text No. 821, <http://promo.net/pg/_authors/redirect.cgi?site=mu&dir=97&file=domby10&ex t=txtDombey and Son>

30. *Ibid.*

31. 'Never fear, good people of an anxious turn of mind, that Art will consign Nature to oblivion. Set anywhere, side by side, the work of GOD and the work of man; and the former, even though it be a troop of Hands of very small account, will gain in dignity from the comparison. So many hundred Hands in this Mill; so many hundred horse Steam Power. It is known, to the force of a single pound weight, what the engine will do; but, not all the calculators of the National Debt can tell me the capacity for good or evil, for love or hatred, for patriotism or discontent, for the decomposition of virtue into vice, or the reverse, at any single moment in the soul of one of these its quiet servants, with the composed faces and the regulated actions. There is no mystery in it; there is an unfathomable mystery in the meanest of them, for ever. Supposing we were to reverse our arithmetic for material objects, and to govern these awful unknown quantities by other means.' From Dickens, C. *Hard Times*, Gutenberg, No. 786.
<ftp://uiarchive.cso.uiuc.edu/pub/etext/gutenberg/etext97/hardt10.txt>, 10 October 1999.

32. Turner, F.M. (1981) *The Greek Heritage in Victorian Britain.* New Haven: Yale University Press, 188.

33. Grote, G. (1869) *A History of Greece: A New Edition.* London: John Murray, Vol. 4, 104–5, in Turner, F.M. (1981) *The Greek Heritage in Victorian Britain.* New Haven: Yale University Press, 219.

34. Grundy, G.B. (1911) *Thucydides and the History of His Age.* London: John Murray, 106, in Turner, F.M. (1981) *The Greek Heritage in Victorian Britain.* New Haven: Yale University Press, 250.

35. Zimmern, A.E. (1915) *The Greek Commonwealth: Politics and Economics in Fifth Century Athens.* Oxford: Clarendon Press, 365–6, in Turner, F.M. (1981) *The Greek Heritage in Victorian Britain.* New Haven: Yale University Press, 262.

36. Witzel, M. 'China: The World's Oldest Brand' in 'Asian Culture and the Global consumer', *Financial Times Mastering Management Review*, 24, <www.ftmas-tering.com/p/oc7c7.html>, 15 May 2000.

37. *Ibid.*, 24–7. The quotation is from p. 27.

38. Bryant quoted in Wiener, M.J. (1982) *English Culture and the Decline of the Industrial Spirit, 1850–1980.* Cambridge: Cambridge University Press, 75.

39. Courtauld quoted *ibid.*, 127.

40. *Ibid.*

41. Dunning, J.H. 'Changes in the Level and Structure of International Production: The Last One Hundred Years' in Wilkins, *International Library of Critical Writings in Business History*, Volume I, *The Growth of Multinationals*, 96.
42. In the words of Professor Stopford, where it was 'relatively easier to develop exports to previously underdeveloped regions than it was to compete directly with the technically and competitively more energetic firms in the developed world'. Stopford, J.M. 'The Origins of British-Based Multinational Manufacturing Enterprises', 169.

14

The Second Global Economy

America's 'Legionary Capitalism': 1800–1970

BRITISH business in its heyday conjures up Athens; American business is very suggestive of ancient Rome. Signers of the American Constitution looked to Roman examples. 'A Republic, madam, if you can keep it,' was wily old Ben Franklin's rejoinder to a lady who had asked him what kind of state was emerging from the deliberations of 1789.

Like Rome, the United States began with a free market of farmers who laid the foundations of a trading colossus where partnerships evolved into giant continental firms. Standard Oil of the Rockefellers, J.P. Morgan's US Steel and many other American firms followed the same bias for patriarchal leaders. Most significantly both Rome and America excelled in military capitalism, or 'military Keynesianism', as some have called it.

Despite professed allegiance to free-market credos, American business was nurtured by national security spending and defence contracts. As early as 1798 President John Adams asked Eli Whitney to make 10 000 muskets for the army. The first thing Whitney built were the machine tools made so a part of one musket would fit any other musket and large numbers could be assembled in record time. This would become an American value: make them fast, make them cheap and make plenty of them![1]

The pattern set in the days of Adams set the tone for the American business experience. 'There was not', according to historian Geoffrey Perret, 'a single important element in the American system that did not derive from an arms contract.'[2] The War Department provided roads, maps and the US cavalry to aid settlers moving westward. The Erie Canal and the National Road were built with funds from state governments. By 1860 the frontier stretched from Minnesota to Texas and America had 30 million people. Stocking arsenals like Springfield and Harper's Ferry spurred production of machine tools and interchangeable parts all across the country, but especially in the Connecticut River Valley, the Route 128/Silicon Valley of pre-Civil War America. Machine tools made wheels, gun handles, axles, shoes, sewing machines, clothing, railway cars and rails and other interchangeable items. Ploughs, reapers and threshers launched a horsepower revolution in the Midwest, allowing wheat and corn to displace cotton as America's prime export crop. Wheat production in the Midwest rose from 28 million bushels in 1840 to 44 million in 1850, 95 million in 1860, and 194 million in 1870.

Some industries already foreshadowed the muscle of the Gilded Age and even the auto age. The Studebakers of Indiana made carriages; Charles Goodyear perfected rubber tyres. The rotary steam press made possible mass-circulation newspapers and mass literacy sustained by public education. Most important were the railroads, which forged a national market joining the farms of Minnesota, Iowa and Wisconsin to the factories of New York and the mines of Pennsylvania.[3] The rail, steel and telegraph grew together in mutual dependence. Peter Cooper's Trenton Iron Company built most early American rails until British competition drove them into the brand-new market of making cables for the telegraph lines, which ran alongside the railways. Telegraph companies themselves multiplied in the 1840s and 1850s much as today's Internet service providers, with the North American Telegraph Association creating a near monopoly by 1859. A national market was impossible without a net of railways, and efficient running of railways was impossible without instant telecommunications.

> A national market was impossible without a net of railways, and efficient running of railways was impossible without instant telecommunications

America's military capitalism ensured victory for the Union in the Civil War of 1861–1865. General Ulysses S. Grant managed war as a nationwide business. Yankee firms expanded enormously on the contracts for supplying, arming and clothing Mr Lincoln's army. Northern wheat and wool, not Southern cotton, were now king as factories in New York and Pennsylvania turned out one million blue uniforms and farms in the Midwest fed not only the Union but a Europe plagued with bad harvests.

Andrew Carnegie and John D. Rockefeller became war millionaires. Grant himself possessed 'a manager's temperament and an executive's outlook' and ran the Army of the Potomac in 1864 and 1865 like a company operation, sending out concise memos by telegraph. Grant's Army of the Potomac 'embodied the bureaucratic, organizational culture of the North at its most energetic and progressive'. Lee's brilliant army, in contrast, was so chaotic in its logistics that many a Yankee unit escaped certain doom when the Rebels failed to carry out their orders before dusk.[4]

America emerged from the Civil War with almost double the amount of business establishments – some 250 000 – than it had in 1850. During the 1860s the number of US manufacturing companies grew by almost 80 per cent and the industrial workforce by almost 60 per cent. Grant well understood how the link between business and war dragged humanity forward at terrible cost: 'War is progressive,' he said 'because all the instruments and elements of war are progressive.'[5] America grew even faster after 1865, becoming the richest and most powerful nation in history. Population tripled from 23 million in 1850 to 76 million in 1900 and the value of manufacturers grew elevenfold from $1 billion to $11 billion. In the first decade of the 20th century, the United States produced half of Europe's output and twice that of Britain. The spectacular growth of American industrial production was truly staggering – 1800 per cent between 1859 and 1914 and 3300 per cent between 1859 and 1919. This was due to a number of advantages, outlined in Table 14.1.[6]

> In the first decade of the 20th century, the United States produced half of Europe's output and twice that of Britain

The story of Trimalchio, the obnoxious parody-figure of the self-made Roman from the 1st century, was being repeated again and again, though his 19th-century heirs made their wealth in industry rather than in agriculture. The code of Samuel Smiles, slowly being downplayed in Britain, now found a new home in America, his ideas saturating the culture in the stories of Horatio Alger. In Alger's lay sermons a young man, typically through hard work, hustle, luck and risk-taking, usually rose to great wealth – a Dick Whittington updated for the industrial era. William Dean Howells' *The Rise of Silas Lapham*, written in 1889, mirrored the rise of an upwardly mobile class of self-made business leaders, far more entrepreneurial than the traditional New England elite: 'Tall hats and long coats disappeared ... New names appeared at the head

Table 14.1 United States business advantages

1	Liberal patent laws encouraging entrepreneurial innovation.
2	Scarce, high-cost labour encouraging investment in technological innovation and machinery.
3	Standardization of machinery and parts.
4	A horsepower revolution in agricultural production based upon investment in reapers and other machinery.
5	Abundant deposits of iron ore and petroleum and cheap sources of energy: coal, water, wood, electricity.
6	Pro-business government policies: *laissez-faire*, railway subsidies and grants, high external tariffs.
7	A continent-sized market unified by navigable rivers, telegraph and railways.

of great industrial enterprises. Boys who had gone to the War as junior officers had brought back honourable titles which vouched for responsibility, character, and daring ... You can't, if you will, hold down a captain, a Colonel ... who has earned and won the admiration of the public, and who has tested his worth.'[7] Mark Twain's and Charles Dudley Warner's 1873 novel *The Gilded Age* satirized the new industrial business culture, giving its name to the era. Philip Sterling, the hero, is a self-reliant coal entrepreneur. The villain, Colonel Beriah Sellers, one of the new breed of professional public-relations advertisers, persuades a railroad company to build a worthless line so he can prosper. Twain's portrait of Washington scandals described the politics of financiers such as Jay Gould, Daniel Drew and Jim Fisk.

The driving industry in the industrial expansion of the Gilded Age continued to be railroads: the 64 000 kilometres of lines in 1865 grew to 420 000 in 1915, one third of all the railway tracks in the world, more than all of Europe combined! The New York Central, Pennsylvania, Erie, Baltimore and Ohio, and Grand Trunk lines monopolized the routes east of Chicago and, with the cash proceeds, virtually ran state legislatures. In the West, the Federal Government provided lines such as the Union Pacific, Central Pacific and Northern Pacific with ownership of huge chunks of Minnesota, Washington, Wisconsin, Iowa, Kansas, North Dakota, Montana, Nebraska, California and Louisiana, a total area bigger than Germany or France. Settlement of the Great Plains fed a demand for railroads that fed a demand for iron, steel and oil. Large corporations everywhere copied the structure of the railways. As late as 1898 they issued 60 per cent of public stock in the country. That would drop to 40 per cent in 1914 and, as the auto triumphed, to 17 per cent in 1925 and 13 per cent in 1957. The railroad empires were linked to the oil and steel industries. Neither United States Steel nor Standard Oil could have existed without the rails and telegraph lines that had facilitated their rapid expansion.

The economy began to shift as railways reached saturation point. Realising in 1859 that underground oil was a new source of light and energy, young John D. Rockefeller created the Standard Oil partnership. Aware of the dangers of market failure in a very risk-oriented business, Rockefeller sought to corner the market in oil refining. Standard Oil applied the Eclectic Paradigm of internalization within the American market with a vengeance. Standard shipped kerosene in its own barrels. Rockefeller bought up local refineries in Ohio and others in Baltimore, Pittsburgh, Philadelphia and New York. He also set up subsidiaries such as the South Improvement Company, which undercut his competitors by exacting a refund of his shipping costs on the New York Central, Erie and Pennsylvania rail lines. By 1899 Standard Oil monopolized oil production in the United States, had grown from $10 million to $110 million and had stock in over 40 other companies. In the United States it marketed 75 per cent of crude oil, 80 per cent of kerosene and 90 per cent of railway lubricants, controlled over 50 per cent of railway tank cars and even had its own fleet of almost a hundred ships. Its power was so great that in 1906 President Theodore Roosevelt initiated an antitrust suit, which led to its break-up and the creation of Exxon, Chevron, Sohio, Amoco, Conoco and Sun. While American business culture would be uncomfortable with monopoly, it would become less worried about oligopoly.

The giant trusts would be restrained less by the Justice Department than by the rise of whole new industries and markets. In 1901 oil was discovered at Spindletop in Texas. Almost overnight the Lone Star State began to produce annually 136 million barrels of oil, more than all of Russia and double the 58 million barrels produced in the rest of the United States. By 1902 some five hundred oil companies were operating in Texas and the Rockefeller monopoly was challenged even before the 1906 suit. 'Spindletop alone', according to David Halberstam, 'changed the nature of the American economy ... [it] inaugurated the liquid-fuel age in America. If the energy of the new age was to be oil, then America suddenly was rich in it.'[8] Cleaner, more storable and cheaper than coal, oil empowered small firms and individuals who owned their own lorries and autos, thus hastening a shift away from trains. Cheap Texas oil helped Henry Ford build a car so affordable he could sell it to the millions. Ford, like Eli Whitney before him, turned to a new version of an old Roman idea. Mass production existed in the ancient Roman clay industry, where jugs and lamps had been turned out by the thousands. Its modern version had its own prophet, Frederick W. Taylor.

Taylor, in his 1911 *Principles of Scientific Management*, advocated the use of time studies to make production as rapid and as efficient as possible. Instead of depending on a floor-walking foreman, companies would be run efficiently by systematic procedures. Employees would now be evaluated and given performance appraisals on the basis of objective standards. Factory production would be organized by experts to produce the maximum amount of goods with the least resources in the minimum amount of time. Ford applied – and perhaps misapplied – Taylor's principles ruthlessly. He set up an assembly-line procedure that reduced the time needed to make a Model T from 13 hours to a mere hour and a half by 1914. Ford made only a $100 profit on each car, but between 1908 and 1928 he sold 15 million of them. Quantity became a qualitative factor. A Model T cost $780 in 1911 but only $360 in 1914. By this time Ford Motor Company had utterly dominated the American car industry. By 1914, Ford had 13 000 employees and produced 267 000 cars. All other companies combined, some 300 of them, employed 66 000 and produced only 287 000 cars. Ford's share of the market in the early years grew and grew: 9.4 per cent in 1908, 20.3 per cent in 1911, 39.6 per cent in 1913 and, after its assembly line was up and running, a staggering 48 per cent in 1914. The company's earnings in 1915 were $100 million; its net worth in 1908 was $2 million, by 1927 $673 million. Ford recognized the revolution he had created: 'Mass production precedes mass consumption, and makes it possible by reducing costs and thus permitting both greater use-convenience and price-convenience.'[9]

> American business in the 20th century was dominated by hierarchical mass-production firms

American business in the 20th century was dominated by hierarchical mass-production firms. America's entry into World War I in 1917 only accelerated this trend. Firms not only supplied the legions but became legions themselves. Ford, GM and IBM often applied mass-production, assembly-line and Scientific Management techniques in a very regimented, conformist fashion. Agents, brokers and salesmen, dressed in seemingly lookalike dark suits, were often trained with a military efficiency in which individual personalities were forced into a rigid mould. The new mass-production corporations went to war in the spirit of the Roman *publicani*. Ford, GM, US Steel and others, with no more experience in war production than Scipio's Romans had in building their navy, quickly retooled. GM's Cadillac division made Army staff cars, Buick tanks and lorries for Pershing's army. Henry Ford converted his own assembly lines to military cars, lorries, aeroplane motors, subchasers, tanks and arms. American firms working from government contracts built a Merchant Marine from scratch, raised iron ore production from 41 to 75 million tons and helped the United States emerge in 1919 as the world's leading creditor nation, with a $3.8 billion trade surplus.

> The motor vehicle and its lifeblood, petroleum, not only helped win the Great War for the Allies, but – along with the widespread application of electricity – transformed the Second Global Economy and the entire culture and even the landscape of the United States

The motor vehicle and its lifeblood, petroleum, not only helped win the Great War for the Allies, but – along with the widespread application of electricity – transformed the Second Global Economy and the entire culture and even the landscape of the United States. In California a slogan ran: 'Electricity is the road to the health, wealth and happiness of mankind.' Its metal cousin, the motor vehicle, saved Paris in 1914 when 'the Taxis of the Marne' rushed French troops to the front lines. Motorized reinforcements aided the defence of Verdun in 1916 and massed lorries helped break the back of Germany's final offensives in 1918. Shell's visionary executive, Henri Deterding, quickly spotted that the 20th century would be the century of the automobile: 'This is a century of travel, and the restlessness which has been created by the war will make the desire for travel still greater.'[10] Nowhere was this to be truer than in the jazzed-up, Charleston-dancing America of the 1920s, now the first large nation in history with a majority living both in cities and on wheels. There were eight million cars in America in 1920; by 1930 there were 26 million, one for every five Americans. The highways grew faster than the cars. Where there had mostly been dirt roads in 1919, a series of state and Federal bills funded the building of dozens of concrete highways. It took the railways 50 years to link every corner of America. These modernized versions of the Appian Way were paved in less than a decade. Roadside stands, motels, billboards, thousands of Texaco stars, Shell scallops and Gulf discs all competed for the eyes.

The car culture was taking over! Even in the 1920s, the auto became pivotal to the American way of life, consuming 90 per cent of the oil and spawning whole new industries such as fast foods, filling stations and motels. The car culture inspired popular songs such as 'Take Me on a Buick Honeymoon' and 'You Can't Afford to Marry Me If You Can't Afford a Ford'. Suburban America, which grew from 5 to 13 million in the 1920s, was essentially the creation of the motor car. It helped create new population belts around the cities of the Northeast, Midwest and southern California. Miami, Los Angeles and Dallas doubled in population. Real estate boomed in places such as California and Florida, now accessible by car, and the speculation inspired by this motorized boom eventually found its way into the stock market. It was the car that created a real-estate boom in American suburbs, as promoters urged people to own their own homes and municipal governments rushed in to fund public utilities.

Not surprisingly, American business philosophers in the 1920s recast the boot-strapism of Trimalchio, Samuel Smiles and Horatio Alger for the Jazz and Auto Age. Government efforts to enforce the eight-hour day, which even Henry Ford went along with, aroused the wrath of not a few modern conservatives in the tradition of Cicero and Cato. George Markland, Jr, of Philadelphia Gear Works saw concessions to workers as a threat to personal responsibility and property itself: 'Rome did that and Rome died ... The men of our country are becoming a race of softies and mollycoddles; it is time we ... turned out some regular he-men ... Any man demanding the forty-hour work week should be ashamed to claim citizenship'.[11]

A reaction was already in full swing. The 1920s entrepreneur is mocked in Sinclair Lewis's *Babbitt* (1922). The portly George F. Babbitt is no Rockefeller or Carnegie, but a suburban real-estate promoter who made 'neither butter nor shoes nor poetry' but was quite adept at 'selling houses for more than people could afford to pay'.[12] His views on charity and labour unions are purely mid-Victorian or late Roman Republic: the sooner one learns 'he isn't going to be coddled, and he needn't expect a lot of free grub ... the sooner he'll get on the job and produce-produce-produce'.[13] Relatively honest and diligent for the times, Babbitt made his sales pitch in thousands of breathless form letters: 'I just want you to know can I do you a whaleuva favor? Honest! No kidding! I know you're interested in getting a house ... did you ever stop to think that we're here to save you trouble? That's how we make a living – Folks don't pay us for our lovely beauty!'[14]

Cars, and the status they represented, bewitched a whole new class of American equestrians who saw in their 'streamline bodies, hill-climbing power, wire wheels, chrome steel, ignition systems and body colors ... an aspiration for knightly rank'.[15] In *Babbitt*, the issues of mass production and Taylorism are debated by the lawyer Doane, proud to 'get a better tool for less money', and the scientist Yavitch who deplores what he sees as America's 'standardization of thought' and 'traditions of competition'.[16] For Babbitt himself, the hero of the age is the nattily dressed booster devoted wholly 'to the cosmic purpose of Selling – not of selling anything in particular ... but pure Selling'.[17]

> The Twenties boom was based on the automobile and the new electric industry

The Twenties boom was based on the automobile and the new electric industry. According to Paul Johnson, no country had achieved such a lead in total world production as the United States in the 1920s. The American share was 34.4 per cent of the total, compared with Britain's 10.4 per cent, Germany's 10.3 per cent, Russia's 9.9 per cent, France's 5 per cent and Japan's 4 per cent. Workers found it difficult to keep up with the soaring prosperity. The enormous gains in productivity were frittered away on outer appearances, office towers, gadgets, and increased gains for shareholders with the object of drumming up the share price and making capital gains. The crash, when it came, was traumatic – but not fatal! The Depression of the 1930s inspired new forms of 'legionary capitalism'. The American love affair with the car continued even with half of the auto plants in Michigan shut down and one in every three dealers out of business.

President Franklin D. Roosevelt's (1933–45) remedies were very much geared to a country dependent upon cars. Eighty per cent of the New Deal's make-work expenditure went to doubling the road mileage in the country. Downtown construction came to a near halt, but the sprawling suburbs of Detroit, Chicago and other cities grew by 10–20 per cent. The 1939 General Motors (GM) World Fair *Futurama* showed a vision of high-speed expressways, already in existence in the form of the Pennsylvania Turnpike and the Pasadena Freeway. The 1930s brought forth super-markets, roadside restaurants and new approaches to management that would spread well into the 1950s. For example, the GM Corporation under Alfred Sloan combined systematic management with divisional responsibility. Its 30 departments were grouped around Chevrolet, Pontiac, Oldsmobile, Buick and Cadillac, each of whose management teams had near autonomy while the head office managed policy and administration. GM's units were permanent, specialized corporations in themselves, joined together by a bureaucracy.

Ford relied on intuition, Sloan upon organization. GM's style was Babbitt writ large: unpretentious, conformist, hard-working, hardly conducive to flamboyant, freewheeling entre-preneurs but more geared to men in grey-flannel suits. GM hired not high-tech geniuses, but 'solid Midwestern citizens whose work lives oddly mirror that of their products ... putting in more time and more effort to turn out more product'.[18] Fewer than 10 per cent of GM foremen had college degrees. Managers rose from within, usually from the Flint-based General Motors Institute. One reason the big automotive industries survived was that the market was primarily domestic. In spite of hard times, the average American still believed in the future and an ever-growing standard of living. Cars were part of that 'conspicuous consumption' that social theorists would soon write about. Thus the automotive giants weathered the Depression with severe scars, ultimately to emerge as the models for a new post-war economy.

> The crash, when it came, was traumatic – but not fatal!

IBM, another of those models, prospered in the 1930s, largely due to the programmes of the New Deal. IBM's prosperity during the Depression was hardly due to free-market practices. It specialized in large customized adding machines, designing them so they would operate only with IBM punch cards. Even as the Justice Department pursued an antitrust case against IBM – it controlled 85 per cent of the keypunch, tabulating and accounting market in the United States – the new Social Security Admin-istration was ordering 400 IBM adding machines and 1200 keypunchers.

Americans had seen the future and it would work. The future very definitely seemed to lie with large, hierarchical organizations and systems capable of processing the data they needed.

World War II did for America what the wars with Carthage did for Rome, but with some very different social results. It ended the 1930s' Depression, mobilized the economy of the United States as never before and made the vast republic the most powerful nation in history. Some have said that the atomic bomb – developed under the auspices of the Manhattan Project – was the most characteristic single product of American entrepreneurial energy and organising ability. The world war helped consolidate the gains of labour and lifted millions from destitution into the middle class. It also confirmed ongoing parallels to the Roman models of mass production, a mixture of drivers: entrepreneurs, big companies and 'military Keynesianism' in America's post-war business culture. Defence contracts would underwrite American affluence and prosperity. During the war the federal government bought half the goods produced by American industry and agriculture. President Roosevelt, however, made every effort to treat business as a partner, not an adversary, putting CEOs on war production boards. American mobilization was far more market-oriented and democratically spirited than in any other major warring country. The draft and the all-out 'can-do' spirit showed 'a remarkable entrepreneurial spirit in sharp contrast to the situation in Germany or in socialist, centrally planned economies.'[19]

By 1945, American Big Government was bigger than ever, but the country did not become a command economy. Workers went to war-production jobs on the basis of market demand and their own free choices. Businesspeople were now seen neither as rugged individualists nor as villains, but as patriotic citizens. In 1942, Ford, GM and Chrysler turned from cars to Sherman tanks, tank destroyers, trucks, jeeps, gliders and hundreds of thousands of tyres. Ford's giant Willow Run plant outside Detroit turned out one B-24 bomber per *hour*. Henry Kaiser's shipyards in Fontana, California, produced one Liberty Ship per day. Lingerie makers made camouflage nets, lipstick makers turned to bomb cases, beer-can makers converted to making hand grenades. The economy grew by 10 per cent a year during the war, but reconversion to consumer production was much easier and quicker than in 1919.

For millions of Americans, the immediate post-war years were the best years to work and raise a family. The economy held steady. The pursuit of happiness never seemed more within reach for so many. The industrial powerhouses geared up for peacetime ways. Patterns of growth in America's petroleum economy, set in 1900–1930, resumed full-throttle in the 1950s. America completed its transformation into a society of highways and suburban middle-class commuters. There were 50 million cars on the road by 1960. State governments built a series of super-highways allowing motorists to get from Maine to Chicago in two or three days. The National Interstate and Defence Highways, begun by President Dwight Eisenhower in 1956 and completed by the early 1970s, became the sacred space of the car culture. It would eventually cost $76 billion – the largest public-works project in the nation's history. Like the Roman roads of old, the interstates were a product of military necessity – President Eisenhower saw the need to move men and material quickly. Caesar would have approved. The interstate highway system affected the American way of life even more radically than did the highways of the 1920s. The 41 000 miles of high-speed travel arteries cut wide swathes across farmlands, hills, seacoasts, deserts and prairies, hiking real-estate prices where they went and depressing neighbourhoods where they did not go. Downtowns became ghettos. Interstate exits became concrete *emporia* drawing in businesses and 20 000 new shopping malls.

Whole enterprises owed their fortunes to the interstate explosion. Colonel Harland Sanders' Kentucky Fried Chicken chain was but one example. When an access road routed traffic away from his Kentucky restaurant, Sanders marketed his secret recipe at the foot of interstate exit ramps. By 1963, he had 600 outlets in the South and the Midwest. Ray Kroc made as much money buying and leasing interchange properties as he did marketing fast foods. Motel franchises such as Holiday Inn out of Memphis, Tennessee, Howard Johnson's and Ramada mushroomed. Interstates helped lure over 600 000 Americans a year to what would become known as the Sunbelt. American companies led the way, eager to leave unionized high-tax states with cold winters and high energy costs such as New York, Massachusetts, Ohio and Michigan. The temptation to relocate or to retire to the warmer climate and more business-friendly Sunbelt played its own part in the rezoning of America. The South was truly rising again!

By 1975 the Southern Rim of the United States, stretching from

> Whole enterprises owed their fortunes to the interstate explosion

Arlington, Virginia, to Los Angeles, California, had become the heart and core of American wealth and power. The old Confederacy, with the addition of Arizona, New Mexico and southern California, was now a $400 billion superpower with a GNP larger than that of any country save the Soviet Union. Its population had grown from 40 million to 80 million: Texas by 100 per cent, California by 200 per cent, Florida by 400 per cent and Arizona by 450 per cent. Houston rocketed from 385 000 to 1.4 million, Phoenix from 65 000 to 755 000. In spite of a strong anti-government ideology, tracing from the botched federal programme of 'Reconstruction' after the disastrous Civil War, the rise of the Sunbelt was an even greater triumph of 'legionary capitalism' than the highway system that spurred its growth. In World War II some $60 billion of the $74 billion spent for the war effort went into the states of the Southern Rim. After World War II, the contracts of the Cold War economy fuelled an escalation in defence spending, which soared from $12 billion in 1945 to $50 billion in 1960 and $86 billion in 1975. Artful Southern politicians in Congress – the archetype was the future President Lyndon Baines Johnson from Texas (1963–69) – made sure that most defence money was spent in the Sunbelt states. Defence contractors were also attracted to the Southern Rim by the warm climate, open space, weak unionism and the already existing aerospace industries.

In the period 1952–1962, the income of California, Arizona, New Mexico and Mississippi, together with Colorado, Utah, New Hampshire and Kansas, grew by more than 20 per cent due to defence spending. Meanwhile the Northeast and especially the Great Lakes regions – about to be designated the Rustbelt in the 1970s – lost income. From 1962 to 1972, the years of the moon race and the Vietnam War, the trend intensified. Some $80 billion was invested in aerospace development, mostly in California (site of Vandenberg Air Force Base), Texas (site of NASA's manned Space Flight Center in Houston), Alabama (site of the Huntsville rocket centre) and Florida (site of Cape Canaveral). California, Texas and Florida each had at least 30 major aerospace plants. By 1970 Southern Rim states accounted for 44 per cent of all defence expenditure, with California and Texas (now the second biggest state) accounting for 28 per cent of all military contracts. The majority of military installations (142) were in the Sunbelt, as were the majority of military and civilian defence payrolls: 49 per cent of Pentagon research and development funds went there. During that time, 70 California firms alone received a full 25 per cent of defence funds, and much of the prosperity of Texas would be related to NASA and firms such as Convair and Ling-Temco Vought. Louisiana, Georgia, Mississippi, Tennessee and New Mexico all relied upon defence industries as their largest single payroll.

Thus was President Eisenhower's prophecy of a military–industrial complex fulfilled. The top ten defence contracting firms in 1970 (Lockheed, General Dynamics, General Electric, AT&T, McDonnell-Douglas, United Aircraft, North American Rockwell, Grumman, Litton and Hughes Aircraft) concentrated heavily in the South and Southwest. According to writer Kirkpatrick Sale, the preponderance of the defence industry in the Southern Rim 'has almost by itself allowed that region to develop the industrial might that today can challenge the traditional industrial power of the Northeast'.[20] The trend would continue into the later 1970s and the 1980s, with the states of the old Confederacy the stalking horses for the Cold War economy. In 1980, out of 46 major military posts in the United States, 24 were located in the South, along with 48 per cent of all military personnel (District of Columbia included) and 40 per cent of all defence expenditures.

Thus the main lines of American business converged closer to government activities than ever before. Retired generals and admirals often took jobs on company directorates, and military contracts were just as important to vast numbers of American firms as they had been to the Roman *publicani*. Boeing, General Dynamics, Convair, Bell, Lockheed, McDonnell Douglas – those corporate behemoths had absolutely no fear of market failure as long as the country seemed locked in an interminable struggle for research, development and procurement with the Soviet Union. The Soviet superpower, despite its spotty economy, seemed for many years to be leading the United States in the creation of missiles and satellites. American companies themselves consciously emulated military management structures, and became ever more concentrated. In the United States the 200 largest firms owned 47 per cent of American manufacturing assets in 1947. This became 56 per cent in 1963 and 61 per cent by 1968. Most of the shares in these firms were owned by pension funds and insurance companies, not small, viscerally connected

> A not-so-subtle change had occurred, which would be strategic for America's economic future. Capitalism, even in free-market America, was intrinsically tied to government

investors. This allowed directors to run their companies without much interference ... and feedback.

A not-so-subtle change had occurred, which would be strategic for America's economic future. Capitalism, even in free-market America, was intrinsically tied to government. It was more honest to describe American business, in the words of historian William Berman, as a system of *regulated capitalism*. Something else, too: American business now had a managerial instead of an entrepreneurial image. Many, if not most, of its managers were highly conventional, generally of British stock and Protestant upbringing: good chaps on the golf course, and Republican in political affiliation at a time when the party was still strongly entrenched in both the Midwest and Wall Street (1945–70). The managers of IBM, Boeing, General Motors, Esso and AT&T – for all their prestige, perquisites and power – were usually reluctant to take risks. Few of them had a true proprietary interest. Most were now from business school backgrounds. This less visceral approach at the top played well to the conformist nature of American business culture, and America itself, in the 1950s. The period style was noticeable and described in a spate of writings, both fictional and non-fictional. David Riesman's prescient study, *The Lonely Crowd*, appearing in 1950, was followed in 1956 by the equally famous *The Organization Man*. In this study William H. Whyte described an American business culture dominated by a group ethic in which most strove to fit in, conform and serve the company in return for a decent salary, reasonable job security and a growing array of company benefits. Yet corporate America in the 1950s only reflected the society as a whole. Many of the GI generation, now entering middle age, were all too happy to bury their individuality in exchange for a house in suburbia, a secure job and a Norman Rockwell-style family, believing that the Depression was gone and would never return. Besides, hadn't Senator Joseph McCarthy's scare- and smear-campaign between 1950 and 1954 shown that too much radical thinking and ideological questioning might be dangerous and unprofitable as well as un-American?

Creeping complacency began to choke the cowboy spirit of innovation that had been associated with Henry Ford and his competitors. The largest, most established American companies – now run by teams of salaried managers – jealously guarded their public image. Even major oil firms, once run with privateering wildcat instincts, now opted for safe, cautious managers. General Motors, whose president Charles Wilson became Secretary of Defense in the Eisenhower Administration, became the model American corporation of the 1950s. In spite of its enormous success, and likely because of it, GM clung to its traditional interpretation of Taylorism and a now outmoded application of Scientific Management. There were warnings. One secular prophet was management consultant Peter Drucker. As early as 1946, Drucker had recommended that GM, and all the other firms that followed it as a model, should grant its workers more responsibility and its plants more autonomy, and make its assembly lines less repetitive. Drucker's recommendations – published in 1946 under the title *The Concept of the Corporation* – called for a return to the original spirit of Scientific Management as Taylor had conceived it, as a spur to productivity and not as a call to treating workers as little yellow pencils lined up in a row. Drucker counselled that corporations could not be run like armies, that they had to assume a certain amount of social responsibility, and that workers should be seen as an investment and not just a cost. Mesmerized by their own success in Cornucopia America, neither GM's management nor its well-paid unions found Drucker's ideas to their liking. Not only Wilson, but his successors, James P. Roche, Richard Gerstenberg and Thomas Murphy, were all Midwestern committee men who continued to push the company way. Henry Ford II, his company losing $10 million a day in the late 1940s and desperately struggling to survive as a result of his father's chaotic interference, was more open-minded, as was General Electric. 'The truly important events on the outside are not the trends,' warned Drucker, 'they are changes in the trends.' Some in America were listening, but Drucker's largest audiences were in the rebounding economies of Central Europe and Japan.[21]

NOTES TO CHAPTER 14

1. Perret, G. (1989) *A Country Made by War: From the Revolution to Vietnam – The Story of America's Rise to Power*. New York: Random House, 95–7.
2. *Ibid.*, 194.
3. Faulkner, H.U. (1925) *American Economic History*. New York: Harper & Brothers, 202–11, 326–30, 334, 338.
4. Perret, G. (1989) *A Country Made by War: From the Revolution to Vietnam – The Story of America's Rise to Power*. New York: Random House, 229–30.
5. *Ibid.*
6. Johnson, P. (1997) *A History of the American People*. London: Weidenfeld & Nicolson, 441–3.

7. Howells quoted in Chamberlain, J. (1963) *The Enterprising Americans: A Business History of the United States*. New York: Harper and Row, 142.

8. Halberstam, D. (1987) *The Reckoning*. New York: Avon Books, 76.

9. *Ibid.*, 73–4.

10. Deterding quoted in Beaton, K. (1957) *Enterprise in Oil: A History of Shell in the United States*. New York: Appleton-Century Crofts, 171, in Yergin, D. (1991) *The Prize: The Epic Quest for Oil, Money, and Power*. New York: Simon and Schuster, 208.

11. Markland, G., Jr, quoted in 'The Five Day Work Week: Can It Become Universal?', Pocket Bulletin, Vol. 27, No. 6, October 1926, 6, in Warren Prothro, J. (1954) *The Dollar Decade: Business Ideas in the 1920s*. Baton Rouge: Louisiana State University Press, 10.

12. Lewis, S. (1980) *Babbitt*. New York: New American Library, 6.

13. *Ibid.*, 17.

14. *Ibid.*, 33.

15. *Ibid.*, 63.

16. *Ibid.*, 85.

17. *Ibid.*, 119.

18. *Ibid.*, 311.

19. Goodwin, D.K. 'The Way We Won' in *The American Prospect*, Vol. 3, No. 11 (Autumn 1992), 66–70, <http://epn.org/prospect/ 11/11kear.html>, 1 November 1999.

20. *Ibid.*, 31.

21. Sampson, A. (1995) *Company Man: The Rise and Fall of Corporate Life*. New York: Random House, 94–100.

15

World-class rivals

The paternalistic capitalisms of Germany and Japan

OTH the American and the British economic systems had survived the collapse of the Second Global Economy, a crisis triggered by the unprecedented world depression of the 1930s.

This depression was one of the last consequences of World War I (1914–1918). The ferocious and costly conflict seriously weakened the British pound and helped dethrone the monetary stability provided by the projection of Britain's worldwide power.

Another factor buffeting Anglo-American leadership of the Second Global Economy was that of stiff competition from overseas. The rise of two rival forms of business organization based in Germany and Japan in the later 19th century provided competitors for the British and American models of business origination. If, as argued previously, Anglo-Saxon economic structures resembled earlier Greek and Roman precedents, those of Germany and Japan resurrected much older Near Eastern practices.

How so?

Adam Smith rejected: the alternative capitalism of Friedrich List

Enormously large and complex, German and Japanese corporations were to be intentionally integrated with government at the highest levels as well as with one another. The American capitalist can be caricatured as the individualistic cowboy striding off to blow away the competition at the OK Corral; the German capitalist resembles a grouse-hunting baron, hound's-tooth cap on his head, pipe between his teeth and rifle carried at a safe angle in a most genteel manner, covering up his prodigious energy with his genial good cheer. In Japan's revolving directorates, anonymity is the norm, with decisions going round and round and then percolating upwards for the final, infallible decision. German and Japanese companies are traditionally paternalistic, with serious investment in the individual worker hired for life, systematically trained and paid extensive benefits.

Some of the German states began to industrialize in the 1840s. Flooded by cheap British goods, the glassware, arms, pottery and furniture industries of Prussia and her neighbours faced extinction. Adam Smith was of little value to Germans, who turned instead to their own Friedrich List (1789–1846), a teacher at the University of Tübingen. List's 1841 *National System of Political Economy* argued that the free-market model was a prescription for Germany's national suicide. Neither markets nor individual consumers automatically operate in the interest of their country. Germany's survival depended upon businesses that were *German*. A nation is not a bazaar, and those buying and selling within it were *Germans* as well as consumers. The classical economists saw a game of individuals playing by the rules of the market; List saw an economic war of all against all in which *nations* either captured and held markets or perished or others fell behind. Listian economics saw the nation as the natural unit of society and measured success by production in German factories instead of buying abroad.[1]

> The classical economists saw a game of individuals playing by the rules of the market; List saw an economic war of all against all in which *nations* either captured and held markets or perished or fell behind

List provided the theory for what Prussian officials and capitalists were already doing. Berlin's Minister of Industry and Trade, Peter Beuth (1781–1853), actively encouraged factory owners to adopt new technologies of machines, rails and steam. He co-ordinated industry and government, promoted textbooks and trained pioneer industrialists at the Berlin Technical Institute. Under Christian von Rother the Prussian Overseas Trading Corporation financed roads, industry and the search for new Prussian markets. When Bismarck united Germany in 1870–1871, the Second Reich amplified Prussia's Listian practices.[2]

The legacy of Germany's medieval craft guilds was as important in shaping German capitalism as List's doctrine.[3] The long centuries of Germany's fragmentation allowed these self-governing corporations to survive long after their French, Spanish and English counterparts.[4] Not even the coming of giant factories and department stores in the 1880s prevented the guilds from remaking Krupp Siemens and Bayer in their very image. The apprenticeship tradition of training for a lifelong vocation endured and enabled the most forward-looking industries to acquire an expert workforce for a new age of electricity and professional management.[5]

Krupp and Siemens: industrial *tamkāru*

The Krupps of Essen embodied the tradition of craftsman-turned-merchant-prince. Having learned his trade in his grandmother's iron foundry, Friedrich Krupp started up his own in the early 19th century. The Krupp works passed to Alfred, aged 14, in 1826. Alfred improved his knowledge of metalworking by visiting small plants along the Ruhr. When the German states began to organise a free-trade zone called the *Zollverein* in 1834, Alfred bought a German-made steam engine, employed 50 workers and sought markets in Bavaria, Saxony and Berlin. The real take-off for Krupp and German industry came in the 1850s as railroads began to link the German states. Alfred made the steel for August Borsig's locomotives, the cars they pulled and the rails they rode upon from Berlin to Bavaria. Krupp quickly diversified into armaments: he supplied the Prussian army with the heavy artillery, breech-loading rifles, mortars and machine guns that unified Germany and made it the most feared nation in Europe. By 1870 Alfred employed 6000 workers and operated his own iron and coal mines. Typical of this modern German capitalism, his operation was highly paternalistic. Krupp introduced employee welfare schemes in 1836, adding health and life insurance in 1853 and pensions in 1855. Hostels were erected in 1856 and schools, stores and a hospital in the 1860s. When Alfred died in 1887, the Krupp operation was a new established hereditary baronetcy of 20 000 people ruled by a dynasty of merchant-princes. Friedrich Alfred Krupp (d. 1902) further expanded the domain into a vast integrated empire of 43 000 workers with a machine-tool firm, shipyards, a number of mines and the huge and very modern Rheinhausen Steelworks.[6]

Werner Siemens (1816–1892) and the giant concern he founded further illustrate Germany's key role in the second phase of the Industrial Revolution. After 1880, steel, electricity and large bureaucratic firms (eventually petroleum would enter the picture) became the driving forces of the late-19th-century economic expansion. Germany's Listian system, with its heavy public investments in science and education, was much better positioned for leadership in these new industries and technologies than a Britain resting on her laurels and trusting in steam power, free-standing family firms and the public school ethos. Siemens, educated in the Berlin artillery school, began to design rubber-insulated wires for telegraph lines. By the end of the late 1840s Siemens was laying lines for the Ministry of Commerce, connecting Berlin to the Rhineland. Disgusted with the Government's neglect of his advice, Siemens in the 1850s turned to his own devices, laying cables in Russia, the Mediterranean and the Near East and, in the 1860s, from London to Calcutta. Siemens invented the dynamo in 1866. By the 1880s his firm had perfected the electric tramways that began to appear not only in Berlin but also across Europe and even in North America. Finally, in 1883, Siemens merged his company with the German Edison Company of Emil Rathenau. This paved the way for the formation of the giant electrical firm Allgemeine Elektrizitäts Gesellschaft (AEG).[7]

> Germany's Listian system, with its heavy public investments in science and education, was much better positioned for leadership in these new industries and technologies than a Britain resting on her laurels and trusting in steam power, free-standing family firms and the public school ethos

Based upon mutual consensus and mutual aid in troubled times, cartels were encouraged in Imperial Germany. Sharing investment costs, strategies, plans and even recession markets, they grew from 4 in 1875 to 385 in 1905. By 1900 AEG had almost 120 offices, only one third of which were in the fatherland, making it one of the most extensive multinationals in the world. Alliances between cartels like Siemens' electrical combines and investment banks such as the Berliner Handelgesellschaft, whose representatives sat on Siemens' board, were the norm. Typical too were the links between the Diskontogesellschaft and Darmstädter banks and German railroads. These early cartels were replaced in the 1920s and 1930s by more informal trust arrangements called *Interessengemein-*

schaften – 'communities of interest'. Here, families or other associations held stock in several firms. Krupp made locomotives, lorries and farm machinery. Bayer, Hoechst and BASF formed the IG Farben chemical cartel. German steel companies merged into the Vereinigte Stahlwerke.

Nazi management: serfdom in the Steel Age

Listian economics went berserk under the Third Reich. Most German industrialists disliked Adolf Hitler, but after 1933 adapted to a radical regime whose rhetoric championed peasant and craftsman. The Third Reich did have its 'medieval' aspects: everyone owed some form of allegiance to some form of Nazi guild controlling everything from peddlers to fruitsellers. Hitler's new serfdom froze workers in jobs and curtailed the free market. Nazi bureaucrats approved all new enterprises, controlled their prices and forcibly shut down 170 000 of them. Big business was co-ordinated through Industrial Groups manned by firm executives, army officers and appointed Nazis. Government and business were more intertwined than ever. Berlin ordered an end to all companies with capital under $40 000. In 1937, 70 per cent of German heavy industry was monopolistic, one third of it dominated by the Kierdorf-Thyssen-Vögler steel and arms combine. Krupp, Klöckner, Flick, Haniel, Mannesman, Wolff and the state-run Hermann Göring Steelworks controlled the rest. Shareholders and bankers no longer ran company policy. The Reich gave special favour to the chemical industry, notably IG Farben. The firm acquired the German patent for synthetic oil from Standard Oil of New Jersey in 1929, but the process was very uneconomical. Hitler, though, circumvented market failure by guaranteeing Farben markets and prices in return for a large supply of the man-made oil. Half of Hitler's oil supply and 95 per cent of the Luftwaffe's fuel supply came from 20 giant Farben plants, factories that fed the blitzkrieg. Farben's workforce grew 50 per cent between 1938 and 1943 to some 330 000. Many of these workers included slaves in plants such as the one at Auschwitz, which supplied not only fuel but also the Zyklon-B gas used in the Holocaust.[8]

> **Listian economics went berserk under the Third Reich. Most German industrialists disliked Adolf Hitler, but after 1933 adapted to a radical regime whose rhetoric championed peasant and craftsman**

Hanseatic revival: Ludwig Erhard's guild capitalism

The post-war German Federal Republic preserved Listian capitalism with a strong dose of free-market medicine administered by Bonn's first Finance Minister Ludwig Erhard. Erhard let the market set prices and output, but melded a loose free-market economy with a strong welfare state. Federal, state and local government held shares in scores of German companies. Within 20 years of her total devastation in 1945 Federal Germany was the third-largest trader on earth. Germany's big firms played to their strengths, according to Peter Drucker: of DM690 billion of German exports in 1994, some DM339 billion was in machinery, DM110 billion in manufactured goods, and DM92 billion in chemicals. Daimler-Benz, Siemens and Volkswagen were the three leading firms, employing a total of about one million and boasting total sales between them of around DM250 billion. German firms did not dominate single industries but had a strong presence in many niche markets. In 1985 some 345 German companies had a share in world exports of over 10 per cent. According to Michael Porter, no other country has such a width and depth of strongly competitive firms: 'Germany does not have dominant positions in large industries but has strong positions in many, many industries' with a tendency

> German business has traditionally accepted markets and individualism, but does not see them as central as Anglo-Saxons do

towards specialized industries in chemicals and machinery with high levels of productivity. Even in the Berlin Republic of the 21st century, German capitalism continues to embrace both List and traditions of medieval craftsmanship. Whilst war, depression and Hitler have tarnished so much of German life, the engineer and apprentice are cherished as a strong source of German identity. German business has traditionally accepted markets and individualism, but does not see them as central as Anglo-Saxons do. Labour–management partnerships, job security and long-term planning remained almost as important as profits until the 1990s, 'a degree of social commitment unheard of in the United States'.[9] German companies were responsible to more than just shareholders, and ranked success not only by sales and dividends but also by job creation. Employees are considered co-workers, and firms issue reports, detailing – along with earnings – job and productivity improvements. When a German firm was in trouble, others would step in and guarantee the jobs of the troubled firm, but were not always successful in doing this: Siemens in 1969 was only able to save 48 000 out of 51 000 Nixdorf computer jobs.

German firms will still ally with banks and state governments. Workers sit on company boards, and the tradition of apprenticeship endures. Training is rigorous. Future sales-clerks learn exchange rates and taxation as well as selling; future mechanics study the engineering and design concepts behind automobiles along with environmental-impact studies: 'Every job, however menial it may seem, is considered part of a larger picture. Apprentices learn to think about what they are doing and how it fits into a larger scheme.'[10] The 'stakeholder' system with its banking ties lets German firms plan strategically. American firms could not endure the short-term losses incurred to sell luxury cars in Japan; Bavarian Motor Works could. Even though BMWs cost 30 per cent more than their Japanese Acura counterparts, the firm still established a toehold in the Japanese market by setting up their own on-site dealer network. Costly as this investment was, it positioned BMW to control its own marketing in the host country. According to company head Hans Peter Sonnenborn, organization, perseverance and the BMW brand name did the rest: 'We were able to build our own showrooms here ... Japanese buyers are very status conscious. It's not so much like in the United States, where you're considered clever for buying cheaply. The Japanese feel that if they pay more, they are getting better quality.'[11]

Most German investment takes place within the European Union. Significant is the rise of German 'Eurofirms' such as the pump maker KSB, which merged in 1986 with the French Pompes Guinard. The new transnational, with its joint Franco-German board of directors, became a strong competitor to both Japanese and American pump makers. 'Eurofirms' KSB, Aerospatiale and Airbus Industrie now play a key role in the European Union's vast internal market, where, free from buyouts or quarterly dividends, they concentrate on capturing market shares from American rival firms Boeing and Bell Helicopter.

THE VECKINGCHUSENS

A LESSON IN BUSINESS ALLIANCES

THE brothers Hildebrand and Sievert Veckingchusen of Westphalia formed several of the many German business alliances that arose in the towns of the Hanseatic League in the late 14th and early 15th centuries. Their business careers began in the German *Kontor* (merchant colony) of Reval in Estonia. They were, like many Hansa merchants, part of a family network that stretched from the English Channel to the eastern shores of the Baltic.

Hildebrand, after marrying the daughter of another Baltic German merchant, fell out with his father-in-law and relocated first in Lübeck and, attracted by the Flemish textile market, shortly thereafter in Bruges. Sievert would remain in Germany alternating between Lübeck and Cologne. Both brothers operated their own enterprises while forming their own partnerships. From his base in Bruges until his death in 1426, Hildebrand traded everywhere. His agents bought salt in Bordeaux, wool in London, cloth in Flanders, fish in Holland and the spices and silk of the Orient in Italy. These goods were usually shipped to and from the North Sea and Baltic in 30-metre ships with big, wide sails called cogs, whose contract captains carried 200 tons of goods per voyage.

Hildebrand's career presents a sad lesson in how not to manage a business alliance. He habitually and recklessly overinvested in costly ventures in the hope of reaping windfall profits in commodities like French salt and Russian fur. He loaned money to the emperor, who was very slow in repaying him. The business climate of the time posed very high risks for Hansa partners. The turbulence of Flemish politics threatened German merchants with labour strife and, on one occasion, seizure of goods and even arrest if they tried to relocate. The Emperor Sigismund banned trade with Venice in 1417, on top of which conflict broke out between the Hanseatic League and Spain in 1419.

In spite of the extent and expansion of his enterprise, Hildebrand lost money in a fur-trading partnership with two other Baltic German merchants, Heinrich Tyte and Wösten of Dorpat. Another major partnership, the 'Venetian Company' entered into with Peter Karbow in Venice, prospered at first, doubling its capital from 5000 to 11 000 marks. Karbow was soon exporting 70 000 marks' worth of spices and other goods from Venice. Trust and co-operation are essential in business alliances and partnerships. Karbow began buying spices and, through the medium of the new bills of exchange, charging it to his Bruges partner. Other partners, one of whom was robbed and imprisoned, and one of Karbow's suppliers swindled the enterprise. The partnership began to lose money. Hildebrand and Karbow went to court with each other and liquidated an enterprise that might have lasted a lot longer with wiser management. By 1422 Hildebrand was in prison for debt where he remained until 1425. He died shortly after his release.

Sievert was a wiser and much more cautious manager. Returning to Lübeck in 1418, he invested in mining, landed property and even rosary manufacturing. By 1431 he was prosperous enough to join the patrician Circle society. He died in 1433.

Regimented individualism

German business culture represents a middle ground between American notions of rugged individualism and Japanese-style conformity.[12] Professor Martin suggests that the German ideal is the symphony orchestra: many diverse performers, each an individual, join together under the will of the conductor. Solo players stand out from time to time, but they do not steal the thunder of the rest. Hard work and ambition are prized, but aggressiveness and open self-promotion are in bad taste: 'Like the soloist, the business person adds to the concerted efforts but is not the centre of attention.'[13] Executives dealing with American companies approach the top manager; in Germany they are politely directed to the subordinate in question. Information does not easily flow between departments, allowing German managers to be barons in their own right. Privacy, distance, formality and space are central to German business life. Office doors are transgressed at one's peril. Invitations to homes for strangers are rare. German business meetings are highly detailed and formalized. German advertising stresses craftsmanship and detailed information in place of the celebrification, image-making and lifestyle appeals of American advertising. A Volkswagen may not win you a dream date but it will provide many years of safe, fuel-efficient transportation. American materialism is that of conspicuous brand-name consumption and public image; German materialism tends towards the ownership of durable, high-quality goods, which are treated with the respect accorded to valuable musical instruments.[14]

List's Asian disciples: Fukuzawa the teacher and Iwasaki of Mitsubishi

Listian principles also took root in Japan. For centuries, the Land of the Rising Sun had remained in a more or less splendid isolation, inward-looking and with a rare sense of cultural uniqueness. Portuguese and Spanish traders reached the Japanese islands in the 16th century, where they encountered a less bureaucratic culture than that found in China. With the Emperor little more than a figurehead, the country was divided into a number of small feudal *han*, or kingdoms. Each of these was ruled by Samurai, a warrior class of fierce combatants who resembled medieval European dukes.[15] The Samurai spirit of all-out assault at the strategic time and place helped the Japanese leapfrog into the electric and oil age in the space of a few decades after Commodore Perry's famous 'black ships' arrived in 1853.

Japan's feudal system and maritime location suggest parallels with the great seagoing traders of antiquity, the Phoenicians. Sporadic European incursions meant that Japan in 1854 already operated with paper money, complex credit arrangements and large merchant houses such as the Mitsui. These houses resembled medieval European firms, being owned and operated by the large clans who governed Japan under the Shogunate and who recruited and trained professional managers. Unlike the European merchant houses, those of Japan produced for their native market, permitting only a few merchants to trade abroad through the port of Nagasaki.[16]

Now, suddenly, in the middle of the 19th century, Japan confronted an aggressive, free-trading Anglo-Saxon capitalism attempting to force open its markets. The response chosen by the young Emperor Meiji was to apply Western expertise to defend Japanese values. Fukuzawa Yukichi, a Samurai economist, studied American and European management and concluded that Japan's major resource was intellectual capital. Instead of a company, he founded Keio University to train professional managers for Japan's hastily emerging companies. Fukuzawa's management philosophy combined the Samurai code of honour, loyalty and concern for one's subjects with the adoption of the latest corporate management and accounting techniques.[17] Fukuzawa inspired the new breed of Japanese executives starting to emerge in the 1870s and 1880s, men such as Shibusawa Eiichi and Minomura Rizaemon. Shibusawa founded the

Daiichi National Bank. Accepting market competition as necessary, he also believed corporate profits must be entwined with the duty of making Japan strong. Minomura joined a 300-year-old family trading firm and turned it into a professionally managed joint-stock company. Mitsui also began to form alliances with both the Meiji Government and other Japanese firms.

Iwasaki Yataro became a modern Japanese version of Sinaranu of Ugarit who, as mentioned in Chapter 5, was given monopoly privileges for trading in the Aegean. Iwasaki invested the wealth of the Todo clan of Samurai in his NYK company, which grew into the giant Mitsubishi. Iwasaki waged economic war in true Samurai fashion, creating a vast Pacific trading concern. The aristocratic, warrior capitalism of Japan had a naval cast. Iwasaki lent the emperor his own ships to wage war on China in 1894–1895; the emperor responded by granting Mitsubishi monopoly privileges in trading. Iwasaki vanquished his lesser rivals, then faced off against Mitsui, beginning an exhausting battle between two business alliances lasting many years. Mitsui embraced free markets and joint-stock forms while Mitsubishi represented what Morgen Witzel of the *Financial Times* terms 'new Japanese entrepreneurs, steeped in the Samurai traditions and conducting business ... as their ancestors had conducted war'.[18]

Mitsubishi helped shape the culture of the Japanese *zaibatsu* (cartel) of the early 20th century. Both joint-stock enterprises and owner-run Japanese businesses adopted a feudal structure in which a core company was supported by a network of semi-independent associates. 'Linkages of companies based on family ties persisted,' according to Witzel, 'even in the *zaibatsu* (company groups) of the early 20th century.'[19] We have shown already how in ancient Phoenicia and Carthage the trading companies formed temporary and sometimes lasting alliances with each other and with the government. Nor were the temple and its vigilant priests left out of this arrangement. Intelligence-gathering had been a key function of this co-operative alliance system in the Mediterranean world and now in modernising Japan where 'alliances between businesses, between business and government, became early on a key focus of Japanese business strategy ... corporations had to be focused and use information well if they were to survive in an "alien" environment. Alliances proved to be an effective coping strategy and have been a feature of Japanese business ever since.'[20]

Some Japanese businesses became multinational enterprises, investing heavily in East Asia. By 1914, Japan had almost $300 million invested abroad, both directly and indirectly, around one eighth of its GNP. The investments were concentrated heavily, around 80 per cent of them in China. In 1902, the branch manager of Mitsui, Jotaro Yamamoto, acquired a textile mill in Shanghai, and soon picked up others. Japanese cartels also invested in coal and iron, setting up the Hanychping Coal and Iron Company near Hankow to provide the iron ore for the Yawata works in Kyushu.[21]

'Rugged collectivism' and strategic investment: Japan's *kata*-based business culture

Japan's imposing and quickly built industrial superstructure was erected upon the social foundation of a nation that possessed a rare and sensitive love of nature. Being part of nature is at the centre of a Japanese worldview that treasures beauty and aesthetics.[22] Shinto is based on the worship of pure spirits; *haiku* poetry is full of references to the landscape and the seasons, as is the Japanese language itself. Japanese gardens show nature as it is, with no perfect rocks, trees or streams. The delightful Japanese gardens can function as a metaphor for Japanese business just as the orchestra does for the German.

Consider: in a Japanese garden every element is part of a greater whole. Foreigners can make a ripple in the garden pond but the ripple soon vanishes within the confines of a harmonious system whose other parts work

> Mitsubishi helped shape the culture of the Japanese *zaibatsu* (cartel) of the early 20th century. Both joint-stock enterprises and owner-run Japanese businesses adopted a feudal structure in which a core company was supported by a network of semi-independent associates

to strain out the intrusion. The goal is always the restoration of harmony. So, as the Japanese see it, the *way* business is conducted is as important as the final results. Everyone seeks to work together harmoniously, acting in the proper manner and striving for improvement. *Shikata* (procedure) in the form of thousands of *kata* (rules) dominates life in and out of the corporate office. Innumerable *kata* exist for exchanging greeting cards, making telephone calls, gripping baseball bats, exchanging *meishi* (business cards) and every other sphere of Japanese life. The social penalty for violating these strict social codes can be severe. Corporate training programmes restrict sleep and impose hard physical activity to instil discipline, devotion to the firm and positive inner attitudes developed by 'rugged collectivism' instead of 'rugged individualism'. One American businessman made the mistake of praising a Japanese subordinate to his superiors. The subordinate lost face, for, in Japan, the saying goes that 'the nail which stands out gets hammered'. This rigid training starts early. University students identify with their school for life and there build the networks that will sustain them in the world of companies, which are seen as families and providers as well as sources of income.

Mitsui, Mitsubishi and the other original giant *zaibatsu* of Japan were based on family ownership. Their post-World War II reincarnations, the *keiretsu*, are more non-family. Work and decision-making within the *keiretsu* firms are viewed as group efforts and there are few formal job descriptions for individuals outside these workgroups. Rewards are often given on a group basis, and managers do not have their own offices but more often work right on the shop floor. Decisions are often made in a group context, with proposals coming from middle or lower management and circulated for everyone to affix their stamp of approval. Japanese culture stresses the total social context in which business is carried out. Feelings, 'saving face' and loyalty are more important than the letter of the law or formal business agreements. Conflict-resolution takes precedence over individual rights. American managers see contracts as a written code of moral absolutes; Japanese see a broad agreement of trust that can always be modified.[23] Everything in the garden and the Japanese firm has its natural place. Title, status and rank in the group are permanent and more important than one's name. Businesspeople carefully read one another's *meishi* and much non-verbal communication takes place in Japanese board meetings.

Led by the Ministry of International Trade and Industry (MITI), Japanese executives since 1945 have tackled growth and trade with the fervour of a Phoenician naval campaign. MITI officials, knowing that mass production meant national power, determined to build a powerful Japanese auto industry. Toyota and Nissan were given loans, tax write-offs, protection from imports and other concessions. In 1950, Japan made only 32 000 vehicles a year; by 1960 that total was up to 482 000. By

1970, 5.3 million cars a year were pouring off Japanese assembly lines, an astonishing annual growth of 30–40 per cent. By 1974, Japan was the leading car exporter and by 1980 *the leading car maker*, overtaking the United States. That year Japan produced more than 12 million Toyotas, Datsuns, Hondas, Nissans and others, exporting over half of them. The reckoning about which Peter Drucker and others had warned had arrived. Americans were buying Japanese cars in record numbers, threatening Chrysler with bankruptcy and even forcing General Motors into the red. The key to Japanese success was their ability to plan strategically, target special markets and shift models as markets shifted. Japanese auto makers fought the economic wars not as armour-plated battleships but as swift-turning destroyers.[24]

> The key to Japanese success was their ability to plan strategically, target special markets and shift models as markets shifted. Japanese auto makers fought the economic wars not as armour-plated battleships but as swift-turning destroyers

Through the 1950s and 1960s Japan's economy grew at a staggering rate as alert managers poured the rich profits into research, modernization and investment. The Japanese GNP in 1950 was $10 billion and by 1955 $20 billion. In 1965, it reached $100 billion and by 1970 $200 billion. It climbed to $300 billion in 1975 and by 1978 reached almost $450 billion. The signs of the times were already being posted in the 1960s. By the end of that decade Japan had overtaken every industrial country in the West except the United States. She had a GNP of over $250 billion and was challenging American leadership in radios, televisions and telephones. Steel production rose from 10 million tons in 1956 to 40 million in 1965 and 60 million by 1967. Japan's business–government combine, using a quasi-military strategy of gaining and hoarding product knowledge and technological breakthroughs and then supporting co-ordinated campaigns to capture foreign markets, swept through the Postwar Global Economy like a divine wind of victory. One by one the hurdles in front of it swiftly fell. Japan won crushing victories over the American textile industry in the 1950s, the American electronics industry in the 1960s and the American auto industry in the 1970s and early 1980s.

The US computer and semiconductor industries became the next target. The first transistor had been perfected in 1956. Almost immediately MITI planners went to work, consulting with executives, selecting products to develop, setting targets in production, quantity and cost, and directly subsidising and directing various *keiretsu* banks for the long haul ahead. Cartels could be set up if they needed to be to fuel the effort and an Electronics Industry Deliberation Council co-ordinated businesspeople, academics and journalists. MITI raised tariffs against American computers and compelled IBM, Texas Instruments and other US firms to license their patents to Japanese firms if they wanted to do business in Japan. MITI funnelled capital from Japanese banks to Hitachi, Fujitsu, Nippon Electric Company, Mitsubishi Electric and Oki Electric, all eager to spearhead Japan's effort in the computer race. These firms were given a guaranteed market through the public Japan Electronic Computer Corporation, which bought the new computers and prevented price competition. MITI pressured auto makers and steel makers to buy Japanese computers. American firms, the Japanese discovered, could easily be played off against one another to extract technology licences and other concessions. United States executives were learning little, it seemed, from the fate of Ford, GM and Chrysler. Some computer companies were so confident of their technological lead that they gave the Japanese older technology, which the Japanese then proceeded to refine and make better and cheaper.

By 1978 and 1979 Japanese 16K memory chips were being marketed aggressively and quickly captured 40 per cent of world share. The Japanese home market was totally under Japanese control, and the surging demand in the world market was exploding so quickly that it left a vacuum. Quality counted, too. The performance abilities of Japanese microchips – they failed only 20 per cent as often as American chips – boosted sales and encouraged many American firms to choose Japanese firms as their second suppliers. The thinking was that Japanese microchip suppliers would be less dangerous competitors than other American firms. That thinking was wrong. Howls went up in America when the Japanese began 'dumping' their chips on the American market in violation of US trade laws. Business writer John C. Condon referred to the Japanese–American trading relationship by the term 'the odd couple'. He concluded: 'No nation is more different from America than Japan.' The Japanese, with no ideological background in the rules of free-market competition, believed that all was fair in trade and war. Cutting prices to get the maximum in foreign sales in the company's and national interest and underselling the *gaijin* (foreigners) were just good business.[25]

By 1980, the Japanese victory in the computer wars became even more evident. They had beaten Intel, Motorola and Texas Instruments to the 64K chip by six months to a year. They had done this by producing a chip based on the older standard design in place of the sophisticated designs put forth by the Americans. Later in 1980, moreover, Nippon Telephone and Telegraph announced that it had developed the world's first 256K chip, whereupon Japan began to sweep the microchip market. In the October 1981 issue of *Scientific American*, an advertorial by Toshiba, Sony, Mitsubishi and 14 other Japanese companies declared victory in the semiconductor war, symbolically raising the Rising Sun flag over Silicon Valley much as Toyota and Nissan were raising it over Detroit. The article attributed the Japanese victory to the alleged superiority of its *keiretsu* system to the free market. In terms of the actual statistics, in 1981 Japan controlled only 33 per cent of the semiconductor market; the US still held the lead at 57 per cent. Japan's leading firms, however, felt that if they captured the lead in chips, they would eventually capture the lead in all the other products based upon microchip technology.

Though the United States had a larger share of the market, the Japanese share was growing at a much faster rate. Eventually, they would have the larger share and be the lower-cost producer, squeezing American profits and discouraging American investment in new plants and technology. American computer companies then faced the stress of shareholders pressuring American firms to abandon the long-term technological race for something more profitable in the short term. The five Japanese firms involved in semiconductor development – Hitachi, Toshiba, NEC, Mitsubishi Electric and Oki Electric – were, in contrast, supported by their *keiretsu*, banks and MITI. This gave them the capability to plan long-term and invest even when markets were depressed. By 1983, the Japanese passed the Americans in total investment in semiconductors, an issue critical for the United States given the dependence of its sophisticated weaponry on a technology now increasingly in Japanese hands. American strategic planners were not amused.

By the end of the 1980s it seemed that Japan was sweeping all before it. Thousands of manufacturing jobs in the American Midwest had gone, victims of imported Japanese steel and cheaper Japanese cars – many of them now being built in North American factories hungry for work. Japan exported $6.8 billion in foreign capital in 1982, $49 billion in 1985 and

$86.6 billion in 1986. The exports in long-term capital rose even faster, reaching $137 billion in 1987. Japan's trade surplus with the United States, buoyed by a weak yen, ballooned from $20 billion in 1983 to nearly $100 billion in 1987. Japanese overseas assets rose at the same time from $25 billion to $240 billion. Japanese overseas investment in 1985 was $24.4 billion and the production from Japanese multinationals abroad reached $240.9 billion. Their subsidiaries employed 800 000 people.

Economic Guadalcanal: the triumph and retreat of Japanese business

In 1988, historian Paul Kennedy wrote that by comparison with Japan, *every* other large power seemed economically sluggish! By 1987 Honda was selling more autos in America (738 000) than in Japan. By 1979 Toyota was exporting ten million cars, and during the 1980s Japanese manufacturers, encouraged by a high yen and low interest rates, plunged into foreign direct investment on a gigantic scale, investing $280 billion overseas. This staggering sum matched the whole economic output of Australia! About half of this investment was in auto plants. From 1982 onwards Toyota, Datsun, Nissan, Honda and others dotted the American Midwest with factories. *Japanese multinationals in America made more cars than the entire British or Italian car industry.* Some 300 000 Japanese managers settled abroad on several-year stints, bringing their families, living near their factories and eating in Japanese restaurants. Other Japanese investors began buying American properties. Sony took over Columbia Pictures; Matsushita went for Universal Studios. In spite of the attempt to portray this investment as an invasion, many Americans and Europeans liked working for the Japanese, who humanized the assembly-line process and treated workers with the same job security and benefits that Japanese workers enjoyed.[26]

This export revolution did not go without comment. During the 1980s, a virtual cottage industry of American books was written on the Japanese triumph. Some, like Marvin Wolf's *The Japanese Conspiracy*, saw this success as a deliberate plot to reverse the outcome of World War II. Others, like Daniel Burstein's *Yen! Japan's New Financial Empire and its Threat to America*, Clyde Prestowitz's *Trading Places: How We Allowed Japan to Take the Lead* and Ezra Vogel's *Japan as Number One*, suggested that

Japan was well on its way to overtaking the United States as the world's leading economic power.[27] Others, noticeably William G. Ouchi's *Theory Z: How American Business can Meet the Japanese Challenge,* examined the American business model and found it wanting. *The Art of Japanese Management: Applications for American Executives* by Richard Tanner Pascale and Anthony G. Athos was in the same vein.[28] Writing in 1981, Pascale and Athos concluded that Japan must have been doing something right. A country the size of Montana, it had an investment and growth rate twice that of America and was quickly overtaking American leadership in steel, shipbuilding and electronics. Not even the oil crisis could stop the Japanese, who merely increased their exports, productivity and competitiveness. The United States, Pascale and Athos insisted, was not out of the running, but could learn something from Japan. The key to Japanese success, they asserted, was in managerial skill. American companies were based upon the Roman 'legionary' model in which the ethos of the first important organizations – political, religious and military – was the matrix from which 'our first concepts of leadership, the chain of command, co-ordination, control, and functional specialization were formed'.

According to this analysis 'the Roman Empire and the Catholic Church were particularly influential'.[29] Pascale and Athos went on to show that, in the medieval tradition, the Holy Roman Emperor had charge of men's affairs in this life, the Pope in the next. Gradually, spiritual and business matters were pushed into separate compartments. When the Industrial Revolution came, labour was viewed as a commodity and individualism intensified. There was more and more stress on one's private life outside the workplace. In Japan, however, there was no such separation. The Samurai land-owning class had exercized total control over their subjects' lives both on and off the job, but they had also felt responsible for the totality of their servants' lives. There was no differentiation between private life and the workplace in Japan. The same pattern persisted in the 1980s, contended Pascale and Athos. The Japanese, however, have not become Americanized, and nor will Americans become Japanized. Morale and discipline and the ability to sacrifice for the good of the company, the good of the nation – these were virtues the Japanese possessed in spades. Writers such as Pascale and Athos in the 1980s still felt that Americans could respond to the Japanese challenge by adapting what they could from the Japanese just as the Japanese had adopted much from the Americans: 'We can't ape the Japanese system. But we can incorporate some of their approach, which still will strengthen our areas of weakness.'[30]

One book, published in January 1989 by the *Economist*'s Bill Emmott, dissented from the conventional wisdom that Japan was on the way to world hegemony. In *The Sun Also Sets: The Limits to Japan's Economic Power*, Emmott clearly pinpointed Japan's hidden weaknesses before many other authors did. He boldly predicted that Japan could never overtake the United States. Within a year after Emmott's book was published, the Japanese stock market crashed, bringing on a Tokyo-led recession, which has persisted and at times even threatened to become a full-blown depression. Through the 1990s the Japanese economy has grown very slowly. Even a MITI report in 1996 now admitted that the 'economic system that has supported the fifty years of economic development following World War II is ill-suited for future growth'. Once growing at 4 per cent a year, the economy in 1992–1997 completely stagnated, growing by less than 1 per cent a year. The *keiretsu* system, seemingly so well suited to bring growth in the 1950s and 1960s, suddenly seemed to be working no longer. The Friedrich List-style policies, designed to jump-start a newly industrialising country, did not operate so well once industrialization matured and the rules of the world economy began to change:

> *'The "Japanese economic model" that we see today is not, as some have suggested, a different kind of capitalism. It is rather a holdover from an earlier stage of capitalism. It is the spectacle of a country vainly trying to carry into maturity economic patterns better suited to its adolescence. For Japan, this turned into a recipe for debilitation. Instead of turning infant industries into export stars, the same tools created a cocoon that protected inefficient – but politically connected – industries from competition, domestic as well as foreign.'[31]*

According to Professor Richard Katz, 'the essence of Japan's malaise is that it gradually shifted from promoting winners to protecting losers'. Lingering xenophobia played its part. Chronic protectionism turned its economy into a dual one where spectacularly efficient multinational exporters operated alongside unproductive domestic industries shielded from foreign competition. The system worked as long as firms like Toyota earned enough to prop up domestic industries in rubber and steel. This effort was proving very costly. It drove many of the productive firms into exporting and investing in places like Korea, Taiwan and America rather than in Japan. Deprived of investment yen, some firms began to stagnate. Few were alert to this subtle shift, especially in 1989, as Japan continued to conquer market after market and run up huge trade surpluses. In reality, the massive investments overseas, some 35 per cent of GNP, yielded diminishing returns through faulty growth projections, with Japan on an economic treadmill. The money for the Toyota, Matsushita and other plants spreading around the world came from a stock market where the price of shares had no relationship to real profits. Loans could be repaid in stock rather than in cash, and the cost of capital was virtually zero. Japan's investment offensive, so imposing on the surface, in fact rested on a gigantic pyramid of bad debt.

> The *keiretsu* system, seemingly so well suited to bring growth in the 1950s and 1960s, suddenly seemed to be working no longer. The Friedrich List-style policies, designed to jump-start a newly industrialising country, did not operate so well once industrialization matured and the rules of the world economy began to change

The chickens came home to roost in December 1989, with the Nikkei falling from 45 000 to 13 000. Banks went under, though most were propped up by billions of dollars of government money. Job security became a thing of the past, with a million jobs vanishing between 1992 and 1996 and another million in danger by the year 2000. The leadership in microchip technology, so coveted by the Japanese, went to Korean competitors as well as Microsoft and Intel. In 1995 and 1996, Tokyo applied the traditional remedies of deficit spending and a renewed export drive. This was now much more difficult in a new global economy where overseas investors could force governments to cut back spending. By 1997 the economy headed downward again. [32]

Few books were written in praise of the Japanese model in the 1990s. It was instead criticized as a 'system that soured'. Yet to some degree, the Japanese system was a victim of the new emerging global economy it had sought to compete in and had helped create. This Third Global Economy, consolidating after the end of the Cold War, would quickly begin to rewrite many of the rules of international commerce.

NOTES TO CHAPTER 15

1. Fallows, J. 'How the World Works'. Atlantic Unbound, December 1993. <http://www.theatlantic.com/ politics/foreign / fall1f.htm>, 8 December 1999.
2. Henderson, W.O. (1969) *The Industrialization of Europe: 1780–1914*. London: Thames and Hudson, 69–75.
3. Fukuyama, F. (1996) *Trust: The Social Virtues and the Creation of Prosperity*. New York: Free Press Paperbacks, 245.
4. Germany's abiding division 'kept alive a host of feudal communal institutions like the guilds for much longer than in other parts of Europe'. *Ibid.*, 246.
5. *Ibid.*, 247.
6. *Ibid.*; Henderson, W.O. (1969) *The Industrialization of Europe: 1780–1914*. London: Thames and Hudson, 69–75, 98–107; see also the historical survey found on the Krupp website at <http://www.krupp-ag.com/world/worldeng.htm>, 15 October 1999.
7. Henderson, W.O. (1969) *The Industrialization of Europe: 1780–1914*. London: Thames and Hudson, 89–92.
8. Grunberger, R. (1971) *The 12 Year Reich: A Social History of Nazi Germany 1933–1945*. New York: Holt, Rinehart and Winston, 177; Yergin, D. (1991) *The Prize: The Epic Quest for Oil, Money & Power*. New York: Simon and Schuster, 328–33.
9. Glouchevitch, P. (1992) *Juggernaut: The German Way of Business – Why it is Transforming Europe and the World*. New York: Simon and Schuster, 105.
10. *Ibid.*, 126.
11. *Ibid.*, 207.
12. According to Martin Gannon: 'German society is more collective than ... American, but less so than ... Asian societies.' Gannon, M.J. (1994) *Understanding Global Cultures: Metaphorical Journeys Through 17 Countries*. London: Sage Publications, 70.
13. *Ibid.*, 69.
14. *Ibid.*, 66–84.
15. Landes, D.S. (1999) *The Wealth and Poverty of Nations: Why Some Are so Rich and Some so Poor*. New York: W.W. Norton, 356–7.
16. Witzel, M. 'How Japan Leapt into the Modern Age', *Financial Times Mastering Management Review*, n.d. 22–6.
17. *Ibid.*, 23–4.
18. *Ibid.*, 25.
19. *Ibid.*, 26.
20. *Ibid.*
21. See the article by Wilkins, Mira (1991) 'Japanese Multinational Enterprise before 1914', in her *International Library of Critical Writings in Business History*, Volume I, *The Growth of Multinationals*, Aldershot, UK: Edward Elgar Publishing, 218–50.
22. *Ibid.*, 254.
23. *Ibid.*, 263–7.

24. Yergin, D. and Stanislaw, J. (1999) *The Commanding Heights: The Battle Between Government and the Marketplace that is Remaking the Modern World.* New York: Touchstone, 162–9.

25. Prestowitz, C.V., Jr. (1988) *Trading Places: How We Allowed Japan to Take the Lead.* New York: Basic Books, 26–46.

26. Sampson, A. (1995) *Company Man: The Rise and Fall of Corporate Life.* New York: Random House, 162–3.

27. See Vogel, E.F. (1979) *Japan as Number One: Lessons for America.* Cambridge MA: Harvard University Press; Wolf, M.J. (1983) *The Japanese Conspiracy: the Plot to Dominate Industry Worldwide – and How to Deal With It.* New York: Empire Books; Burstein, D. (1988) *Yen! Japan's New Financial Empire and its Threat to America.* New York: Simon and Schuster.

28. Ouchi, W.G. (1981) *Theory Z: How American Business can Meet the Japanese Challenge.* Reading, MA: Addison-Wesley; Pascale, R.T. and Athos, A.G. (1981) *The Art of Japanese Management: Applications for American Executives.* New York: Simon and Schuster. See also Locke, R.K. (1996) *The Collapse of the American Management Mystique.* Oxford: Oxford University Press; Alston, J.P. (1986) *The American Samurai: Blending American and Japanese Managerial Practices.* Berlin: Walter de Gruyer.

29. Pascale, R.T. and Athos, A.G. (1981) *The Art of Japanese Management: Applications for American Executives.* New York: Simon and Schuster, 22.

30. *Ibid.*, 27.

31. Katz, R. (1998) *Japan: The System that Soured – The Rise and Fall of the Japanese Economic Miracle.* N.p.: M.E. Sharpe, Chapter 1. <http://www.businessweek.com/chapter/katz.htm>, 29 November 1999.

32. *Ibid.*

16

The Third Global Economy

Multinationals, microchips and the Information Age: 1970–2000

T**HE** Third Global Economy emerged slowly in the post-World War II world. It achieved speed only after the collapse of communism, signified by happy Berliners dancing on the Berlin Wall in 1989. The Wall's demise symbolized many things, not least of which was its metaphoric pointer to the many barriers to international trade that had fallen in the deregulatory climate of the 1980s and 1990s. 'The globe has become far more of a single operational unit,' wrote the ageing Marxist historian Eric Hobsbawm in 1994. Looking back on the 20th century in his provocative work *The Age of Extremes: A History of the World, 1914–1991*, he argued that through the last two centuries, 'capitalism was a permanent and continuous revolutionizing force'. It was indeed. Even Marx would have been surprised.

> The Third Global Economy emerged slowly in the post-World War II world. It achieved speed only after the collapse of communism, signified by happy Berliners dancing on the Berlin Wall in 1989

The First Global Economy that began around 1500 and lasted till the Napoleonic Wars was based on agriculture, gold, silver and luxury goods. It was the Golden Age of mercantilism. Operating according to principles of naval capitalism, Portuguese, Spaniards, Dutch, French and English competed with each other for the European share of a prosperous Asian trade. The Second Global Economy replaced it around 1844. Based upon what became known as agribusiness and then manufacturing, this second world economic regime was dominated by the British. It operated according to a 'Hellenic' model of an almost free-market economy with multinational enterprises becoming increasingly important.

This economy, however, partially collapsed as a result of world war, depression and the spread of communism during the turbulent years 1914–1919. It was given a glorious Indian summer by the soaring productivity of the United States in the period from about 1947 to 1973. The Third Global Economy is one based upon information technology and capital and led by the 'legionary capitalism' of the United States, but with the potential of very real challenges from both Europe and Asia.

Pax Americana: the multinational ... at its zenith

As previously argued, by 1880 the multinational corporation had assumed its mature form: central direction from a home office, direct investment and production abroad, professional middle-management layers, and swift communication among the various branches of each enterprise. By 1914, Britain accounted for 45 per cent of all foreign investment, the US and Germany for 14 per cent each. In this trading cornucopia where national borders began to matter less and less, the pound sterling, linked to gold, was the world's true reserve currency. Britain supported some 200 multinationals, America 40.[1] After 1914 this Second Global Economy began to totter: 'The borderless world suffered its first setbacks as a consequence of the First World War and its aftermath.'[2] The stability of both the gold standard and the Sterling Bloc was undermined. Many British free-standing firms established in faraway places with strange-sounding names went out of business. Meanwhile, hundreds of US firms established foreign subsidiaries and American direct investment internationally rose from $7 billion to $17 billion.

Then came the stock market collapse on Wall Street in 1929 and the Great Depression of the 1930s. This depression was much worse than that of the business-cycle collapses of the late 19th century because Britain could no longer dominate the Second Global Economy and America was not yet ready to do so. According to Professor De Long 'during the interwar period ... no power could shape the international economic environment through its own actions alone. Britain tried ... and failed. America might have succeeded had it tried.'[3] International trade and investment imploded so much in the 1930s and 1940s that one can speak of the demise of the Second Global Economy. Britain and America abandoned the gold standard; nations engaged in devaluations and protectionist measures that stifled the flow of trade even further, and investment plummeted. Regional blocs formed in the Americas, the Commonwealth, East Asia and Central Europe. Mexico in 1938 expropriated foreign oil companies, terrifying investors everywhere.

The true epoch of the multinational came in the Pax Americana after World War II. By 1980 US firms accounted for 40 per cent of foreign direct investment, with the British down to 15 per cent and the Dutch 8 per cent. After 1975 the overseas impact of the Germans and Japanese could be noted. Together they quickly captured 15 per cent of the world's direct investment share. The decline of colonialism, political instability in the Third World and the rise of a service economy directed 80 per cent of multinational investments in 1980 to developed countries. The United States became a favourite investment haven after 1973, so that by 1980 it harboured 33 per cent of all non-American foreign direct investment. Investment now concentrated not so much in natural resources but in fast foods, hotels, electronics, aviation, aerospace, computers, software and entertainment.

By 1970 over 1200 US firms had opened branches in Europe, Canada and Latin America. Jet airliners, telexes, satellite communications, fax machines and cheap long-distance rates let executives travel overseas at will and helped them easily manage huge transoceanic enterprises. Global direct investment grew at an unprecedented rate, from $90 billion in 1960 to over $500 billion by 1980 and perhaps as much as $2.2 trillion by 1993. The investment boom was encouraged by the new role of the US dollar as the world reserve currency. Japan soon began to encroach upon American dominion, controlling 13 per cent of all foreign direct investment by 1993, by which time the United States accounted for only 26 per cent. The competition for dominance of the Third Global Economy revolved around the control of a tiny silicon disc. From such tiny acorns do mighty oak trees grow.

Postmodern abacus: the microchip and the Information Revolution

A major key to the Third Global Economy is the introduction and strategic possession of the microcomputer. Paradoxically, the origins of such a mighty industry trace back to the ancient abacus of Sumer and the Hindu invention of the zero. The zero made possible the binary system of counting numbers in base two, perfectly compatible with the on–off switches of the age of electricity. Modern calculating machines were first designed by Blaise Pascal (1623–1662) and Gottfried Wilhelm Leibnitz (1646–1716). Charles Babbage (1791–1871) envisioned a steam engine able to store digits and calculate by memory using punch-cards. An American, Herman Hollerith (1860–1929) invented a calculating machine which used Babbage's punch-card idea to calculate the 1890 census in a mere six weeks. Soon Remington Rand and IBM tapped into the nationwide market for adding machines. IBM in the 1930s became a major operation by processing the Social Security, relief and job checks streaming out of the New Deal. World War II and the Cold War inspired the first true computers. Iowa professor John Atanasoff invented a calculating machine that represented any number in binary code electronically. An 'on' switch would be a one, an 'off' a zero. A machine could represent any number as a series of open and closed switches.

Then during World War II the United States Army applied this discovery to create the Electronic Numerical Integrator and Computer (ENIAC). As big as a house, ENIAC, the world's first computer, had 18 000 vacuum tubes and 70 000 transistors, and used enough power to light a whole corner of Philadelphia. The first commercial computer, Remington Rand's UNIVAC, came in the early 1950s. After 1956, transistors replaced vacuum tubes, allowing IBM, Honeywell and others to produce for a small academic and governmental market. By the mid 1960s, printed circuits were replacing transistors and new languages like COBOL and FORTRAN allowed IBM and others to sell mainframe computers to large businesses that could use them for payroll and other functions. The mainframes of the 1960s were still suited for the corporate world of GM and IBM, being too big and cumbersome for small entrepreneurs. Then came the big breakthrough. It was but a short leap from the printed circuit to the silicon microchip, invented in 1971. This allowed all the functions of a computer to be contained on a single chip, making possible the personal computer.

By 1975–1977 entrepreneurs such as Bill Gates, Steve Jobs and Steve Wozniak had perfected the first microcomputer language, BASIC, and the first personal computers with monitors and keyboards. Microchip technology now advanced at an ever-accelerating pace, the chips of the 1970s carrying hundreds of components, those of the 1980s hundreds of thousands, and those of the 1990s millions. Floppy disk drives and application software for word processing, data management and spreadsheets were available, allowing microcomputers to become a business tool, especially for small and mid-sized business owners. The number of personal computers grew exponentially. At first, Radio Shack and Apple led the market until IBM weighed in with its first model in 1980. Thereafter the number of personal computers in the world doubled, from 2 million to 5.5 million between 1981 and 1982, and by 1991, 65 million. Desktops shrank to laptops; software applications such as Word, WordPerfect, Excel and Power Point and the invention and mass marketing of CD-ROMs, mice and icons made computers ever more popular and easier to use.

The spread of the microcomputer coincided with a global telecommunications revolution. The invention of the telegraph and the telephone had led the way to radio and television. Beginning in the 1960s, satellites could instantaneously relay television signals and telephone calls over the broadest oceans. Television broadcasts through cable lines allowed much better quality and many more networks, and faxes allowed printed messages to be sent over phone lines.

The Internet, a spin-off of the Cold War, began in 1969 when the US Department of Defense linked four university computers in California and Utah. A dozen more were added by 1971, 100 by 1977, 1000 by 1984, 50 000 by 1988 and 500 000 by 1991. Then things went wild. One million computer hackers were working the Internet by 1992, two million by 1993 and four million by 1994. Systems such as UNIX and TCP/IP let newsgroups swap information and build global networks. Full e-mail service went online at the end of 1992 and by 1995 America On-Line, Prodigy, Compuserve, Earthlink and other commercial providers had taken over from the Government. Internet hosts reached the total of 8 million in 1995, 22 million in 1996, 30 million in 1997 and 43 million in 1998.[4] A global e-culture – a billion people are expected to be hooked up to the Web by

2005 – has come into being in less than a decade. The consequences are possibly much greater than those of the Industrial Revolution. In the late 1990s the world moved, said *Newsweek*, from 'a culture centered on network television, phones with wires, information on paper and stock prices based on profit [into] a digital society of buddy lists, streaming video and 34-year-old billionaires in tennis shoes.'[5]

The implications of the Web culture for business are staggering. Millions of Americans and other people around the world now shop, invest, bank, converse, court, learn and do practically everything else on the Net. A whole new class of companies and entrepreneurs has made overnight fortunes through Internet commerce, the volume of which is estimated to be $148 billion between 2000 and 2002.[6] Flagship of the new e-firms is Amazon.com, the brainchild of financial strategist Jeff Bezos, who first conceived a company without stores in 1994. Unlike other booksellers who had scores of expensive store outlets, Amazon.com sold books directly over the Web from Seattle. By 1999 Amazon.com was worth $22 billion in comparison with Borders' Book Stores at $1 billion.

Other e-firms soon followed Amazon's lead. Ebay began holding Internet auctions. The inventory was provided by the customers themselves, as were the shipping payments. The customer base became the community, the feedback from loyal consumers becoming the basis for company trust. Jay Walker's Walker Digital patented its own business schemes and sold them to other e-entrepreneurs. Priceline allowed consumers to name their price for airline flights. Other e-firms are expected to do the same for motels, mortgages, cars and even groceries. Europeans, more protected by EC headquarters in Brussels from aggressive marketers, adapted to the Net in their own way, dialling in from their cafés over their cordless phones. Nokia, Vodafone and other European firms are the world leaders in wireless technology. The mobile phone grid in Europe is standardized and is expected to serve 13 million people by 2002. Here cultural differences are shaping the form e-commerce is taking, and the European Web providers have upstaged even America On-Line. European e-firms are making headway by being sensitive to the respective national cultures of their customers. The Swedish furniture firm IKEA, for example, operates a stylish Italian website and a traditional German one.

So just what was this acceleration in techno-scientific capability signifying for the world of globalized, turbo-charged capitalism?

Thomas Friedman's 'Electronic Herd': rewriting the economic rules

The restructuring of capitalism around information technology and the advance in globalization seemed to be synergistically feeding each other. The microcomputer and the Internet appear as fundamental to the Third Global Economy as the factory and the telegraph were to the Second. Journalist Thomas Friedman contrasts the new open global economy, whose symbolic birth he dates from the fall of the Berlin Wall in November 1989, with the more protectionist Cold War economy of the 1950s and 1960s. The Cold War's hierarchical corporations, welfare states and command economies cushioned global market forces, permitting, claims Friedman, IBM, GM, Nissan, Toyota and Volkswagen to provide lifetime job security for their armies of workers. The new information technologies and events of the 1970s and 1980s began to change the rules. Personal computers, fax machines, cable TV, satellites, cell phones and the Web had a cascade effect, placing instant global communications in the hands of creative individuals just as smart cards and teller machines personalized banking and junk bonds individualized investment. Fixed international exchange rates were replaced with a free-float of currencies. Money could move instantly and freely from country to country seemingly at the flick of a cursor. Governments were locked out of the process and few people complained. By 1989, the walls of the post-1945 order began crashing down. Marxism was first to go with the Warsaw Pact countries installing market-oriented regimes and the Soviet Union itself dissolving in 1991. Under Deng Xiaoping China embarked on its greatest market revolution since Song times. The crash of the Iron Curtain coincided with the fall of the Nikkei, the Japanese stock market, which plunged from 45 000 to around 15 000.

Europe was next, as German reunification presented consumers with tax bills and currency dislocations they would pay for throughout the decade. The shockwave finally hit the United States in the white-collar recession of 1990–1991. By 1996, even the Democratic President of the United States, Bill Clinton, and Britain's Labour Prime Minister, Tony Blair, had accepted the demise of the welfare state and the triumph of the

> The microcomputer and the Internet appear as fundamental to the Third Global Economy as the factory and the telegraph were to the Second

global free market. 'The driving idea behind globalization', says Friedman, 'is the spread of free-market capitalism to virtually every country in the world.' Its rules 'revolve around opening, deregulating and privatizing your economy'.[7] It remains for us to sketch out in some fashion what all this might mean.

One thing is already clear. The Third Global Economy puts a premium not on job security but on competitiveness. More than ever, the global market is rewarding efficient companies and destroying inefficient firms. 'Those countries that are most willing to let capitalism quickly destroy inefficient companies, so that money can be freed up and directed to more innovative ones, will thrive in the era of globalization. Those which rely on their governments to protect them from such creative destruction will fall behind in this era.'[8]

In the Third Global Economy, innovation is an asset, tradition a liability. There are no longer friends or foes, only competitors and interests, and the impersonal forces of a shifting global marketplace. The downside is obvious – jobs, communities and ways of life can be destroyed very rapidly. With the Internet, 'a symbol that we are all connected but nobody is totally in charge', the nation-state is no longer the force it once was. What Friedman calls the 'Electronic Herd' of millions of investors concentrated in the capital 'Supermarkets' of New York, London, Frankfurt, Tokyo and Hong Kong, move money around the globe instantly. Not only does money flow instantaneously, but also its control is in far more hands. Thus already low-rated 'junk bonds' have created a global market for high-risk loans. To cite one example, the nation of Mexico was rescued by 20 New York bankers in 1982. In 1994 it was at the mercy of a multitude of investors who could instantly switch their money anywhere in the world.[9] Conceivably, the Herd can topple governments that do not play by global market rules by downgrading their bonds. By wiring the world into networks, globalization has allowed companies such as Long-Term Capital Management to gain from financial bets than all the foreign reserves of China. It permits individuals such as Osama bin Laden to wage private war upon the United States. You will never understand globalization, argues Friedman, 'unless you see it as a complex interaction between ... states bumping up against states, states bumping up against Supermarkets, and Supermarkets and states bumping up against Super-empowered individuals.'[10]

Also, in the Third Global Economy corporations cannot so easily define themselves in traditional nationalist terms as before. Companies are no longer linked by territory but by modem and fax. A firm in California can outsource software production to a contractor in Hong Kong or India. Established firms, such as the Ford Motor Company, now consolidate design operations from three continents operating from a workstation in Michigan that is linked to sites in Britain, Germany, Italy, California, Japan and Australia. Traditional concerns of keeping wealth in one's country and internalising trade and production in semi-public firms are frustrated by a host of technocratic nomads in cyberspace. The hiring of fellow nationals, job security and health benefits are fast becoming an anachronism. Expediency rules more than ever in this new age of globalization.

Table 16.1 Richest ten companies in the United States by market value, 1917–1997[14]

	Year				
	1917	*1945*	*1967*	*1987*	*1997*
1	US Steel	AT&T	IBM	IBM	General Electric
2	AT&T	General Motors	AT&T	Exxon	Coca-Cola
3	Standard Oil (New Jersey)	Du Pont	Kodak	General Electric	Microsoft
4	Bethlehem Steel	Standard Oil (New Jersey)	General Motors	AT&T	Exxon
5	Armour & Co.	General Electric	Standard Oil (New Jersey)	General Motors	Intel
6	Swift & Co.	Union Carbide	Texaco	Du Pont	Merck & Co.
7	International Harvester	Humble Oil & Refining	Sears, Roebuck	Ford	Philip Morris
8	Du Pont	Sears, Roebuck	General Electric	Merck & Co.	IBM
9	Midvale Steel & Ordinance	US Steel	Polaroid	Amoco	Procter & Gamble
10	US Rubber	Texas Co.	Gulf & Western	Digital Equipment	Wal-Mart Stores

The transformation of the workforce is most clearly evident in the largest and most prestigious US companies. The 1990s were the years of 'downsizing'. Between 1990 and 1995 Sears cut 185 000 jobs, IBM 122 000, General Electric 76 000, Boeing 57 000, and General Motors 52 000.[11] Many of the job cuts were matched by job creation in newer companies: industries such as telecommunications and entertainment. Thus, while IBM bled, Intel and Microsoft added 140 000 workers.[12] The vast majority of the 7.7 million new US jobs generated in the early 1990s came from companies with fewer than 20 workers. Big firms over 5000, in contrast, eliminated 3.4 million jobs.[13] Even the large corporations reflected the changed nature of American business. At the time of World War II, the largest companies were concentrated in steel and autos; oil and electricity had taken over. By the time of the Vietnam War, IBM reflected the rise of the new technocracy, a trend that continued into the Reagan years (1981–89). By the late 1990s, however, IBM and General Motors had slipped down the list on the Fortune 500 and new giants such as Microsoft and Intel signalled the triumph of the Information Age (see Table 16.1).

A return of Dark Age economics?

The pace of turbo-charged capitalism is not slowing down. The volume of global trade, now $3.5 trillion, has increased tenfold since 1950. Tariffs have fallen worldwide from 40 per cent of average prices to 5 per cent.[15] Even Japanese companies are forced to play by the rules of the Third Global Economy where imports and exports and a positive trade balance no longer carry the weight they once did.[16]

Toyota now makes one fifth of its cars overseas, and almost all the workers in Mabuchi Motors are cheap labour outside Japan. Fair concerns about deficits, downsizing, foreign imports and the public interest are seen as violating the inexorable laws of the global market where 'old *laissez-faire* notions re-emerge with a new force'.[17] The economies of antiquity, the Middle Ages and the early modern era contended with some form of federal or state control. A traditional conservative, US President Theodore Roosevelt (1901–1909) made his reputation as a noted trust-buster. The young Winston Churchill was an early advocate of workers' pensions and some form of social compensation. National governments of the past had the jurisdiction to govern commerce. This is not so true today. With no global authority in the new economy, a *laissez-faire* ideology more individualistic than Adam Smith could possibly have dreamt of has become the new orthodoxy.

In its most extreme form, this new hard-edged ideology is being articulated by radical libertarian thinkers such as David Boaz, Charles Murray and Robert Ringer, who believe unfettered markets should manage just about everything. Government should abolish all public welfare and end all subsidies, grants, controls and protective tariffs. Free-market capitalism is seen as a *moral* as well as an economic system in which all human relationships are governed not by broader concerns of mutual obligation, honour or trust but by 'value-for-value' considerations of mutual self-interest. Society itself becomes one vast market; all human relationships are contractual, not personal.[18] In England, financial consultants Lord William Rees-Mogg and James Dale Davidson share similar views, but put them in historical perspective. The coming of the microchip is seen to be as revolutionary as the coming of the stirrup, which created feudalism, or gunpowder, which destroyed it and ensured the rise of managed enterprise, democracy and welfare states. Some critics contend that the chip is recreating Dark Age conditions in a newer form. Entrepreneurs operate in cyberspace, where trading restrictions cannot operate as effectively and welfare states have no way of being sustainable.

> If the First Global Economy parallels the ancient Phoenician experience, and the Second Global Economy the Classical Greek and Roman systems, the Third may well parallel some aspects of the Dark and Middle Ages

The worst-case scenario is already being envisioned: business accountability, company loyalty and job security will disappear; millions of unskilled people will be reduced to a subsistence level harsher than medieval serfdom.[19] What Benjamin Barber calls 'McWorld' and the global downsizing it engenders resurrect the Western world of 400–1000 CE, where prosperity, social welfare, citizenship and civility unravelled and personal gain and self-indulgence came to the fore. Managed companies, depending on strong states and high-trust cultures, do not operate well in such worlds:

> *'The invisible hand … takes on new significance in the setting of invisible cyberspace, where virtual corporations defeat real nations. [T]he space in which they operate is as invisible as the market's phantom hands … the free market ideology … is a battering ram against the walls of the nation-state.'*[20]

Traditionalist historians in the 1970s, such as John Lukacs and Leften Stavrianos, also worried about a low-trust, high-risk Dark Age condition in an up-to-date form. This was before advances in computer technology made it all too feasible. Indeed, if the First Global Economy paralleled the ancient Phoenician experience, and the Second Global Economy the Classical Greek and Roman systems, the Third may well parallel some aspects of the Dark and Middle Ages. (See Table 16.2.)

Table 16.2 **Is history repeating itself?**

Parallels	*Regional/hemispheric world economies*	*Global economies*
'Near Eastern'	Mesopotamian/Canaanite: 3500–300 BCE. Phoenician voyages of discovery and managed trade through merchant-princes	First Global Economy: 1500–1800 CE. European voyages of discovery and managed trade through joint-stock companies
'Hellenic'	Greek: 800–150 BCE. Greek colonization, independent enterprise and ironworking revolution	Second Global Economy (steam): 1800–1880. British colonization, independent enterprise and industrial revolution
'Roman'	Rome: 500 BCE–500 CE. Roman expansion, large-scale enterprise, mass production and 'legionary' capitalism	Second Global Economy (Auto): 1880–1970. American expansion, large-scale enterprise, mass production and 'legionary' capitalism
'Dark Age /Medieval'	Dark Age and Medieval business culture: 500–1500 CE. Independent traders, partnerships and dominant Asian markets	Third Global Economy: post-1970. Independent e-commerce, partnerships and strong Asian markets

Historical remembrance may help here. Grim as they were, the centuries after the fall of Rome were also centuries of surprising innovation in which old bureaucratic institutions collapsed and more effective and responsive institutions were born. The centralized Roman system – resting as it did on slave labour, high taxes and a swollen state – eventually crumbled under its own weight. That dismal collective experience eventually made way for local, private initiative. 'The analogy is relevant for our age', says Professor Stavrianos, 'for modern civilization is undergoing a disintegration–reintegration experience similar to those precipitated by the barbarian invasions and the World War II bombings.'[21] In the 500s and afterwards, Roman managers gave way to mobile peddlers, and slaves turned into serfs who could manage more of their own time and act as an embryonic entrepreneur. 'Medieval serfs engaged in more self-management than did the slaves of the Roman Empire,' argues Stavrianos. This 'participatory impulse is today a central feature of the emerging ... Age'. Stavrianos claims that 'the idea of popular participation is now worldwide in scope ... implying self-management in all phases of life ... for all segments of society.'[22]

Globalization ... with Mickey Mouse ears

In general, the world associates globalization with Americanization. The microcomputer, junk bonds and the free-market cybernaut flourish in America as nowhere else. The chief gathering-place for the Electronic Herd is Wall Street. Most adept at riding the global tiger they raised, America's freebooting computer geniuses are the heroes of the hour. They insist that everyone else get on their backs or be left behind: 'On top of it all, globalization has a distinctly American face. It wears Mickey Mouse ears, it eats Big Macs, it drinks Coke or Pepsi and it does its computing on an IBM or Apple laptop ... In most societies most people cannot distinguish anymore between American power, American exports, American cultural assaults, American cultural exports and plain vanilla globalization. They are now all wrapped into one.'[23]

Many European and Asian-based market cultures are struggling to adapt to this made-in-America Third Global Economy. The United States boasts the most 'individualistic' business culture in the world. In no other countries are corporate swashbucklers such as Lee Iacocca, Ted Turner and Bill Gates exalted so highly. In Britain, Canada and Australia rampant individualism is tempered with some forms of 'Tory democracy', paternalism and pro-labour egalitarianism. Italian individualism rests on family networks, while Germans stress order, procedure and conformity more than other Europeans. The Japanese enforce conformity by unspoken tradition and a web of age-old customs of politeness and respect, even if the company is often put before the individual. Chinese cultures with pronounced kinship ties and Confucian traditions are highly collectivist, as are the Indian ties of caste and group.[24] But in the New World Economy it is the New World calling the shots, especially after the 'Asian contagion' economic scare of the mid-1990s. Europe and Japan are forced to come to terms with the new American model of doing business, with its sudden periods of downsizing, high-pressure entrepreneurialism, penchant for short-term profits, restless shareholders and belief in the cult of competition.

Adjustments in the Third Global Economy have been painful for Japan in particular. As of early 1997 the equivalent of $2 trillion was lost on the Nikkei in what was still a $5 trillion economy. Toyota, Toshiba and other multinationals shifted production overseas, leaving thousands of domestic suppliers – employing 70 per cent of the Japanese workforce – to fend for themselves. Tokyo's pump-priming efforts failed to impress the Electronic Herd. There is a feeling that MITI can no longer manage the system. By 1995 30 million Japanese were living on fixed personal assets with slight margins of security for the basics of life. As in 1854 and 1945 many Japanese again see Americans as the aggressive outsiders, forcing them to adopt alien ways. Japanese executives recognize the need to restructure and deregulate their firms if they want to survive in the star-spangled present. Japan's top executives now sound like the Reagan Cabinet. Toshiba president Taizo Nishimuro sees 'no other choice but to globalize and market world wide'. Steel maker Hiroshi Ono knows 'there needs to be a deregulation of the economy. People can't live the same as they have before.' Shosaku Yasui of Teijin Ltd confessed: 'The Japanese system of doing business has hit a wall.' Author Noriyuki Ueda meanwhile lamented 'the collapse of our cultural and spiritual values' rooted in Japanese Confucianism and economic growth.[25]

Change in Japan is coming, albeit slowly. Prime Minister Ryutaro Hashimoto in 1996 deregulated stocks, banks, brokerages and life insurers, threatening to put one third of the country's financial players out of business. The Ministry of Finance shut down the Hanwa Bank that was sinking under $700 million in bad property loans. Foreign insurers were granted licences, the competition causing premiums to fall by 20 per cent. Japan Air Lines' charter subsidiary hired foreign crews. Easier rules on petrol imports lowered pump prices while endangering 50 000 filling stations. Sony, Minolta, Toshiba and Nippon Electric use foreign suppliers, threatening the jobs of Japanese suppliers.[26] The harshest medicine was swallowed by Nissan. After six years of losses and shrinking market share, in 1999 Japan's number-two auto manufacturer formed an alliance with Renault. Renault gave Nissan $5.4 billion in return for 37 per cent of its shares. Nissan president Yoshikazu Hanawa then cut 21 000 jobs – 14 per cent of the workforce – reduced domestic output by 30 per cent, and closed 10 per cent of dealerships. Nissan tried stalling as many lay-offs as possible through attrition and early retirement. The greatest costs fell on Nissan's 500-odd suppliers. Some, such as car seat manufacturer Taichi-S, no longer see independence from *keiretsu* ties as disloyalty. According to Teijin's Yasui: 'The system of cross-shareholding is coming to an end.'[27] While many Japanese firms downsize, growth in the new information and technology sectors is outstripping that in the old industrial sector by a ratio of three to one. Sales of personal computers, foreign brokerages and online trading are now booming in Tokyo. High-tech firms such as Rakuten, owned by Hiroshi Mikitani, 34, and the e-firms Cyber Agent and Indigo show that Japan, too, can produce brainy young entrepreneurs. The push for a more free-market system is coming from executives as well as government. From $40 billion in 1998, foreign investment in Japan has now reached $125 billion. In 1989, only 5 per cent of the shares on the Nikkei were in foreign hands; now it is up to 15 per cent, $3.7 trillion out of approximately $25.9 trillion.[28]

Germany's 'social market' economy – a free market balanced by paternalism – has also buckled in the headwinds of the Third Global Economy. Germany in the 1990s experienced the lowest job growth in the European Union. Critics blamed a number of uncompetitive practices: payroll taxes of 52 per cent, mandatory closings in evenings and on Sundays, forbidding pension funds to invest in stocks, and discouraging price competition.[29] Just as in Japan, downsizing came to the fore as new firms were starting up. Start-up biotech companies capitalising on German strength in chemistry and pharmaceuticals are clustering in markets from Aachen to Cologne and Munich. Simon Moroney, head of Munich's MorphoSys, remarks that: 'Germany is moving toward much more of an American model: dynamic, high turnover, fast growth.'[30] Germany, like Japan, is splitting into a two-tiered economy of successful and unsuccessful companies. Daimler-Benz (now DaimlerChrysler), Volkswagen, Bayer and others have begun to restructure, cutting labour costs by 10 per cent since 1997. While Deutsche

Telekom shed 11 500 jobs, other telecommunication companies were adding 40 000 to the workforce. Germans were entering the new entrepreneurial cyber-economy with a vengeance. In 1984 Jurgen Peter and Sasha Hanke launched a German branch of Dell Computer, which now has 280 employees and $90 million in annual sales. The new German economy is, nonetheless, still oriented to state intervention. Many of the 500 biotech firms in Cologne, Düsseldorf, Munich and Heidelberg profited from government funding that attracted venture capital. Music and entertainment companies such as Munich-based EMTV & Merchandising AG are also heavy-growth industries. EMTV's share value rose by 3400 per cent between 1997 and 1998.[31]

If globalization invokes medieval parallels with its weakening of traditional hierarchical structures and winnowing the effectiveness of the nation-state, it is good to note that there are redeeming features. The medieval economic systems held forth a partnership/alliance model that might be relevant to the complexities involved when considering the European, Asian and American business cultures. The reality of globalization was evident when Jurgen Schrempp, CEO of the most revered company in Germany, Daimler-Benz, negotiated a merger with Robert Eaton of Chrysler. At last there was a truly *global* auto company. Blunt and emotional, Schrempp symbolized a revolution in German management style. Taking over Daimler in May 1995 when the company was losing $3.45 billion, he applied American-style medicine to this most German of all companies. Schrempp cut head-office staff by 75 per cent, workers by 63 000 and divisions from 35 to 23. By 1996 Daimler-Benz was no longer in the red. DaimlerChrysler may represent an experiment in a new approach to global competitiveness. Daimler contributes its brand name and engineering expertise, Chrysler its expertise in utility vehicles and North American market share. Both intend to create a low-cost car they can sell in Asian markets. Mercedes and Chrysler brand names are kept

> If globalization invokes medieval parallels with its weakening of traditional hierarchical structures and winnowing the effectiveness of the nation-state, it is good to note that there are redeeming features. The medieval economic systems held forth a partnership/alliance model that might be relevant to the European, Asian and American business cultures

separate and sold in separate showrooms owned by the same dealer. Servicing, warehousing and technical training are pooled. This alliance between the upscale, procedure-driven Daimler and the middle-class, democratic mini-van culture of Chrysler will require a great deal of corporate trust between Schrempp and Eaton.[32] But perhaps it beats the alternative.

Global business alliances

The merger-alliances linking DaimlerChrysler and Nissan/Renault hint at a new business model for the Third Global Economy. So do the writings of Japanese management expert and globalization advocate Kenichi Ohmae. In the Dark Ages many, though not all, large hierarchical organizations disappeared. Business was conducted in Europe, the Muslim world and China by temporary joint ventures. The more lasting partnership alliances were between *individuals*. Something like that, suggests Ohmae, may be arising now between *companies* in the Third Global Economy. In a complex world where companies may lack the resources to go it alone, but cannot afford the fixed costs of opening overseas branch plants, genuine strategic alliances between companies based on different continents offer a solution. 'Globalization mandates alliances, makes them absolutely essential to strategy,' argues Ohmae.[33] Alliances offer a number of advantages for managers with the patience and commitment to use them. In the Third Global Economy companies need to be deployed in all the important markets at the same time, but not all of them have the time, money and luck to accomplish this, for 'Globalization will not wait as companies need alliances and need them now'.[34] When a US firm forms an alliance with a Japanese or European one and vice versa, it allows that firm access to markets on other continents without having to start from scratch and build them up one by one.

   The key to establishing such alliances, however, is that one cannot set up such a global alliance through control of one's partner any more than one 'controls' a mate in a happy marriage. In a good intercontinental alliance, mutual trust and confidence between or among the partnering firms deepen with time. Trying to control a partner corporation through buying its stock will quickly poison the relationship. The 'you work for me' attitude stifles the development of intercompany management skills, 'critical for success in today's global environment'.[35] Interestingly, the Japanese *keiretsu* system, in which each firm owns 3–5 per cent of the shares in its partners, could work quite well among intercontinental partners dividing up the markets of the US–Europe–Japan triad. Peter Bonfield of International Computers Ltd has set down other rules for the new *commenda* of the 21st century, all of which imply trust and long-term thinking (see Table 16.3).

Table 16.3 Bonfield formula for intercontinental business alliances[36]

1	Treat collaboration as a personal commitment.
2	Be willing to invest managerial time in the alliance.
3	Mutual trust and respect are essential.
4	Both partners must benefit.
5	Draw up an explicit contract, then put it away.
6	Recognize circumstances and markets change.
7	Have mutual expectations of the collaboration.
8	Get to know opposite numbers socially.
9	Appreciate that cultures are different.
10	Recognize partner's interests and independence.
11	Make sure managers have company approval for decisions.
12	Celebrate achievements together.

Increasingly it is factors of corporate culture and basic business ethics that will determine the future. Communication is a must. Alliance ventures can flourish when each company understands the goals and mission of the other, when the goals are well defined, competent managers are in charge, and informal channels of communication are regularly used. Numerous examples of alliances already existed at the beginning of the 1990s. Nissan distributed Volkswagens in Japan. Volkswagen sells four-wheel-drive Nissan cars in Europe. Mazda and Ford, and GM and Toyota collaborate and compete. Despite much of the nationalist rhetoric flying back and forth across the Atlantic, Japanese and American industries, even in the semiconductor realm, are engaging in many forms of alliance, swapping licences aggressively.

The Japanese construction firm Hitachi Kenki had too narrow a product line to set up its own distribution network. It formed an arrangement with Deere & Co. in the American market and Fiat-Allis in the European. The alliance between the American PPG and the Japanese Asahi Glass began with a joint venture in Japan in 1966, opening an automotive-glass joint venture in the United States in 1985. A second American plant with another joint venture in Indonesia was agreed upon in 1988 with the Mitsubishi Trading Company. All the while, PPG and Asahi remained fierce competitors in the sheet-glass business. The British trading firm Inchcape, with branches in Hong Kong, Singapore and China, has an arrangement with Toyota and Ricoh. Inchcape serves as the distributor for the Japanese through traditional British ties in Asian markets, with the Japanese providing the British new competitive products to market. Even IBM Japan, in the late 1980s, became a major player in the Japanese market through its *keiretsu* alliances with Ricoh, Nippon Steel, Fuji Bank, Omron and hundreds of smaller local firms. These smaller firms handled IBM's Japanese sales, service, engineering and manufacturing. With few fixed costs, IBM Japan in 1988 had $8 billion in sales.[37]

Some Japanese companies have already adapted the alliance strategy so well to the new economy that they are increasingly able to reconquer some of the ground lost by Japanese industry in the 1980s. Such is the rising Internet empire of Masayoshi Son. Long-term planning is far from dead in Japanese business. Son, 42, has a *300-year plan* to control, through his Tokyo holding company, Softbank. He hopes this will give his company the lion's share of e-commerce on the globe, and he is making progress: 'Our 300-year plan is the long-term structure we need to fit our goals; long horizons change your priorities.' Softbank already controls 23 per cent of Yahoo and about $40 billion in investments in about 130 other companies. An estimated 10 per cent of those are doing business on the Web – names such as GeoCities, People PC, Webvan and Global Sports. In effect, Son is creating the world's first Internet *keiretsu*, in which the participating firms would encompass the globe, support each other and undercut the competition. Son would not own his companies outright or even run them. He would hold a 20–30 per cent stake in each, enough to build a web of cross-investments, sales, marketing and supply in the classic Japanese pattern. By 2004, Son hopes to have 780 companies in his Softbank *keiretsu*. The corporate empire is already worth almost $80 billion, more than Sony, and is extending its alliances into Europe through France's Vivendi and Britain's News Corporation.

Son, Japan's newest corporate superstar, is in fact a Korean by heritage, educated at Berkeley. His entrepreneurial zeal may arise in part as a reaction to the discrimination he faced as a *gaijin*, growing up in Kyushu but never being fully accepted as Japanese. Founding Softbank in Tokyo in 1981, Son laboured many years until his Internet vision began to fall into place in 1993. By 1995 he was in Silicon Valley, armed with almost $1 billion from Japanese banks, desperately scouting new investment opportunities. Out of this trip came Softbank's key American player, the San José-based Softbank Technology Ventures, to which Son added Comdex, the computer industry's biggest convention, Kingston Technology, and Ziff-Davis Publishing. Softbank Technology Ventures poured investment into Silicon Valley companies, investing in 55 companies during four months in 1996 alone. Kleiner Perkins and David Weatherell's CMGI have responded by forming their own alliances, with Lycos competing with Yahoo and Kleiner Perkins' online supermarket WebGrocer doing battle with Softbank's Webvan. According to Yankee Group consultant Howard Anderson, 'These *keiretsu* are going to face off like football teams.' This implies that the Japanese have decided to play the American game ... *by Japanese rules*. The impulsive Son has already made bad investments. He was forced to sell unprofitable firms such as Ziff-Davis and Kingston, but he sees the value of taking risks. Despite the freewheeling nature of e-commerce in 1999, Son knows that eventually only the firms with the most staying power will survive. Taking a long view, he also recognizes that, while Americans excel at starting up companies, Japanese excel at preserving them.[38]

Today, Calvin Coolidge needs upgrading: 'The business of the *world* is business.' Thus, the evidence seems conclusive that the Third Global Economy is forcing non-American business cultures to adapt to the American model. Yet most competitors are trying to adapt in their own way, trying to preserve their own ways of doing business as much as possible. Germans invest in cellular phones, biotech and 'Eurofirms', Japanese in Internet *keiretsu*, while both seek to minimize the social costs of painful downsizing. A key underlying issue raised by the Third Global Economy is crucial for the new century: should the world become American? Does one size really fit all, or is the diversity of business cultures a living, unchangeable reality? To these questions we must now finally turn.

NOTES TO CHAPTER 16

1. Jones, G. (1996) *The Evolution of International Business: An Introduction*. London: Routledge, 37–9.
2. *Ibid.*, 39.
3. De Long, J.B. (February 1997) *Slouching Towards Utopia? The Economic History of the Twentieth Century, 1991–1998*. <http://econ161.berkeley.edu/ TCEH/1998_Draft/fourteen /Slouching2_14roaring.doc>, 2 November 1999.
4. *Ibid.*; 'Computers: History and Development'; Howe, W. 'A Brief History of the Internet', <www.delphi.com>, 3 July 1998, in Young, G., ed. (1998) *The Reference Shelf*, Vol. 70, No. 5, *The Internet*. New York: H.W. Wilson, 3–7; 'Microcomputer History'; 'The FHTE Web History of Telecommunications' in (1996) *Fachhochschule für Technik*. Esslingen, Germany. <http://www-stall.rz.fht-esslingen.de/telehistory>, 19 October 1999; Hobbes Zakon, R. 'Hobbes' Internet Timeline v. 4.2', 15 August 1999. <http://www.isoc.org/zakon/Internet/History/HIT.html>, 19 October 1999.
5. 'The Dawn of E-Life' in *Newsweek International*, Online Edition, 11 October 1999. < http://www.newsweek.com/nw-srv/printed/int/wb/ov0115_1.htm-2.htm>, 20 October 1999.
6. *Ibid.* According to *Newsweek*: 'It's crucial to assess the impact of this shift, because the digital revolution is much more profound than a mere change of tools. The Internet is built on both a philosophy and an infrastructure of openness and free communication; its users hold the potential to change not just how we get things done, but our thinking patterns and behavior. Bound together by digital mesh, there's hope we may thrive together – if some nagging, unanswered questions find felicitous answers. Can a spirit of sharing be maintained in the face of the need to recoup huge investments? Will persistent security holes – both personal and national, with the threat of cyberwar – erode our confidence in this new medium? Is it really possible for governments to forgo their impulses to regulate the Net with their usual heavy-handedness? How will the bounty of the digital age be distributed fairly?'
7. Friedman, T.L. (1999) *The Lexus and the Olive Tree: Understanding Globalization*. New York: Farrar, Strauss and Giroux, 8.
8. *Ibid.*, 9–10.
9. *Ibid.*, 49–51; 'Microcomputer History', 19 October 1999; Hobbes Zakon, R. 'Hobbes' Internet Timeline v. 4.2', August 15, 1999, <http://www.isoc.org/ zakon/Internet/History/HIT.html>, 19 October 1999.
10. Friedman, T.L. (1999) *The Lexus and the Olive Tree: Understanding Globalization*. New York: Farrar, Strauss and Giroux, 12–13.

11. Cox, W.M. and Alm, R. (1999) *Myths of Rich and Poor: Why We're Better Off than We Think*. New York: Basic Books, 131.
12. *Ibid.*, 114.
13. *Ibid.*, 115.
14. *Ibid.*, 122.
15. Barber, B.R. and Schulz, A., eds. (1996) *Jihad Vs McWorld: How the Planet is Both Falling Apart and Coming Together*. New York: Ballantine Books, 30.
16. *Ibid.*
17. *Ibid.*, 31.
18. For an introduction to libertarian ideas see Boaz, D. (1997) *Libertarianism: A Primer*. New York: Free Press; Boaz, D. and Crane, E.H., eds. (1993) *Market Liberalism: A Paradigm for the 21st Century*. Washington, DC: Cato Institute; von Mises, L. (1996) *Human Action: A Treatise on Economics*. Irvington-on-Hudson, NY: Foundation for Economic Education; Murray, C. (1988) *In Pursuit of Happiness and Good Government*. New York: Simon and Schuster; *idem* (1997) *What it Means to be a Libertarian: A Personal Interpretation*. New York: Broadway Books; Rand, A. (1957) *Atlas Shrugged*. New York: Random House; *idem* (1961) *For the New Intellectual: The Philosophy of Ayn Rand*. New York: Signet; *idem* (1964) *The Virtue of Selfishness: A New Concept of Egoism*. New York: New American Library; *idem* (1966) *Capitalism: The Unknown Ideal*, with additional articles by Branden, N., Greenspan, A. and Hessen, R. New York: New American Library; Ringer, R.J. (1977) *Looking Out for Number One*. New York: Funk & Wagnalls; *idem* (1979) *Restoring the American Dream*. New York: Harper & Row; *idem* (1983) *How You Can Find Happiness During the Collapse of Western Civilization*. New York: Harper & Row.
19. Davidson J.D. and Rees-Mogg, Lord W. (1997) *The Sovereign Individual: How to Survive and Thrive During the Collapse of the Welfare State*. New York: Simon and Schuster, 11–60. See also *idem* (1987) *Blood in the Streets: Investment Profits in a World Gone Mad*. New York: Summit Books and (1993) *The Great Reckoning: Protect Yourself in the Coming Depression*. New York: Simon and Schuster.
20. Barber, B.R. and Schulz, A., eds. (1996) *Jihad Vs McWorld: How the Planet is Both Falling Apart and Coming Together*. New York: Ballantine Books, 32.
21. Stavrianos, L.S. (1976) *The Promise of the Coming Dark Age*. San Francisco, CA: W.H. Freeman, 2–3.
22. *Ibid.*, 7.
23. *Ibid.*, 309.
24. Gannon, M.J. (1994) *Understanding Global Cultures: Metaphorical Journeys Through 17 Countries*. London: Sage Publications, 340–1.
25. Bremner, B. *et al.* 'Two Japans: The Gulf Between Corporate Winners and Losers is Growing' in *Business Week Online*, 27 January 1997, US Edition. <http://www.businessweek.com/search.htm>, 24 November 1999; Bremner, B. *et al.* 'A New Japan?', *ibid.*, 25 October 1999, US Edition. <http://www.businessweek.com/search.htm>, 24 November 1999.
26. *Ibid.*, 25 October 1999.

27. 'Nissan To Slash 21,000 Jobs, Close Plants' in *Reuters*, 18 October 1999; Strom, S. 'Cuts by Nissan are Deeper than Foreseen' in *The New York Times Online*, 19 October 1999.
    <http://www.nytimes.com/yr/mo/day/news/financial/nissan-cutback.html>, 19 October 1999; Bremner *et al.*, *ibid.*, 25 October 1999.
28. Bremner *et al.*, *ibid.*, 25 October 1999.
29. Ewing, J. 'Wanted: A Turnaround Artist for Germany' in *Business Week Online*, International Edition, 21 June 1999.
    <http://www.businessweek.com/search.htm>, 24 November 1999.
30. Peterson, T. and Miller, K.L. 'Germany enters the New Economy' in *Business Week Online*, International Edition, 15 February 1999.
    <http://www.businessweek.com/search.htm>, 24 November 1999.
31. *Ibid.*
32. Miller, K.L. and Muller, J. 'Jurgen Schrempp: The Auto Baron', *ibid.*, 16 November 1998. <http://www.businessweek.com/search.htm>, 24 November 1999.
33. Ohmae, K. (1990) *The Borderless World: Power and Strategy in the Interlinked Economy*. New York: HarperBusiness, 114.
34. *Ibid.*, 117.
35. *Ibid.*, 120.
36. *Ibid.*, 121.
37. *Ibid.*, 125–31.
38. Gibney, F. Jr 'Emperor of the Internet' in *Time Magazine*, Time.com, 6 December 1999.
    <http://www.pathfinder.com/time/magazine/articles/0,3266,35062,00.html>, <http://www.pathfinder.com/time/ interstitials/inter.html>, 1 December 1999.

17

Should the world become American?

THE rapid consolidation and growth of the global economy at the onset of the 21st century pose the question of questions for the world's business managers, politicians and even citizens: *If the American model is so successful, must and should we all become Americans?*

Few asked this question even in the 1980s, when Americans were buying books like William Ouchi's *Theory Z: How American Business Can Meet the Japanese Challenge* and *The Art of Japanese Management: Applications for American Executives* by Richard Pascale and Anthony Athos.[1] In the Carter and early Reagan years Americans, mired in recession and seeing their steel mills closing down, thousands homeless and Toyota and Nissan pushing Chrysler to the point of bankruptcy, looked to emulate the apparent success of a Japanese model that seemed to bring rapid economic growth, high-quality production, job security, high wages and productivity, workplace harmony and very low unemployment. Then, in 1989, Japan's economy burst and the stocks on the Nikkei declined to one third of their value. A decade later, with Asia sliding into severe economic problems, Europe still wrestling with high unemployment in many regions, and the United States not only enjoying the lowest unemployment (4.2 per cent) since the 1960s but almost single-handedly holding the rest of the world back from a global depression, the free-market Anglo-American model is back in favour. Even Japanese firms like Nissan now embrace corporate downsizing, while governments of the European Left trim social benefits.

The first decade of the Third Global Economy has accelerated a major shift in economic thinking in which defenders of the free market now feel vindicated against their critics. These include libertarians like P.J. O'Rourke, neo-conservatives like Lord William Rees-Mogg, Democrats like

US President Bill Clinton, and journalists like Thomas L. Friedman and the editors of *The Economist* and the *Wall Street Journal*. The present triumph of Anglo-American shareholder capitalism has caused a great deal of soul-searching among foreign – particularly European and Japanese – executives, economists, statesmen and intellectuals. Many, particularly in countries like France, Sweden and Finland, have serious misgivings about the Anglo-American model. Examining their misgivings an American observer would quickly conclude that perhaps these Europeans were merely jealous of American success and trapped by their own unwillingness to embrace the *laissez-faire* economics that would guarantee their prosperity. Europeans (and Japanese) nevertheless remain troubled, for there is a price and a downside to globalization, American-style, that many of them are reluctant to pay.

America is deploying its traditional economic strengths of agility and openness to reassert its century-old global economic supremacy

Financial Times, *20 December 1999*

It is safe to say that we are witnessing this decade, in the United States, history's most compelling demonstration of the productive capacity of free peoples operating in free markets.

Alan Greenspan, chairman of the Federal Reserve

We think this clash of business cultures can be best captured with the story of an imaginary Finnish telecommunications executive whom we'll call Timo Tormanen. Tormanen arrives in a growing American city in the Sunbelt for a business meeting and negotiation. Many American and other firms have located in this state because its climate is pleasant, wages and taxes are low, its Republican governor is very pro-free-market and anti-welfare, and right-to-work laws long ago discouraged the formation of unions.

Tormanen, arriving at the airport, notices the presence of several panhandlers (beggars) who accost him as he takes a taxi to his motel, which cannot be reached by the city's sparse public transportation. At his motel, he is warned never to leave his baggage unattended. Even though the economy is booming, for those who are skilled or have cars to take them to where the jobs are, there is no welfare for the able-bodied. As he relaxes for a few moments in his hotel, Tormanen watches the stock market report on the local business channel. It has been a good day on both Wall Street and

Helsinki. The American components company, Galt Computers, with whom he has come to bargain, has posted reasonable earnings for the second quarter. Tormanen catches an interview with the firm's new CEO, Russell Howard. Even though the company is securely in the black, the CEO, whom the media have nicknamed 'Russ the Reaper' is announcing the lay-off of another 1500 employees, including half of the middle management. When asked if there was any need to do this, Howard, a flamboyant self-educated entrepreneur replies that his duty is, first of all, to save the jobs of the firm's remaining 27 000 workers and, second, to increase the firm's dividends to its shareholders by as much as possible, as quickly as possible.

Tormanen hears similar words in person from Howard in his office a few hours later. His Helsinki-based Konia Telecommunications, a rising Finnish multinational with 40 000 employees and branches in 35 countries had chosen to deal with the US firm because its labour costs are lower and its components cheaper than those of the high-quality Swedish firm that Tormanen wanted to purchase from, but, after heated discussions, he was overruled. Tormanen finds Howard, the American boss, quite personable and friendly, but becomes uncomfortable when, in the midst of dinner, Howard leads the discussion to the merits of American versus European management. Howard, an aggressive risk-taker and a self-professed free marketeer, waxes eloquent on the superiority of American business and the 'hard knocks' school of management:

'Listen, Mr Tormanen. You criticise my labour practices but it's people like me who don't pay people more than they deserve who have put America on top and are going to keep it there. While you guys were patting yourselves on the back for all the featherbedding, giveaways, lavish benefits and other nonsense you saddle your companies with, so they wouldn't hire anybody in a million years, people like me were churning out jobs by the thousands. We created more jobs in America last year than Finland has people. We don't give people help; we give them jobs, if they want to take them, but of course you Finns, Swedes, French and Germans have coddled people so much, including your managers, that they wouldn't know hard work or an opportunity if it hit them in the head. Even the Brits are too soft!'

Silent in the Finnish manner, Tormanen listens intently as Howard continues to expound his philosophy, offering his quick solution to Finland's and Europe's chronic joblessness. For Russ Howard, the world economy is really very simple: inside every European and Asian businessman is a *wannabe* American hustler. Loosened up after a couple of beers, Howard becomes quite blunt with Tormanen. If firms were run like Galt Computers and Europe and Japan like his home state, lean and mean, joblessness would disappear:

'If I was running your company, I'd sack half the people tomorrow, then sack another third and rehire them ... without your fat company benefits and at half the salaries. If they didn't produce they'd be out the door. If we brought good Yankee know-how to Finland we'd halve your jobless rate in three years, particularly if we got rid of welfare and your expensive socialized medicine. Why, we'd slash taxes and government to the bone. Just think – if people paid their own way instead of expecting a free ride. Mr Tormanen, I've got the most cost-effective job-creation plan your country would ever see. I'd just end all handouts for the able-bodied, period. If they were hungry enough, they'd have a job in a week and be pulling their weight. Why, it happens in our country every day. Asian and Latin American immigrants come here with nothing and in a few years become millionaires while people whose families came on the *Mayflower* are whining because they think everybody owes them a living and they won't take a job at the local burger joint because they think it's beneath them. The boss simply won't pay them more than their worth ...'

'Enough!' Tormanen finally interrupts. Normally a very controlled person given to long periods of silence in business dealings, he is visibly irritated with the monologue of his host. In his ten years with Konia, he has dealt with managers from many countries, and it has been a learning process for him. He made many mistakes. Mustering all his patiently acquired negotiating skills, Tormanen looks Howard straight in the eye and voices his own opinions, trying to control his emotions as he describes his business philosophy, quintessentially Nordic and European:

'Mr Howard, I recognise that your company and your country are doing very well. I certainly don't doubt that we now live in a global economy and no one has adapted better to the rules than America. Nonetheless, if you think that Finland, Europe or Japan are going to follow American rules fully, you are mistaken. I have been all over the world and have negotiated with executives from many different countries, including your own. If there is one constant I have seen, it is that no two countries do business in the same way. Mr Howard, when I went to Harvard, I studied history as well as marketing and management. I would really recommend anyone dealing in international business to do so. The one thing you learn is that business culture is inseparable from all other forms of culture.'

'Can't you see it, then? It's obvious,' says Howard. 'When you don't conform to the rational laws of the market, you pay a price in taxes, inflation, unemployment and loss of investment. Look at that computer over there, our latest model. You don't see me working on a 20-year-old PC or Mac. The world's moved beyond that. If you don't upgrade, you die. If you Europeans and the Japanese don't upgrade the operating systems of your society, you too will become one of our theme parks.'

Tormanen takes his time in replying: 'Mr Howard, I don't want to waste your time with a history lesson, but please give me a few minutes. Do you see your collection of plants over there next to your computer? Your view is that all management systems are like that computer: they all work the same way, and if it becomes obsolete you junk the computer and buy a new one. Business cultures, though, are not like machines, but more like those plants. You can prune them, graft in new branches, rearrange them and change their environment, but if you try to rip them apart, they will die.'

The Finn then launches into a discussion of the proper role of the market in society while the American listens with a blank expression on his face: 'You seem to be saying, Mr Howard, that the market should be the central institution in society and everything else conform to it. For you, as for Mrs Thatcher, there is no such thing as a society or even a culture, but only individuals and, hopefully, families. The lesson of history, though, is that while markets have always been there, they have always operated in the context of geography, religion, language, folkways, families, armies and governments, never in a vacuum. This "rational" *laissez-faire* system you praise has never existed, not even in Hong Kong.

'If history gives us any lessons, it is how cultures have changed over the centuries, and yet somehow each developed its own rules. Government, whether you want to admit it or not, has always been involved. In the Sumerian era before 3000 BC, commerce began with temple merchants. Then, as in Taiwan today, it became more privatized in the hands of merchant-princes who exercized public functions. By the time of Babylon and Assyria, these merchant-princes were operating multinationals. They used the market, but the supervision of their temple priests and royal and family connections kept them honest. If people like yourself had waited for the unregulated market, there would have been no Phoenicia, Assyria, Babylonia or Persia. Tyre and Carthage survived and Solomon built up Israel because the public and private sectors worked together; they always did.'

'What about the Greeks and Romans?' asks Howard. Tormanen admits that, yes, they were more free-market, but not from the beginning. Furthermore, they were mostly agrarian to begin with, and evolved the concept of citizenship. The Greek city-state regulated most commerce, as eventually did Rome. The freer markets and independents grew up in the Aegean partly as a result of newer iron technology that empowered entrepreneurs, as the microchip does today. 'In spite of this,' the Finn insists, 'the older, more hierarchical business cultures survived for centuries, in Tyre, Carthage and the rest of the ancient East. Hellenic culture regulated the market through the city-state, which promised the rights of all and the general persistence of farming values. On the maxim of "nothing too much", traders were encouraged not to let their desire for profit override their civic duties as citizens or, more likely, immigrants. Even at its height, entrepreneurial Athens taxed its traders and provided a welfare safety net and ample job opportunities through its navy.

'Greek and Roman capitalism worked because it was found in a society in which the family, the clan and the civic duties of patriotism set the rules. When large firms rose up in Rome, they were able to do so because their knightly managers had roads, ports and huge markets created by the wars of the Republic. Asian models of capitalism were far more collectivist than anything in Greece or Rome. Merchants in India were regulated by the rules of caste, and in China a long tradition of state enterprise and self-sacrifice inspired by Confucius endures to this day. Even the most entrepreneurial Chinese are bound by the rules of the extended family. As for the Japanese, they have adapted Confucian principles to their own traditions of Samurai feudalism, creating a corporate family.'

Tormanen then talks about the Muslim culture of the Middle Ages – far more friendly to the entrepreneur than most of the cultures of antiquity. 'In some ways,' he said, 'free enterprise flourished far more in the Middle Ages than it had in antiquity. It worked, however, because people could trust family members or fellow Muslim, Christian or Jewish believers. Caliphs, in the meantime, promoted state as well as private enterprise in industries such as papermaking. Even in Europe during the Dark Ages, Frankish, Anglo-Saxon and Viking kings promoted trade and money whenever they could by setting up trading towns. Kings granted lords and towns the privilege to set up fairs. Lords and monks invested in waterwheels, woodmills and land clearance. From medieval partnerships and business alliances would grow the large Italian firms that foreshadowed the first modern business organizations. Again, ventures were encouraged by the city-states of Genoa, Venice and Florence, and by the Hansa towns of Germany, whose merchants pooled their resources and created branch offices all over Europe.'

Whether out of curiosity or simple desire to close a lucrative deal with a Finnish firm breaking ground in portable computer-phones, the American continues to listen to the Nordic's monologue, which is becoming more like a long-winded history lecture than a corporate bargain. 'By early modern times the nations of Europe began to enter world trade through the use of state and joint-stock companies like the Dutch and English East India Companies, which, like the firms of the late medieval Italian city-states, unconsciously took after the Tyrian model of signposted enterprise. By using this model to exploit the New World and enter the trade of the Old, Europeans used mixed enterprise to create the First Global Economy,' continues Tormanen. When he gets to the Industrial Revolution, the Finn relates how Adam Smith's theory was partly inspired by Newtonian physics and how the free-market system was itself created by parliamentary legislation. Total *laissez-faire*, though, never got off the ground in Britain as concern over urban sanitation, social unrest and strong religious traditions produced factory legislation and a social safety net in the Athenian tradition. Free trade, the Finn says, was good for Britain, giving it a dominant position in the Second, or Industrial, Global Economy, but the resulting collapse of British agriculture threatened Britain with starvation in the U-boat blockade of 1917. Tormanen really gets Howard's attention when he turns to the United States, the supposed paragon of unrestricted freewheeling entrepreneurship:

'Mr Howard, if you'd studied your own history more, you'd see that there is much more to the American tradition of business than meets the eye. If your Presidents, Congress and entrepreneurs had practiced the kind of *laissez-faire* that you want to push at Finland, you would have had no arms industry, no mass production, no railways. The state we're meeting in would still be a territory, possibly of Mexico or of the Confederate States of America. You would not have any interstate highways, satellites, microcomputers, software or Internet, and we would probably be negotiating this deal under a portrait of Queen Elizabeth, Jefferson Davis, Kaiser Wilhelm or, I shudder to think, Adolf Hitler. Entrepreneurs like yourself became rich because your Uncle Sam provided you with good roads and infrastructure, and good markets. Eli Whitney got rich making army muskets; Carnegie and Rockefeller by supplying the Union armies and the Great White Fleet; Ford and GM by saving Europe; Tom Watson and Ross Perot by supplying the government with systems to keep track of the welfare programmes you despise so much. What would you do without the interstates and the Internet, both hatched in Washington? How could your dad afford to live in the suburbs without the GI Bill and a government-guaranteed mortgage? Your own business history is so like the Romans' ... pure military Keynesianism. I don't even need to mention what Ronald Reagan's defence build-up did for your company.'

Finally, the Finn concludes: 'You expect Europe and Japan to abandon ways of doing business that are as much a part of their societies as their landscapes, religions and languages, all of which shaped their business culture. We may have to adapt, yes, while you're calling the shots in the global marketplace. We might not be able to guarantee lifetime employment or cradle-to-the-grave social insurance as we did in the past, but we won't run our companies or countries like casinos or sweatshops, either. I may have to pay more taxes to Helsinki and maybe Brussels than you do to Washington, but at least my taxes are visible. Yours are not. You don't want to pay for government healthcare, pollution control, unemployment insurance, welfare, mass transit, public education, universities and so on. Instead, you are paying for things like more jails, private detectives, security systems, run-down highways, various cancers, traffic gridlock and lawyers. I know I can trust my employees. We give them a stake in our company and consider them a valuable asset of intellectual capital. I don't have to worry about them pilfering from me like your firm does. Because we have a vested interest in our employees and our customers, instead of just our share-holders, we can think long-term. We're way ahead of you people in the mobile phone market and we'll exploit this niche to the full. Another thing: the marketplace is not as global as you think it is. Most of your business you do with Mexico and Canada. Fully 80 per cent of ours is with Europe and Russia. The Japanese I know are now investing 90 per cent in Asia. Scratch the global economy and you will find huge regional blocs – NAFTA, the EU, Asia – within which we can manoeuvre and be ourselves. Keep in mind, too, you're doing so well in America in part because your car makers learned from the Japanese without becoming Japanese. For us it is the same. We will learn from you how to compete globally, but we will do it our own way and, eventually, we will both benefit.'

In the end, the deal was never really in jeopardy. Howard and Tormanen sign the contract, with the American firm in his shareholder-model convictions despite the history lesson, and the Finn equally firm in his own belief in the 'stakeholder' model as best for Finland. Both sides have nevertheless gained a grudging admiration for the other's vantage point.

The fictional discussion above summarises the history of nearly 4000 years of world business traced in this book. We have found in history a great variety in the forms of economy or capitalism. What we feel stands out are three central factors that are critical to the form of economy that will work best for a given nation: culture, social institutions and national history.

> What we feel stands out are three central factors that are critical to the form of economy that will work best for a given nation: culture, social institutions and national history

From our reading of over 4000 years of economics and international business history it is obvious that the business cultures of today are very rooted in the ancient, medieval and recent past. They are also very different from one another. The question posed at the start of this chapter thus leads to another of today's critical issues: globalization is riding on another free-market revolution that is sweeping all before it, demolishing all centralized structures and pressuring everyone to play by American rules of entrepreneurialism, free trade and minimal government. To what degree can Europeans, Canadians, Australians, New Zealanders, Russians, Japanese, Indians, Chinese, Koreans, Latin Americans, Turks, Arabs and Africans adapt to this revolution and yet remain themselves? Many think they cannot. Many others are prepared to say that they can, although it will not be easy.

Conventional wisdom at the end of the 1990s says universal adoption of the free-market 'shareholder' American model is the inevitable wave of the future. Chris Patten, former British Governor of Hong Kong and now European Union Commissioner for External Relations, insists: 'The Asian crash and subsequent recovery have reasserted the validity of classical liberal ideas everywhere,' and believes that the most influential thinkers of the 21st century will not be 'the gurus of the left' who 'will lie forgotten as the millennium turns', but economic individualists like Friedrich Hayek.[2] Martin Sorrell, CEO of the advertising giant WPP, was even more blunt, in 1999: 'There is not a global way of marketing, rather there is an American way,' as 'America's business methods have become the world's.' One of us submitted an editorial to the *Wall Street Journal Europe* and, in discussing it with an editor, was informed that American values are universal values and when Europeans come to their senses they will adopt the same values!

The reality of different business cultures deeply grounded in history still remains a truism. The United States free-market model grew out of American history and generally works, although not for everyone, in the American context due to political, economic and social institutions that are quintessentially American, namely a dynamic entrepreneurial capitalism, often harsh, balanced by strong traditions of citizenship, government regulation, and a charitable voluntarism that has strong religious roots. Harsh inequalities and relentless individualism are traded for a high degree of freedom and mobility. Short-term thinking and the importance of immediate shareholder returns march hand-in-hand with the willingness to take risks. This model, hopefully mitigated by some form of safety net, may, perhaps, be the only rational one for Americans, but it remains our view that any effort to persuade the rest of the world to adopt it in its entirety, in spite of its seeming efficiency, is bound not only to fail but also to generate a very unpleasant backlash. A leading British thinker, Will Hutton, makes that point eloquently: 'All capitalisms have a different way of reconciling private property, profit and markets to the different concerns and value systems of the wider civil society. The United States represents a particular solution to these dilemmas. But it is this model that is being thrust down the throat of the rest of the world, with huge risks that no part of the American debate seems to recognise.'[3]

What Americans see as a global economy superseding the nation-state is seen by many Europeans, Asians and others as one nation's approach and system being imposed on them. Leading academic thinkers are now discussing the debate about the impact of globalization in new ways. Undoubtedly the biggest change in thinking is the recognition that the biggest economic activity is taking place in regions. For example, Alan Rugman of Oxford, in a recent book, points out that the vast bulk of trade takes place within the trading zones of the EU, NAFTA or ASEAN, and the vast bulk of foreign direct investment (FDI) takes place between these three dominant economic regions.[4] This important trend suggests to us that we will continue to see different approaches to organising the economies in various regions of the world economy. The NAFTA area will probably continue to be the most homogeneous, as it is dominated by the US economy with the second economy in the region, Canada, not far from the US model. In the ASEAN region we see greater diversity of models, from Hong Kong's very *laissez-faire* approach to China's evolution from communism to a more market-driven capitalism. The fact of two radically different models in one country reinforces our view that culture, social institutions and history are the defining factors of how a national system will evolve. Will mainland China ever be a giant Hong Kong? On the other hand, will Hong Kong ever fully adopt the mainland model? Our view is that the former will simply never occur, only if Beijing formally decrees it, though this would kill the golden goose that Hong Kong has become for Beijing and the Party appears fully to understand. Though they share thousands of years of Chinese culture, over the last few hundred years Hong Kong has developed a culture of virtual *laissez-faire* capitalism, a matching set of social institutions and history of its own, which tell us that Hong Kong is a different creature from its northern cousins.

In the EU we find the greatest difference between the UK and the continent. The hottest issue in UK politics is whether the UK should adopt the euro. The Tory party, at the time this book was written, was firmly on the side of staying out. At the heart of the debate is the question of the UK's adopting more continental economic approaches. Even within continental Europe there is considerable debate about the best approach. An excellent example of the differences between nations on the continent is found in Djelic's 1999 book *Exporting the American Model* (OUP), which carefully studied the impact of the Marshall Plan on three European economies: France, Germany and Italy. This extremely generous plan, a gift from the US to Europe, brought great economic assistance to Europe after the massive destruction of World War II. What the author found was that each country made very considerable adaptations of the American system.

Are we arguing that the Japanese, Germans, Swedes and others don't have to change? Not at all! We believe that the formerly more socialistic countries should continue on their course of reforming, of making work pay more than welfare for healthy adults, of putting their banking systems in order, paying off long-standing government debt, reducing tax burdens that severely penalise innovation, and the other aspects of freeing up an economy for the 21st century. However, what we do argue is that Anglo-American capitalism in all its full-blown glory is only one model of capitalism, one that is firmly and irrevocably rooted in the Anglo-American cultures. If, as some suggest, we were to take that system and impose it on other countries, it would fail miserably. Why? Because it goes against most other societies' views of the world and how to live. A widely held view in America is that anyone can succeed and, if they don't, it is solely their fault. This view simply is not accepted in a society like Finland or Japan, where an individual is seen as part of a group. In those cultures, if a person becomes an alcoholic it is seen as a group failure as well as individual. It goes against social institutions, the way management and workers relate and the relationship between universities and business. I remember well arriving in Gothenburg in Sweden and being driven to the corporate headquarters by a senior manager. He looked troubled and explained that his company was in the midst of corporate downsizing. What I found intriguing was that before the people were cut they had to discuss the list with the union; not something one would usually do in the UK or the US. But then again, in Sweden the social network is different. Finally, history has a trajectory in any nation, which tends to go in certain directions and not others.

The Japanese, in the midst of their equally painful restructuring, remain determined to do it Japanese-style and remain, above all, Japanese even as they launch their own entrepreneurial and high-tech alliances. Downsizing proceeds, with an estimated 4.5 million 'overemployed' workers on firm payrolls and some three million unemployed. Some companies, like Yokogawa Electric, are determined the lifetime system can survive and adapt by introducing a merit system of promotion in which workers will compete against one another to improve quality. Unlike many North American CEOs who believe that job security turns a good employee into a mediocre one, Yokogawa officials argue that in Japan it makes them more responsible. Toyota chairman Hiroshi Okuda, who also heads the Nikkeiren, or Japan Federation of Employers' Associations, is also trying to defend the lifetime employment system, deeming it 'suitable for Japanese who highly value stability and teamwork,' and expressing doubts about whether the downsizing being attempted at Nissan would work in Japan.

It is important to remember that the tradition of job security in Japan dates back over two centuries to when children began work as apprentices and were given an allowance when they retired. Still, 55 per cent of companies plan to maintain the lifetime employment system, seeing in it a source of mental stability and strong loyalty. Firms approach American consultants to obtain advice on how to implement early retirement plans in place of lay-offs. According to Kazuhiro Arai, Professor of Economics at Hitotsubashi University, American-style hire-and-fire management is not an option for most Japanese firms, for it runs deeply against the grain of Japanese culture: 'The traditional value for Japanese is the spirit of *wa* [harmony]', and the 'lifetime employment system pulls out a co-operative attitude and loyalty among Japanese employees who originally have Japanese values'. Arai's view is shared by Hosei University's Professor Masaru Kaneko, who recognises that many workers have been trained to work only for their companies. They specialise in Toyota or Nissan, not in wheel or transmission assembly, so it is harder for them to take their skills with them to another firm or start their own as do some in America or even Europe. Too much American-style job-cutting would be a social disaster in Japan and more training for adaptability should be encouraged: 'Merely pushing drastic downsizing of labor forces would lead to the ruin of the nation because a sufficient safety net has not been arranged in Japan.'[5]

In this book we have looked at the history of some of the leading business cultures from the beginnings of civilization. What we have discovered is that the basic models of doing business over the last 5000 years were and are quite diverse, some being very much organized from the top down, others being very entrepreneurial. We found as well that there was no one 'right' organizational form, but that business management reflected, and reflects, the culture it came out of. Down through the centuries, similar cultural patterns produced broadly similar responses in management. The Mesopotamians solved their trading problems with a system of merchant-princes, and so have medieval and modern Germans. Phoenicians and Carthaginians ran their mercantilist trading system as an extension of naval warfare, and so, to some varying degree, did medieval Italians, 16th-century Spaniards, 17th-century Dutch and 20th-century Japanese. The Greek entrepreneurial model was adopted by the British and the legionary entrepreneurialism of Rome recurs in the mass-production, military-industrial economy of America. The tributary and family models of Chinese capitalism are ageless, and understanding the medieval Arab and European partnership may hold the key to the trust-based business alliances of the postindustrial age.

Another theme we developed was the slow journey of cities, nations and peoples towards a global economy. The first economies of the Bronze Age were regional, developing in Mesopotamia, Egypt, India and China. By 1000 BCE, a regional economy stretched from the Aegean to the Indus, and the spread of ironworking encouraged its extension into Europe, Africa and Central Asia. By Hellenistic times, the world economy spread from the Atlantic to the Indian Ocean, and China entered this sphere in the time of the Roman Republic and Empire. In the Dark Ages, the Muslim caliphate became the heart of a hemispheric Old World economy, which Europe itself began to rejoin after the year 1000. This Asian-dominated economy flourished between 1250 and 1350, contracted briefly during the time of the Black Death, but then became the First Global Economy with the opening of the Americas to European conquest and settlement. From 1850 on, Europe itself, led by Britain, formed the Second Global Economy of the Industrial Revolution, an economy eventually taken over by American leadership in mass production and the internal-combustion engine. Since this collapsed during the 1930s, a new and Third Global Economy, dominated by multinational enterprises, capital and information, has arisen and consolidated itself in the late 20th century, which has some parallels with medieval times.

What we have seen and, in our opinion, will continue to see, is that companies and nations will respond to new challenges in their own ways, conditioned by their own histories and values. Markets, even in places such as Hong Kong or today's New Zealand, do not work in a vacuum. While all nations will have to come to terms with the more 'entrepreneurial' environment imposed by globalization, it will also be recognized that markets alone do not provide economic and social stability, but must operate in societies where social, religious and familial ties dictate codes of honesty, trust and co-operation,

> Companies and nations will respond to new challenges in their own ways, conditioned by their own histories and values

as well as competition, without which markets could not function. The German social market and the Japanese *keiretsu* may become more like the American model in terms of deregulation and competition, but the German symphony will likely still play a recognizable score and the Japanese garden will remain a harmonious whole as much as Americans will continue to huddle on their 'level playing field'.

NOTES TO CHAPTER 17

1. Ouchi, W.Z. (1981) *Theory Z: How American Business Can Meet the Japanese Challenge*. Reading, MA: Addison-Wesley; Pascale, R.T. and Athos, A.G. (1981) *The Art of Japanese Management: Applications for American Executives*. New York: Simon and Schuster; Locke, R.K. (1996) *The Collapse of the American Management Mystique*. Oxford: Oxford University Press; and Alston, J.P. (1986) *The American Samurai: Blending American and Japanese Managerial Practices*. Berlin: Walter de Gruyer.

2. Patten, C. 'Philosophers for the Future' in (1999) *The Economist: The World in 2000*. London: The Economist Newspaper Limited, 38.

3. Hutton, W. 'America's Global Hand' in *The American Prospect*, 6 December 1999. <http://www.prospect.org/archives/V11-2/hutton.html>, 3 December 1999.

4. See Rugman, A. (2000) *The End of Globalization*. New York: Random House; Cantwell, J.A. and Iammarino, S. 'MNCs, Technological Innovation and Regional Systems in the EU: Some Evidence in the Italian Case', *International Journal of the Economics of Business*, Vol. 5, No. 3 (1998), 383–407. The 1999 Academy of International Business Conference and the 1999 European International Business Academy Conference, the two major international business academic conferences, both featured a number of sessions that explored the importance of region over the entire globe.

5. Hisada, K. *et al.* 'Japan Sticks to Lifetime Job System' in *Asahi Evening News*, 2 December 1999, Online Edition. <http://www.asahi.com/english/enews/enews.html#enews_26298>, 3 December 1999.

Suggestions for further reading

Chapter 1: Introduction: *la Longue Durée*

The twin topics of globalization and the emerging knowledge-based economy both have extensive literatures that have developed around them over the last 20 years. To understand globalization better, two key books are important to consider: first, Yip, G.S. (1995) *Total Global Strategy: Managing for Worldwide Competitive Advantage*, Englewood Cliffs, NJ: Prentice Hall, gives an excellent overview of the key forces that have driven globalization; second, another seminal book is Bartlett, C. and Goshal, S. (1989) *Managing across Borders: The Transnational Solution*, Boston, Mass.: Harvard Business School Press, which presents some of their extensive research into the key advantages for a firm that adopts a global strategy. Articles by the same two authors in the *Harvard Business Review* and the *Sloan Management Review* are also useful on the topic.

Key contributions concerning the role of knowledge in firms would include those by Nonaka, I. and Takeuchi, H. (1995) *The Knowledge Creating Company*, Oxford: Oxford University Press; Hedlund, G. 'A Model of Knowledge Management and the N-Form Corporation', *Strategic Management Journal*, Vol. 15, 1995; Quinn, J. *et al.* 'Managing Professional Intellect: Making the Most of the Best', *Harvard Business Review*, March–April 1996; and Moore, K. and Birkinshaw, J. 'Managing Knowledge in Global Service Firms: Centres of Excellence' in *Academy of Management Executive*, November 1998.

Chapter 2: International business and the Eclectic Paradigm

For the non-international business scholar, that is many readers of this book, there is probably no better starting place than Chapter 4 of Dunning, J. (1993) *Multinational Enterprises and the Global Economy*, Wokingham, UK: Addison-Wesley. Those interested in further reading are recommended to consider the work on location or country-specific advantages by Porter, M. (1990) *The Competitive Advantage of Nations*. New York: The Free Press. For internalization advantages *see* Buckley, P. (1987) *The Theory of the Multinational Enterprise*. University of Uppsala; and Casson, M. (1987) *The Firm and the Market*. Oxford: Basil Blackwell; and on ownership or firm-specific advantages, see Dunning, J. (1988) *Explaining International Production*. London: Unwin Hyman.

Chapter 3: Cradles of civilization … and capitalism. The international economy of the Bronze Age: 3500–1600 BCE

Saggs, H.W.F. (1984) *The Might that was Assyria*, London: Sidgwick and Jackson, is still the most thorough account of Assyria available and a good source for the rediscovery of Nineveh. The author attempts to present the Assyrians in a more sympathetic light than most historians, arguing that the Assyrians were no worse, and perhaps a good deal better, than other Near Eastern peoples. Budge, E.A. (1925) *The Rise and Progress of Assyriology*, London: M. Hopkinson, is very old but still useful in reconstructing much of the story of how we know what we know about ancient Mesopotamia, as is Wiseman, D.J.'s published 1962 Oxford lecture *The Expansion of Assyrian Studies*, London University: School of Oriental and African

Studies. On the Kanesh finds see Özgüç, T. 'Early Anatolian Archaeology in the Light of Recent Research', (1963) *Anatolia*, VII, 1–21; 'The Art and Architecture of Ancient Kanesh', (1964) *Anatolia*, VIII, 27–48; the unpublished 1980 Ph.D. philosophy dissertation from Columbia University of Gunter, A.C. 'The Old Assyrian Colony Period Settlement at Bogazkoy-Hattusa in Central Turkey: A Chronological Reassessment of the Archaeological Remains' and Volume 1 of Kuhrt, A. (1994) *The Ancient Near East, c. 3000–330 BC*. London: Routledge.

Chapter 4: Cradle of multinational enterprise. Assyria and Babylonia: 2000–1000 BCE

Kuhrt's (see Chapter 3) is the best and most recent survey of Mesopotamian history available, and makes a fair mention of commerce. The most interesting general interpretation, linking legend, literature and archaeology is Hallo, W.J. and Simpson, W.K. (1971) *The Ancient Near East: A History*. New York: Harcourt, Brace and Jovanovich. A provocative revision of ancient chronology, which shortens pre-1000 BCE dates by several centuries is James, P. *et al.* (1993) *Centuries of Darkness: A Challenge to the Conventional Chronology of Old World Archaeology*. New Brunswick, NJ: Rutgers University Press. Rohl, D.M. (1995) *A Test of Time, Volume One: The Bible – From Myth to History*, New York: Crown, and (1999) *Volume Two: Legend – The Genesis of Civilization*, London: Century, argue for an even lower chronology. Postgate, G.N. (1992) *Early Mesopotamia: Society and Economy at the Dawn of History*, London: Routledge is an excellent overview of the Mesopotamian economy from its beginnings to its full development. Larsen, M.T. 'The Tradition of Empire in Mesopotamia' in (1979) *Power and Propaganda: A Symposium on Ancient Empires*, Copenhagen: Institute of Assyriology, University of Copenhagen, 75–105, provides a geographical explanation as to why Mesopotamia became 'capitalist' and Egypt 'socialist'. Kramer, S.N. (1963) *The Sumerians: Their History, Culture and Character*, Chicago: University of Chicago Press and 'Commerce and Trade: Gleanings from Sumerian Literature', (1977) *Iraq*, 39, part 1, 59–66, give good literary evidence on Sumerian 'temple capitalism'. See also Stetch, T. and Pigott, V.C. 'The Metals Trade in Southwest Asia in the Third Millennium BC', (1986) *Iraq*, 48, 39–64. For Akkadian commerce see Forster, B.R. 'Commercial Activities in Sargonic Mesopotamia', (1977) *Iraq*, 39, part 1, 31–44 and Westenholz, A. 'The Old Akkadian Empire in Contemporary Opinion' in Larsen, M.T. (1979) *Power and Propaganda: A Symposium on Ancient Empires*. Copenhagen: Institute of Assyriology, University of Copenhagen, 107–24. The Neo-Sumerian prelude to Old Assyria is treated in Limet, H. 'Les Schemas du Commerce Neo-Sumerien', (1977) *Iraq*, 39, part 1, 51–8.

The leading writer on Old Assyrian trade remains Larsen, M.T. Consult his (1976) *The Old Assyrian City-State and Its Colonies*, Copenhagen: Akademisk Forlag, and 'Partnerships in the Old Assyrian Trade', (1977) *Iraq*, 39, part 1, 119–43. Also essential are Orlin, L.L. (1970) *Assyrian Colonies in Cappadocia*, Mouton: The Hague, and the works of Veenhof, K.R.: 'Kanesh: An Assyrian Colony in Anatolia' in the second volume of Sasson, J. *et al.*, eds. (1995) *Civilizations of the Ancient Near East*. New York: Scribner, 859–71; (1972) *Aspects of Old Assyrian Trade and its Terminology*, Leiden: E.J. Brill; and 'Some Social Effects of Old Assyrian Trade', (1977) *Iraq*, 39, part 1, 109–18. The story of the Assyrian merchant Pusu-Ken is found in Larsen, M.T. (1976) and Orlin, L.L. (1970) as well as the first volume, *Economic Foundations*, of Goitein, S.D. (1967) *A Mediterranean Society*, Berkeley, CA: University of California Press.

Chapter 5: The multinational becomes intercontinental. Ugarit and Tyre: 1500–600 BCE

A comprehensive survey of Phoenician history is still hard to find. See Aubet, M.E. (1997) *The Phoenicians and the West: Politics, Colonies and Trade*. Cambridge, UK: Cambridge University

Press. Aubet has good material but stresses overseas commerce. The second edition of Harden, D. (1963) *The Phoenicians*, New York: The Free Press, is still worth reading, but quite out of date. For Ugarit see Rainey, A.F. 'Business Agents at Ugarit', (1963) *Israel Exploration Journal*, vol.13, 313–21; Linder, E. 'Ugarit: A Canaanite Thalassocracy' in Young, G.D., ed. (1981) *Ugarit in Retrospect: Fifty Years of Ugarit and Ugaritic*, Winona Lake: Eisenbrauns, 31–42; and Astour, M.C. 'Ugarit and the Great Powers'. McMillan, C.J. (1996) *The Japanese Industrial System*, New York: Walter de Gruyter, is an essential introduction to the modern *keiretsu*. James, P. *et al.* (1993) *Centuries of Darkness: A Challenge to the Conventional Chronology of Old World Archaeology*, New Brunswick, NJ: Rutgers University Press, argues that Ugarit is dated too early, implying a much closer relationship between its business culture and that of Tyre. Evidence in Markoe, G.E. 'The Emergence of Phoenician Art', *Bulletin of the American Schools of Oriental Research*, no. 279, August 1990, 13–26, lends some support to James's contention.

Aubet, M.E. (1997) *The Phoenicians and the West: Politics, Colonies and Trade*, Cambridge UK: Cambridge University Press, is the essential guide to Tyrian commercial expansion. The Israel–Tyre relationship is illuminated by Elat, M. 'The Monarchy and the Development of Trade in Ancient Israel' in Lipinski, E., ed.(1979) *State and Temple Economy in the Ancient Near East*, Louvain, Belgium: Catholic University of Louvain; Stern, E. 'New Evidence from Dor for the First Appearance of the Phoenicians along the Northern Coast of Israel', *Bulletin of the American Schools of Oriental Research*, no. 279, August 1990, 29–30; and Gal, Z. 'Hurbat Rosh Zayit and the Early Phoenician Pottery', (1992) *Levant*, XXIV, 173–85. Silver, M. (1995) *Economic Structures of Antiquity*, Westport CT: Greenwood Press, shows the crucial role of the Melqart hierarchy in Tyrian enterprise. On the Tyrians in Assyria and Babylonia consult Lipinski, E. 'Les Pheniciens à Ninive au temps des Sargonites: Ahonbasti, portier en chef' in the (1983) *Atti del I Congresso Internazionale di Studi fenici e punici, Roma, 5–10 Novembre 1979*. Rome: Consiglio Nazionale della Ricerche, 125–34. Tyrian settlement in Sardinia is the subject of Barreca, F. 'The Phoenician and Punic Civilization in Sardinia' in Balmuth, M.S., ed. (1989) *Studies in Sardinian Archaeology, Volume II, Sardinia in the Mediterranean*. Ann Arbor MI: University of Michigan Press, 145–70.

The Phoenician operation in Spain is all-important. In addition to Aubet, who devotes the major portion of her very fine book to it, there is the most up-to-date survey of ancient Iberia by Castro, M.C.F. (1995) *Iberia in Prehistory*, Oxford: Blackwell. Harrison, R.J. (1988) *Spain at the Dawn of History: Iberians, Phoenicians and Greeks*, London: Thames and Hudson, openly argues for 'multinational' business hierarchies in Phoenician Spain, as does Gamito, T.J. (1988) *Social Complexity in Southwest Iberia: 800–300 BC: The Case of Tartessos*, B.A.R. International Series no. 439, Oxford: B.A.R. A technical perspective on Rio Tinto by two archaeologists, who are also professional engineers, is found in Blanco-Freijeiro, A. and Rothenberg, B. (1981) *Exploración Arqueometalúrgica de Huelva (EAH)*, Barcelona: Editorial Labor. For a longer account of our argument please see our article 'Multinational Enterprise in Ancient Phoenicia' in *Business History*, Volume 42, Number 2, April 2000.

Chapter 6: Birth of free enterprise. The Aegean market revolution: 1000–336 BCE

There has been important revisionist writing dealing with the Archaic and Classical Greek world in the last decade. Osborne, R. (1996) *Greece in the Making: 1200–479 BC*, London: Routledge, is absolutely indispensable. Building upon the latest demographic studies as well as traditional literary and pottery studies, Osborne discards the notions of rapid Iron Age population growth taught by earlier historians. He also suggests that market-seeking behaviour played more of a role in Archaic Greek colonization than previously supposed. Another interesting revisionist work is Sallares, R. (1991) *The Ecology of the Ancient Greek*

World, Ithaca, NY: Cornell University Press. Sallares provides a 'green' interpretation of Archaic Greece, based in part upon climatological studies and comparisons with modern Greece. In his view, the Greek market transformation was caused by the importation of the olive tree as well as ironworking. The ascendancy of Greece over Persia was, he argues, ultimately due to a population explosion in the former. Martin, T.R. (1996) *Ancient Greece: From Prehistoric to Hellenistic Times*, New Haven: Yale University Press, is an excellent survey.

The Euboeans and their role in the origins of the market revolution are treated in the revised edition of Murray, O. (1993) *Early Greece*, Cambridge, MA: Harvard University Press. Papadopoulous, J.K. 'Phantom Euboians', (1997) *Journal of Mediterranean Archaeology*, vol.10, no. 2, 191–219, offers an interesting corrective to the traditional view of Euboean primacy in early Greek trade, stressing the role of Phoenicians and others in bringing the Iron Age to Greece. On the Euboeans and Pithekoussai see also Buchner, G. 'Pithekoussai: Oldest Greek Colony in the West', *Expedition: the Bulletin of the University Museum of the University of Pennsylvania*, vol. 8, no. 4, summer 1966, 4–12; Ridgway, D. 'The First Western Greeks: Campanian Coasts and Southern Etruria' in Hawkes, C. and S., eds. (1973) *Archaeology into History*, I: *Greeks, Celts and Romans: Studies in Venture and Resistance*. London: J.M. Dent, 35–8; Sackett, L.H. and Popham, M.R. 'Lefkandi: A Euboean Town of the Bronze Age and Early Iron Age (2100–700 BC)', *Archaeology*, January 1972, vol. 25, no. 1, 8–19. Starr, C.G. (1977) *The Economic and Social Growth of Early Greece, 800–500 BC*, New York: Oxford University Press, is older but still useful in discussing the strengths and weaknesses of comparing economic growth in Greece to that of medieval and modern Europe. Volume I of reprinted Heichelheim, F. (1965) *An Ancient Economic History from the Palaeolithic Age to the Migrations of the Germanic, Slavic and Arabic Nations*, Leyden: A.W. Sithoff, provides an interesting, if dated and overly deterministic, interpretation of the spread of the Iron Age beyond the Near East. In his view, now largely modified or discarded, iron ploughs made possible the intensive farming of European lands and the rise of European cities. On Corinth see Salmon, J.B. (1984) *Wealthy Corinth: A History of the City to 338 BC*, Oxford: Clarendon Press. For Athens see Mattingly, H.B. (1996) *The Athenian Empire Restored: Epigraphic and Historical Studies*, Ann Arbor, MI: University of Michigan Press, and Rankin, D.I. 'The Mining Lobby at Athens', (1988) *Ancient Society* (Louvain) vol. 19, 189–206.

Redfield, J.M. 'The Development of the Market in Ancient Greece' in Anderson, B.L. and Latham, A.J.H., eds. (1986) *The Market in History*, London: Croom Helm, 29–58, looks at Homer, Hesiod and other writers for subtle evidence of the market revolution and its effect on Archaic Greek culture. The story of the slave-entrepreneur Pasion is told in Casson, L. (1964) *The Ancient Mariners: Seafarers and Sea Fighters of the Mediterranean in Ancient Times*, New York: Macmillan. Scholarship on the origins of the Peloponnesian War has been more or less in limbo since the publication of de Ste Croix, G. (1972) *The Origins of the Peloponnesian War*, Ithaca, NY: Cornell University Press, but check Macdonald, B.R. 'The Impact of Attic Pottery to Corinth and the Question of Trade during the Peloponnesian War', (1992) *Journal of Hellenic Studies*, CII, 113–23.

Chapters 7 and 8: Overture to world economy. India, China and the heirs of Athens and Tyre: 331–146 BCE
Rendering unto Caesar. Roman multinationals in a world economy: 146 BCE–476 CE

The Hellenistic economy represents an important transition between that of Classical Greece and later Rome. Little documentation on economics, however, is available outside of Ptolemaic Egypt. A good place to begin is Chapter 21 of Green, P. (1990) *Alexander to Actium: The Historical Evolution of the Hellenistic Age*, Berkeley, CA: University of California Press. Bagnall, R. and Derow, P., eds (1981) *Greek Historical Documents: The Hellenistic Period*, Chico,

CA: Scholars Press for the Society of Biblical Literature, has excellent primary sources on Ptolemaic Egypt's state capitalism. On Carthage the definitive work is Lancel, S. (1997) *Carthage: A History*, Oxford: Blackwell.

The most up-to-date work on the early Roman Republic is the monumental study, Cornell, T.J. (1995) *The Beginnings of Rome: Italy and Rome from the Bronze Age to the Punic Wars (c. 1000–264 BC)*, London: Routledge, which does for Rome what Osborne's work does for Archaic Greece. Cornell integrates archaeology, demography and literature to argue that Rome was not a commercial desert before 200 BCE. Frank, T.'s six-volume (1975) *Economic Survey of Ancient Rome*, especially Volume I: *Rome and Italy of the Republic*, New York: Octagon Books, c. 1933–1940, is a goldmine of information on individual Roman industries and literary evidence, in spite of its age and long-outdated interpretations of Roman enterprise.

Good primary source documents, some of them relating to trade, appear in Lewis, N. and Reinhold, M., eds. (1966) *Roman Civilization: Sourcebook I: The Republic* and *Sourcebook II: The Empire*, New York: Harper and Row.

The parameters of Roman trade and economic development, as traced by artefacts, can be discovered in Greene, K. (1990) *The Archaeology of the Roman Economy*, Berkeley, CA: University of California Press, and Potter, T.W. (1990) *Roman Italy*, Berkeley, CA: University of California Press, which traces the export ventures of the Sestii through their wine vessels. See also Manacorda, D. 'The Ager Cosanus and the Production of the Amphorae of Sestius: New Evidence and a Reassessment', (1978) *Journal of Roman Studies*, vol. 68, 122–31. D'Arms, J.H. (1981) *Commerce and Social Standing in Ancient Rome*, Cambridge, MA: Harvard University Press, is a good introduction to the debate on how much Roman senators took part in commerce. Aubert, J.J. (1994) *Business Managers in Ancient Rome: A Social and Economic Study of Institores, 200 BC–AD 250*, Leiden: E.J. Brill, analyses the Roman management structure, notably the clay industries in the light of Roman business law and archaeology, suggesting the presence of partnerships and agents. The rise and structure of the publican companies are well treated by Badian, E. (1983) *Publicans and Sinners: Private Enterprise in the Service of the Roman Republic*. Ithaca, NY: Cornell University Press. The marble trade, another good candidate for multinational enterprise, is described by Ward-Perkins, J. 'The Marble Trade and its Organization: Evidence from Nicomedia' in D'Arms, J.H. and Kopff, E.C., eds. (1980) *The Seaborne Commerce of Ancient Rome: Studies in Archaeology and History*. Rome: American Academy in Rome, 325–38. Dodge, H. 'Ancient Marble Studies: Recent Research', (1991) *Journal of Roman Archaeology*, vol. 4, 28–50, revises some of the geography of earlier scholarship in this area.

Chapter 9: Dark Age Capitalism. Faith meets economics in the age of Muhammad and Charlemagne: 500–1000

Chapters 3 and 4 of Cameron, R. (1997) *A Concise Economic History of the World: From Paleolithic Times to the Present*, Oxford: Oxford University Press, are a quick, up-to-date introduction to medieval economics and those of the non-Western world. Postan, M.M. and Miller, E. eds. (1988) *Cambridge Economic History of Europe*, 2nd Edition, Vol. 2, *Trade and Industry in the Middle Ages*, Cambridge: Cambridge University Press, is more thorough. On the decline of Rome see Brown, P. (1989) *The World of Late Antiquity, AD 150–750*, New York: W.W. Norton, which shows the role of the Persian Sassanids and of monasticism in the transition from the ancient world to that of the Dark Ages. MacMullen, R. (1988) *Corruption and the Decline of Rome*, New Haven, CT: Yale University Press, gives a revisionist view that business corruption and privatization, not big government, were the cause of Rome's decline. Ashtor, E. (1976) *A Social and Economic History of the Near East in the Middle Ages*, Berkeley, CA: University of California Press, has a good survey of economic history in the Islamic world, as does the relevant section in Abu-Lughod, J.L. (1989) *Before European Hegemony: The World*

System AD 1250–1350, New York: Oxford University Press, which places the Abbasid Caliphate in a world-system context. Goitein, S.G. (1967) *A Mediterranean Society: The Jewish Communities of the Arab World as Portrayed in the Documents of the Cairo Geniza*, Berkeley, CA: University of California Press, and Goitein, S.G. (1973) *Letters of Medieval Jewish Traders*, Princeton: Princeton University Press, provide the most detailed discussion and documents of Fatimid commerce. See also Labib, S.Y. 'Capitalism in Medieval Islam', *Journal of Economic History*, Vol. XXIX, No. 1, March 1969, 79–96. On Dark Age Europe, Thompson, J.W. (1966) *Economic and Social History of the Middle Ages*, New York: Frederick Ungar, 2 vols., has a lot of marvellous detail but it is very dated. Hodges, R. and Whitehouse, D. (1983) *Mohammed, Charlemagne and the Origins of Europe*, Ithaca, NY: Cornell University Press, is more up to date and uses more archaeological evidence from coin hoards to link European and Near Eastern trading developments. Hodges' previous work, (1982) *Dark Age Economics: The Origins of Towns and Trade AD 600–1000*, New York: St Martin's Press, is a more in-depth discussion of the revival of capitalism in the towns of England and Scandinavia. The most current examination of European Dark Age economy in the light of archaeology is Webster, L. and Brown, M. eds. (1997) *The Transformation of the Roman World AD 400–900*, London: British Museum Press.

Chapter 10: Merchants of Venice, Inc. Europe's road to the multinational: 1000–1450

Hunt, E.S. and Murray, J.M. (1999) *A History of Business in Medieval Europe, 1200–1550*, Cambridge: Cambridge University Press, is the most recent survey of medieval business, and is quite good on the response of merchants to the changed economic circumstances of the 1300s. Favier, J. (1998) *Gold and Spices: The Rise of Commerce in the Middle Ages*, New York: Holmes & Meier, goes into much more detail on business organization. Thompson, J.W. (1996) *Economic and Social History of the Middle Ages* (cited above under Chapter 9) quotes many original sources, but was written originally in 1928. Gies, J. and F. (1972) *Merchants and Moneymen: The Commercial Revolution, 1000–1500*, New York: Thomas Y. Crowell, is a good introduction to the subject and has excellent biographical vignettes. Braudel, F. (1992) *Civilization and Capitalism 15th–18th Century*, Volume 3, *The Perspective of the World*, Berkeley, CA: University of California Press, presents a fascinating discussion of both medieval and modern commerce from a geographic and demographic standpoint. Gimpel, J. (1976) *The Medieval Machine: The Industrial Revolution of the Middle Ages*, New York: Holt, Rinehart and Winston, stresses the role of technology in transforming medieval Europe. Abu-Lughod, J.L. (1989) *Before European Hegemony: The World System AD 1250–1350*, New York: Oxford University Press, shows how Europe reintegrated itself into Asian world economy.

Chapter 11: China's chance. The enduring decree of heaven

Hucker, C.O. (1975) *China's Imperial Past: An Introduction to Chinese History and Culture*, Stanford: Stanford University Press, is a good popular survey. Temple, R. (1998) *The Genius of China: 3,000 Years of Science, Discovery and Invention*, London: Prion Books, lists all China's inventions and shows how advanced the Middle Kingdom really was. Gates, H. (1998) *China's Motor: A Thousand Years of Petty Capitalism*, Ithaca, NY: Cornell University Press, is written from a radical Marxist and feminist perspective. Gates provides a lot of good material on the sociology of Chinese family capitalism and the growth of both public and private sectors in medieval China. See also the following works by Shiba, Y.: (1970) *Commerce in Sung China*, Ann Arbor, MI: University of Michigan, Center for Chinese Studies; 'Sung Foreign Trade: Its Scope and Organization' in Rossabii, M., ed. (1983) *China Among Equals: the Middle Kingdom and its Neighbors, 10th–14th Centuries*, Berkeley, CA: University of California Press, 89–115; and 'Urbanization and the Development of Markets in the Lower Yangtze Valley' in Winthrop

Haeger, J., ed. (1975) *Chapter Crisis and Prosperity in Sung China*, Tucson, AZ: University of Arizona Press, 13–33. Fukuyama, F. (1996) *Trust: The Social Virtues and the Creation of Prosperity*, New York: Free Press Paperbacks, explains the low-trust nature of contemporary Chinese business cultures. Levathes, L. (1994) *When China Ruled the Seas: The Treasure Fleet of the Dragon Throne, 1405–1433*, New York: Simon and Schuster, is the detailed story of Zheng He's armada. Abu-Lughod, J.L. (1989) *Before European Hegemony: The World System AD 1250–1350*, New York: Oxford University Press, again integrates Yuan and Ming China into the world economy.

Chapter 12: A global economy. The age of the chartered trading company: 1450–1800

The 'Rise of the West' controversy in world history has provoked a heated debate. Much of this debate is coloured by political ideology. McNeill, W.H. (1991) *The Rise of the West: A History of the Human Community*, Chicago: University of Chicago Press, is a good place to start. The 1991 book is a reissue of the 1963 original, which stressed the role of contact between cultures as the key to economic progress. McNeill focused heavily on Europe and downplayed the importance of China and Asia. Landes, D.S. (1999) *The Wealth and Poverty of Nations: Why Some are so Rich and Some so Poor*, New York: W.W. Norton, finds the success of the West in the geography and in the moral and cultural values acquired by Europeans, which gave them an advantage. Rosenberg, N. and Birdzell, L.E., Jr (1986) *How the West Grew Rich: The Economic Transformation of the Industrial World*, New York: Basic Books, has a good chapter on the Roman roots of many medieval and modern business forms. The McNeill school has been challenged in recent years by a school of 'world-system' historians. Often of Marxist orientation, these writers claim that Europe rose to power not by any innate advantages but by exploiting non-Western cultures. Wolf, E.R. (1982) *Europe and the People Without History*, Berkeley, CA: University of California Press, has a good overview of the world economy in 1400. Wolf stresses the role of slavery and conquest and depicts Africans, Asians and others as full participants in a global economy of the 1500s and 1600s, which heavily oppressed them. Wallerstein, I. (1976) *The Modern World System: Capitalist Agriculture and the Origins of the European World-Economy in the Sixteenth Century*, New York: Academic Press, presents a strong case for a Europe-centred imperialistic global economy existing in the 16th century. The most radical 'world-system' argument is that of Frank, A.G. (1998) *ReORIENT: Global Economy in the Asian Age*, Berkeley, CA: University of California Press, which says Asia continued to dominate the world economically until the 1800s. Lach, D.F. and Flaumenhaft, C., eds. (1965) *Asia on the Eve of Europe's Expansion*, Englewood Cliffs, NJ: Prentice-Hall, has some eye-witness accounts of Asian commerce from the 1500s. Bernstein, P.J. (1996) *Against the Gods: The Remarkable Story of Risk*, New York: John Wiley, shows how mathematical discoveries in India and the Arab world allowed Europeans to calculate risk and build modern business organizations. Carlos, A.M. and Nicholas, S. 'Giants of an Earlier Capitalism: The Chartered Trading Companies as Modern Multinationals', *Business History Review*, 62, Autumn 1988, 398–419 in Wilkins, M., ed. (1991) International Library of Critical Writings in Business History, Volume I, *The Growth of Multinationals*, Aldershot, UK: Edward Elgar Publishing, Article 18, 450–71, is a good introduction to the study of joint-stock firms. Boxer, C.R. (1979) *Jan Compagnie in War and Peace 1602–1799: A Short History of the Dutch East India Company*, Hong Kong: Heinemann Asia, covers the Dutch East India Company. On the English East India Company see Lawson, P. (1993) *The East India Company: A History*, London: Longman Higher Education.

Chapter 13: The Second Global Economy. The 'Hellenic' free-trade world of the *Pax Britannica:* 1800–1931

Landes, D.S. (1999) *The Wealth and Poverty of Nations: Why Some are so Rich and Some so Poor*, New York: W.W. Norton, covers the Industrial Revolution. Harley, C.K. 'Transportation, the World Wheat Trade, and the Kuznets Cycle, 1850–1913' in (1980) *Explorations in Economic History*, Vol. 17, 218–50 looks at the Second Global Economy. On British multinationals see Jones, G. 'Origins, Management, and Performance', excerpt from *idem* (1986) *British Multinationals: Origins, Management, and Performance*, Aldershot, UK: Edward Elgar Publishing, Article 9, 251–73; *idem*, 'The Growth and Performance of British Multinational Firms before 1939: The Case of Dunlop' in Wilkins, *ibid.*, Article 19, 475–93; Stopford, J.M. 'The Origins of British-Based Multinational Manufacturing Enterprises' in (1974) *Business History Review*, 48, 303–35, Article 6, 159–91; and Wilkins, M. 'European and North American Multinationals, 1870–1914: Comparisons and Contrasts', (1988) *Business History*, 30, 8–45, Article 3, [52–89] all in the Wilkins anthology mentioned above. For free-standing companies see Wilkins, M. and Schröter, H., eds. (1998) *The Free-Standing Company in the World Economy, 1830–1996*, Oxford: Oxford University Press. Turner, F.M. (1981) *The Greek Heritage in Victorian Britain*, New Haven, CT: Yale University Press, covers the cultural and intellectual parallels between Britain and Athens.

Chapter 14: The Second Global Economy. America's 'Legionary Capitalism': 1800–1970

Perret, G. (1989) *A Country Made by War: From the Revolution to Vietnam – The Story of America's Rise to Power*, New York: Random House, surveys American military history from the point of view of 'military Keynesianism'. Chamberlain, J. (1963) *The Enterprising Americans: A Business History of the United States*, New York: Harper and Row, is old but still a good survey. Johnson, P. (1997) *A History of the American People*, London: Weidenfeld & Nicolson, is a conservative, pro-free-market interpretation of American history by a British journalist–historian. Yergin, D. (1991) *The Prize: The Epic Quest for Oil, Money, and Power*, New York: Simon and Schuster, is very perceptive on the Rockefellers and the role of the oil industry. Sampson, A. (1996) *Company Man: The Rise and Fall of Corporate Life*, New York: Random House, is a very readable look at the change in management cultures in the US, Britain, Europe and Japan over the last century. On the car industry: Halberstam, D. (1987) *The Reckoning*, New York: Avon Books, tells the story of Ford and Nissan and how Japan came to challenge Detroit in the 1980s; Kay, J.H. (1998) *Asphalt Nation: How the Automobile Took Over America and How We Can Take It Back*, Berkeley, CA: University of California Press, is a critical treatment of the car culture with a lot of good historical material, as is Goddard, S.B. (1996) *Getting There: The Epic Struggle between Road and Rail in the American Century*, Chicago: University of Chicago Press. Kanter, R.M. (1984) *The Change Masters: Innovation and Entrepreneurship in the American Corporation*, New York: Touchstone, looks at the business culture of General Motors. Goodwin, D.K. 'The Way We Won', *The American Prospect*, Vol. 3, No. 11, autumn 1992, 66–70, applies the 'legionary' thesis to World War II from a pro-interventionist perspective. Sale, K. (1975) *Power Shift: The Rise of the Southern Rim and its Challenge to the Eastern Establishment*, New York: Random House, has a New Left perspective but nonetheless is insightful in the role of military spending in creating Sunbelt power and prosperity. Grantham, D.W. (1994) *The South in Modern America: A Region at Odds*, New York: Harper Collins, is less radical but makes a similar point.

Chapter 15: World-class rivals. The paternalistic capitalisms of Germany and Japan

Landes (cited above under Chapter 13) has good chapters on Europe and Japan. Henderson, W.O. (1969) *The Industrialization of Europe: 1780–1914*, London: Thames and Hudson, has a section on German entrepreneurs. Stolper, G. *et al.* (1967) *The German Economy: 1870 to the Present*, New York: Harcourt, Brace and World, looks at German industrialization. Grunberger, R. (1971) *The 12 Year Reich: A Social History of Nazi Germany 1933–1945*, New York: Holt, Rinehart and Winston, has a chapter on business in the Third Reich. Glouchevitch, P. (1992) *Juggernaut: The German Way of Business: Why it is Transforming Europe and the World*, New York: Simon and Schuster, is a good introduction to the German 'social market' economy. Porter, M. (1990) *The Competitive Advantage of Nations*, New York: The Free Press, has lots of good hard data on strategies and differences in German, Japanese and US business cultures. Gannon, M.J. (1994) *Understanding Global Cultures: Metaphorical Journeys through 17 Countries*, London: Sage, and Trompenaars, F. and Hampden-Turner, C. (1998) *Riding the Waves of Culture: Understanding Diversity in Global Business*, New York: McGraw-Hill, both explain the differences in US, European and Asian business cultures. Gannon uses cultural metaphors: American football, German symphony, Japanese garden, English house, etc.; Trompenaars uses hard data from surveys. The literature on Japanese business has been massive. Wilkins, M. 'Japanese Multinational Enterprise before 1914', (1968) *Business History Review*, No. 60, 199–231, Article 8, 218–50 in her 1991 anthology, gives some historical background. Prestowitz, C.V., Jr (1988) *Trading Places: How We Allowed Japan to Take the Lead*, New York, Basic Books, Vogel, E.F. (1979) *Japan as Number One: Lessons for America*, Cambridge MA: Harvard University Press; Wolf, M.J. (1983) *The Japanese Conspiracy: The Plot to Dominate Industry Worldwide – and How to Deal With It*, New York: Empire Books; Burstein, D. (1988) *Yen!: Japan's New Financial Empire and its Threat to America*, New York: Simon and Schuster. Ouchi, W.Z. (1981) *Theory Z: How American Business can Meet the Japanese Challenge*, Reading, MA: Addison-Wesley; Pascale, R.T. and Athos, A.G. (1981) *The Art of Japanese Management: Applications for American Executives*, New York: Simon and Schuster; Locke, R.K. (1996) *The Collapse of the American Management Mystique*, Oxford: Oxford University Press; and Alston, J.P. (1986) *The American Samurai: Blending American and Japanese Managerial Practices*, Berlin: Walter de Gruyter, all pointed to the Japanese model as a threat to America and a positive example Americans needed to learn from. Since 1989 writers have been far more critical of the Japanese model. See Emmott, B. (1989) *The Sun Also Sets: The Limits to Japan's Economic Power*, New York: Times Books, and Katz, R. (1998) *Japan: The System that Soured: The Rise and Fall of the Japanese Economic Miracle*, Armonk, NY: M.E. Sharpe.

Chapter 16: The Third Global Economy. Multinationals, microchips and the Information Age: 1970–2000

On the history of multinationals see Jones, G. (1996) *The Evolution of International Business: An Introduction*, London: Routledge, and Sampson, A. (1996) *Company Man: The Rise and Fall of Corporate Life*, New York: Random House, as well as Dunning, J.H. 'Changes in the Level and Structure of International Production: The Last One Hundred Years', Article 4, 90–148 in Wilkins, M., ed. (1991) International Library of Critical Writings in Business History, Volume I, *The Growth of Multinationals*, Aldershot, UK: Edward Elgar Publishing.

The best book in a growing literature on globalization is Friedman, T.L. (1999) *The Lexus and the Olive Tree: Understanding Globalization*, New York: Farrar, Strauss and Giroux, which offers a tentative historical perspective. Barber, B.R. and Schulz, A., eds. (1996) *Jihad Vs. McWorld: How the Planet is Both Falling Apart and Coming Together*, New York: Ballantine Books, is more philosophical. Yergin, D. and Stanislaw, J. (1999) *The Commanding Heights: The Battle Between Government and the Marketplace that is Remaking the Modern World*, New York:

Touchstone, looks at how globalization has weakened welfare states worldwide. Cox, W.M. and Alm, R. (1999) *Myths of Rich and Poor: Why We're Better Off than We Think*, New York: Basic Books, is a triumphant celebration of American 'shareholder' capitalism as the most successful business system of the 1990s. Rugman, A. (2000) *The End of Globalization*, New York: Random House, is by a leading scholar who has studied multinationals and their impact on the world for almost 30 years. In this book he argues that regional economies are now more important than the global economy. Stavrianos, L.S. (1976) *The Promise of the Coming Dark Age*, San Francisco, CA: W.H. Freeman, deals with Dark Age parallels, as does Davidson, J.D. and Rees-Mogg, Lord W. (1997) *The Sovereign Individual: How to Survive and Thrive During the Collapse of the Welfare State*, New York: Simon and Schuster, from a harsher, Malthusian perspective. See also *idem* (1987) *Blood in the Streets: Investment Profits in a World Gone Mad*, New York: Summit Books, and (1993) *The Great Reckoning: Protect Yourself in the Coming Depression*, New York: Simon and Schuster. The subject of global alliances is dealt with by Ohmae, K. (1990) *The Borderless World: Power and Strategy in the Interlinked Economy*, New York: Harper Business, and *idem* (1995) *The End of the Nation State: The Rise of Regional Economies – How Capital, Corporations, Consumers, and Communication are Reshaping Global Markets*, Boston, MA: Harvard Business School.

Chapter 17: Should the world become American?

This debate is one that is very much on the agenda. Articles appear regularly in the major 'thoughtful' press, such as *The Economist, Financial Times, The New York Times, The Wall Street Journal, The Globe and Mail* and *The Times*, as well as the 'not so thoughtful' media, which tend to be more polemic in nature.

There have also appeared a number of excellent books on the topic of differing forms of capitalism or economies. Scholars in the area include Richard Whitley of Manchester University, Richard Wade of Brown University in the US and Marie-Laure Djelic of ESSEC in Paris. Four books from the academic world stand out in our minds: Whitley, R. (1999) *Divergent Capitalism*, Oxford: Oxford University Press; Djelic, M.-L. (1998) *Exporting the American Model*, Oxford: Oxford University Press; Marco, O. *et al.* (1997) *The Economic Organization of East Asian Capitalism*: London: Sage; and Zeitlin, J. and Herrigel, G., eds. (2000) *Americanization and its Limits: Reworking American Technology and Management in Post-war Europe and Japan*, Oxford: Oxford University Press.

Professor Whitley, in his latest book mentioned above, presents a comparative business-systems framework for describing the major differences between the various market economies in the late 20th century. He suggests six major types of business system and points out the strong ties to different institutional arrangements in countries and regions in which they operate. In her book, Djelic discusses how the Marshall Plan after World War II was instrumental in exporting the American model of corporate capitalism to Europe. She focuses on France, Germany and Italy and shows how the transfer of the American model met with varying success, depending on the degree of resistance it met and how it was, to varying degrees, adapted to the national conditions in each of the three nations studied.

An allied set of literature looks at the importance of national culture to doing business internationally. Among the best books in this growing area is the excellent Gannon, M. (1994) *Understanding Global Cultures: Metaphorical Journeys Through 17 Countries*, London: Sage. In it he uses metaphors to capture each culture. Written by a highly experienced international businessperson, Lewis, R. (1999) *When Cultures Collide*, London: Nicholas Breadly, is also highly recommended. Finally, Trompenaars, F. and Hampden-Turner, C. (1998) *Riding the Waves of Culture: Understanding Diversity in Global Business*, New York: McGraw Hill, explains the differences in US, European and Asian business cultures using empirical data.

Index